William Pencak

History, Signing In

Essays in History and Semiotics

PETER LANG
New York • San Francisco • Bern • Baltimore
Frankfurt am Main • Berlin • Wien • Paris

Library of Congress Cataloging-in-Publication Data

Pencak, William.
   History, signing in : essays in history and semiotics / William Pencak.
      p. cm.—(Semiotics and the human sciences; v. 4)
   Includes bibliographical references and index.
   1. History—Philosophy.   2. Semiotics.   I. Title.   II. Series.
D16.9.P34   1993   901—dc20   92-4143
ISBN 0-8204-1838-2   CIP
ISSN 1054-8386

Die Deutsche Bibliothek-CIP-Einheitsaufnahme

Pencak, William:
History, signing in : essays in history and semiotics / William
Pencak.—New York; Berlin; Bern; Frankfurt/M.; Paris; Wien: Lang,
1993
   (Semiotics and the human sciences ; Vol. 4)
   ISBN 0-8204-1838-2
NE: GT

The paper in this book meets the guidelines for permanence and
durability of the Committee on Production Guidelines for
Book Longevity of the Council on Library Resources.

For my friends, students, and colleagues, at Penn State and elsewhere:

Especially:

James Smith Allen	Carole and Harlan Kutscher
Marguerite Anthony	Shirley Marchalonis
Devy Barnet-Buchen	Jordan and Marie Max
Jim Boyer	Ray and Cathy Mazurek
Dmitry Bronov	Dorothy McKenzie
Irving Buchen	Dennis Merryfield and Amy Jackson
Matt Caldwell	Linda and Randall Miller
Bryan Charap	Jeffrey Morris
Robert and Melissa Close	Breen Murray
John Colyer	John Murrin
Margaret Cote	Leonard Mustazza
Ralph Crandall and Family	On-cho Ng
Gary Cross	Bill Parsons
John Deely	Brad Phinney
Michael De Thomas	Jeffrey Polizzotto
The Elizondo Family	Terry Prewitt
Tim England and Family	Peter Rebane
Lisa and Tom Faranda	Mike Riley
Stephen and Rhonda Fitz	Carl and Diana Royer
John Frantz	Richard Ryerson
Cate Fiorillo	James and Tish Sandos
Bill Frohlich	Kurt Seidel
Gary Gallagher	Suzanne and Fred Stutman
Paul Gilje	Jeffrey and Marta Stewart
Tom Gombar	Christopher Takacs
Claire Hirshfield	Tramble Turner
Cory Heller and Kathy Owens	Ruth Vitale
Mark and Sheri Hiester	Rosemary Warden
Natalie Isser	Brooke Williams
Sandy Keim	David Zeeman
Roberta Kevelson	

TABLE OF CONTENTS

HISTORY, SIGNING IN: STUDIES IN HISTORY AND SEMIOTICS

Chapter 1

Introduction

I chose the title of this book, *History, Signing In* because it conveys my dual purpose. First, I offer some examples of how signs work in history, how a historian aware of semiotics but unwilling to become a semiotic theorist -- or drown his writing with semiotic jargon incomprehensible to his normal audience -- can employ semiotics in historical work. Second, while semiotics has made a considerable impact in fields such as philosophy and literary criticism, it is still terra incognita, and territory that is usually feared or reviled at that, when it comes to history. Much of the work on 'history and semiotics' -- as in two special issues of *Semiotica* published in 1982 and 1984 -- consists of the musings of non-historians about the meaning of history. The special issue I co-edited with Brooke Williams in 1991, the contents provided by practicing historians, has begun to reverse the process. It shows how historians can use semiotics to ask and answer better the sorts of questions and interpret the sorts of data they usually do, rather than using history as a springboard for semiotic theorizing. This book, consisting of papers I delivered at various semiotic and historical conferences between 1984 and 1992, is another initial effort by a historian in the semiotic field.

Historians can be especially useful to semiotics, I think, for semiotics is in danger of being confused with and subsumed by deconstruction and its overlapping fellow-traveller, post-modernism. Now before I deconstruct deconstruction, let me admit that it does have its place, in deflating the dogmatisms the human race trumpets whenever it gets ahold of something it really cares about. But it is one thing to argue that human beings construct a specifically human world from the greater universe. It is another thing to say that therefore they are intentionally or unintentionally lying, that meaning is arbitrary or found only in texts, or that we cannot know what is really out there.

Semiotics is in fact a powerful weapon against deconstruction when history is brought into play. Certain signs have retained their power throughout human history. People feel affection, anger, hunger, joy, and fear. They worship a god or gods and believe in causes. They form families and communities to which they devote great care. They engage in agriculture and construct trade networks. They create music, art, literature, and ceremony. They symbolize their loyalties through flags, monuments, and dress. They construct moral codes which define permissible and impermissible uses of violence, property, and sexual activity.

What can we do with these signs? We can go the 'nothing else but' route of Hobbes in *Leviathan*, where the phrase appears dozens of times, to reduce man and the state to mechanisms. We can deconstruct social symbolisms from Nietzschean ('nothing else but' the will to power), Freudian (sexuality), feminist (domination of men over women), or Marxist (class struggle) perspectives, or we can point out intellectual inconsistencies in any societal symbolization and sigh with Hans Sachs: 'Wahn! Wahn! Überall wahn!' (Everywhere folly).

Or we can be historical semioticians and trace the transformations in meaning of human (or non-human) signs. When we look at a cross, we see not only the Nietzschean revolt of the slaves or the Marxist opiate of the masses, but also a symbol of social order and human brotherhood which has resonated for nearly two thousand years. This fact was brought home to me most powerfully when in June 1992 I visited two exhibitions in Washington D.C. One, at the Smithsonian Institute, of Eastern European anti-Communist posters, used a great many Christian symbols to tap into the forces which ultimately toppled seemingly invincible governments. The other, on Chicano Art at the National Museum of American Art, showed the importance of both Christian and pre-Columbian Native American symbols in mobilizing Chicano resistance to injustice in the late twentieth-century United States. The persistence of the great religions over thousands of years, and the power they and the historical figures and traditions, or myths, associated with them still exert over the world's peoples, suggest these symbols do express the fundamental concerns of human existence. Thus, understanding their change and continuity, their transformations in meaning as history moves on, is the fundamental task of the historian. We can say the same about states, families, the arts, and economic systems: fundamental experiences are symbolized in ways both consistently recognizable yet constantly changing.

I am most taken with Roberta Kevelson's metaphor of reality as a kaleidoscope. The world is constantly changing not only from one perspective but from every possible perspective; but in our kaleidoscope there are still shapes and colors, the symbols which allow us to talk meaningfully about the nature of this change. We will never get a 'fix' on reality. Thank God, or the adventure of seeking knowledge stops as surely as if we deny that the shapes and colors of the kaleidoscope exist or have meaning. In that case we must either stop talking or simply guess what we're lying about and why.

Semiotics, I contend, is simply the theoretical explanation of the way people have always thought and acted who were not intellectuals, and even they think and act that way although they pretend not to. Jesus did not argue in syllogisms: he presented his teachings through stories, in which the actors served as signs of the underlying moral reality. Plato and his mentor Socrates did argue logically, but their ultimate argument was that reality could only be grasped in a blinding vision. Speech, writing, theater, and other forms of representation were the signs which enabled us, however distantly, to get something of a sense of that reality and understand it.   When the saints wished to convert the heathen, they healed the sick, turned the other cheek, and preached about Jesus and his stories: they did not explain the *Summa Theologica*.   Flags and civic ceremonies to invoke and evoke national loyalty are offered by contemporary statesmen along with ritual incantations of the greatness of the country in question: we rarely hear disquisitions on Marx, Madison, or Mill.   I am less troubled than most by complaints that civic discourse in America is now reduced to television spots and images: except when the Founding Fathers were talking to each other or Abraham Lincoln was trying to make sense of the Civil War, this has always been the case. Teddy Roosevelt did not cast such a great shadow because he wrote numerous books and served as President of the American Historical Association -- he was a symbol of dynamic nationalism.

If semiosis is the way humans think and act, deconstruction -- the denial that action is what it purports to be -- is the product of a historical situation which has lost faith in its society's symbolization of human experience.   Admittedly, this is not an unreasonable reaction to the world of the late twentieth century.   Capitalism has proven unsatisfactory, and thus discredited democracy for many, because, in Churchill's words, it is the unequal distribution of the wealth.   Socialism has also failed, again to quote Churchill, because it was the (somewhat) equal distribution of the misery.   Successful mixed economies still depend on impoverished and exploited internal and external proletariats.   Nothing seems to work: as Francis Fukayama has written in *The End of History and the Last Man*, published in 1992, with the collapse of Communism bourgeois liberalism has the field to itself.   Any nation which would prosper must adopt it.   Yet it does not work terribly well, and its ideal of a comfortable life based on production of goods offers little to the mysterious yearnings of the human heart for meaning.   Hence the continued appeal of nationalism -- sometimes in fascist form -- and fundamentalist religions, especially among those denied the comfortable life.

Intellectuals have a reasonably comfortable life, at least by the standards of most of the world's people. But their existence depends on thinking, speaking, and writing in order to make sense of human experience. When for good or ill civilization has lost confidence in its mission and ideals -- one sign of this is the contemporary obsession with 'diversity,' that is, each group clamoring for its place in the sun -- what is left is the intellectual thinking, speaking, and writing to a specialized audience. By asserting that there is no meaning outside the text or that meaning is arbitrary, the deconstructionist is advancing the idea that meaning comes from intellectuals imparting significance to texts and undermining the validity of any other source (society, religion) which claims to do likewise. To put it uncharitably, deconstruction is the justification of the leisure of the theoried class, at least as long as the much-reviled western democracies continue to support it.

But let us not be only uncharitable. Many things can be profitably deconstructed -- advertising, political campaigns, legal injustice, insidious forms of racial, class, and sexual exploitation. But the man on the street cannot stop there. He needs his symbols to live for as much as the deconstructionist needs them for his text and tenure.

So what then does the semiotician do? Briefly, she looks at the way signs arrange themselves, 'abducts' (guesses) a pattern based upon her training and historical situation, and tries to figure out what they mean. This requires sensitivity to the different meaning of signs over time based upon the audience, communicator, and place of the sign in an overall code. It also requires sensitivity to one's own historical context as reinterpreter of the sign's meaning, and awareness that no interpretation will ever be definitive. As Charles Peirce taught us, the truth is something that an infinite community of dedicated inquirers adhering to scientific methodology will arrive at in the indefinitely long run -- that is, never. We can approximate it, not attain it. We can describe, we cannot define. We may deconstruct, but then we *must* reconstruct.

My own imperfect understanding of semiotic theory is best found in chapters two, five, and the first part of thirteen. The essays in this book deal with a variety of items which illustrate or may influence the conjunction of historical and semiotic inquiry. First I reprint a review of John Deely's *Basics of Semiotics*. Deely, Brooke Williams, and Roberta Kevelson have been the key people who introduced me to semiotics and whose enthusiastic proselytizing has converted me. Next I include two essays on the American philosopher Charles Sanders Peirce. The first situates his semiotic philosophy in the context of his own magnificently tragic life; the second looks at Peirce's historical writing, some of which is almost totally unknown, and explains why a semiotician would possess a particular philosophy of history. Peirce's 'anancastic' evolution argued strongly that history did not evolve -- it erupted in cataclysms and catastrophes (much like those in his own life) and brought forth representative figures whose movements created new orders out of chaos -- for a while.

Next I look at three thinkers whose approach to reality was decidedly semiotic: Carl Becker, Eric Voegelin, and Thorstein Veblen. Treating the greatest human ideals as signs made concrete in different systems over time, they sensitively explored the transformations of society and politics on a grand scale. Rejecting dogmatisms and insisting that 'by their fruits (signs) ye shall know them,' the liberal Becker, conservative Voegelin, and radical Veblen all offered important critiques of societal flaws and appreciations of the value of a civilization's cooperative work and thought.

Chapters nine through twelve deal with my major historical field, American history. The Founding Fathers, I maintain, set up a republic which offered Americans, much like a Peircean community of inquirers, the flexibility to maximize justice, freedom, and equality. Their own interpretations of the Declaration of Independence and the Constitution bear this out. I take strong exception to the periodically fashionable notion that they were elitists out to hoodwink the people and stifle democracy -- that came after the Civil War. Rather, they institutionalized as much popular rule as was consistent with their understanding of the fate of republics in history and the limitations of human nature. I next examine the semiotic jurisprudence of the fascinating nineteenth century philosopher Francis Lieber, whose work on *Legal and Political Hermeneutics* could still serve as a basic text for a course on legal semiotics. Then I apply semiotic analysis to the symbolisms both middle-class Americans and radical opponents of their values have used to define themselves. I here illustrate a thesis borrowed from Professor Kevelson, that 'legitimacy' (what a community will assent to as law) interacts with and is sometimes opposed to 'legality' (the letter or judicial interpretation of the law).

Essays thirteen through fifteen look at historical texts which reject dogmatic reality in favor of offering the reader the freedom to think deeply about basic problems of the state, morality, and religion. My interpretations of Thucydides, Plato (which I suspect will be controversial if anyone pays attention), and the fundamental articles of the Anglican Church present them as intending to create 'good' or 'thinking' people by offering a spectrum of possible answers to the great issues which have vexed humanity, and leaving us to wrestle with these insoluble problems.

Essays sixteen through twenty-one are on music and film. I hope to show the value of looking historically at how music, film, film-makers, and musicians all function in worlds of complex symbolisms which raise the same basic human issues as the other essays in the book.   The essay on Ernesto Cardenal, a Nicaraguan poet acutely aware of how you can judge a society by its symbols, was placed here to facilitate reading the two essays on Central America together.   I conclude with a somewhat whimsical piece on postage stamps as symbols of national identity, an easy way to illustrate how semiotics may be done.

Semiotics can be fun, as when a friend and I amused ourselves figuring out why yuppies in Philadelphia would go to a jungle-style nightclub on the Delaware River.   It can be dangerous, too: if you get too involved in semiotics and start trying to interpret everything from every possible perspective and then criticize your interpretation, it can take the ginger out of a musical performance or social gathering.   But it is essential: essential to save us from the Scylla of dogmatism and the Charybdis of deconstruction.   Have I therefore become symbolically Ulysses?   Oh, stop it . . . .

This book is for my friends and colleagues, but I would like to thank especially Cindy Palecek, 'A Perfect Secretary' and her staff for whatever attractiveness the volume possesses.   Funding from Penn State's Berks and Ogontz Campuses, College of the Liberal Arts, the College's Dean for the Commonwealth Educational System Margaret Cote, and most of all my incredibly generous and loving parents, Charles and Harriett Pencak, who have always provided all the moral and financial support I needed to do my work, facilitated publication of the book.   Michael Flamini and the staff at Peter Lang have been expert in assisting me in preparing the volume and removing rather than creating hurdles.

While I will not hierarchize my friends, four persons have especially inspired me over the years.   Bill Parsons showed me how persistent one can be in his quest to become a historian.   Carl Royer taught me about total devotion to one's writing.   Roberta Kevelson first involved me in semiotics, and suggested many of the topics in this book either directly or indirectly in what seems in retrospect one prolonged, beautiful discussion over the past ten years. She also invited me to collect my essays and publish them in her series, for which I am most grateful. And there is Jeffrey Polizzotto, my spiritual brother and a modern hero. Had he lived in the Athens of Pericles, people would remember him as one of the most admirable of men, and the kindest and best friend anyone ever had.

Glenside, Pennsylvania

Chapter 2

Semiotics is Not, Necessarily, Deconstruction: A Review of John Deely, *Basics of Semiotics*

Having attained notoriety as a preacher of the semiotic gospel to historians, I am frequently asked two questions by my colleagues: 'What is semiotics?' and 'Why are you fooling around with all that deconstruction stuff?' My usual answer to the first question is a less elegant approximation of two phrases from John Deely's *Basics of Semiotics*: 'The whole of our experience, from its most primitive origins in sensation to its most refined achievements of understanding, is a network or web of sign relations' (p.13) and '. . . semiotic studies investigate. . . . The action of signs.' (p.22).[1] To the second question, I respond that deconstruction and the glamorous figures associated with it are engaged in what at best is an offshoot ('the minor tradition', as Thomas Sebeok calls it) at worst a perversion of the real semiotic enterprise. 'The contemporary teaching of semiotics is severely, perhaps cripplingly, impoverished by the utter, frightening innocence of most practitioners of semiotics about the natural order in which they and it are embedded' (Sebeok, 1990:82).

Now I can stop mumbling and simply tell my friends to invest a mere ten dollars to embark on what should be the beginning of the greatest intellectual adventure of their lives. John Deely has written a great book that deserves the widest possible circulation and translation for three reasons. First, as Sebeok notes on the cover blurb, his is 'the only successful modern English introduction to semiotics . . . a clear, creative, and provocative synthesis of major trends, past and present.' (I am bold to say, unless something in Albanian or Guarani has escaped me, this is the only successful introduction to semiotics in *any* language.) What, you may ask, of earlier introductions by Deely (1982) and Sebeok (1979) themselves, not to mention Umberto Eco (1976)? These estimable tomes are fine for explaining the semiotic enterprise to practitioners. The layman, especially the skeptical academic or the educated man in the street, has long required a book in which jargon is explained, usually more than once, using diagrams and down-to-earth examples, where the *basics* (hence Deely's title) and importance of the subject are emphasized to the exclusion of more complicated theoretical material.

Second, Deely here conveys as does no other book I know the excitement of practicing semiotics and its absolute necessity for understanding the universe in which we live. Deely's central chapters give us, in roughly equal proportion, anthropo -- (signs and man), zoö -- (signs and animals), physio -- (signs and inorganic matter) and phyto -- (signs and plants) semiosis, amply proving his contentions that 'The objects of experience as such, thus, depend in every case on signs. . . .' (p. 53) and 'semiotics tends to function as an antidote for overspecialization, by imposing an objective awareness of the common processes of signification on which the most specialized achievements of knowledge depend.' (p. 107). Deely gives us a semiotics of the stars as only one dazzling element in his 'A Matrix for All the Sciences' (p. 74). He takes us on a breathtaking ride through philosophical history from Augustine to the present in fifteen pages, showing us how great minds through the ages have looked at the universe in terms of sign relationships.[2] He frees us from having to argue over false dichotomies: nature/culture (quoting Thüre von Üexkill: 'Man is led, from his extravagant position as the observer positioned outside nature and as its unscrupulous exploiter, back into nature') -- (p. 103), mind/body, idealism/realism, subject/object (p. 17). Once we adopt the semiotic point of view (not method, Deely insists; semiotics is rather a means of linking methods) and realize 'Signs . . . are required not only for any given method in philosophy or in the sciences, natural or human, but for the very possibility of there being such a thing as method or inquiry of any kind.' (p. 11); once we realize that the observer selects, creates, and interacts with the observed to transform a constantly changing universe composed of an infinity of sign relationships, the Gordian Knots of traditional philosophy are not so much cut as leaped over: '. . . semiotics puts an end, long overdue, to the Cartesian revolution and to the pretensions of scientific thought to transcend, through mathematical means, the human condition.' (p. 118).

Now does this sound like deconstruction, a word Deely does not use once in his entire book? Properly understood, distinguished from the 'semiology' of Barthes, Saussure, Derrida, etc. (to whom Deely gives short or no shrift), semiotics is reconstruction, or, as Deely puts it 'revelation' (p. 11). Its task is '. . . renewing the history of thought and restoring unity to the ancient enterprise of so-called philosophical understanding,' (p. 118) as Deely writes of semiotic pioneer John Poinsot, whose *Treatise on Signs* (1632) he has translated. Limiting texts to the literary, or modelling an artificial universe on the 'primary' system of linguistics, French or Saussurian semiology has indeed given us a dessicated, deconstructed, jargon-laden universe. 'The question', both for Deely and for anyone concerned with the future of human thought, '. . . is whether, in coming into its own, semiotics will continue modern philosophy's obsession with method or will it establish its theoretical framework with sufficient richness and flexibility to accommodate itself to the full range of signifying phenomena.' (p. 9). In other words, is semiotics equal to the universe it purports to describe? Not if semiologists keep writing more and more about less and less; not if philosophers and scientists keep trying to define and measure constantly changing relationships as through they were 'objects'.

Fortunately, on the other side there are the mighty figures of Charles Peirce, Thomas Sebeok, founding father and present godfather of the Semiotic Society of America, and now John Deely fighting the phantom dragon and seeking to restore to us the significant (intentional double-entendre) universe in its full glory. *Basics of Semiotics* will bring to the reader the insight which flashed in Martin Esslin's mind when he discovered semiotics: '. . . I felt rather like Molière's M. Jourdain who was surprised to discover that he had been talking prose all his life.' (p. 120): we have all been practicing semioticians all our lives, constructing an *Umwelt* (world of significant relationships which enable us to function) from the *Lebenswelt* (the infinity of worlds possible).   What Deely has done is make it possible for the uninitiated layman (and academic) now to be a *conscious* semiotician: '. . . semiotics must first, in order to achieve its history, identify and hierarchize those moments where the sign comes to be *recognized* for the role it plays in its own right and not just *deployed* quasi-invisibly in dealings with objects.' (p. 106). 'Then, . . . semiotics . . . expands outward over the whole realm of knowledge and belief to elicit from within each of the disciplines objectively constituted an actual awareness, more or less reluctant, of the semioses and semiotic processes virtually present within them by their very nature as finite knowledge.' (p. 107).

Freeing philosophy from the bogeymen of deconstruction, enforced separation of disciplines, and false dichotomies, semiotics possesses exciting possibilities for action in the world. As mentioned above, it restores man to nature and nature to man, increasing awareness of mutual dependence. It is the fierce foe of intolerance and ideology, the Procrustean beds onto which zealots of every description have attempted to confine both their universes and their opponents. It is the point of view of the free, choosing, interactive person, as opposed to the determined, passive, enslaved person, for when we become aware that the contexts and codes confronting us are infinite in number and develop through our manner of dealing with them, we can embark on the adventure for which our grey matter obviously exists. John Deely has written a book which one can only hope will become a landmark of intellectual history: the clear and exciting explication of why the semiotic point of view and only the semiotic point of view adequately describes man's interaction with his universe.

ENDNOTES

1.   For convenience, references to the book under review are indicated by page only in the text. *Basics of Semiotics*, Indiana University Press paperback, 1990, $9.95.

2.   In the second edition this book surely deserves to have, may I suggest Deely add an historical appendix of leading figures in semiotics and a brief discussion of their theories, along with lists of their major works. It would, for instance, be useful to know about Greimas's semiotic square and Saussure's distinction between langue and parole, and the contributions of Lacan, DeMan, Barthes, Foucault, etc., as anyone delving further into semiotics will encounter these names and probably be frustrated by their inability to understand them easily. Also, the Prague School and Roman Jakobson need some attention, as they were important influences on Sebeok and, thus, on Deely himself. Even if Deely disagrees with many of the continental writers, his ability to clarify complex material and make it exciting would undoubtedly serve the 'semiologists,' as he calls them, very well in initiating novices into their difficult world.

REFERENCES

Deely, John, 1982, *Introducing Semiotic: Its History and Doctrine*, Bloomington: Indiana University Press.

Eco, Umberto, 1976, *A Theory of Semiotics*, Bloomington: Indiana University Press.

Poinsot, John, 1632, *Tractatus de Signis*, trans., John Deely in consultation with Ralph A. Powell, Berkeley: University of California Press, 1985.

Sebeok, Thomas A., 1979, *The Sign and Its Masters*, Austin: University of Texas Press; corrected reprint 1989. Lanham, MD: University Press of America.

_____, 1990, 'Semiotics in the United States,' introduction to *American Signatures*, Norman: University of Oklahoma Press. Page reference to manuscript version.

Chapter 3

Charles S. Peirce and Arisbe

The life of Charles Sanders Peirce (1839-1914), one of the United States' finest philosophers and the major pioneer of pragmatism and semiotics, can accurately be described as a tragedy in the classic Greek sense. Peirce was a great man undone by his greatest strength -- his unwillingness to constrict his life and thought to horizons recognized and rewarded by his contemporaries. He preferred voluntary exile for the last quarter-century of his life even when Arisbe, his dream of a flourishing community of true scholars, deteriorated into a perpetually unfinished shambles. Rejected by and rejecting the traditional academic and social circles of the late nineteenth century, Peirce sought to create something like a cross between a free university and a 'think tank' on the banks of the Delaware River, just outside Milford in extreme northeastern Pennsylvania, decades before either materialized.[1] But instead of serving as an example to the world, Peirce's rambling villa became a trap for the aging philosopher. The final years of his life were marked by increasing bitterness, poverty, illness, and isolation.

This paper hopes to convey the tragedy of Peirce's life at Arisbe and to demonstrate its effects on his philosophy. Peirce referred to concrete events from his life and surroundings only rarely in his formal writings. However, the cumulative effect of his tragic personal life caused him to emphasize four ideas in his later works only hinted at or not mentioned earlier: the 'brutality' of experience; the 'surprising fact' as the beginning of doubt which initiates thought; 'anancastic' or 'cataclysmic' change as more important than progressive evolution;

and the test of self-sacrifice, practical uselessness, and rejection to distinguish the true lover of knowledge from the seeker after power, money, and popularity. Ironically, Peirce had earlier sought academic appointments and lived a luxurious -- by contemporary standards scandalous -- life. At Arisbe, he transformed his personal tragedy into a psychological and philosophical triumph.

If Arisbe ended in catastrophe, it began with the highest of hopes. Peirce moved to this site, which his wife Juliette purchased in her name on May 10, 1888, for three major reasons. First, he hoped to show American universities how true education and scholarship ought to proceed. Second, the nearby village of Milford contained a sophisticated French community which he hoped would grant Juliette the social acceptance previously denied her. Finally, Pike County provided a rare combination of spectacular scenic beauty, peace, and isolation with easy access to both a lively local society and the railroad station at Port Jervis, New York. A two and one-half hour ride took Peirce to the Manhattan ferry in Jersey City.

By the mid-1880s, Peirce and the American university had no more use for each other. In his 1880 Fourth of July Address to the American community in Paris, Peirce deliberately subverted the typical function of this patriotic oration. Instead of indulging in 'self-glorification of our ancestors,' he decided to 'submit ourselves to a little self-humility,' arguing that 'my faith in a love for America is not of so skin-deep a kind that I am afraid to look her faults in the face.' He then launched a scathing condemnation of the American college and even the newly emergent university to explain 'why has science made so little progress in America'? Distinguishing foolishly between the 'practical and theoretical,' colleges had been 'positively frowning upon' scientific research 'as tending to interfere with proper pedagogical activity.' Peirce singled out Harvard (where he had taught briefly but was refused a permanent appointment) and Columbia for special censure. He only praised the Johns Hopkins University (where he was currently employed and seeking tenured status): 'it has here alone been recognized that the function of a university is the production of knowledge, and that teaching is only a necessary means to that end.'[2] By 1900, having been fired from Hopkins in 1884, Peirce re-discovered 'the most elevated ideal of any university in the world' at Clark University, which pursued 'science as its first object, with teaching . . . as only a secondary or subordinate subject.' Since this praise appeared in Peirce's review of a history of Clark, perhaps he was still trying for academic respectability.[3] But in general, as he wrote about 1896, 'wherever there is a large class of academic professors who are provided with good incomes and looked up to as gentlemen, scientific inquiry must languish.' He only added that 'wherever the bureaucrats are the more learned class, the case will still be worse.' (1.51)[4] Peirce had found his duties at the Coast and Geodetic Service, from which he was forced out in 1891 after thirty years' service, as confining as the university requirements that he teach subjects and students in which he had little interest.[5]

Uncomfortable with the restrictions in both his conventional careers, Peirce created Arisbe as an alternative:

Our American universities have, one and all, a narrowly and rigidly prescribed end, that of education . . . for the individual advantage of the students. And what, I pray, is the individual advantage which refuses to look beyond the individual? . . . that they should lead luxurious lives. Wretched business! They had better spare themselves their years of bad habits at the university, content themselves with a course at a commercial college, go about the world, and look for a chance to make money.

In place of these training schools for greed, Peirce proposed 'not a school, but a brotherhood,' comprised of 'the sort of persons who are consumed with the desire of learning what they do not know and of correcting the errors what they now hold for knowledge.   They would and must be animated by a pure passion for increasing the available fund of understanding of God's universe more and more, forever and ever.'   He was hopeful, he wrote in an unpublished letter, that 'embodied in such an institution as I would plan, they [the brotherhood] would prove one of the greatest agents of enlightenment in all history.'   Peirce went so far as to predict that 'the XXIst. century would say that nothing in the world had been so good for it and the XXth. as this brotherhood in Arisbe.'[6]

Clearly, as Juliette Peirce told her neighbors after Charles' death, 'he had great possibilities.'   'He had wonderful dreams,' Milford resident Elmer Roberts recalled.[7]   Peirce planned a correspondence school to supplement residential instruction, hoped to develop acetylene as a source of energy, and even proposed to begin experiments in flying.[8]   If in 1909 he could write of 'having deliberately buried myself in this wild country in order to devote myself more completely to the study of logic,' Peirce was giving an incomplete account of his motives based on the activity to which his life eventually shrunk.[9]   He had also wished to turn his estate into a center of the high life he had known and enjoyed in both the United States and on trips to Europe:[10]

> I propose to set up three pretty cottages of about four rooms each and
> make the house a sort of Casino for fashionable people of 'cultural
> tendencies' to spend the summer, have a good time, and take a mild
> dose of philosophy. . . . My ultimate aim is to get a going institution
> for the pursuit of pure science and philosophy which will be self-
> supporting.

At the beginning, Peirce had every intention that a life of social grace and luxury would complement rather than inhibit his scholarly endeavors.   It is no wonder that he named his residence 'Arisbe.'   The first record of this name dates from September 9, 1891. Peirce had at first preferred the old name of 'Quicktown,' as 'Tom Quick [the area's pioneer and an Indian scout] was 'a rather romantic figure.'[11] But Arisbe served several purposes. In the *Illiad* (II, 836-839), we read that 'Axylos . . . from well-built Arisbe,' a Greek colony on the coast of Asia Minor, was 'a man of substance and loved by all men, for his home was on the high road there, and welcomed all who came by.' Peirce's estate similarly was on the road connecting the fashionable summer resort of Milford with Port Jervis's rail terminal; he also hoped to welcome learned and interested people. Second, Arisbe appears later in Greek history as a colony of Miletus, the latter city being the home of the earliest philosophers. Not only was Peirce's Arisbe obviously a 'colony of philosophy' in its own right, but Max Fisch has demonstrated Peirce's increasing interest in the Greek thinkers in his later life.[12]

Peirce not only modelled Arisbe on an ancient Greek community. It was also founded on the two real communities which most influenced his thought. At his father's house 'he was forced to think hard and continuously' by the assemblage of intellectuals who visited including Longfellow, Emerson, James Russell Lowell, Charles Norton, George Bancroft, Daniel Webster, Rufus Choate, Judge Joseph Story, Margaret Fuller, and Charles Sumner. Later, in the 1870s, he and a group of friends including William James, Chauncey Wright, John Fiske, Nicholas St. John Green, and Oliver Wendell Holmes set up a 'Metaphysical Club' in Cambridge. Given the intellectual stature of these groups, and the free-flowing conversation and constructive criticism found among groups of friends, it is easy to understand why Peirce believed such a setting far more conducive to the pursuit of wisdom than a traditional university classroom.[13]

A congenial social atmosphere mattered at least as much to Peirce as a chance to pursue his studies. Peirce and his second wife -- Juliette Pourtalai (née Froissy) -- had been snubbed by his family and respectable society ever since they had become companions. Beginning in 1877 -- after his first wife Melusina Fay (later a prominent women's rights activist) left him -- Peirce had travelled extensively in Europe and America with a widowed Frenchwoman about twenty years his junior. They finally wed in 1883 after 'having been so intimate for some years as to cause great scandal,' according to Peirce's Hopkins colleague Simon Newcomb. There were two main objections to Peirce's behavior with Juliette. First, the mere fact of divorce was unusual in Victorian America. Peirce's brother Herbert wrote to his sister Helen that 'society wouldn't be too good if every man could get divorced from his wives (say only a couple of them) and marry his mistress.' And Herbert liked Juliette personally: 'She is kind, pleasant, always ready to help Charlie (too ready) and seems most discreet. Yet there is the great fact of their imprudence.'[14]

Most of all, no one knew who Juliette was. This fact greatly offended Peirce's proper Bostonian family. The Peirces had immigrated to Massachusetts in 1635, married into the Lodges, and boasted Peirce's father Benjamin, America's finest mathematician of the early nineteenth century. Peirce always maintained that although his wife enjoyed 'the most intimate relations with the most celebrated people of Europe,' still, 'nobody but me knows who she really is and I have always protected her against questions and have, when pressed, simply refused to give any information.' Peirce's Milford neighbors saw her beautiful furs and jewels, and recalled her claiming relations with the royal houses of Austria, Germany, and Russia. She apparently had been 'Princess Juliette' who had played as a child with the future Kaiser Wilhelm II. Pennsylvania's Governor Gifford Pinchot -- a fellow inhabitant of Milford and friend of the Peirces -- insisted that 'she knew too much that was reliable to have been fabricating the whole thing.' A memorandum of attorney Henry James, Jr., who handled the Jameses' gifts to the Peirces, stated that 'she could not establish her identity without compelling other members of her family to acknowledge the selfish and scandalous course which had led them to sacrifice her.' In a letter to Pinchot written about 1930 she claimed to have signed away two fortunes and travelled to America to save her brother (a prominent diplomat) 'from disgrace and her father from shock,' only to have her brother commit suicide and her father die almost immediately.[15]

Nevertheless, some of Peirce's neighbors and, most especially, his family, did not believe any of it. Members of the Gassmann family thought she and Peirce were involved in smuggling, and observed 'a constant flow of unidentified foreign visitors to the Peirce household.' 'Papa' Gassmann, a neighbor at whose house Juliette would drink beer sometimes, once responded to one of her regal stories: 'I know where you came from -- a crow dropped you on the fly.' Neighbors also thought she might be a gypsy: she called Peirce 'Bapa', a gypsy nickname, read tarot cards, and had psychic powers. Gypsies passing through the area invariably visited the Peirces, and Peirce took some interest in the gypsy language. Peirce's family preferred to believe the worst as well. Herbert considered her 'an absolute humbug,' claimed that she had 'bewitched' Charles, and 'if she had lived in Salem during witch time she would have been tried as a witch.' Peirce's sister Lizzie (Charlotte Elizabeth) termed her 'absolutely disagreeable.'[16]

Milford, the Peirces hoped, would prove a congenial location where Juliette, who was French, could enjoy the company of a genteel, long-established Huguenot community including the Pinchots. Juliette's friendship with the future governor's mother in fact prompted the Peirces to investigate Milford in the first place. They originally stayed at the Hotel Fauchère, named for another leading local family, and the gourmet Peirce was especially delighted at the presence of French chefs who 'have disseminated good cooking wonderfully.'[17]

Furthermore, in the summer, when the small town of 500 was augmented by its high society vacationers, it offered a summer theater. The Peirces hoped it would mark Juliette's debut as an actress. Peirce wrote to his mother in 1887 that the then-famous actor Steele MacKaye 'told some gentlemen that there had not been her equal on the stage in our day.' He went so far as to translate the French play *Médée* by Legouvé into English for his wife. Peirce inscribed as a dedication two lines of Creusa's dialogue which obviously described Juliette: 'What noble accents and what sovereign brow; she remains an exile yet she stands a queen.' Even in her old age, neighbor Bob Blood described Juliette as 'theatrical' and 'the greatest conversationalist in the world.'[18]

Finally, the Peirces settled at Arisbe because it was spectacularly beautiful. Peirce claimed that 'the valley of the Delaware where I live will compare with any country I have seen -- and I have seen many -- for picturesqueness.' Writing in an unpublished manuscript of 1913, Peirce waxed poetic:[19]

> What chiefly makes me delight in it is the fine view from it. For the ground slopes down, or rather descends by three short jumps and a pretty lofty one, to the picturesque Delaware River, beyond which one sees two ridges parallel to the river. . . . It is a charming spot looking far and wide over a smiling and civilized looking country; and all but at the very tip top lies a most poet-inspiring tarn that makes one weep for joy to catch sight of. So a man of wealth has established a large house there [Grey Towers, built in 1886 by Amos Pinchot] and apparently very near the house has erected a sort of less ambitious *tour d'Eiffel*, which stands up above the skyline with very good effect.

On at least three occasions, though, Peirce referred to his new residence as 'wild' -- 'the wildest country I could reach.' Yet by wild he undoubtedly meant isolated (the nearest neighbors were a mile away) and undeveloped.[20] In 1904 he spoke lovingly of the improvements Juliette designed for the house, modelled on the chateau she had lived in as a child, as 'exquisitely soft without the faintest suggestion of ambition. The house is entirely unlike any other and breathes a spirit of deep peace.'[21] When interviewed in 1976 as to why Peirce came to Milford, Caroline Depuy, who had known him as a little girl, agreed: 'The quiet. The fresh air. The forest, which he loved, and the river. There was a quiet and peace that he couldn't find anywhere else.'[22]

Arisbe began well. Peirce originally had an income of about $6000 a year and his wife $4000, which made them very wealthy indeed by the standards of the 1890s.[23] They immediately began demolishing shacks and refurbishing the main house, so that by May of 1892 *The Home Journal* could remark that 'in the past year, Mrs. Charles Sanders Peirce has brought her exquisite French taste and continental experience to the building of a picturesque villa not in the least pretentious, which forms as it were the prelude to the feast of grand river and interior view which fill the eye and stimulate the mind.'[24] Peirce even made a practical scholarly impact: Gifford Pinchot credited him with the inspiration in 1887 or 1888 to go to Germany to study scientific forestry, a pressing need in Pike County which had been devastated by forest fires. There were apparently a couple of students from Harvard who visited Peirce, and many years later Juliette recalled to Frank Manuel how the house 'was once full of the voices of brilliant and talkative men' such as William James and Josiah Royce.[25]

But things began to go wrong almost from the start. The Peirces' problems may be grouped under no fewer than five categories: their extravagant plans for Arisbe; the financial distress which made them impossible to fulfill; repeated illnesses for both Charles and Juliette, plus assorted disasters; their consequent inability to care for the place; and difficulties with their neighbors. At the time of Peirce's death in 1914, the villa itself had deteriorated along with his health and his dreams.

Peirce's desire to recreate his wife's childhood chateau fell victim to a lack of architectural knowledge and incompetence.   Gifford Pinchot recalled that 'Peirce was extremely impractical. He submitted to her plans for alterations in the house loyally and cheerfully, living in one room while all the others were in turmoil.'   Pinchot termed the alterations 'of an absurd character,' a judgment confirmed by an anonymous observer in 1907 when Peirce was engaged in another round of modifications.   He insisted on drawing up all the plans himself, but 'really, a person who knows so little about buildings as Mr. Peirce ought not to attack such a problem.'[26]   At times the roof leaked so badly that the Peirces had to wear rubbers in the house.[27]   Neighbors remarked that he sometimes paid twice over for work done on the house.[28]   Despite his increasing poverty, Peirce undertook extensive alterations in 1909 and 1913; at the time of his death Arisbe had no fewer than twenty-five guest rooms and twenty-four baths (many subsequently dismantled by Robert Phillips after Juliette's death in 1934) in the hopes that it could either be sold for a price of $30,000 to $40,000 (Peirce paid $3200 for the original) or run as a profitable inn.[29]

Peirce might have survived his experiments in construction had both he and his wife not 'lost every cent within a fortnight of one another and without the slightest -- without a day's warning.' The cause of the Peirces' financial demise is unknown, although it can be dated with considerable confidence to 1892. The Peirces acquired a great deal of property adjoining the house in Juliette's name in 1891, but in November, 1892 Peirce drafted a letter, stating that 'all my difficulties have to be kept secret from my wife, or she would be wanting to compromise her prospects in a way I would never consent to.'[30] From then on, we read of debts, of mortgages, sheriffs visits,[31] unpaid bills,[32] and complaints of extreme poverty which included protestations that Juliette only had 'rags' to wear, that Peirce could not afford ink to write with, or a candle to see by, and that they were practically starving. In 1909, Peirce confessed himself 'devoid of business habits, experience, or natural faculty. I am still a perfect three year old in such matters. I turn every penny over to my wife and wonder how she contrives to make ends meet.'[33]

Juliette not only handled the Peirces' finances -- all the deeds and mortgages are in her name -- but she obtained money secretly from Europe. Neighbors noted she periodically journeyed overseas; in 1914 she wrote that she had just lost an income of $300 annually. It may have been, as Edna Green recalled, that she was required to spend all the money at once, on the house and immediate expenses, rather than to build up a fortune. This would account for the fact, Bob Blood remarked, that 'she would put up a certain amount of renovation, have so much demolition done on the front, and then in the next few years she would tear that down and do it again. It became quite a joke.'[34]

The Pinchots and William James also helped the Peirces. William James assumed the burden of the Peirces' mortgages. The Pinchots even provided the Peirces with a small gravestone in their family plot in the Milford Cemetery.[35]

In addition to their financial woes, both Charles and Juliette were ill much of the time, sometimes simultaneously. This made caring for the house and Peirce's continuing with his writing almost impossible for long periods. As early as January 1882, before they were married, Peirce noted in his diary that Juliette had serious pelvic trouble. In 1887, she was ill again. In 1889 she was spitting 'lots of blood.'[36] In the last decade of Peirce's life, letters and diary entries concerning illness appear with heartbreaking regularity. On April 10, 1904, Peirce informed Lady Welby that 'the reason I have not written for so long is that my dear wife has been ill and for five weeks I hardly left her bedside, and even now that she is up, I am continually worried about her too great energy, besides myself being in a state of nervous fatigue about it all.' In February, 1905, he 'was suddenly collapsed with nervous prostration' and could only do half a day's work as late as April. Later that year, he found Juliette without a pulse stretched on the floor. In 1908, he thought Juliette was dying: 'my dear wife constantly though slowly loses ground and her disposition not to spare herself is most distressing.' By 1911, aged 72, he claimed to be 'suffering from an early old age, the case with all the males of my ancestors,' and was sure that his wife 'who was constructed to be a princess,' would not survive another winter.[37]

Peirce's final diary entries from 1911 to 1914 record his bouts with what turned out to be fatal stomach cancer along with such miscellaneous vexations as a broken rib; a bite from his dog, Zola; a fire which nearly reached the house; a bout with an itch; cold spells which lowered the temperature in the house to the forties; frozen pipes; and continued illnesses for Juliette. Peirce's suffering in his bowels, first noted on November 26, 1911 must have been the onset of the cancer which plagued him for the last two and a half years of his life, but as early as April 27 of that year he had written: 'I am terribly unhappy. I long to die but mustn't desert J.' On New Year's Day 1914 he recorded that 'my eternal stomach ache continues' while Juliette also 'suffers greatly.' The final entry in his diary, dated March 30, 1914, only three weeks before his death, was: 'Of course a good deal of pain.'[38]

As a result of their repeated illnesses, the Peirces' house became a shambles. Although the neighboring Gassmanns noted they always had servants, it appears from their letters they only did intermittently and at any rate had to do a good deal of work themselves. In 1911, Peirce recorded 'rows with the servants', but he, Juliette, and the neighbors commented on how household chores and the burden of caring for each other took their toll on both their constitutions.[39] As a result, 'the weeds got the best' of their garden. By 1909, Peirce realized he would have to thoroughly repair the house to obtain a reasonable price for it. He told Lady Welby that 'it looked so forlorn that nobody could be persuaded that the inside is worth looking at.' On May 25, 1911, he wrote that 'it is ridiculous for us to live in such a place,' and predicted its sale would fetch almost $40,000.[40]

Yet for all his hints and protestations about the burden Arisbe had become, neither Peirce nor Juliette ever moved out. As early as 1901, Peirce's family was thinking he might sell the place and move to St. Petersburg in Russia. In 1904 he was trying to obtain a consular appointment in Ceylon, and at various times for the rest of his life he entertained hopes of going abroad and resuming his travels. In 1909, Peirce added that his wife 'has never felt at home here' and hoped 'to make her remaining years more tolerable.'[41]

Yet even after Peirce's death, Juliette refused to give up the place. She became indignant when the James family lawyer, Henry, Jr. (Harry) suggested, as did her neighbors in future interviews, that she could have lived very well from the sale of the property in a more modest place: 'I am pained and shocked at your continued injustice to me. In one of your letters you accuse me of having misappropriated the pension in spending it on the property.' She complained that 'I have struggled hard ever since with my own resources to maintain the place at no end of sacrifices,' and refused to surrender at a bargain price an estate she claimed was 'superior to anything between Philadelphia and Pittsburgh.' Orra Gassmann commented that Juliette's tragedy was every bit as great as her husband's. 'The woman suffered everything to take care of this house and what was in it, and after she died [in 1934], people went through it, and pulled it this way and that way.'[42]

Juliette Peirce undoubtedly clung to the house out of her great devotion to her husband. Until the day she died she dressed in black and wrote letters on black-edge cards. Caroline Depuy summed it up best: 'If ever a woman adored her husband, Madame Peirce adored him.' This resident of Milford termed her 'a most remarkable woman. Without her love, tenderness, and care, Charles Sanders Peirce would have departed this life long before 1914.' Other neighbors agreed: Elmer Roberts told how she would come around and 'tell you how wonderful he was.' Walter Gassmann noted 'everything was Bapa. [Her pet name for Peirce.] She thought a lot of Bapa.'[43] Peirce reciprocated his wife's feelings. In 1894, responding to a letter from his brother James asking him to leave her, he called her 'a saint and an angel besides a most skillful manager ever since. Her genius, her courage, her probity has so enslaved my heart, that it is no more use asking me to leave her than asking me to be chopped in two.' In 1904, he wrote to Lady Welby of 'my exceptional dependence upon her . . . a person whom all men reverence and all women love and of whom it is impossible to tire.'[44]

For all their personal affection, however, Juliette could never fathom the point of her husband's research, although she was very proud of him. On February 23, 1909, she wrote to Mrs. William James: 'My husband works with all his might and strength on his logic. But *entre nous*, I *detest* logic. There don't seem to be anything practical to it.' Peirce, for his part, especially admired his wife's culinary abilities -- 'Juliette is a veritable cordon blue' -- and her fascinating if unorthodox conversation. On February 14, 1889, for instance, 'Juliette talked in a very interesting way at dinner. Everybody had genius in some line. Mixed races were the finest. Californians a fine people.'[45]

Both Charles and Juliette made tremendous sacrifices to stay together. Peirce would write that 'while free all along to be rich and leave me, [she] has stuck to me and to the most grinding poverty.' And Juliette was acutely aware that their marriage estranged Peirce from his family. In 1921 she wrote 'When I married Mr. Peirce he had *embarrass de choix*. But he refused, insisting he would not abandon his country.' Peirce's brother James also found it strange that he gave her half his earnings and allowed her to own their property.[46] But Juliette summed up the basis of their mutual devotion in a draft of a letter she may have sent to Lady Welby:[47]

> You call him a genius. Never mind about me. I have been for the last twelve years accustomed to suffering of endless privations and humiliations and miseries but what is hardest of all is to bear to think I have married a man that must depend more or less on charity. For in other countries a man of his abilities would be eagerly sought out, instead of being called too old at sixty years for a well deserved post in his own country.

Peirce was not only scorned by his prominent countrymen. He did not always get on very well with many of his Milford neighbors. Most noticeable was his aloofness. Gifford Pinchot, who found 'the presence of the Peirces in Milford added much to the pleasure of life there [as] there was not any intellectual society,' noted that 'Peirce's generation regarded social distinctions as important. He did not get on well with country people.' Local lawyer Alfred Marvin complained that Peirce 'never paid any attention to anyone that he passed as he drove about the country.' Farm boys would snicker and throw rocks sometimes as he passed in his buggy. Caroline Depuy agreed that 'the Peirces did not enter into the social life of Milford; just a few close friends, their life was secluded.' Peirce had trouble with the natives in Milford. He did not like them to trespass, and he argued over bills from local merchants. Yet the few who really knew the Peirces loved them. Mrs. Frank Ludwig called him 'the most wonderful man I've ever known'; Walter Gassmann noted that 'Mr. Peirce never mingled much with any of the neighbors or they with him, as he seemed to revolve in a world of his own. But as you became familiar with him, to the point when, as a saying goes, one lets down his hair, he became an entirely different man, made himself easy to converse with, and made you feel at ease.' He even offered to teach the studious Frank Gassmann 'everything he knew' in an hour or two after school each day, which the latter's chores prevented. Peirce ultimately gave Frank some engineering books when he went off to school. Peirce's doctor G. Alto Pobe termed him 'a model man, soft-toned, always writing,' and the Peirces a 'devoted couple, good and kindly.' Pinchot called him a 'thoroughly charming gentleman with an old world manner,' although after the initially friendly relationship of the two families 'there developed a certain coolness.' In short, it seems the Peirces related quite well to the few sympathetic and intellectually inclined people in the area, but put off a good many of the ordinary folk by their reserved manners and efforts to live in a style they could no longer afford.[48]

Between problems with the neighbors, illness, financial distress, and neglect of his work, it is understandable Peirce began to view himself as a martyr for the sacred cause of truth. Although he tried to interest Hopkins President Daniel Coit Gilman in operating Arisbe as a sort of extension university in 1895, and even as late as 1905-1907 thought about obtaining pupils, Arisbe became more and more the St. Helena where the intellectual Napoleon wrote as much as he could between his bouts with illness and his efforts to fix up the place and sell it. As he wrote to William James in 1909: 'If she [Juliette] doesn't live, I don't think I shall feel much like benefitting Beacon Street. I don't care a tinker's damn what becomes of me. All the message I had for mankind will be where it can be unearthed if anybody has the sense to look for it, and I don't think it is my part to give them that sense, since I have received from humanity no gift for making myself appreciated by the world at large, but an almost insurmountable aversion to the applause of fools.'[49]

In his last years, Peirce not only repudiated the academic community. He found his work and life burdensome and sometimes looked forward to death as a release. When asked to record his membership in scientific and learned societies, he responded: 'I don't amount to a row of pins (according to any such mode, or *any* mode of estimation); the distinctions of which I am proudest are the devotions of friends, especially my wife and several women whom I have never seen and never shall see.'[50] One of these women was the philosopher Lady Victoria Welby, with whom he shared his most intimate thoughts in his final years. He predicted that 'much of my work will never be published' and only wished that 'before I die, [to] get so much made accessible as others may have a difficulty in discovering.' He concluded that 'Philosophy can only be passed from mouth to mouth, where there is an opportunity to object and cross-question and that printing is not publishing unless the matter be petty politics.' Such disillusionment from someone who rarely discussed philosophy with anyone verbally and yet kept writing when he could! In one of his last letters, of May 25, 1911, Peirce summed up what he viewed as his failure within his lifetime. He felt he could only write sensibly on assurance through reasoning, since he could no longer obtain books which would make his pronouncements on other topics valuable. He 'thought that would be of great use to the world and that nobody is likely for a very long time to reach the same truths; and yet owing to my obscurity and lack of information, I had better seek the tomb as quietly as possible.'[51] Concluding that 'I came within an ace of teaching men something to their profit,' Peirce summed up his shattered dreams for Arisbe. Pinning his faith that his writing would be discovered and found valuable by an 'infinite community' after his death, Peirce's life and philosophy came together in the bitter experiences of his final years.

Peirce did not often illustrate his philosophy using direct examples from his personal life. When he did, though, the effect on those familiar with his thoughts and biography can be striking. In 'How to Make Our Ideas Clear,' for instance, Peirce compares the folly of holding too tenaciously to an 'unclear' idea with the fable of the beautiful Melusina in Greece, who did not exist corporeally and vanished into the air. The passage becomes especially poignant when we realize that in 1878, when it was written, Peirce's own marriage to Melusina Fay was breaking up:

> Many a man has cherished for years as his hobby some vague shadow
> of an idea, too meaningless to be positively false; he has,
> nevertheless, passionately loved it, has made it his companion by day
> and night, and has given to it his strength and his life. . . and then he
> has waked up some bright morning to find it gone, clean vanished
> away like the beautiful Melusina of the fable, and the essence of his
> life gone with it. I have myself known such a man . . . (5.393)

In 'On the Doctrine of Chances,' written the same year, Peirce uses his famous illustration of a man damned eternally because he had unfortunately if rationally chosen one black card from a deck of twenty-five red and one black, rather than hoping to catch the one red in a deck of twenty-six black. Such a man would still have the 'consolation' of knowing he had acted both logically and morally: 'logicality inexorably requires that our interests shall *not* be limited. They must not stop at our own fate, but must embrace the whole community . . . [which] must extend to all races of beings.' Peirce undoubtedly chose this example because he enjoyed performing card tricks based not on sleight of hand, but on the calculation of mathematical probabilities, as Walter Gassmann remarked. (2.54)[52]

Peirce continued to use such illustrations from time to time after he came to Arisbe. 'The Architecture of Theories' was published in 1891 at the same time he and Juliette were redesigning their house. Peirce's amateur effort as an architect may have inspired his comparison of the tremendous intellectual preparation required for constructing a new philosophical theory (including 'a complete survey of human knowledge' and a consideration of the faults and strengths of each type of science), with that required for 'partially rebuilding a house' (6.8):[53]

> The faults that have been committed are, first, that the repairs of the
> dilapidation have generally not been sufficiently thoroughgoing, and
> second, that not sufficient pains had been taken to bring the additions
> into deep harmony with the really sound parts of the old structure.
> When a man is about to build a house, what a power of thinking he
> has to do, before he can safely break ground! With what pains he has
> to excogitate the precise wants that are to be supplied! What a study
> to ascertain the most available and suitable materials, to determine the
> mode of construction to which those materials are the best adapted,
> and to answer a hundred such questions!

Peirce's difficulties with the construction and frequent remodelling of Arisbe come through vividly in this passage. Also obvious in retrospect is that for all his theoretical and intellectual preparations, he failed to construct a sound usable structure.

The most important effect of Peirce's life on his philosophy, however, did not lie in his infrequent if vivid use of personal examples. Rather, during his years at Arisbe, Peirce's conceptions of experience and knowledge changed to reflect his increasingly unhappy existence. He began to regard experience as 'brute' or 'brutal'; emphasize 'surprising facts' which initiated the doubt which gave rise to thought; introduced the concept of 'anancastic' or cataclysmic evolution; and postulated not merely self-sacrifice in the interest of a universal community as the condition of advancing knowledge, but insisted that the true thinker would in fact be persecuted and rejected by his world.

Peirce did not consider experience 'brutal' in his great early essays. In 'Questions Concerning Certain Faculties Claimed for Man,' (1868), he emphasizes how perceptions of reality are mediated by previous experiences. Peirce's most startling example of this is how the retina of the eye contains a blind spot. We compensate through experience to perceive objects as continuous rather than containing dark ovals. Peirce provides further instances -- how we distinguish musical tones or the texture of cloth. All of these examples are fairly innocuous. Moreover, they stress the continuum rather than the disjunction of experience which Peirce emphasized once his own life took on a tragic cast. In 'The Fixation of Belief' (1877), Peirce criticizes the notion that 'experience alone teaches anything.' (5.360) He does so by discussing the advantages and drawbacks of various methods of thought, concluding that 'the genius of a man's logical method should be loved and reverenced as his bride, whom he has chosen from all the world. He need not torment the others; on the contrary, he may honor them deeply.' (5.387) At this stage, Peirce can with impartiality and equanimity regard various conceptions of the relationship of matter and mind. In fact, he makes such equanimity itself a major scholarly virtue.

In his late writings, however, Peirce is not much concerned with the continuity of experience or with looking impartially at various ways of knowing. In a manuscript written in 1903 where he is describing Firstness, Secondness, and Thirdness, Peirce considers 'actuality, and [to] try to make out just what it consists in.' He argues it consists in 'its happening *then* and *there*.' He then provides a most 'arresting' example from his own life (1.24):

> A court may issue *injunctions* and *judgments* against me, and I care
> not a snap of my fingers for them. I may think them idle vapor. But
> when I feel the sheriff's hand on my shoulder, I shall begin to have

a sense of actuality. Actuality is something *brute*. There is no reason
in it.

Between November 4, 1895 and December 8, 1896, the Sheriff of Pike County in fact called on Peirce at least four times to require him to post bail of $1000; he was, states the court record, either 'hiding out or out of town.' Depending on which neighbors one believes, Peirce may have had a trap door in Arisbe which enabled him to conceal himself. Hazel Gassmann did recall Juliette had a 'secret panel' in which she kept her most beautiful gowns, furs, and other valuables. It is no wonder that writing about 1896, in the midst of his financial crisis, Peirce used the words 'bitter, tedious, hard, heartrending, and noble' -- which relate immediately to his personal circumstances -- to illustrate Firstness as 'qualities of phenomena.' In the same essay, his description of Secondness reads like a *cri du coeur*: 'We feel facts resist our will. That is why facts are proverbially called brutal' (1.418-419).[54]

Peirce's fullest discussion of the 'brutality' of experience occurs in the letters written to Lady Victoria Welby during the last decade of his life. By this time his experiences had become brutal indeed. In a letter of May 7, 1904, he laments 'the circumstances that prevented me from writing to you,' offering as his excuse that 'living in the country on this side of the Atlantic, unless one is a multimillionaire, is attended with great friction.' Then he brings back the sheriff once more to illustrate Secondness as 'brute action . . . because in so far as any law or reason comes in, Thirdness comes in':

> The law of gravitation is the judge upon the bench who may
> pronounce the law till doomsday, but unless the strong arm of the
> law, the brutal sheriff, gives effect to the law, it amounts to nothing.

Peirce's fullest discussion of 'brutality' occurs in his letter of December 14, 1908.   After dismissing the Latin connotation of 'brutal' as 'immovable' or 'heavy,' he goes on to say:

> In English, I think *brute* matter, and the like are the familiar applications of the adjective . . . when the lower animals are called 'brute,' the meaning is that they are irrational, that is to say, are incapable of *self-control*, which is relatively the case.   So that, far from any *blame* being implied in the epithet, their being *brute* is a valid excuse for any conduct whatever.   I am not far from using the adjective in this same sense when I speak of *brute force*, meaning force in *no measure derived from reason*; like the muscular force of the policeman's or huissier's (bailiff's?) arm, even if it obeys reason; just as a dog is none the less brute for obeying a master who taught him by force of habit, if not by bruter means.[55]

Why the emphasis on the word brute, and this elaborate explication, in Peirce's later philosophy?   He could have used 'irrational,' and without the connotations of force and unpleasantness 'brute' conveys.   Peirce clearly intended to stress such elements -- symbolized in the sheriff's visits -- as crucial to experience.   In 'A Neglected Argument for the Reality of God' (1908), he again defined 'an experience' as 'a brutally produced conscious effect that contributes to a habit, self-controlled, yet so satisfying on deliberation, as to be destructible by no positive exercise of internal vigor.'   (6.454)

In his discussion of brutality Peirce mentions a dog.   How he trained his French poodle Zola is open to speculation.   On the one hand, Walter Gassmann remembers him calling the dog repeatedly from the porch which suggests the dog retained considerable independence.   On October 20, 1911, we find a trembling, outraged scrawl in Peirce's diary that 'Zola bit me!'   The wound on his hand required at least two doctor's visits to heal. Still, Elizabeth Heisser recalls that Peirce was very fond of Zola, and Juliette lamented in a letter to Mrs. William (Alice) James that her 'doggy [was] lost same time as husband.'[56]

Peirce's emphasis on 'brutal' strokes of fate to illustrate experience led to his emphasis on 'surprising facts' to spur genuine thinking. Besides the sheriff, he sometimes used the interruption of his peace and quiet by a railway whistle. This must have occurred frequently at Arisbe, as a train whistle would be audible four and one-half miles away in the stillness of the Pike County wilderness. Since Peirce was an insomniac in his last years who fell asleep writing in his chair he must have been awakened and disturbed and felt it keenly. Whether he ever took a balloon ride like the one he described to Lady Welby, however, remains unknown:[57]

> Imagine yourself to be seated alone at night in the basket of a balloon,
> far above earth, calmly enjoying the absolute calm and stillness.
> Suddenly the piercing shriek of a steamwhistle breaks upon you, and
> continues for a good while. The impression of stillness was an idea
> of Firstness, a quality of feeling. The piercing whistle does not allow
> you to think or do anything but suffer.

At another point, Peirce described an approaching train whistle as 'disagreeable' and a 'shock.' Around 1905, he summarized his mature view of experience by arguing that 'were it not for this garment [of contentment and habituation], he would every now and then find his internal world rudely disturbed and his fiats set at naught by brutal inroads of ideas from without. I call such forcible modification of our ways of thinking the influence of the world of fact or experience.' (1.321)

Peirce's most sustained application of the 'surprising fact' occurs in 'A Neglected Argument for the Reality of God.' (6.469)

Every inquiry whatsoever takes its rise in the observation of some surprising phenomenon, some experience which either disappoints an expectation, or breaks in upon some habit or expectation of the inquisitor's. . . . The inquiry begins with pondering these phenomena in all their aspects, in the search of some point of view whence the wonder shall be resolved.

Earlier in the same essay, Peirce traced how his habit of taking walks -- 'passages' as he refers to them in his late diaries -- led to the neglected argument. He recommends that philosophers indulge in 'Musement,' or a form of intellectual 'Pure Play' for 'some five to six per cent of one's waking time, perhaps during a stroll.' This entails 'no purpose save that of casting aside all serious purpose,' obeying 'no rules except this very law of liberty,' and letting one's thought 'bloweth where it listeth.' Peirce found 'the dawn and the gloaming most invite one to Musement,' but any time of the day would do. He then came upon the following 'wonder.' Three 'Universes' existed -- 'mere Ideas, those airy nothings'; 'Brute Actuality of things and facts'; and that 'which establishes connections between different objects, especially objects in different Universes.' Then he began to wonder 'why is all nature -- the forms of trees, the compositions of sunsets -- suffused with such beauties throughout, and not only nature, but the two other Universes as well?' He contemplated 'the unspeakable variety of each Universe,' which coexists with 'homogeneities of connectedness in each; and what a spectacle will unroll itself!' The variety, beauty, and harmony of the Universes thus suggest the hypothesis of God's reality. (6.455-456)[58]

Peirce always maintained we reason to relieve doubt. But there is a world of difference between the matter-of-fact illustrations of the young philosopher, with a great career supposedly before him, and the existential agonies of the alienated old man. In 'How to Make Our Ideas Clear,' where he argues 'the action of thought is excited by the irritation of doubt, and ceases when the belief is obtained,' Peirce used two trivial examples to illustrate doubt: whether a man should pay for his horse-car fare with a nickel or with five pennies; and how an individual passing time in a railroad station will compare the 'advantages of different trains and different routes . . . merely fancying myself to be in a state of hesitancy, because I am bored.' (5.394) Later, he used more meaningful and 'brutal,' 'surprising facts' such as sheriffs' visits and disjunctions and connections among the three universes.

Just as he believed surprising facts which raised doubts lead an individual to think, Peirce came to believe that radical discontinuities in experience, rather than a progressive social evolution from less advanced modes of thought to higher ones, characterized the development of intellectual history. In the conclusion of his History of Science Lectures, written in 1892 after he had moved into Arisbe, Peirce stipulated that 'there are three ways by which human thought grows: by the formation of habits, by the violent breaking up of habits, and by the action of innumerable fortuitous variations of ideas combined with differences in the fecundity of different variations.' He then went on to insist that 'the last mode of development, which I have called Darwinism . . . in the history of science it has made . . . no figure at all, except in a retrograde motion.' (7.769) From radical disjunction as the wellspring of knowledge it was only one step to catastrophe, both in Peirce's risky Arisbe experiment and in his thought. In some notes made about 1896, Peirce distinguished Darwinian, Lamarckian, and 'cataclysmic evolution, according to which the changes have not been small and have not been sudden.' He maintained that 'the last of these has been most efficient.' (1.104) In 'Evolutionary Love,' published in 1893, he termed this 'anancastic' evolution, or evolution by 'mechanical necessity,' which 'advances by successive strides with pauses between. . . . A habit of thought having been overthrown is supplanted by the next strongest. Now this next strongest is sure to be widely disparate from the

first, and as often as not its contrary.' (6.312) Peirce went on to conclude that
'the evolution of history is in considerable part of the nature of internal anancasm.'
(6.314) He tried to show in manuscript how these historical disruptions occurred
about every thirty years on the small scale, and about every five hundred years on
a larger scale. He also hoped that a period of 'agapistic' or selfless evolution
would succeed the present 'tychastic' era of competitive evolution through
'fortuitous variation.'[59]

Peirce's lifelong dedication to 'agapism' in theory became, during his years
at Arisbe, a compulsory dedication to its practice. In 'On The Doctrine of
Chances' (1878), he insisted that 'he who would not sacrifice his own soul to save
the whole world is, as it seems to me, illogical in all his inferences.' Yet he
immediately went on to qualify this identification of philosophy with St. Paul's
'famous trio of Charity, Faith, and Hope.' 'It is *not* necessary for logicality that
a man should himself be capable of heroism or self-sacrifice. It is sufficient that
he should recognize the possibility of it, should perceive that only that man's
inferences who has it are really logical, and should consequently regard his own
as being only so far valid as they would be accepted by the hero.' (2.654-655)
Living luxuriously in Europe and America, Peirce was unwilling to recognize at
this stage that if he really believed his own philosophy it would in fact require that
he give up his worldly pursuits. When he added 'Later Reflections' to the essay
in 1910, Peirce curtly made the point that 'no man can be logical whose supreme
desire is the well-being of himself or any other existing person or collection of
persons.' (2.664)

When Peirce did in fact consider self-sacrifice in the 1870s, he utilized
military metaphors, emphasizing the active, heroic quest of a combatant for logic
and truth. In 'On the Doctrine of Chances,' he compared the logician to 'the
soldier who runs to scale a wall [and] knows that he will probably be shot, but that

is not all he cares for. He also knows that if all the regiment with whom in feeling he identifies himself, rush forward at once, the fort will be taken.' (2.654) While self-sacrifice and worldly failures exist as possibilities, victory is at least a likely outcome. In 'The Fixation of Belief,' written about the same time, the logician fighting for his method is compared to a knight defending his lady's honor (5.387):

> But she is the only one that he has chosen, and he knows that he was right in making that choice. And having made it, he will work and fight for her, and will not complain that there are blows to take, hoping that there may be as many and as hard to give, and will strive to be the worthy knight and champion of her from the blaze of whose splendours he draws his inspiration and courage.

If Peirce in the 1870s is a fearless knight, confident of some worldly success, Peirce in the 1890s and 1900s is an embittered saint. He regards his rejection by the world as a proof of his virtue and of the world's corruption. Beginning with the Lowell Institute Lectures on great scientists, Peirce stresses not only that the true devotee of knowledge must pursue his course unflinchingly, but that in his work he must be completely aloof from everyday, practical concerns. He distinguishes the great nineteenth century men of science upon whom he modelled himself from those of all previous ages through their 'devotion to the pursuit of truth for truth's sake.' And the truths they found, 'those wonderful new substances, helium and the rest, that seem the connecting link between ordinary matter and the ether,' were precisely those that 'sapient good sense pooh-poohs,' and in thorough disaccord with the older 'good sense.'[60]

Peirce made the same point even more emphatically in his interesting review in *The Nation* of Paul Leicester Ford's biography of Benjamin Franklin, published in 1899. Peirce goes straight for the jugular, criticizing Franklin much as Perry

Miller or D.H. Lawrence would in the twentieth century, for daring to ask the blasphemous question: 'what signifies philosophy which does not apply itself to some use':[61]

> The true devotee of science, so long as he enacts that role never
> thinks or cares about Philistine utility. In his mind, to learn the ways
> of Nature and the reasonableness of things, and to be absorbed as a
> particle of the rolling wave of reasonableness, is not *useful*, but is the
> *summum bonum* itself towards which true usefulness tends.

Peirce is here describing himself; one can only wonder if in the contrasting portrait of Franklin he was thinking of John Dewey and even more so William James. He believed these philosophers had transformed and popularized 'pragmatism', which Peirce conceived as the scientific inquirer's disinterested search for truth, provisionally holding his judgments in suspension pending their ratification by the long-term investigations of a like-minded community. Instead, they held truth as relative, as 'what works' psychologically for a person or community at a specific point in historical time:

> At the same time, when one descends to the question of food and
> raiment, warmth, and cleanliness, to decree that the scientific
> investigator shall pursue utility alone, it can only mean that he shall
> pursue nothing but what appears to be useful in advance of
> investigation, usually among the less useful class of inquirers, even
> in the most grovelling sense. Dr. Franklin ought to have considered
> that before he asked -- 'what signifies philosophy which does not
> apply itself to some use?' -- that utilitarian spirit was what made the
> eighteenth century a scientific desert.

In fact, by 1905 Peirce was so annoyed by the way 'pragmatism' had been abused that he changed its name. 'To serve the precise purpose of expressing the original definition, he begs to announce the birth of the word 'pragmaticism,' which is ugly enough to be safe from kidnappers.' (5.414) Peirce even turned the final paragraphs of his 'Neglected Argument' into a not altogether relevant critique of F.S.C. Schiller's and, especially, William James's use of the term. It grated Peirce by 1908 that not only had James usurped his rightful position at Harvard and taken the credit for pragmatism, but he was in the humiliating position of being partially dependent on James's charity for his own survival. (6.484-486)

At Arisbe, Peirce's life and theory of knowledge merged in his insistence that the pursuit of the '*UTTERLY USELESS*,' (1.76) self-sacrifice, and disinterested 'agapism' distinguish the scholarly quest. 'True science is the study of useless things. . . . To employ those rare minds in such [useful] work is like running a steam engine to burn diamonds,' he remarked around 1896. (1.76) In the 'Neglected Argument,' he describes how a belief in God will console a man 'of small instruction with corresponding natural breadth, intimately acquainted with the N.A., but to whom all logic is Greek.' Peirce, most of whose logic was indeed 'Greek'-inspired in his later years, then illustrates the sufferings of an 'ignorant' man with his own and Juliette's misfortunes (6.478-479):

> Though his desperate struggles should issue in the horrors of his rout,
> and he should see the innocents who are dearest to his heart exposed
> to torments, frenzy, and despair, destined to be smirched with filth,
> and stunted in their intelligence, still he may hope that it be best *for
> them*, will tell himself that in any case the secret design of God will
> be perfected through their agency, and even while still hot from
> battle, will submit with adoration to His Holy will.

Instead of using the image of a heroic knight he had three decades earlier, in 1908 Peirce refers to the need to keep one's faith in the midst of a 'rout.' And in 'Evolutionary Love,' Peirce stresses the theme that 'self love is no love,' that you should 'sacrifice your own perfection to the perfectionment of your neighbor,' and that growth comes from 'I will not say self-*sacrifice*, but from the ardent impulse to fulfill another's highest impulse.' Peirce insists that we cannot make our ideas grow by 'dealing out cold justice,' but only 'by cherishing and tending them as I would the flowers in my garden.' (6.288-289) In his last years, Peirce not only could not care for his wife's beloved roses, he could not even work as much as he would have liked.[62]

If Peirce's earthly existence ended in tragedy, the late twentieth century has witnessed his posthumous vindication by a community of inquirers who have studied and applied his methodology to a variety of disciplines, interacting with the master much as he had hoped students would in his life time.[63] And he expected to be discovered in due course. Juliette's final moving recollection of Peirce was that 'in handing me his last writings,' he stated, 'my book is finished and will make a revolution in the sciences.'[64] In the long run, Peirce's dedication and self-sacrifice paid off, even if he drew the one black card out of twenty-six.

Furthermore, Peirce's insistence on utter dedication to the pursuit of truth serves not only as an inspiration -- and a warning -- but also as a paradigm. We see over and over again that men such as Peirce make history and advance knowledge: that the great thinkers, humanitarians, revolutionaries, religious leaders, artists, and scientists risked everything in pursuit of their vision, and in the final analysis cared not for the things of this world. Peirce's life and epistemology thus bring into focus the possibilities and dangers of the pursuit of knowledge as a heroic endeavor performed for the benefit of an unthinking, and usually uncaring world.

Editor's Note: I thank Max Fisch for his hospitality at the Peirce Papers Project, Indiana University -- Purdue University, Indianapolis, and for his kindness in showing me how to use the papers collected there. I dedicate this essay to him.

ENDNOTES

1. 'Recalling Charles Peirce,' unpublished ms. dated March 10, 1981 containing Preston Tuttle's 1976 interviews with several neighbors of Charles and Juliette Peirce, 28. The two best accounts of Peirce's life and thought are by Max H. Fisch, 'Peirce's Place in American Life,' *Historia Mathematica* 9, 1982, 265-287, and R. Jackson Wilson, *In Quest of Community: Social Philosophy in the United States, 1860-1920*, New York: Oxford University Press, 1968, 32-59.

2. Ms. 1330 of the Peirce Papers in the Houghton Library of Harvard University, as numbered by Richard S. Robin and described in his *Annotated Catalogue of the Papers of Charles S. Peirce*, Amherst: University of Massachusetts Press, 1967, microfilm edition.

3. Charles S. Peirce, book review of *Clark University, 1889-1899: Decennial Celebration, Science*, April 20, 1900, 620-622.

4. Charles S. Peirce, *Collected Papers*, 8 volumes, eds., P. Weiss, A. Burks, C. Hartshorne, Cambridge: Harvard University Press, 1931-1958. References to this collection are indicated by volume and paragraph number in the text, and CP in the endnotes.

5. Max H. Fisch, 'Peirce's Arisbe: The Greek Influence in His Later Philosophy,' *Transactions of the Charles S. Peirce Society*, 7, 1971, 187-211, at 200, and Wilson, *In Quest of Community*, 49.

6. Peirce Papers, Harvard, Ms. 1329, 27, 76-78.

7. 'Recalling Charles Peirce,' 20.

8. Diary excerpt from the 1880s in 'Charles Peirce-Juliette Froissy and the Peirce Family,' in Data Concerning the Second Wife of Charles S. Peirce folder, hereafter cited as 'Juliette Peirce' folder; on acetylene, St. Lawrence Power Company folder; and draft of letter to Samuel P. Langley, September 28, 1894, in 'Milford' folder, all at the Peirce Papers Project, Indiana University -- Purdue University, Indianapolis.

9. Draft of letter from Charles S. Peirce, November 13, 1909, Juliette Peirce folder, Peirce Papers, Indiana. Peirce also refers to Pike County as 'the wildest county of the Northern States, South of Adirondacks and East of the Alleghenies.' Fisch, 'Peirce's Arisbe,' 199, quoting Ms. 842, Peirce Papers, Harvard.

10.   Charles S. Peirce to F.C. Russell, September 17, 1892, reprinted in 'A Report on the Physical Condition of Arisbe,' prepared by Woollen Associates, Inc., Architects, Fort Wayne, Indiana, 1975, 41-42, Peirce Papers, Indiana.

11.   Charles S. Peirce to James Mills Peirce, November 29, 1888, 'Report on Arisbe,' 29, and note in Arisbe Chronology, Peirce Papers, Indiana.

12.   Fisch, 'Peirce's Arisbe.'

13.   Charles S. Peirce, 'The Law of Mind,' *CP* 5. 12-13; 6. 102; *Charles S. Peirce's Letters to Lady Welby*, ed., I.C. Leib, New Haven: Whitlock's Inc., 1953, 37, January 31, 1909. Hereafter cited as *Welby Letters*.

14.   See generally Juliette Peirce folder, Peirce Papers, Indiana, and the following letters therein: Simon Newcomb to Mrs. Newcomb, October 14 and November 21, 1883, from Newcomb Papers, Library of Congress; Herbert Peirce to Helen Peirce Ellis, March 18, April 10, and April 25, 1884.

15.   Peirce worked out his family's history in Ms. 1601, Peirce Papers, Harvard. See Juliette Peirce folder, specifically drafts of letters from Charles S. Peirce, March 14, 1898, and November 13, 1900, Peirce Papers, Indiana. In the same collection, Memorandum of Henry James for November 28, 1921; Juliette Peirce to Gifford Pinchot, n.d., and Henry S. Leonard Interviews, c. 1933, with Peirce's neighbors, in Milford folder. Also see 'Recalling Charles Peirce,' *passim*.

16.   Henry S. Leonard interviews with Gassmann family; V.F. Lenzen, 'The Identity of Juliette Peirce,' January 3, 1973, has material on the gypsies; Herbert Peirce to Helen Peirce Ellis, March 18, 1884 and Charlotte Elizabeth Peirce 'Lizzie' to Helen Peirce Ellis, February 15, 1886, all in Juliette Peirce folder, Peirce Papers, Indiana. See also 'Recalling Charles Peirce.'

17.   Interviews of Henry S. Leonard with Gifford Pinchot and Juliette Peirce in Milford folder, the latter of which has the material on the hotel. The diary of Mrs. J.W. Pinchot, the governor's mother, recalls many visits from the Peirces, including performances of amateur theatricals and charades, in 1887. Library of Congress, transcribed in Milford folder. Peirce's letter mentioned the chefs to F.C. Russell, September 17, 1892, in 'Report on Arisbe,' 41-42, all in Peirce Papers, Indiana.

18.   Note on *Médée* and Charles S. Peirce to his mother, Sara Mills Peirce, April 3, 1887, Juliette Peirce folder, Peirce Papers, Indiana. The best history of Milford, on which I rely for information about the community, is by Norman Lehde, *Milford, Pennsylvania: 1733-1983*, n.p., n.d., a fine work of local history. 'Recalling Charles Peirce,' 56.

19.   Peirce to F.C. Russell, September 17, 1892, in 'Report on Arisbe,' 41-42, Peirce Papers, Indiana; Ms. 682, 29, 1913, Peirce Papers, Harvard.

20. See Fisch, 'Peirce's Arisbe,' 199-213, and 'Report on Arisbe,' 29.

21. Juliette Peirce to Mrs. McArthur, c. 1928, Juliette Peirce folder, Peirce Papers, Indiana, and *Welby Letters*, 15, May 7, 1904.

22. 'Recalling Charles Peirce,' 70-71, Peirce Papers, Indiana.

23. Draft of Charles Peirce letter, November 13, 1909, Juliette Peirce folder, Peirce Papers, Indiana.

24. *The Home Journal*, May 4, 1892, Milford folder, Peirce Papers, Indiana.

25. Henry S. Leonard interview with Gifford Pinchot, Milford folder; Frank Manuel to Max Fisch, December 5, 1973, Juliette Peirce folder; 'Recalling Charles Peirce,' 25-27, all at Peirce Papers, Indiana.

26. Henry S. Leonard interview with Gifford Pinchot, Juliette Peirce and Milford folders; Penelope Hartshorne Batcheler, 'Charles S. Peirce House, Historic Structure Report,' Boulder, Colorado: Department of Interior, 1976, citing an unpublished ms. of December 15, 1907, 10, in Delaware and Hudson Canal folder, all in Peirce Papers, Indiana.

27. Juliette Peirce to Mrs. William (Alice H.) James, February 23, 1909, Juliette Peirce folder, Peirce Papers, Indiana.

28. Juliette Peirce to Mrs. William James, June 30, no year, Juliette Peirce folder, Peirce Papers, Indiana.

29. 'Report on Arisbe,' 31-34, 43; Juliette Peirce to Henry James, Jr., October 6, 1914, Juliette Peirce folder, Peirce Papers, Indiana; 'Recalling Charles Peirce,' 12-16; Charles S. Peirce to William James, September 3, 1909, Juliette Peirce folder; *Welby Letters*, 46, May 25, 1911.

30. Draft of Charles S. Peirce letter, November 13, 1909 and probably November 1892, 12 and 22, Juliette Peirce folder, Peirce Papers, Indiana.

31. For the Peirces' financial difficulties, see the entries under their names in the Civil Court Records, Pike County Courthouse, Milford, Pennsylvania, 8: 38, 46, 180, 295. Peirce had to borrow $2000 from his brother James Mills Peirce in 1895, 8:46, and most of the Peirces' mortgages were assumed and ultimately paid by Henry James, Jr. See Mortgages Index, Pike County Courthouse, 10:449, 11:280, 12:341, 12:389. The deeds whereby Peirce acquired his estate are in the Pike County Deeds, 45:92; 46:139; 47:1, 186, 434; and 49:413. The sheriff's visits are recorded in the Civil Court Records 8:161, 172, 178.

32. For neighbors' complaints that the Peirces did not pay their bills, see 'Recalling Charles Peirce,' 22.

33. Charles S. Peirce to William James, June 13, 1907, quoted in Wilson, *In Quest of Community*, 50; same to same, September 3, 1909, and draft of Charles S. Peirce letter, November 13, 1909, Juliette Peirce folder, Peirce Papers, Indiana. See also notes 35 and 37-38 below.

34. Juliette Peirce to Mrs. William James, October 29, 1914, and Charles Hartshorne interviews, Juliette Peirce folder and Henry S. Leonard interviews, Milford folders, Peirce Papers, Indiana; 'Recalling Charles Peirce,' esp. 57-58.

35. Charles S. Peirce to William James, September 3, 1909; Juliette Peirce to Lady Welby, c. 1905-1907, to Mrs. William James, February 23, 1909, and to Henry James, Jr., May 7, August 24, October 6, 1914 in Juliette Peirce folder and Henry S. Leonard interview with Gifford Pinchot, in Milford folder, Peirce Papers, Indiana; 'Recalling Charles Peirce,' 68.

36. Charles Peirce's Diary for January 1 1882, noted in 'Charles Peirce, Juliette Froissy, and the Peirce family,' and Charles S. Peirce to his mother, April 3, 1887, Juliette Peirce folder, Peirce Papers, Indiana. Diary for 1889, Ms. 1616, Peirce Papers, Harvard.

37. *Welby Letters,* 5, April 10, 1904; 18, April 16, 1905; 32, December 14, 1908; 42, May 20, 1911; and Charles S. Peirce to William James, September 23, 1905, Juliette Peirce folder, Peirce Papers, Indiana.

38. Diary of Charles S. Peirce, Ms. 1623, Peirce Papers, Harvard. Diaries for 1911-1914 are sparse with only occasional entries.

39. See generally Charles Hartshorne 1928 interview with the Gassmans, Juliette Peirce and Milford folders, Peirce Papers, Indiana; 'Recalling Charles Peirce,' esp. 15-19; Ms. 1623, Charles S. Peirce Diary, entries for July 30 and August 2, 1911, Peirce Papers, Harvard. See also Charles and Juliette's frequent complaints about household work in their letters to Lady Welby and Mrs. William James, respectively, Juliette Peirce folder.

40. *Welby Letters*, 34, October 24, 1909, and 46, May 25, 1911.

41. James Mills Peirce to Herbert Peirce, February 1, 1901, Juliette Peirce folder, Peirce Papers, Indiana; *Welby Letters*, 15, December 16, 1904; draft of letter by Charles S. Peirce, November 23, 1909, Juliette Peirce folder.

42. Juliette Peirce to Henry James, Jr., October 10, 1914, Juliette Peirce folder, Peirce Papers, Indiana; 'Recalling Charles Peirce,' esp. 37.

43. 'Recalling Charles Peirce,' esp. 8, 19, 31, 57. Caroline Depuy to Max H. Fisch, October 20, 1979, Milford folder, Peirce Papers, Indiana.

44. Charles S. Peirce to James Mills Peirce, November 18, 1894, Juliette Peirce folder, Peirce Papers, Indiana; *Welby Letters*, 5, April 10, 1904.

45. Juliette Peirce to Mrs. William James, February 23, 1909, Juliette Peirce folder, Peirce Papers, Indiana; Charles S. Peirce Diary, Ms. 1616, February 14, 1889, and February 2, 1912, Ms. 1623, Peirce Papers, Harvard.

46. Draft of letter by Charles S. Peirce, November 13, 1909; Juliette Peirce to J.H. Woods, January 15, 1921; James Mills Peirce to Herbert Peirce, February 1, 1901, all in Juliette Peirce folder, Peirce Papers, Indiana.

47. Juliette Peirce to Lady Welby, c. 1905-1907, Juliette Peirce folder, Peirce Papers, Indiana.

48. Charles Hartshorne interviews, Juliette Peirce folder, Peirce Papers, Indiana; Henry S. Leonard interviews and Victor Lenzen to Max H. Fisch, July 11, 1961, Milford folder, Peirce Papers, Indiana; 'Recalling Charles Peirce,' esp. 1-11, 61.

49. Charles S. Peirce to Daniel Coit Gilman, April 19, 1895, quoted in 'Report on Arisbe,' 33; Juliette Peirce to Lady Welby, c. 1905-1907, and Charles S. Peirce to William James, September 3,1909, Juliette Peirce folder, Peirce Papers, Indiana.

50. Biographical Statement, Ms. 1613, Peirce Papers, Harvard. In another statement, Ms. 1612, Peirce listed under honors conferred -- 'never any, nor any encouragement or aid of any kind or description in my life work, except a splendid series of magnificent promises.' But Peirce vowed to continue his research 'as long as I retain my faculties and I can afford pen and ink.'

51. *Welby Letters*, 15, December 2, 1904, and 46, May 25, 1911.

52. For other examples of Peirce's references to playing cards, see 'The General Theory of Probable Influence,' 1883, *CP* 2.696, and a manuscript from 1898, *CP* 6.3. For Peirce's card trick ability, see Victor Lenzen to Max H. Fisch, July 11, 1961, Milford folder, Peirce Papers, Indiana.

53. Neighbor Elmer Roberts reported 'he didn't know nothing about building,' 'Recalling Charles Peirce,' 20.

54. Pike County Civil Court Records, 8:161, 172, 178. The denial of the trap door and revelation of the secret panel are in 'Recalling Charles Peirce,' 32, 69-70. Similarly, in the 1903 Lectures on Pragmatism, Peirce's second lecture after 'Presentness' is 'Struggle.' *CP* 5.41. See also *CP* 5.48 for the sheriff again.

55.   *Welby Letters*, 9, May 7, 1904 and 22-23, December 14, 1908.

56.   'Recalling Charles Peirce,' 4; Charles S. Peirce Diary, Ms. 1623, Peirce Papers, Harvard; Elizabeth G. Heisser to Max H. Fisch, Milford folder, Peirce Papers, Indiana; Juliette Peirce to Mrs. William James, October 6, 1914, Juliette Peirce folder, Peirce Papers, Indiana. Peirce also mentions his dog in *CP* 7.369 where he explains even the dog is not an automation, and in *CP* 7.484, where he notes the dog expects to find his master when he hears his voice.

57.   *Welby Letters*, 8, May 7, 1904.

58.   Peirce also mentions the relation between walks, musing, and his belief in God in *CP* 6.501, 'The Reality of God': 'I have often occasion to walk at night, for about a mile, over an entirely untravelled road, much of it between open fields without a house in sight. The circumstances are not favorable to severe study, but are to calm mediation. . . . Let a man drink in such things as come to him in contemplating the physico-psychical universe without any special purpose of his own. The idea of there being a God over it all of course will often be suggested, and the more he considers it, the more he will be enwrapt.'

59.   Ms. 1325, Peirce Papers, Harvard.

60.   The quotation is from Peirce's article 'Review of the Nineteenth Century,' in the *Annual Report of the Smithsonian Institution for the year ending June 30, 1900*, Washington: The Smithsonian, 1901, 696.

61.   Charles Sanders Peirce, *Contributions to The Nation, Part Two: 1894-1900*, Lubbock: Texas Tech University Press, 1978, 218-221.

62.   On the Peirces' decaying garden, see 'Recalling Charles Peirce,' 17, 27.

63.   'Charles Peirce-Juliette Froissy and the Peirce family,' Juliette Peirce folder, Peirce Papers, Indiana.

64.   See Eugene Freeman, ed., *The Relevance of Charles Peirce*, LaSalle: The Monist Library of Philosophy, 1983.

Chapter 4

Charles S. Peirce,
Historian and Semiotician

Had he wished, the great American philosopher Charles Sanders Peirce could probably have become an equally great historian. Since his ideas on history were every bit as combative and against the contemporary grain as his writings on logic and semiotics, he would probably have found it just as impossible to teach in the history departments of Harvard and Johns Hopkins as he did in philosophy. Evidence for Peirce's historical acuity exists not only in the Lowell Institute lectures on the history of science, but even more vividly (for those of unscientific bent such as myself) in three fragments on Rienzi (Peirce c.1892b: 550-554), Napoleon (Peirce c.1893a), and the Middle Ages (Peirce c.1892c). Peirce's historical works illustrate some of the crucial elements of his philosophy in broad, general terms. They also challenge historians even today to rethink seriously some of their fundamental assumptions about causation and human nature, to the extent professional historians seriously examine their philosophical assumptions at all.[1]

Peirce is especially acute on three points. First, history does not 'evolve,' it erupts -- suddenly transforming itself under the pressure of surprising events. Second, at such conjunctures, great men do make a difference, men who cannot possibly be considered 'products' of 'forces.' And third, these men do in fact shape history, *to the extent that* they wholeheartedly and unselfishly dedicate themselves to a higher ideal.

During the years Peirce lectured in logic at the Johns Hopkins University (1879-1884), that institution, which was transforming the American college from a place of instruction for undergraduates to a center for scholarly research, also revolutionized historical scholarship in the United States. A history department led by Herbert Baxter Adams sought to redirect the discipline toward the methodology of the modern social sciences as practiced in the German universities. In effect, this meant a conservative variety of Social Darwinism. Adams and his followers stressed 'the continuity of human history,' arguing that 'the political history of the world should be read as a single whole.' The Hopkins scholars particularly interested themselves in New England local history, demonstrating to their satisfaction how American democratic institutions evolved organically from the 'germ' of Aryan, Anglo-Saxon communities of free warriors during the first millennium. If they rejected the idea of American exceptionalism and the role of Providence in history put forth by George Bancroft and earlier nationalist scholars, their message was similarly patriotic and presentist. As Adams wrote, 'what the world needs is historical enlightenment and political and social progress along existing institutional lines. We must preserve the continuity of our past life in the State' (Ross 1985).

Peircean scholars need read no further. When it came to science and philosophy, two things raised the master's hackles more than anything else: the idea that *anything* worthwhile evolved smoothly and continuously; and the subordination of the pursuit of knowledge and truth to anything else, be it the State, personal wealth, or whatever. Having limited use even for Darwinism as natural science, Peirce took on the crude forms of Social Darwinism current in his day wherever he found them.

For instance, in the conclusion of the History of Science lectures, Peirce argued 'that there are three ways by which human thoughts grow: by the formation of habits, by the violent breaking up of habits, and by the action of innumerable fortuitous variations of ideas combined with differences in the fecundity of different variations.' Peirce emphatically claimed that 'the last mode of development, which I have called Darwinism . . . in the history of science it has made, as far as we have been able to see, no figure at all, except in retrograde movements.' 'In all these cases it betrays itself infallibly by its two symptoms of proceeding by insensible steps and of proceeding in a direction different from that of any strivings' (Peirce 1892a: 287). Much as Thomas Kuhn would several decades later in his work on *The Structure of Scientific Revolutions* (1962), Peirce insisted that science did not evolve. It proceeded 'by the violent breaking up of habits,' by 'leaps,' 'by new observations and reflections' (Peirce c.1896: 1.101-109), through the efforts of great individuals able to sense and correct problems in habitual modes of thinking, thereby explaining phenomena in more elegant and satisfactory ways. Peirce termed this 'abductive reasoning' -- an educated guess that apparently comes from nowhere but forms the basis of major scientific discoveries. Peirce considered Kepler's discoveries and Mendeleef's (Mendelev's) periodic table the two greatest feats of abductive reasoning in history (Peirce 1895: 456).

In his studies of scientists' lives, Peirce had even harsher words for the subordination of scholarship to 'practical' matters. In a review of the nineteenth century, he found that 'the glory of the nineteenth century has been its science.' Why? Because 'the distinctive characteristic' of its great men 'has been the devotion to the pursuit of truth for truth's sake.' Peirce launches into a tirade against practicality and common sense at this point:

> I dare say, sapient 'good sense' pooh-poohs those wonderful new substances, helium and the rest, that seem the connecting link between ordinary matter and the ether. So it could be useless to point out that

their discovery was entirely due to Lord Rayleigh's fastidiousness in the determination of the density of nitrogen. . . . But it has to be noted as a characteristic of great physicists of the nineteenth century that their *reverence* for each feature of the phenomenon, however minute, has been in thorough disaccord with the older 'good sense.' (Peirce 1901a; emphasis added)

Had he lived to see the age of the atom and relativity, Peirce's insight would be even more appropriate. Paradoxically, the greatest 'practical' advances in technology (Peirce cites Marconi's wireless) do not come from those who seek wealth, fame, or practical ends, but from a new breed of saint, one who holds his work in 'reverence':

The man of science, eager to have his every opinion regenerated, his every idea rationalized, by drinking at the fountain of fact, and devoting all the energies of his life to the cult of truth, not as he understands it, but as he does not yet understand it. . . . To an earlier age knowledge was power, merely that and nothing more; to us it is life and the *summum bonum*. (Peirce 1901a)

'Fountain of fact'; 'cult of truth'; '*summum bonum*.' Peirce will find kindred spirits in the medieval philosophers and architects who lived for their ideals and not for themselves.

If we transfer Peirce's theory of scientific change to historical change in general, his selection of topics, his methodology, and his quarrel with the Hopkins history department become clear. First, in his philosophy, Peirce concentrated a great deal on what he termed 'The Surprising Fact': 'some experience which either disappoints an expectation, or breaks in upon some habit of expectation of the inquisitor; and each apparent exception of this rule only confirms it' (Peirce 1908: 6.469). Thought in science and change in history begin when something surprising occurs which creates doubt and causes questioning as to the habitual way of doing things. No theory of gradual evolution or development could explain Rienzi, the son of a saloonkeeper and washerwoman, who rose to be master of Rome in 1347; or how a Corsican solider became master of Europe four and a half centuries later; or how the never to be duplicated miracles of Gothic architecture and scholastic philosophy sprang into existence around 1200 A.D. Peirce's notion of intellectual and historical change anticipate Henri Bergson's 'quantum leap' in *Creative Evolution* (1911) and *The Two Sources of Religion and Morality* (1935) as opposed to the gradual organicism of the Darwinists.

But if significant change and great figures do not 'evolve,' what accounts for them? Doubt -- 'the irritation of doubt causes a struggle to attain a state of belief,' Peirce writes in 'The fixation of belief.' 'There must be a real and *living* doubt and without this all discussion is idle' (Peirce 1877: 5.374, 376). Doubt caused by a breakdown in the accepted way of doing things creates the occasion for change and the possibility for a great man -- or a great school of art or science -- to emerge. But it is equally crucial that people are present who have prepared to be great. How? By adhering to the selfless, systematic pursuit of their vision of truth in a manner similar to the nineteenth-century scientists' single-minded devotion to knowledge. Rienzi, Napoleon, and the anonymous Gothic architects thus serve as signs -- to borrow another Peircean term -- of a type of person appearing throughout history, in different fields of endeavor (arts, science, politics, music), who has a chance to initiate something new under the sun.

The conjunction of uncertain circumstance with the dedicated genius is necessary for a new era in history or a new stage in a mode of thought or art to begin; neither alone is sufficient. Peirce voiced his frustration that while he was creating a new system of logic and opening the path to a new era in the history of philosophy, the time was not ripe and hence his contemporaries rejected him (Peirce c.1892c):

> God creates millions of potentialities that might grow into mighty things were circumstances favorable. And in the one case of the million where the circumstances are favorable, the potent seed will not be wanting.

> I am an officer awaiting orders which will never come to me. The world has got to know that services are wanted before they can be rendered. To teach the world what is wanted is not the task which I was put together to perform.

In contrast, Rienzi (1313-1351) was a genius for whom the circumstances were indeed ripe. This self-educated poor lad turned revolutionary hero humbled the Roman nobility and church. He then set up a short-lived republic founded on imitation of classical virtue, only to perish in a counterrevolution. Something of a cult figure in the early nineteenth century, when Romanticism and dreams of revolution were in vogue, Rienzi was the subject of a novel by Bulwer-Lytton which inspired a grandiose opera by the young revolutionary Richard Wagner. But by the time Peirce wrote his eight-page unpublished fragment in (probably) the last decade of the century, nation-states were consolidating in Germany, Italy, and the United States. Positivist and neo-Darwinian intellectuals looked askance at those aberrant souls who questioned the justice of existing arrangements.

Nevertheless, Peirce found in Rienzi's career a parable for his most important philosophical ideas. This apparently casually tossed-off essay (Peirce put at its head a note, found only in manuscript [Peirce c.1892d: Ms. 1318] to a 'proof reader -- Don't undertake to correct grammar!') also contains some of his most inspired prose:

Four centuries before the French Revolution, something like it was instigated in Rome by Cola di Rienzo. Cola is the nickname for Nicholas, Rienzo for Laurienzo, or Lawrence, surname he had none. 1313 was his birth in a dirty alley near the Tibur, where papa was saloon-keeper, mama washerwoman. No pope was then in Rome, the see having been removed to Avignon. Emperor Henry of Luxembourg and Robert King of Naples, Guelph Chieftain, were warring through Italy. Rome was sunk into deepest barbarism, justice and order forgotten, every outrage to humanity perpetrated by day in open streets, under no restraint but fear of private vengeance. For safety of one's goods, of one's handsome wife, who might be dragged from her chamber any time by marauders, a man must depend on his own arm and his friends. All this story, understand, I am merely condensing from a contemporary chronicle, with great detriment by vividness. (Peirce c.1892b: 550-554. I use this source for all material on Rienzi.)

Peirce begins with a sense of chaos, a total breakdown of justice and law, which prepares the conditions under which a great man may creatively restore order. Peirce's depiction of fourteenth-century Rome, in fact, remarkably resembles his critique of late nineteenth-century 'Darwinian' society, which he hoped his own essays urging selfless commitment to the long-term interests of humankind would correct. The struggle for survival, praised by contemporary historians as the pinnacle of the evolution of civilization, Peirce condemned in the essay 'Evolutionary love,' published in 1893 (Peirce 1893b: 6.290):

The conviction of the nineteenth century is that progress takes place by virtue of every individual's striving for himself with all his might

and trampling his neighbour underfoot whenever he gets a chance to
do so. This may accurately be called the Gospel of Greed.
Darwinism, Peirce claims, 'merely extends politico-economical views of progress
to the entire realm of animal and vegetable life.' The brief opening of 'Rienzi'
symbolizes Peirce's contempt for pseudo-sciences which would transform such a
chamber of horrors into a model for social evolution.

To the 'surprising fact' of Rome's social and moral collapse Peirce adds the
equally surprising fact of Rienzi. Despite his background, he 'somehow . . .
learned to read, and did read passionately.' After learning Latin, 'he devoured the
prose of Livy, Seneca, Cicero, Valerius Maximus, and Caesar.' These bulwarks
of disinterested patriotism -- who also inspired America's Founding Fathers to
reject the perceived corruptions of English colonialism -- served as Rienzi's
models, much as Peirce found solace in disinterested great scientists. As one of
a small literate class, Rienzi obtained an appointment as a notary. 'He was a
dazzlingly handsome young Roman, his face full of meaning and fire, his voice
with a sort of laugh in its tones.'

Rienzi became a revolutionary when his beloved half-brother was murdered
by the barons and he could not obtain redress. For reasons Peirce does not
mention, he then obtained an appointment in a delegation to visit Pope Clement VI
in Avignon, where he promptly got into trouble for attacking the nobles.
However, the poet Petrarch, 'a veritable power in the polite and frenshy [sic]
court,' saved him by interceding with the pope. Clement then sent Rienzi back to
Rome as 'notary to the Camorra de Roma, that is, second in the governing council
of the city.' Rienzi 'continued his verbal attacks on the aristocracy' in the 'very
seat of power,' where council members slapped his face and walked out on his
speeches making 'vulgar gestures.'

Rienzi's early career, therefore, demonstrated perseverance in the face of adversity and even danger. It also illustrated the potential of intellectual idealists such as Rienzi and Petrarch to have practical influence not by trying to be 'practical,' but by fearlessly pleading for ideals they believed in, regardless of the consequences. At this stage of his career, 'Rienzi swerved not,' Peirce writes, identifying with his heroic stand for truth and justice. 'Gradually gaining ascendancy over the papal vicar, he acquired practical control of the government.'

Once ensconced in power, Rienzi became an educator and semiotician. He realized that the 'ignorant, unthinking people, their minds confined by the fetters of centuries,' would have difficulty understanding that 'the Roman nobles had not the right to do what they pleased, but that they, the Roman people, had the right, duty, and power too, to restrain all crimes.' Given popular ignorance, Rienzi mediated his message through the use of easily accessible 'signs.' Since his 'speeches would have been interrupted [and] there was no press, neither could the people read, Rienzi, therefore, prepared a great allegorical picture and set it up for public gaze and ponderment. . . . It set forth the people's distressful condition and imminent danger, and indicated bad men, especially barons, as the authors of their woes.' He then

> convened the public in the splendid new-built church of St. John in Lateran, for a lecture on an ancient inscription. This sounded so innocent, nobody prepared to interrupt him. Beginning beautifully garbed, by interesting the audience in a stone he had set up in the nave, with an inscription relating to the election of Vespasian as emperor, he went on to point out how the emperor's authority derived its sanction from the voice of the people of Rome, and made all there feel inwardly what the old pride of the Roman was, but finally turned

and brought their thoughts to existing misery, and sent them home with burning hearts.

Finally, Rienzi secured his popular authority on May 27, 1347 by leading a procession, accompanied by one hundred knights and the papal vicar, bearing three banners: the first red, representing liberty; the second white, for justice; the third blue, for peace. Peirce notes that 'this anticipates *liberté, égalité, fraternité,* for justice means equality, and fraternity means peace.' Having prepared the populace for his message through theatrical and historical 'signs,' 'Rienzi set forth the people's woes and slavery, then their majestic rights and power, and read the laws which he proposed they should then and there enact -- a sort of *magna charta*. It was done; the Senate was closed and Rienzi and the papal vicar were invested with the title 'Tribuni de la popolo e liberatori.' Barons, judges, notaries, and last the merchants took the oath of allegiance.' 'The revolution was accomplished without blood shed, without the raising of a finger.'

At this point, Peirce is clearly sympathetic to Rienzi, who began as a selfless, dedicated individual. Rienzi rose solely through his intellectual abilities -- his powers of persuasion with the elite, and his ability to convey his ideas in a symbolic and effective form to the common people. In this respect, Rienzi brings to mind Peirce's sense of his own mission. Having failed to obtain permanent academic appointments at Harvard and the Johns Hopkins Universities, Peirce condemned the contemporary academic societies of his day and the latter-day 'robber barons' much as Rienzi condemned the world of the Roman barons (Peirce c.1892c):

Our American universities have, one and all, a narrowly and rigidly prescribed end, that of education . . . for the individual advantage of the students. And what, I pray, is the individual advantage which refuses to look beyond the individual? What sort of morality is that teaching these young men? It teaches them that what is meant by their individual advantage which a vast institution undertakes as its ultimate end . . . is that they should lead luxurious lives. Wretched business! [Wonderful double entendre.] They had better spare themselves their years of bad habits at the university, content themselves with a course at a commercial college, go about the world, and look for a chance to make money.

Peirce found English universities, which considered the welfare of the nation as a whole rather than emphasizing self-aggrandizement, somewhat better. (And 'in her struggle with Germany,' Peirce notes, 'England is the hope and standby of the human race, in great measure, as the exponent of individual freedom, etcetera.') Nevertheless, 'in those schools, it is not what England stands for in civilization that is studied, it is just England's [presently perceived] needs without looking further.'

American universities corresponded to the America of Social Darwinism and the unreformed Rome Rienzi confronted. Individuals went about their business without regard for the greater good. English universities presented an intermediate type of society, where the individual existed to serve the immediate interest of a particular community which identified itself with the *summum bonum*. Peirce proposed instead an academic version of Rienzi's vision of Rome: 'not a school, but a brotherhood . . . [comprising] the sort of persons who are consumed with the desire of learning what they do not know and of correcting the errors what they now hold for knowledge. They would and must be animated by a pure passion for increasing the available fund of understanding of God's universe more and more, forever and ever.' He was sure that 'embodied in an institution such as I would plan, they would prove one of the greatest agents of enlightenment in all of history.' Peirce planned his villa, Arisbe, in Milford, Pennsylvania, as the prototype of such a community of scholars -- a harbinger of the modern 'free university' -- and predicted 'that the XXIst. century would say that nothing in the world had been so good for it and the XXth. as this brotherhood at Arisbe.'

Rienzi's dream of an uncorrupted Rome began as nobly as Peirce's dream of an alternative college at Arisbe. He organized a house of peace and justice 'where enemies came together and acknowledged the evil they had wrought, asked pardon, kissed, and made friends.' So successful was Rienzi at first 'that one man who had blinded another begged for his own eye to be put out' (which the latter refused); 'thieves, homicides, adulterers, and all persons of ill fame fled the city'; even established monarchs submitted their disputes to Rienzi's arbitration, and 'all Christendom, says the contemporary chronicler, expressed an emotion, and seemed to be roused from sleep.' Peirce compared the 'noble feeling and hope [that] abounded' to the atmosphere at the beginning of the French Revolution.

But Rienzi's utopian effort to undo the feudal anarchy of the fourteenth century proved quixotic, as unfortunate as Peirce's dream of establishing a university dedicated to pure scholarship to serve as the model for a society based on the selfless pursuit of goodness and truth. Whereas Peirce blamed his own failure on his contemporaries' indifference, he attributed Rienzi's to his own incompetence and lack of perseverance. Having come into power, 'Rienzi did not know what to do next. His success had been so sudden, that he was quite unprepared for the situation it created. Besides, it was found that notwithstanding the great revival of elevated sentiment, misery had not altogether disappeared. Nay, all this had cost money, much money, and taxes had to be increased. Things were far better than before, all allowed; still, clearly, no millennium was at hand.'

Rienzi's downfall was as precipitous as his rise. It occurred from lack of tenacity. For Peirce, who clung to his decaying vision and villa for the last twenty-seven years of his life, this was an unpardonable sin. Having put down some rebellious barons and killed several members of the Colonna family, Rienzi lost his nerve when he roused his followers to counter the return of the exiled Count Janni Pipino. 'But the weather was chilly, hearts were cold, no particular danger from Pipino was apprehended, nobody meant to desert Rienzi, but still nobody answered the tocsin.' At this 'infinitesimal reversal,' Peirce writes that Rienzi 'went into a blue funk. . . . He resigned everything, and fleeing into the wildest parts of the Appennines, adopted the life of a hermit, and devoted himself to penitence.' (Could Peirce be identifying with this exile also? He regarded Arisbe as located in the 'wildest' part of the eastern states, and it clearly marked his abandonment of a traditional career [Fisch 1971: 199-211].) The barons returned; Rienzi's revival of the Roman republic endured less than seven months.

If Rienzi's fall was tragic, his final days were pathetic. In 1351, after three years in solitude, he journeyed to Prague and proposed to share the world with Holy Roman Emperor Charles IV. Charles responded by sending him for trial to the pope at Avignon. Condemned to death, Rienzi was again saved by Petrarch. In 1353, a new pope, Innocent VI, sent him to Rome to restore order once again. 'Welcomed with enthusiastic affection,' he did the job, but was then exiled to Perugia. There he fell in with some robbers who funded an army of mercenaries with which he reconquered the city. He promptly murdered his benefactors, 'opened a tyrannical course,' and was soon assassinated in a popular uprising.

Rienzi's career illustrates a key point Peirce hoped to make about both men of science in general and his own life. By adhering unswervingly to his ideals, devoting himself unsparingly to his vision of the good, Rienzi accomplished much. But when he refused to stay the course and descended to the practical politics of his adversaries, he failed not only on his own exalted terms, but even on their 'pragmatic' grounds. Peirce concludes with a summary assessment of Rienzi:

Rienzi was clearly what is called a genius -- a vigorous, unsymmetrical mind. He also makes upon us the impression of greatness; but among great men we must reckon him the smallest. He was not great in action; not in reason, but belongs to the category of the great emotionalist. Even his speeches seem now cold and artificial. He was a more studious and brilliant Robespierre, but with less staying power.

Rienzi thus appears as a potentially great man who was granted an opening by chaotic historical events. He could have created something of lasting impact comparable to the French Revolution, but he failed when he descended to the level of his age. Peirce is suggesting that contrary to the evolutionary determinism of his contemporaries, a great man could have engineered something like the French Revolution in the fourteenth century, and brought a rebirth of popular enlightenment and government. Nothing inevitable or environmental dictated either Rienzi's failure or the French Revolution's success. Both were products of a breakdown in authority which created possibilities for dramatic change.

If Peirce viewed Robespierre as Rienzi's counterpart in the French Revolution, he envisaged Napoleon as a truly great man who in fact took advantage of that unprecedented situation to reshape the world. Peirce collected a great many 'Materials for the study of Napoleon' as a by-product of a review of Arthur Levy's *Napoléon Intime*. Since Levy's book was published in 1893, one year after Peirce's Lowell lectures, and in the same year as 'Evolutionary love,' it makes sense that the Rienzi and medieval essays were also products of this period of Peirce's life, when he was interested in the problems of great men and history (Peirce c.1893a: Ms. 1319; I use this source for all material on Napoleon).

Peirce's research on Napoleon was prodigious. He apparently examined numerous memoirs and biographies in French or English, including Napoleon's own 32 volumes of correspondence. His fragmentary study ultimately makes three points. First, Peirce became fascinated with the tremendous variations in the way different scholars and observers judged Napoleon. He finally concluded that they let their prejudices dictate their conclusions, and dismissed much historical writing on this count. Significantly, almost all of those he condemns are anti-Napoleon. Second, he attributes the majority of Napoleon's negative qualities to the 'savage' Corsican national character, which he still finds admirable in its fierceness and loyalty to friends and kin. Finally, he concludes with sweeping praise for Napoleon as one of those 'surprising facts' that alter the course of history, his flaw being not in his genius or execution of his plan but in the fact that he did not look beyond 'conquest and triumph' to more exalted, selfless ends. Still, Napoleon demanded more subtle, sophisticated, and exalted treatment than Peirce found in any biography from the nineteenth century.

Peirce begins his analysis with the interesting problem that in purely factual terms, we know more about Napoleon than anyone in history. After listing all the sources for research he could discover, Peirce asks:

> Is it not true that no man's life was ever more spread before us in so
> great detail? Besides these sources of facts, many elaborate analyses
> of his character, founded on this mass of information, are at hand to
> aid us. We daily form our judgments of men and consign them to the
> backseat of the community upon information amounting to one one-
> thousandth of what is known about Napoleon.

But to what end has all this knowledge been amassed? 'The question arises how it is possible for such utterly divergent characterizations as those of [Hippolyte] Taine [negative] and Levy [positive] to coexist?' Peirce cuts his way through this historiographical Gordian knot with a stroke of a pen:

On the one hand, there were in Napoleon, as the penetrating eye of
Metternich clearly saw, two men, the private man, the man of home
and domesticity, and the public man, the schemer. The same thing
is true of every person who has vast and intimate projects to carry
out. Now M. Levy, as his title page proclaims, only busies himself
with one of these two characters -- a picture on the whole ridiculously
false, although the more positive of the traits of his portrait really
existed in life. M. Taine is too cultured a scholar to fall into so
[illegible] a self-deception. But, like most other Napoleonographers
[a Peircean term], he has a political purpose to promote.

Peirce's glib assertion that historians are biased and their biases tend to
dictate their methodologies and areas of interest will not strike late twentieth-
century scholars as earth-shaking. But we should remember that in the 1890s,
historians were under the influence not only of Darwin, but also of the Positivism
of Auguste Comte. Comte preached that the scientific accumulation of facts could
result in both scholarly objectivity and human betterment. History was still largely
a gentleman's profession which believed knowledge and Western civilization
evolved cumulatively for the good of the human race (Ross 1985). Peirce instead
relegates most Napoleonic (and hence most) nineteenth-century history to the
dustheap as too biased to be worthy of serious consideration: 'The historical and
general descriptions of Napoleon . . . continue, one and all, to be completely
dominated by their writers' politics.'

Peirce gave two especially amusing examples of such bias in Taine's work.
The first concerns the time Napoleon purportedly kicked his friend Volney in the
stomach. Napoleon had remarked 'France desires a religion'; Volney replied,
'You might as well say France desires the Bourbons,' which prompted the physical
retort. Peirce goes on to show that Volney and Bonaparte remained friends, and

fulminates at Taine: 'Such a ridiculous tale needed four citations to bolster it up' -- one from a biased primary source, the other from three secondary works which cited it! Would Taine have so overfootnoted this absurd anecdote had he really believed it? Peirce also attacks Taine's charges that Napoleon 'never had a generous sentiment' and 'was incapable of love.' He points to how Napoleon ate only one meal a day and sent money instead to support his brother and mother when he was a poor young officer; 'seriously endangered his throne by his weak indulgent laxity toward the faults of his friends'; 'never forgot an old companion or failed to help him'; 'provided splendidly for his family, and tolerated conduct on their part which contributed to his fall'; and loved Josephine ardently until she began to have extramarital affairs.

Peirce attributes most of Napoleon's flaws to his Corsican heritage. His devotion to family and willingness to reward friends and carry out 'vendettas' against enemies were Corsican traits. 'Corsicans resemble real savages in their deep cunning and mendacity, and in this respect it is needless to say that Napoleon was the Corsican of Corsicans.' Napoleon's 'burst of rage,' which he practiced to 'heighten the performance to terrifying style,' Peirce similarly links to the fact that 'Corsicans are men of volcanic passions, and respond to the whole gamut of human emotions from the fiercest to the tenderest.'

However, if Napoleon's defects arose from his heritage, Peirce is quick to point out his unique virtues. Much as he argued in 'Great men of science' that Darwinism only manifested itself 'in retrograde motion,' Peirce finds the atavistic traits and weaknesses which caused Napoleon's downfall in his cultural heritage. But his virtues, which Peirce praises passionately, were exceptional and consciously developed. 'He made his own brain obey him . . . with military discipline.' 'His greatest intellectual capacity was his comprehension and grasp of every intricate problem,' which included 'absolute instant command of all he had ever pondered over.' In concluding his essay, Peirce denies the ability of conventional historians to deal with a phenomenon such as Napoleon (would he had lived to see Abel Gance's 1927 film!); an 'epic poet' would be required to do him justice:

> These seem to be some of the traits of Napoleon's character. To put
> them together, the admirable and the evil, in their proper collocation
> and reproduce the man would be a theme for the lyre of an epic poet.
> Napoleon was veritably an epic hero, heroic in his greatness of heart
> and head, heroic in his brutality, heroic in the worship of his people,
> heroic in his subjective merging of destiny, of France, and of self.

Napoleon's real, individual flaw, as Peirce views and expounds it in his next-to-last paragraph, was that he was not selfless. Far from putting his genius to work for the betterment of mankind, he subordinated peaceful reform and human betterment to what the French call *la gloire*:

> He was pre-eminently a man of imagination. Indeed, he was quite an
> aerial castle-builder. Only, his castles once elaborately erected in the
> air, he had a way of patiently copying them on solid earth. His
> fancies were neither very elevated nor very artistic. They were
> dreams of conquest and triumph. However, they intoxicated him.
> They caused his rise and they caused his fall. They puffed him up,
> and made him rash. He understood his enemies, he looked upon the
> rest of mankind as inferior beings; he despised them.

Peirce demanded love and charity as the prerequisites of disinterested thought if the human race were truly to progress. If Rienzi failed because he pursued a noble vision with insufficient tenacity, Napoleon failed because he clung too strongly to an egotistical ideal.

In his essay on the Middle Ages, reprinted as 'Remarks on the history of ideas' (Peirce c.1898: 350-355; I use this source for all material on the Middle Ages), Peirce points to yet a third pitfall that awaits men of genius who can seize the moment and create a new order of things. Here, architects and philosophers indeed selflessly submitted their work to the consideration of a community of inquirers. But medieval Christendom, for all its virtues, represented a limited, temporal community. Much like the English universities Peirce criticized, the unfettered, disinterested pursuit of truth became subordinate to the parochial needs of a group. Nevertheless, Peirce found much to admire in Gothic architecture and Scholastic philosophy. He used them to refine and make explicit many of the points about historical causation which can be deduced from the essays on Rienzi and Napoleon.

Peirce considers the spirit which led to Gothic architecture and Scholastic philosophy 'the most extraordinary break in people's ideas that modern history reveals -- except perhaps at the French Revolution.' He waxes rhapsodic over 'one of the most wonderfully original creations that the history of man shows.' The rich and beautiful but not deeply emotional Romanesque was suddenly replaced by the extremely chaste but devotional Gothic:

> There was a spirit of rationalism, of thinking for oneself which served
> to wake the people out of their slavish faith. The non-fulfillment of
> the prophecy about the end of the world in 1000 A.D. also helped.
> It was one of those *surprising* events -- in this case a negative one --
> which break association and increase the vividness of life.

Peirce curtly dismisses the idea of influences. Gothic architecture could not have come from the 'the Mohammedans, who never executed a single piece of architecture with the slightest level of sentiment.' From Aristotle? 'Could anything be shallower?' Peirce snarls. Europeans had known about Aristotle for centuries.   Why did his influence assume this form at this time?   From the Crusades?   'Very likely.   But *how*?   That is the question.'

Peirce thus takes the level of discussing historical causation one step beyond where even good historians are frequently content to let it rest.   European history books still talk about how a backward Europe was 'influenced' by contact with Islam and thereby developed the Gothic style and a new appreciation of Aristotle. But that is not enough for Peirce, nor should it be for us.   Peirce's alternative model suggests that the profound *differences* between European and Islamic art and philosophy required a previous psychological alteration in the European mind which would have taken some form or other, even without Islamic contact:

> To my mind the origin of the epoch A.D. 1200 was simply the logical result of the widespread belief of the tenth century that the world would be destroyed A.D. 1000.   For in the first place this belief was bound to be followed by a surprise and that of an exalting tone.   That necessarily created a nationalistic tendency, which in two centuries greatly developed man's intellect and imparted high self-confidence. The logical result of high self-confidence and pride is humility. Humility brings self-consciousness and self-study.   Self-study under humility brings the desire to learn and to correct one's errors and remove one's ignorance.   Now the earnest wish to correct one's errors is the principal factor of originality.

Peirce replaces evolution with earthquakes, disjunctions between expectation and reality so shocking they require people to think.   By thought, Peirce does not simply mean the elaboration of prejudices under the cloak of fashionable methodologies, but the genuine inquiry which arises from the willingness to admit one's own and one's civilization's errors, to examine the rights and wrongs of various positions from a variety of approaches.   And a glance at all the seminal periods in Western thought -- Judaism following the Exodus and in the time of the Prophets; Greece in the wake of the Peloponnesian War; the questioning of religious and monarchical authority following the Thirty Years' War in Europe; and the widespread disillusionment with capitalism and the nation-state following World War I (Peirce was ahead of his time, as usual) -- bears him out.

With what is probably a concise explanation of the manner in which he worked through his own ideas, and why he found the life of thought an exciting quest, Peirce thinks himself into the mind of a Gothic architect:

> The men of that time were not content to go on building as they had always done. They wanted to do better; in order to do better they must have wider aisles. In order to accomplish this they must have oblong compartments. -- These, they had to think, had to solve a new problem, -- harder than they would be able to screw themselves up to doing but for the deep earnestness of their aspiration for improvement. The result was the gothic arch. But they did not stop with simply making a gothic arch. They carried it to its logical conclusion, or lofty roof. A lofty roof implied slender columns. Now how were these slender columns to be acceptably heightened? Only by clusters of cylinders, another most startling medievalism.

At the same time medieval architects were striving to embody a new vision in stone, medieval philosophers articulated their quest for truth on parchment. Peirce views mature Scholastic philosophy as an imperfect approximation of his own conception of knowledge and that of his beloved nineteenth-century scientists: 'that truth be recognized as public -- as that of which any person would come to be convinced if he carried his inquiry, his sincere search for immovable belief, far enough; the opinion which is fated to be ultimately agreed to by all' (Peirce 1903-1911: 26):

The age had passed by an inevitable 'logic of events' from a conception of truth as each man's castle to a conception of truth as the property of the entire congregation of the faithful in its organized church. It was a public thing and of its essence general. Now when truth is regarded as general, reality must be looked upon in the same light.

How did this come about? Or, as Peirce phrases it, 'what is the logical nature of such inferential triumphs of new ideas?':

Take the overthrow of the early fetish that the 'truth' or rather the presupposition a man ought to support was the proposition he had previously heeded. Experience showed:

A man cannot stand against the world.

A man cannot stick through thick and thin to a personal whimsy.

Therefore, no personal whimsy is a proposition for a man to believe.

Peirce looked admiringly at the University of Paris as an institution dedicated precisely to such a communal ideal of truth, and condemned, by comparison, the narrower, utilitarian ends of the schools of his own day:

The founding of the University of Paris is one of the most remarkable examples of the extraordinary love of truth in that age. Compare it for the moment to the hundred universities which have been founded during the enlightened XIXth century in up-to-date America. There are hardly half-a-dozen of these latter that was not intended to be an institution for the defence of a foregone conclusion. . . . But in the early thirteenth century the University of Paris was founded in order that men might go there and learn what was to be learned about divine truth, especially from Aristotle, and to teach the prince and his

people. Education was a merely secondary purpose. The great object
was to find out the truth.

However, the Middle Ages stopped short of full freedom of thought. In
overcoming nominalism, the idea that each man could defend his own conception
of truth, they 'came to conclude that the proposition for a man to defend was the
one which was consonant to the authority of the church.' This led to the notion
that 'any proposition so backed is a proposition fit to be defended.' Still, the
submission of truth to even a restricted community of inquirers marked an
advance:

> The great truth that from a conception of truth as one's own fortress
> reason will infallibly lead to the next step -- though not the final step
> -- to the adoption of truth as the dictum of the church, or the
> organized *force* of society.

In discussing medieval philosophy, Peirce's sense of proportion reveals
itself. If he admired the Gothic cathedral without qualification, he realized only
too well from his personal life how his own creative thought was neglected in
favor of those who wrote more accessibly and in accordance with the 'spirit of the
age,' or the 'organized force of society,' as he put it. When he speaks of 'truth
as one's fortress,' as 'each man's castle,' it recalls his own 'standing through thick
and thin against the world,' confident that in the long run he would be vindicated
by the community of truth-seekers even as he was rejected by the (for him) biased
and insufficiently astute scholarly community of his own day. It speaks volumes
for Peirce's ability to distance himself from his own experiences that he could see
flaws and virtues in both nominalism (freedom to explore, but no need for testing
by communal standards) and scholasticism (testing by communal standards, but no
freedom to go beyond them). He could in fact sympathize with the *communal*

enterprises of medieval architecture and philosophy even as he remained estranged from the fashionable intellectual currents and universities of his own times.

In his essay on the Middle Ages, Peirce casts yet another stone at one of his contemporaries' most cherished concepts. The individual best fulfills himself not though egotistic striving, but through selfless devotion to a communal enterprise. The anonymous and collectively built cathedrals of Mont Saint-Michel and Chartres, and the great *Summae* of Aquinas with their inclusion of all obtainable human wisdom, stand as testimonies to the cooperative nature of art, scholarship, and man's pilgrimage through history. In Peirce, as in Henry Adams, the Middle Ages found a champion who did not hope, as did their contemporaries, to discover an ideal, vanished world of order and stability. The cutthroat Gilded Age looked nostalgically at the medieval period. The late nineteenth century held it up as a model for restless youth and workers by erecting pseudo-Gothic college campuses, fortress-like National Guard armories, and palatial homes (Adams 1904; Jaher 1964). Peirce and Adams held the Middle Ages up to their contemporaries as a rebuke. In a time of infinitely fewer material resources, people put themselves in the service of a vision of the good, the true, and the beautiful, then devoted themselves collectively, humbly, self-critically, and tirelessly to its realization. They thereby created a civilization which modern capitalism, for all its self-congratulation through the dogmas of Social Darwinism and Positivism, sought to imitate artistically, and used as a psychological escape.

Peirce traced the decay and predicted the downfall of a modern capitalist civilization founded on 'The Gospel of Greed.' He condemned a society which 'had come to look upon reason as mainly decorative,' demanded 'that it shall be plain and facile,' and 'if in special cases complicated reasoning is indispensable, they hire a specialist to perform it' (Peirce c.1896: 1.58):

The result of this state of things is, of course, a rapid deterioration of intellectual vigor, very perceptible from one generation to the next. This is just what is taking place before our very eyes; and to judge from the history of Constantinople, it is likely to go on until the race comes to a despicable end.

Peirce substituted 'cataclasmine' for Darwinian evolution as 'the most efficient,' in which 'the changes have not been small and not been fortuitous,' but where 'sudden changes of the environment . . . have put certain organs at a disadvantage' (Peirce c.1896: 1.104). In the essay 'Evolutionary love,' which contains his greatest praise of agapistic evolution (creative love) and his most damning indictment of 'the Economical Century' which produces 'food in plenty and perfect comfort . . . for the greedy master of intelligence,' Peirce modified 'cataclasmine' to 'anancastic' evolution, or 'evolution by mechanical necessity' (Peirce 1893b: 6.290). 'Anancastic evolution advances by successive strides with pauses in between. The reason is that in this process a habit of thought having been overthrown is supplanted by the next strongest. Now this next strongest is sure to be widely disparate from the first, and as often as not its direct contrary.' Condemning 'tychastic' or Darwinian evolution through fortuitous variation as operative 'exclusively in backward and barbarizing moments,' he found 'the evolution of history is in considerable part of the nature of internal anancasm' (Peirce 1893b: 6.312-314).

Peirce detected cycles of a 'rough natural era of about 500 years' in history. These occurred when 'cataclasmine' evolution (external anancasm) set moving a new period of 'internal anancasm' ('logical groping . . . upon a predestined line'). He noted that the intervals between the expulsion of the Tarquins (510 B.C.), Octavius assuming the title Augustus (27 B.C.), the end of the Western Roman empire (476 A.D.), the creation of the Holy Roman Empire (962 A.D.), and the fall of Constantinople (1453 A.D.) were 'rather curiously nearly equal.' They also suggest his use of Constantinople as a symbol of decline -- and therefore modern civilization was only a half century or so away from its next major stage.   In philosophy, Peirce chose three dates: 433 B.C. (the death of Aristotle), 1274 A.D. (the death of Aquinas), and 1804 A.D. (the death of Kant), to establish periods of 1595 (thrice 500) and 530 years.   In the history of thought, he used the beginning of Greek philosophy (535 B.C.), the crucifixion (A.D. 30), the closing of the Athenian schools (A.D. 529), the rise of the medieval universities (A.D. 1125), and the publication of Copernicus' tract on the solar system (A.D. 1534), intervals of 615, 499, 596, and 418 years (Peirce 1893b: 6.312-315).

Peirce also found shorter cycles in history:

If the evolution of history is in considerable part of the nature of internal anancasm, it resembles the development of individual men; and just as 33 years is a rough but natural unit of time for individuals, being the average age at which a man has issue, so there should be an approximate period at the end of which one great historical movement ought to be likely to be supplanted by another. (1893b: 6.314).

Although he did not publish his shorter periods in 'Evolutionary love,' Peirce did work them out in a manuscript (Peirce c.1893c: Ms.1325).

1453 -- Fall of Constantinople.

1492 -- America discovered.

1519 -- Luther's theses.

1547 -- Battle of Muhlenberg.

1572 -- St. Bartholomew's Massacre.

1598 -- Edict of Nantes.

1618 -- Thirty Years' Wars.

1648 -- Peace of Westphalia.

1685 -- Revocation of Edict of Nantes.

1713 -- Peace of Utrecht.

1740 -- War of Austrian Succession.

1763 -- End of Seven Years' War.

1791 -- King's retreat from Varennes.

1815 -- Waterloo.

1848 -- Revolutions.

1871 -- German Empire established.

Of course historians would question Peirce's cycles and periodization. Why the War of the Austrian Succession and not the American Revolution? Why the Edict of Nantes and not the Spanish Armada? Why Copernicus and not Newton? Why Kant and not Darwin? Why Thales and not Plato? The cycles vary in the final table from a high of 39 (1453-1492) to a low of 20 (1598-1618) years. But even if we criticize Peirce's details, two crucial points stand. First, 'cataclasmine,' 'mechanical,' 'anancastic' great events do occur which disrupt predictable developments and initiate a new paradigm, or era of internal anancasm, until the next leap forward. Second, Peirce worked out his cycles so that the world, which had ignored his philosophical and scientific achievements and rejected 'Evolutionary love' for the 'Gospel of Greed,' was due for both a small-scale transformation and a major 500-year cycle:

> The twentieth century in its latter half, shall surely see the deluge
> tempest burst upon the social order -- to clean up a world as deep in
> ruin as that greed-philosophy has long plunged it into guilt. (1893b:
> 6.292)

Ironically, Peirce died on April 19, 1914, barely three months before the deluge began.

To conclude: in his 'General review of the history of science,' Peirce remarked that 'I have been making what my opponents call an onslaught upon the doctrine of necessity; that is, I hold that while there is a certain force of necessity in the universe, there is a certain power of spontaneity too' (Peirce 1892a: 150). In 'Great men of the nineteenth century' he added that 'human greatness has been a favorite study of mine for seventeen years,' because he wished to test whether 'great men are fashioned out of the most ordinary clay and owe their greatness entirely to the fortune of their rearing, environment, and opportunities,' or whether 'circumstances are as powerless to overwhelm the man born great as they would be to subject a human to a nation of dogs.'   Peirce conceded much to the Darwinian necessitarians of his day: he admitted that even through the truly great man is a 'monstrous birth,' 'his development depends mainly on circumstance.' Peirce argued that there might be a half dozen people with the potential of Milton, Euler, or Augustus Caesar in Gilded Age America, but that greatness only became visible 'when there is a demand' (Peirce c.1901b: 872-875).

However, in the *appropriate circumstances* -- of breakdown in the political order, or uncertainty in the scientific -- the great man could emerge and change the course of history. His greatness would be identified not only by native ability, but by tenacity in holding to the truth of his vision come what may. For the scientist, this meant 'the desire to know the truth, for its own sake, independent of its agreeability.' Like the great statesman, the scientist cannot simply assert his propositions -- to the extent they are truly novel and meaningful, he will find 'the whole moral weight of the community will be cast against' him, 'because science implies a desire to learn, and a desire to learn implies dissatisfaction with current opinions' (Peirce 1892e: 1117-1118).   Peirce illustrates both the tragedy -- limitations imposed by contemporaries (necessity) -- and triumph -- ability to do his work (spontaneity) -- of the true scientist in an essay on Galileo:

It is a bitter thing to be put into the world by God to do a special piece of great work, to be hungering and thirsting to do it, and to be prevented by the jealousies and coldness of men. Galileo did something for the world; but he did not do half what he might have done, and would have done, had helping hands been extended to him. (Peirce 1892a: 286)

Concluding that inventions such as the steam engine would have come quicker and 'every individual . . . would have lived a happier and pleasanter life,' Peirce could not resist comparing Galileo's fate implicitly with his own: 'Do not fancy that this blocking of the wheels of progress is confined to by-gone times and to strange countries. There is plenty of it here, today' (1892a: 286).

By recognizing both chance in extraordinary men and ages, and necessity in the behavior of ordinary men and routine eras, Peirce laid the groundwork for a semiotic of history. For if history happens when things break down and reveal creative possibilities for new starts, then great men become the signs of such periods, the keys to determining history's structure. They may be regarded as 'firsts' who only arise in opposition to 'seconds' of chaos or revolution, and in struggle with contemporary ideas, or as 'abductive hypotheses' emerging to be 'tested' on the battleground of their times, to succeed or fail as their 'truth' is useful. They will form part of Peirce's community of 'truth-seekers,' to the extent they actually pursue their visions and are not diverted by the lures of power and wealth, and will provide the basis for a further evolution of thought and society. The Peircean 'third' is the community's judgment and working out of their ideas in the 'routine' period which follows -- the smaller cycle of twenty to forty years when 'a universal movement or struggle of thought, action or feeling, absorbs men's attention and suppresses other tendencies' (Peirce 1901b: 872), or larger cycles in the case of more important developments. Or 'third' can be the ideas' usefulness in understanding history as a whole. Great men, periods of breakdown, and revolution thus become the critical signs of Peirce's philosophy of history, a philosophy which grants to men both the inspiration to remain true to their visions in the hope that they might make a difference, and the sobering realization that real innovation is usually punished rather than rewarded, and that the exhilaration of freedom and creativity is frequently more than balanced by the pain of repression and censorship.

ENDNOTES

1.   This paper does not treat Peirce's 'The logic of doing history from ancient documents' (1901c: 705-800), because that article deals with the entirely different problem of ascertaining the validity of evidence. That problem is discussed by Williams (1985:277-292; 1986:217-233).

REFERENCES

Adams, Henry, 1904, *Mont St. Michel and Chartres*, Washington, DC: private publication.

Bergson, Henry, 1911, *Creative Evolution*, trans. by A. Mitchell, New York: D.H. Holt.

_____, 1935, *The Two Sources of Religion and Morality*, trans. by R. Audra and C. Brereton, New York: D.H. Holt.

Fisch, Max, 1971, Peirce's Arisbe: The Greek influence in his later philosophy, *Transactions of the Charles S. Peirce Society*, 7, 199-211.

Jaher, Frederic C., 1964, *Doubters and Dissenters: Cataclysmic Thought in America, 1885-1915*, Glencoe, IL: The Free Press.

Kuhn, Thomas S., 1962, *The Structure of Scientific Revolutions*, Chicago: University of Chicago Press.

Peirce, Charles S., 1877, The fixation of belief, in *Collected Papers of Charles Sanders Peirce*, vol. 5, C. Hartshorne and P. Weiss (eds.), 374-387, Cambridge: Harvard University Press, 1931-35, (All references to the *Collected Papers* are to numbered paragraphs).

_____, 1892a, Lectures on the history of science commonly known as 'Lowell Institute Lectures,' in *Historical Perspectives on Peirce's Logic of Science*, Carolyn Eisele (ed.), 139-295, Berlin: Mouton de Gruyter, 1985.

_____, c.1892b, Rienzi, last of the tribunes, in *Historical Perspectives on Peirce's Logic of Science*, Carolyn Eisele (ed.), 550-554, Berlin: Mouton de Gruyter, 1985.

_____, c.1892c, Conception of history, MS. 1329, microfilm edition of the Charles S. Peirce papers, Houghton Library, Harvard University, (Catalogued in Richard S. Robin, *Annotated Catalogue of the Papers of Charles S. Peirce*, Amherst: University of Massachusetts Press, 1967. A portion of the essay is reprinted in *Historical Perspectives on Peirce's Logic of Science*, Carolyn Eisele (ed.), 1120-1121, Berlin: Mouton de Gruyter, 1985).

_____, c.1892d, Rienzi, last of the tribunes, MS. 1318, microfilm edition of the Charles S. Peirce papers, Houghton Library, Harvard University, (Catalogued in Richard S. Robin, *Annotated Catalogue of the Papers of Charles S. Peirce*, Amherst: University of Massachusetts Press, 1967).

_____, 1892e, The chief lessons of the history of science, in *Historical Perspectives on Peirce's Logic of Science*, Carolyn Eisele (ed.), 1117-1119, Berlin: Mouton de Gruyter, 1985.

_____, c.1893a, Napoleon, MS. 1319, microfilm edition of the Charles S. Peirce papers, Houghton Library, Harvard University, (Catalogued in Richard S. Robin, *Annotated Catalogue of the Papers of Charles S. Peirce*, Amherst: University of Massachusetts Press, 1967).

_____, 1893b, Evolutionary love, in *Collected Papers of Charles Sanders Peirce*, vol. 6, C. Hartshorne and P. Weiss (eds.), 290-314, Cambridge: Harvard University Press, 1931-35.

_____, c.1893c, Historical chronology, MS. 1325, microfilm edition of the Charles S. Peirce papers, Houghton Library, Harvard University, (Catalogued in Richard S. Robin, *Annotated Catalogue of the Papers of Charles S. Peirce*, Amherst: University of Massachusetts Press, 1967).

_____, 1895, Review of Sir Robert Ball, *The Great Astronomers, The Nation* (December 19), (Reprinted in *Historical Perspectives on Peirce's Logic of Science*, Carolyn Eisele (ed.), 454-457, Berlin: Mouton de Gruyter, 1985).

_____, c.1896, Lessons from the history of science, in *Collected Papers of Charles Sanders Peirce*, vol. 1, C. Hartshorne and P. Weiss (eds.), 43-125, Cambridge: Harvard University Press, 1931-35.

_____, c.1898, Remarks on the history of ideas, in *Historical Perspectives on Peirce's Logic of Science*, Carolyn Eisele (ed.), 350-355, Berlin: Mouton de Gruyter, 1985.

_____, 1901a, Review of the nineteenth century, in *Annual Report of the Smithsonian Institution for the Year Ending June 30, 1900*, 693-699, Washington DC: The Smithsonian Institution Press.

_____, c.1901b, Great men of the nineteenth century, in *Historical Perspectives on Peirce's Logic of Science*, Carolyn Eisele (ed.), 872-876, Berlin: Mouton de Gruyter, 1985.

_____, 1901c, The logic of doing history from ancient documents, in *Historical Perspectives on Peirce's Logic of Science*, Carolyn Eisele (ed.), 705-800, Berlin: Mouton de Gruyter, 1985.

_____, 1903/1911, *Letters to Lady Welby*, I.C. Lieb (ed.), New Haven: Whitlock's, 1953.

_____, 1908, A neglected argument for the reality of God, in *Collected Papers of Charles Sanders Peirce*, vol. 6, C. Hartshorne and P. Weiss, (eds.), 452-493, Cambridge: Harvard University Press, 1931-35.

Ross, Dorothy, 1985, Historical consciousness in nineteenth-century America, *American Historical Review* 84, 909-928.

Williams, Brooke, 1985, What has history to do with semiotic? *Semiotica* 54(3/4), 267-333.

_____, 1986, History in relation to semiotic, in *Frontiers in Semiotics* (= Advances in Semiotics), J. Deely, B. Williams, and F.E. Kruse (eds.), 217-223, Bloomington: Indiana University Press.

Chapter 5

Carl Becker and the Semiotics of History

Although in 1932 his colleagues elected him President of the American Historical Association, and while some of his beautifully written and thought-provoking works remain in print and continue to influence scholarship four decades after his death in 1946, Carl Becker sometimes disparaged both his historical talents and the value of 'history.' 'This certainly is not history. I hope it is philosophy, because if it is not it is probably moonshine: or would you say the distinction is oversubtle?' (1931: 149). So Becker inscribed a copy of his classic, *The Heavenly City of the Eighteenth Century Philosophers* (1932b), in its thirty-fourth printing when I bought my copy in 1970. In his preface to *The Eve of the Revolution* (1921), one of the few books in the 1920s 'Chronicles of America' series still worth reading, Becker 'endeavored to convey to the reader, not a record of what men did, but a sense of how they thought and felt about what they did.' To do so, he sometimes used 'a rather free paraphrase of what some imagined spectator or participant might have thought,' which he freely admitted might not be 'history': 'the point of greatest relevance being the truth and effectiveness of the *illusion* (my emphasis) aimed at -- the extent to which it enables the reader to enter into such states of mind' (1921: vii-viii).

Becker's denials that he was writing *history* might be dismissed as posturing from so distinguished, not to say whimsical, a scholar. But they perfectly complement his serious theoretical effort to force his contemporaries to rethink what history is. Although he did not use the word, Becker was developing a semiotics of history.   Harry Elmer Barnes's statement that Becker's work possessed the 'potential fundamentally to reshape historiography,' and 'may well come to occupy the same position in historical science that the New Physics does in natural science' remains as true today as when it was written over fifty years ago (Barnes 1936: 70).

To assert that Becker was in effect the Albert Einstein of history is a large claim I hope to justify by building upon Brooke Williams's superb paper 'What has history to do with semiotic' (1985) in which she analyzes Becker's writings 'What is the historical fact' (1926) and 'Everyman his own historian' (1932a).   I propose here to look at *The Heavenly City of the Eighteenth Century Philosophers* and *The Eve of the Revolution* to demonstrate how Becker practiced what he preached, and to suggest to historians wary of wading too deeply into the waters of semiotic theory the reverse proposition -- 'what has semiotic to do with history.'

Becker's 'breakthrough,' Williams points out, was 'to treat the historical fact as a sign, or what he termed "only a symbol"' (Williams 1985: 297).   For Becker, 'facts do not really exist until the historian, at the very least, selects and affirms them *in relation* to one another, in order to give them a certain place in a certain pattern of ideas.'   Becker prefers to call facts 'affirmations,' 'representations,' 'symbols' -- even 'illusions.'   For 'without a purpose no one would take the trouble to bring historical facts to mind.'   'The past is a kind of screen upon which we project our vision of the future' (1926: 329, 330, 337).

Becker does not deny that we can know facts in one sense.   To use two of his favorite examples, we can know the day Lincoln was shot or where Charles the Fat was at certain time (1926: 331; 1923a: 249).   But as Williams puts it, if on one level 'history does exist apart from the observer (is mind independent), that level can only be made comprehensible, meaningful, and alive through an engaged historical observer (is mind dependent)' (Williams 1985: 297).   In Becker's words, 'it is not the undiscriminated fact, but the perceiving mind of the historian that speaks' (1932a: 234).

Given such a perception of history, what is the historian to do? Becker's answer, as his presidential address to the American Historical Association insists, is to realize that 'Everyman [is] his own historian.' 'Every normal person . . . does know some history, enough for his immediate purpose.'

> I suppose myself, for example, to have awakened this morning with a loss of memory. I am all right otherwise; but I can't remember anything that happened in the past. What is the result? The result is that I don't know who I am, where I am, where to go, or what to do. . . . My present world would be unintelligible and my future meaningless . . . knowledge of history, in so far as it is living history and not dead knowledge locked up in notebooks, is only an enrichment of our minds with the multiplied meanings of events, places, people, ideas, emotions outside our personal experience, an enrichment of our experience by bringing into our minds memories of the experience of the community, the nation, the race (1926: 338).

To bring out the experiences of 'the community, the nation, the race,' themselves the product of 'Everyman His Own Historian' -- this is the professional historian's mission. Becker insists that 'there is no more fascinating or illuminating phase of history than historiography -- the history of history; the history, that is, of what successive generations have imagined the past to be like. It is impossible to understand the history of certain great events without knowing what the actors in those events thought about history' (1926: 336).

The writing of history thus becomes a three-fold process. The historian looks at men in the past who are themselves *acting* not only in history, but as historians, basing their behavior on their own visions of the past. These visions may be regarded or understood as *signs*, communicated across centuries, which while recognizable to future communities nevertheless change their meaning as different scholars and generations attain and impose their own visions of the future.

The 'Heavenly City' is one of the most important signs in history. For St. Augustine and the Christian ages which followed him, the 'City of God' was literally true, the goal of human history: 'the earthly city would come to an end, the earth itself be swallowed up in flames' and 'the faithful would be gathered with God in the Heavenly City, there in perfection and felicity to dwell forever' (Becker 1932b: 6). One could even go one step back from Becker and show how the Medieval Heavenly City represented a historical mediation and synthesis of those mentioned in the *Bible* and Platonic philosophy. Becker's thesis is that the eighteenth century philosophers, for all their criticisms of the institutional church and the naive faith of the true believers, merely 'demolished the heavenly city of St. Augustine to rebuild it with more up-to-date materials' (1932b: 31). They even borrowed wholesale the terminology and symbolism of the 'infamous one' they hoped to root out. 'What the next world is for the religious man, posterity is for the philosopher,' wrote Diderot. 'Whatever is the beginning of this world, the end will be glorious and paradaisical, beyond what our imagination can now conceive,' rhapsodized scientist and political radical Joseph Priestley. Like 'everyman,' the eighteenth century thinkers 'surveyed the past and anticipated the future.' They reasoned that 'since the present is so much better than the past, will not the future be much better than the present? To the future the philosophers looked, as to a *promised land*, a new *millennium*' (1932b: 118-119 -- my emphasis).

In semiotic terminology, on one simple level of analysis, the Christian 'Heavenly City' may be treated as an icon, an unquestioned 'given' representing itself, which is transformed by the philosophers into an index, an image to represent the world paradise they hope to construct on earth. Each of these two communities share a 'climate of opinion' expressed through a 'code' -- 'magic words' Becker calls it -- 'certain unobtrusive words with uncertain meanings that are permitted to slip off the tongue without fear and without research; words which, having from constant repetition lost their metaphysical significance, are unconsciously mistaken for objective realities.' God, sin, Heaven, grace, and salvation were magic words for the Christian centuries; for the eighteenth, 'the words without which no enlightened person could reach a restful conclusion were nature, natural law, first cause, reason, sentiment, humanity, perfectibility' (1932b: 47).

If the philosophers developed their analysis of society and history in juxtaposition to the 'Heavenly City,' twentieth-century man, Becker insists, has lost the Heavenly City save as an object of nostalgia or scholarly exegesis. It degenerates into a *symbol* of vanished, irretrievable aspirations which a more innocent world confidently cherished. 'For good or ill we must [now] regard the world as a continuous flux, a ceaseless and infinitely complicated process of waste and repair, so that all things and principles of things' are to be regarded as no more than 'inconstant modes of fashions.' No wonder Barnes could compare Becker's repudiation of a clearly discernible historical universe to modern physics' theory of scientific relativity. 'Chance,' 'accident,' man as a 'foundling,' or 'abandoned,' 'relativity, process, adjustment, function, and complex' are Becker's magic words. 'Whirl is king,' 'we have no first premise,' humanity as 'carelessly thrown up between two ice ages by the same forces that rust iron and ripen corn' are his laments for a Heavenly City which, like Nietzsche's dead God, no longer shelters our existence (1932b: 12-16).

But if the death of the Heavenly City is a catastrophic loss for those who cherish the comfort and security of a definable 'world,' a terrible beauty rises from its ashes.   Modern men, reflecting on the transformations of their ancestors' symbols, historically aware to the limits of their courage, vision, and research, may approach ideas as semioticians rather than suppliants, as iconographers rather than ideologues.   To map the content, context, and codes shared by communities of believers, and the whys and wherefores of their transformations, is the historian's task as he endeavors to make the past speak to future generations in novel ways.   If history is not the key to the 'Heavenly City,' as it had been for western man for nearly two thousand years, it remains -- even in spite of itself and where it is scorned -- a means of understanding ourselves as we journey through the earthly one.

To return to the beginning of the paper. 'Moonshine,' Becker described his *Heavenly City*. How apt a description! The moon, a satellite of the earth, itself a satellite of the sun. The third term in the series after the life-giving sun, the living earth, the *dead* moon.   For Becker, the Heavenly City is, literally, moonshine: an image reflected at third hand from the mind and world of Augustine to the mind and world of Voltaire to the mind and world of Becker. 'I hope it's philosophy -- or would you say the distinction is oversubtle?' For modern man, there is no distinction. The Heavenly City continues to shine as the moon, a dead object of investigation rather than a living truth, no longer as paradise, but as paradise forever lost.

In *The Eve of the Revolution*, finished in 1918, a decade before his theoretical writings on history, Becker was already approximating the method he later articulated.   Instead of recounting events in chronological order or marshalling evidence to argue specific interpretive points, Becker presented a series of six paired biographical sketches which depict the changing mentalities accompanying the disintegration of the First British Empire.   After briefly presenting Benjamin Franklin as the symbol of a united empire large enough to accommodate both English and American visions of the good life, Becker discusses George Grenville as the representative of a contradictory, destructive theory. Briton Soame Jenyns and American John Dickinson show how the two sides developed their ideas of sovereignty in the late 1760s. Samuel Adams' victory over Thomas Hutchinson illustrates the triumph of revolutionary zeal over conservative prudence. Becker also includes sketches of William Pitt, Grosvenor Bedford, Robert Livingston and others to augment his canvas, but his interpretation unfolds through the three pairs of adversaries representing the fragmentation of Franklin's grand vision. Each appears as 'everyman his own historian' -- arguing a theory of colonial rights and British power shared by the important historical actors at a given time. But they are more -- they are symbols of mentalities which still prominently effect world history.

Chapter one, which deals primarily with Franklin, is entitled 'A Patriot of 1763.' In his trans-Atlantic travels and influence as well as his writings, Franklin represented the good will shared by the colonies and Mother Country following the triumphant conclusion of the French and Indian War. 'No Briton rejoiced more sincerely than this provincial American in the extension of the Empire. He labored with good humor, and doubtless with good effect, to remove the popular prejudice against his countrymen,' thereby reconciling two continents explicitly and articulating the implicit message of his career. Reflecting on the history of Britain and America, from the perspective of anticipating a glorious future, Franklin found that 'never before . . . were the relations between Britain and her colonies more happy' (1921: 10).

But the 'Heavenly City' that Franklin anticipated would develop from the English-speaking world soon shattered on the reefs of a new vision of Empire, one which looked at the colonies through narrow bureaucratic and cost-accounting bifocals, and saw in their history only disobedience and disloyalty. 'The ablest man of business in the House of Commons,' George Grenville, author of the Stamp Act, had long 'studied the revenue problem with assiduity' and bemoaned the lack of 'system' and the reign of 'easy-going bad custom' in the colonial administration.   His 'first axiom of business was that accounts should be kept straight' (1921: 19, 24, 31).   Replacing Franklin's generous vision of cultural unity with a collection agency, Grenville angered Franklin, who pointed out he was even wrong on his own terms: 'British subjects, by removing to America, cultivated a wilderness, extending the domain, and increasing the wealth, commerce, and power of the mother country, at the hazard of their lives and fortunes' (1921: 50).   The wealth of empire depended not on the balancing of accounts, but on the enterprise and vision of courageous colonials to whom Britain was incalculably indebted.

Furthermore, Becker is presenting Franklin and Grenville as symbols of attitudes toward 'the state' and political obligation present throughout history. Only in his final paragraphs does he explicitly take his historiographical and personal stand.   After quoting from the Declaration of Independence, which proclaimed the 'self-evident' truth of human equality and man's rights to 'life, liberty, and the pursuit of happiness,' Becker concludes not with a remark on the American Revolution, but with a presentist mediation:

> It is to these principles -- for a generation somewhat obscured, it must be confessed, by the Shining Sword and the Almighty Dollar, by the lengthening shadow of imperialism and the soporific haze of Historical Rights and the Survival of the Fittest -- it is to these principles, these 'glittering generalities,' that the minds of men are turning again in this day of desolation as a refuge from the cult of efficiency and from faith in 'that which is just by the judgment of experience.' (1921: 255-256)

Such principles were as revolutionary in the dark days of nationalism run mad during the First World War as they were two hundred years ago. Becker finished his book less than three months after the Bolshevik Revolution. Nevertheless, as he remarks in the preface, these ideas are illusions; in fact, a double sleight-of-hand is being performed. It is an illusion *'not delusion,* O able Critic!' Becker warns, to believe that an author can 'create for the reader the illusion . . . of the intellectual atmosphere of past times.' But the ideas which themselves breathed in this air are also illusions; 'the point of greatest relevance being the truth and effectiveness of the illusion aimed at.' Becker here identifies concepts which many of his colleagues would believe to be mutually exclusive: 'relevance' and the 'effectiveness of the illusion' as a test of 'truth.' What is true is what speaks most meaningfully to the reader of 1918, to modern man who has witnessed the horrors of the Western Front inflicted on their own populations by respectable, conservative gentlemen, and who was right then experiencing another great revolution (1921: vii-viii).

But the case for revolution is not so simple. The subtle and ironic Becker, who could turn ideas inside out and examine them from every possible angle without calling the slightest attention to his methodology or erudition, qualifies his own analysis through the two other principal confrontations of the book.

When John Dickinson took on British apologist Soame Jenyns, revolution won hands down. Becker describes Jenyns as 'logical' and 'versatile,' but representative of the haughty way the British dismissed the colonists' ideas as unworthy of serious consideration: 'in twenty-three very small pages he had disposed of the 'Objections to the Taxation of Our American Colonies' in a manner highly satisfactory to himself and doubtless also to the average Briton, who understood constitutional questions best when they were briefly considered and when they were humorously expounded in pamphlets that could be had for sixpence' (1921: 109).   Against Jenyns' glib pronouncements stood John Dickinson's conscientious efforts.   Although a lawyer, his 'Farmer's Letters' represented the Pennsylvania farmer as ably as the many lawyers among the Founding Fathers articulated the aspirations of their agrarian society.   His 'subtle but clear' book-length production seemed to come from the pen of 'a simple but intelligent and virtuous farmer whose arcadian existence had conferred in him an instinctive love of liberty' (1921: 132-33).   Even as Englishmen erred when they believed America owed much to the mother country, Britain had it wrong again in thinking its political theory superior to the obscure colonials' revolutionary ideas.

But revolutions rarely pose simple choices in retrospect.   Becker drives this point home in his longest and most exciting chapter.   Revolutionary Samuel Adams, who 'thought of the past as chiefly instructive in connection with certain great epochal conflicts between Liberty and Tyranny' was sure 'that a great crisis in the history of America and of the world confronted the men of Boston.'   He was an 'extraordinary man' possessed of 'integrity of character,' of 'that indispensable combination of qualities possessed by all great revolutionaries of the crusading type, such as Jean-Jacques Rousseau, John Brown, or Mazzini.'   But he did not confront the nickle-nursing Grenville or the superficial Jenyns.   Thomas Hutchinson was a worthy opponent, a man of 'outstanding abilities':

> Thomas Hutchinson possessed the efficient mind.   No one surpassed
> him in wide and exact knowledge, always at command of the history
> of the province, of its laws and customs, of past and present practice
> in respect to the procedure of administration. . . .   His sane and
> trenchant mind, habituated by long practice to the easy mastery of
> details, was prompt to pass upon any practical matter, however
> complicated, an intelligent and just judgment. . . .   Of America he

was as proud as a cultivated and unbigoted man could be, extremely jealous of her good name abroad and prompt to stand, in any way that was appropriate and customary, in defense of her rights and liberties. (1921: 168-170)

Confronted with so able and respected an adversary, Adams and his cohorts branded Hutchinson 'an enemy to the Human Race,' 'insidious in plotting the ruin of our liberties,' hoping to 'enslave' his fellow citizens (1921: 164-165). Hutchinson pointed out all the fallacies in their arguments, all the potentially disastrous consequences of taking 'abstract liberty' to its not so logical conclusion. A world in revolution has demonstrated again and again the foresight of Hutchinson's profound political theorizing. No matter that he was a good man and conscientious civil servant whose conception of Americans' real rights resembled his opponents more than his British superiors. The revolutionaries drove him from his homeland; he 'died in England on June 3, 1780, an unhappy and homesick exile from the country which he loved' (1921: 199).

Becker leaves us with the praise of the rights of man ringing in our ears, heaping scorn on the Social Darwinism and lust for greed and power which gave 'civilization' the First World War. But he also leaves us with the long shadow of Thomas Hutchinson, darkly cast across the new birth of freedom brought to the world by the Age of Democratic Revolution. Hutchinson remains a neglected symbol of the price of revolution, an invitation to semiotic reflection on the accompanying efforts to bring the 'Heavenly City' down to earth.

REFERENCES

Barnes, Harry E., 1936, Personal letter to Carl Becker dated March 21, as quoted in Charlotte Watkins Smith, *Carl Becker: On History and the Climate of Opinion*, Ithaca, NY: Cornell University Press, 1956, 70.

Becker, Carl L., 1921, *The Eve of the Revolution*, New Haven, CT: Yale University Press.

_____, 1926, 'What Is the Historical Fact,' paper read at the 41st Annual Meeting, December, of the American Historical Association at Rochester, NY, subsequently published as 'What Are Historical Facts?,' *Western Political Quarterly*, 1955, 327-340.

_____, 1931, Personal letter of Carl Becker to Charles Homer Haskins of October 21, as quoted in *Carl L. Becker and the Genius of History: Selected Letters of Carl L. Becker 1900-1945*, edited by Michael G. Kammen, Ithaca, NY: Cornell University Press, 1973, 149.

_____, 1932a, 'Everyman His Own Historian,' *American Historical Review*, 37, 1932, 221-236, reprinted and cited here from Carl Becker, *Everyman His Own Historian*, Chicago, IL: Quadrangle, 1966, 233-255.

_____, 1932b, *The Heavenly City of the Eighteenth Century Philosophers*, New Haven, CT: Yale University Press, 1932.

Williams, Brooke, 1985, 'What has History to Do With Semiotic?' *Semiotica* 54, 1985, 267-333.

Chapter 6

Dialogues and Dilemmas of Carl Becker:
A Historian's Reflections on
Liberty and Revolution

More than any other major United States historian of the twentieth century, Carl Lotus Becker (1873-1946) was attuned to the philosophical issues raised by history -- the nature of rights, freedom, loyalty, responsibility, and revolution, and even of knowledge itself: what can we, in fact, know about the past, or about the world around us. He was also intensely interested in the role historical writing and teaching played related to action in the world -- what sort of history was written, by whom, and for what end. Brooke Williams has written on Becker's theoretical writings, and found in them both an application of Peircean semiotic to history and a pioneering effort still valuable as a practical, methodological guide for historians today. Also, I have previously discussed how Becker applied his ideas in two of his finest works, *The Eve of the Revolution* (1921) and *The Heavenly City of the Eighteenth Century Philosophers* (1932).[1]

One of Becker's chief interests was to explore those 'unobtrusive words with uncertain meanings that are permitted to slip off the tongue without fear and without research; words which, having from constant repetition lost their metaphysical significance, are unconsciously mistaken for objective realities.'[2] Liberty was such a word, as were its cognates, freedom and the (natural) rights of man, both for the Americans of the revolutionary generation and for many of the historians who memorialized their struggle. Becker wished to explore the complexity of 'liberty' as a sign rather than as a reality -- for liberty not only meant different things to different men and different ages but even changed its meaning for the same men under the pressure of a revolutionary process. He examined such questions as -- Whether deprivation of liberty justifies revolution? What are man's responsibilities to an existing social order? Are liberty (and equality, another ambiguous sign) desirable or possible (and what sort of liberty and equality) and what methods can be justifiably used to transform the signifier into the signified?

For Becker, no historical problem or philosophical issue presented itself without irony and complexity. Hence, the dialogue was a natural form for him. Becker wrote three dialogues in which a revolutionary 'first' (to use Peircean terminology) is confronted by a counter-revolutionary 'second' which invites the reader to render the 'third,' or judgment, which is necessary if 'liberty' is to be understood not as an uncritically accepted sign, but as part of revolutionary and counter-revolutionary codes which develop in specific historical contexts and are addressed to audiences to achieve particular ends. Becker even constructed his general survey of the revolutionary crisis of 1760-1776, *The Eve of the Revolution*, as a series of six short dramas where revolutionaries and loyalists symbolizing the principal debates at key junctures argue the merits of their causes.

In the three dialogues I consider here, Becker personifies his dilemmas as revolutionaries and their opponents explore the meaning of liberty. In the first, 'The Spirit of '76,' Becker pretends that he discovered an anonymous manuscript in which Jeremiah Wynkoop, a moderate, upper-class revolutionary, confronts his father-in-law, 'Old Nicholas' Van Schoickendinck, a loyalist, concerning four key events between 1765 and 1776. The second, 'John Jay and Peter Van Schaack,' Becker creates from the actual correspondence of the future Chief Justice with a former college friend he helped to banish from New York for failure to support the revolution. By juxtaposing two wealthy, well-educated people in each of these dialogues, Becker is also trying to burst the Marxist bubble that ideas are the superstructure of class antagonisms. They are rather the product of a complex context, economic in part to be sure, but only in part, which differs as do the life experiences and temperaments of every individual. And past ideas themselves are part of the context from which future ideas are formed. Finally, 'The Marxian Philosophy of History' presents Becker's own dilemma as a liberal college professor of the 1930s confronted with a fictional representative of a significant American Communist movement seeking ends he approved through means he deplored. Let us examine these dialogues in turn.[3]

The four confrontations of 'The Spirit of '76' personify in a graceful manner four stages through which the American revolutionary ideal of liberty passed and the moral and political dilemmas associated with each. First, at the time of the Stamp Act riots, Wynkoop criticized the British for violating the traditional liberties of Americans by taxing them. The revolutionaries, in short, present themselves as conservative guardians of the sign 'liberty' which is threatened by a government of revolutionary innovators. Old Nicholas, however, finds that the protesters' behavior brands them as liars. If liberty is what they want, then why do 'we get half the windows of Broad Way smashed, and Governor Colden gets his chariot burned. For my part I don't know what Mr. Colden's chariot had to do with the devilish stamps -- it wasn't designed to carry them.' (56) Becker is pointing out that 'liberty' for revolutionaries means collective self-determination, whereas for non-revolutionaries it means the right of people to live safely under the protection of existing laws. But even here, why then is the mode of protest against the Stamp Act the destruction of the property of wealthy British officials? Old Nicholas has the answer: 'It is not windows they aim at but class privileges . . . liberty is a sword that cuts two ways, and if you can't defend your rights against ministerial oppression without stirring the 'people,' you will soon be confronted with the necessity of defending your privileges against the encroachments of the mob.' (57) Revolutionary liberty is a sign of hidden agendas. Those without power would displace those who possess it. To acquire power, revolutionary leaders must mobilize the positively signified 'people,' who also, Becker subtly hints, can be negatively signified as the 'mob'. Through the voice of Old Nicholas, Becker has exposed the key revolutionary terms of 'liberty' and 'the people' as signs rather than objective realities. Signs of what? -- class resentment for 'the people,' 'will to power' for their leaders.

By 1767, Britain had discovered how to tax the colonies through the hitherto traditionally accepted means of regulating their trade, and British thinkers had presented the case for a traditional parliamentary sovereignty, 'in all cases whatsoever' as the Declaratory Act of 1766 put it, as least as effectively as the colonial case that traditional liberties within the Empire were exempted from parliamentary interference. So liberty becomes a shifting sign, as Old Nicholas points out: 'You will be saying that Parliament has no right of legislation for the colonies on any matter whatsoever. And as you can't derive that from precedent you will derive it from the law of nature.' And only God knows what that is. God and Mr. [Samuel] Adams -- it's the same thing.' (61-62) 'Liberty' at this point becomes an immutable law of nature which is nevertheless sufficiently mutable that only an elite of American revolutionaries are aware of it. And even the relevant collectivity in which the supposed rights apply is but a sign -- 'the British Empire'? 'America'? 'Massachusetts?'

The third dialogue concerns the colonists' response to the Boston Port Bill of 1774. Determined to punish the British for cutting off Boston's trade, they did the same with the mother country. Merchants throughout the colonies were compelled to join a so-called 'Voluntary Association' to enforce the embargo. At this point, to obtain 'liberty' the individual is required to participate in the collective struggle, even against his personal will. He is not only denied personal choice but 'forced to be free.'

Finally, when the colonies declare independence, Old Nicholas -- who himself claims to have 'no great love for the Britishers -- Damn them all' sees only one of two futures for America: 'Either we shall be crushed, in which case our last state shall be worse than our first; or if we succeed, we shall be ruled by the mob.' (77) The practical consequence of revolutionary liberty is usually a state far more oppressive to the individual than the one it replaced; those who think the United States has totally escaped such a fate had best look again at Alexis de Tocqueville's *Democracy in America.* 'Liberty' is exposed in revolution's triumph as an empty sign.

'John Jay and Peter Van Schaack' continues to explore the theme whether 'liberty' really is a cause of revolution, and the paradoxical fact that a revolutionary crisis and war reduce personal liberty. In opposition to Jay who argues that *the* paramount issue is the colonists' liberty to tax and govern themselves, Van Schaack replies that on the one hand Britain removed all the taxes save that on tea before the revolution began, and on the other that the colonies had always been willing to contribute to the general expenses of the empire in cases of real need. Van Schaack pleads that 'the article of right is almost out of the question. . . . For refined principles of government, applied to a case so peculiar, can have very little weight. . . . A conflict between different members of the same body is too serious to be upheld for the sake of a punctilio.' (294) Revolution, terror, and war thus arise when people fail to realize signs are signs, and treat them as signified realities. Note Van Schaack also uses the sign of 'the same body' to unite Britain and America.

Jay, on the other hand, insists that 'either Britain was right, and America wrong; or America was right, and Britain was wrong.' (296) Jay must postulate the signs 'right' and 'wrong' and 'America' and 'Britain' as real and diametrically opposite to support revolution. Therefore, since all Americans ought to support the colonial cause, 'it was an easy step to the right of the state to compel the individual.' Revolutionary liberty thus requires loss of judgment, of reason, and of self, the willingness to fight and die for revolutionary signs. As Becker commented:

> The thing that came between them was an aspect of the venerable quarrel between 'the One and the Many'. Their case was a concrete example of the State versus the individual, of personal liberty versus social compulsion, of might versus right. 'America is right,' said Jay. But he identified 'America' with the organized power wielded by government and affirmed the duty of the individual to bow in submission to this right which was might, or this might which was right. 'America is right,' Van Schaack in substance replied, but only insofar as she can win the approval of Americans. I submit to the force which is the State, but I give my first allegiance to reason and conscience. (296)

Becker used the Jay/Van Schaack debate as a vehicle for exploring the nature of the 'loyalty' (yet another sign) a citizen owes his government. Let us remember Becker was friendly to the rights of man and equality. As he wrote at the end of his book on *The Declaration of Independence:*

> It was a humane and engaging faith. At its best it preached toleration in place of persecution, goodwill in place of hate, peace in place of war. It taught that beneath all local and temporary diversity, beneath the superficial traits and talents that distinguish men and nations, all

deploring greed and strife, poverty and injustice, have looked forward to.' (117) Marxism constructs but another version of Heaven, or the *Heavenly City of the Eighteenth Century Philosophers*, about which Becker wrote so elegantly. Mankind uses the same symbols, and men on either side of revolutionary movements become signs themselves, as do the movements, of a long-term historical struggle between opponents and supporters of change in the name of' signs.

But Becker also provides a second criticism of Marxism concerning how signs can themselves become part of the reality they signify.

> Let us assume that up to the time of Marx, men have been submitting
> blindly to the economic class conflict, and that now, thanks to Marx,
> they are in the way of becoming aware of that fact, and that they are
> in a position to modify profoundly the conditions that will determine
> social changes. . . . In short, insofar as Marx has made man aware
> of the influence of the economic class conflict in the past, he has
> destroyed the very conditions that would have enabled him to predict
> the nature of the social revolution in the future. (123)

Man does not achieve 'liberty' through 'class struggle,' Becker says. He obtains it by reflecting (the Peircean third) on the struggle between two definitions of liberty (the reactionary and the revolutionary) and understanding how neither is absolute or real, but both are signs of, among other things, underlying class realities. Advances in human betterment, liberty for both the individual and the group, then follow from reasoned pragmatic adjustment of the differences. This is, in fact, the position of twentieth century welfare state liberal capitalism or the historic course of European socialism.

By becoming conscious of the economic basis of his actions, man can modify them and act otherwise, much as capitalist economies fearing the revolution men are equal in the possession of a common humanity; and to the end that concord might prevail on the earth instead of strife, it invited men to promote in themselves the humanity which bound them to their fellows, and to shape their conduct and institutions in harmony with it.[4]

Yet how could those contending for liberty banish a Peter Van Schaack, who did not oppose them save by privately pointing out the inconsistencies between their practices and ideals? Becker thus sees this loyalist as a superior defender of liberty. If the Americans did not owe loyalty to the best empire on earth -- as most of them admitted -- because it did not square with their ideal liberties, then how could anyone owe loyalty to a newly created United States? Does 'America' or any nation constitute the government and policies of the time? Is it composed of traditions or fundamental principles? Of what is 'America' a sign? Becker concludes with a question, not an answer: 'Whether, all things considered, Jay or Van Schaack was the better American, the better friend of mankind, who shall say?' (298)

In 'The Marxian Philosophy of History,' Becker answers this question, for he puts in the mouth of the 'liberal' college professor with whom he obviously identifies many of the words Van Schaack used to reply to Jay 170 years earlier. Becker's criticisms of the Communist movement of the 1930s parallel Old Nicholas's and Van Schaack's queries concerning revolutionary liberty two centuries earlier. According to Marx, true liberty will be achieved following a revolutionary class struggle. Becker responds: 'If I project this explanation of social change into the future, what does it tell me? It seems to tell me that there will be in the future what there has been in the past -- an endless economic class conflict.' (114) Marx's post-capitalist Utopia of liberty and justice for all is merely 'what during the last two thousand years, all the saints and sages of world, predicted by Marx developed the welfare state. Becker concludes, ironically, that *he*, unlike both reactionaries and revolutionaries, is really working for social betterment because he is not a Marxist. Otherwise, as a college professor, he would have to trumpet the ideology of the master class which pays his salary. He can treat 'class struggle' as a sign as well as a reality, and as such a sign that is mutable. When the Communist tells him that if he 'persists in the futility of expressing his faith in the superior virtues of persuasion' in a Communist state, he 'would be suppressed,' Becker responds: 'I might, as a last resort from imbecility, become a Christian and practice the precept that it is better to suffer evil than to do it. . . . I am a professor, and a professor, as the German proverb has it, is 'a man who thinks otherwise'.' (131)

Where did Becker get this last idea? From the letter of Peter Van Schaack he quoted in his essay of sixteen years before. Compare Van Schaack's response to Jay: 'Upon the whole, as ever in a doubtful case, I would rather be the patient sufferer, than run the risk of being the active aggressor.' (295) Becker thereby projects a community of like-minded men into the past -- a Peircean community of truth-seekers.

In an essay on 'Freedom of Speech,' where Becker declares his allegiance to free, personal inquiry as the primary source of social betterment, he again concludes with the same paraphrase of Van Schaack.[5] On the one hand Becker's critique of the way great wealth in America has become 'socially vicious, to the point of endangering all our liberties,' is virtually identical with the Communists:

Modern methods of communicating thought are more subtle and effective than any ever known before, while the verification of the truth or relevance of the thought so communicated is far more difficult. The result is that there issues daily from the press and the radio a deluge of statements that are false in fact or misleading in implication, that are made for no other purpose than to fool most of the people most of the time for the economic advantage of a few of the people all the time.

Becker concludes that 'this manifestation of free speech is a far greater menace to liberal democracy than the freest dissemination of an alien political philosophy by Nazis or Communists is ever likely to be; and the only defense for it is that to restrict it would endanger the principle of free speech.'[6]

Yet if Becker agrees with the revolutionaries' critique of the malefactors of great wealth (the phrase itself is Franklin D. Roosevelt's), totalitarianism or violence is not the answer: 'If social ills cannot be alleviated by the democratic method of free speech, this very freedom of speech will be used by those whose avowed aim is the abolition of the democratic method.' Becker concludes that 'the real danger, from the liberal point of view, is not that Nazis and Communists will destroy liberal democracy by speaking freely but that liberal democracy, through its own failure to cure social ills, will destroy itself by breeding Nazis and Communists.'[7]

In conclusion, Becker argues that economic justice and free speech are inextricably intertwined as are personal and collective liberty. If we cherish intellectual liberty we must support plans for general social betterment within the system or revolution and/or its concommitants of anarchy and repression will follow. Conversely, for non-revolutionary social betterment to occur it is necessary to develop through free debate alternatives to the status quo. Yet is Becker's theory too neat? Herbert Marcuse argued in *One-Dimensional Man* that the 'democracies' of Western Europe and the United States permit free speech only because it is no threat to the established order; they become repressive when it is.[8] The relationship between speech and action, as Becker would be the first to acknowledge, is extremely complex, and of course the powers that be always enjoy a tremendous advantage in presenting their case.

If John Lennon in 'Imagine' sang that 'There are no problems, only solutions,' Becker would maintain the reverse. He ends the Jay/Van Schaack and Marxist/Liberal dialogues with Van Schaack's commitment to non-commitment. 'The Spirit of '76' ends in mid-sentence after 'perfunctory applause' follows an imaginary speech in the Continental Congress: 'God grant we may so act that the spirit of freedom will ever be synonymous with the Spirit of '76!' (80) Perhaps it is best to end with Becker's dedication of the volume of essays discussed here:

> Dedicated with gratitude and affection to the young people, and some
> not so young now, who have assisted the author in clarifying his
> ideas; partly by listening with unfailing amiability to his expoundings,
> chiefly by avoiding the error of Hway, a pupil of Confucius; Hway,
> said Confucius, is of no assistance to me; there is nothing I say in
> which he does not delight.

Becker dedicated his essays to the real community of thinkers among whom he happily passed his life, the 'seconds' to Becker's 'first' who spurred him on to further reflection. Becker thus in his dedication symbolically presents his vision of the good society, which is essentially Peirce's community of dedicated, skeptical inquirers, rather than the closed community of true believers, either revolutionary or counter-revolutionary, who mistake their signifiers for the signified.

ENDNOTES

1. Brooke Williams, 'What Has History to with Semiotic?,' *Semiotica*, 1985, 267-333; William Pencak, 'Carl Becker and the Semiotics of History,' included in this volume.

2. Carl Becker, *The Heavenly City of the Eighteenth Century Philosophers*, New Haven: Yale University Press, 1932, 47.

3.   Reprinted in Carl Becker, *Everyman His Own Historian*, New York: Appleton-Century-Crofts, 1935, respectively pages 47-80, 284-298, and 114-131; pages in parentheses for the rest of this chapter are from one of these essays.

4.   Carl Becker, *The Declaration of Independence*, New York: Knopf, 1922, reprinted 1942, 278-279.

5.   Reprinted in Becker, *Everyman His Own Historian*, 101-113.

6.   *Ibid.*, 107.

7.   *Ibid.*, 110.

8.   Boston: Beacon Press, 1964.

Chapter 7

Eric Voegelin's
Semiotics of History

As history and semiotic begin their formal rapprochement, evidenced by numerous articles in *Semiotica* during the 1980s on semiotics and history -- including special issues in 1982, 1984, and one in 1991[1] -- and a session on history and semiotics at the American Historical Association Convention in 1987, it is worthwhile to call attention to the immensely learned works of the Austrian-American thinker Eric Voegelin (1901-1985). To call him a philosopher, historian, or political scientist is to diminish his stature: his thought linked these disciplines much as semiotics claims to offer a methodology unifying the realms of knowledge. Moreover, Voegelin's lifelong concern with the symbols through which societies have understood themselves and through which thinkers have sought to interpret human experience foreshadowed modern semiotics. His inquiries were in part inspired by his early encounter with the works of Charles Peirce, William James, George Santayana, and John Dewey -- the last of whom was his teacher at Columbia in the 1920s. I therefore treat Voegelin here as a semiotician of history, and invite scholars in both disciplines to benefit from his exciting, if by no means unexceptionable, approach to history as the creation, questioning, and development of certain symbolisms to represent the fundamentals of human experience.

Voegelin takes as his starting point man's experience of existence 'as a creature and therefore as doubtful.' Feelings such as 'dread, hope, despair, piety, apparent calm, searching, restlessness, outrage, rebellion, renunciation, and so forth,' merge 'somewhere in the depths of the umbilicus of the soul' of a being who senses 'being-thrown-into-life.'[2]

Yet man is also aware of belonging to a 'primordial community of being' with God, the world, and society 'by virtue of his key participation (a major Voegelinian concept) in the mystery of its being.' 'A first ray of meaning falls on the role of man in the drama of being so far as the success of the actor depends upon his attunement (another key term) to the more lasting and comprehensive orders of society, the world, and God.'[3]

The gap between man's sense of his mortality, weakness, and ignorance in a cosmos he experiences as enduring and ordered yet governed by unfathomable laws creates 'a tension for its [the cosmos'] partial revelations in the order of society and the world.' 'Attunement' thus becomes man's effort to 'hearken to that which is lasting in being' and deal with the 'anxiety of existence,' that 'horror of losing, with the passing of existence, the slender foothold in the partnership of being that we experience as ours while existence lasts.'[4]

Man thus experiences his humanity as a 'tension' in the 'In-Between' (or Platonic Metaxy -- two more crucial concepts):

> The flux of existence does not have the structure of order or, for that matter, of disorder, but the structure of a tension between the truth and deformation of reality. . . . If anything is constant in the history of mankind it is the language of tension between life and death, immortality and mortality, perfection and imperfection, time and timelessness; between order and disorder, truth and untruth, sense and senselessness of existence; between love of God and love of self, the open soul and the closed soul; between the virtues of openness toward the ground of being such as faith, love, and hope, and the vices of infolding closure such as hubris and revolt; between the moods of joy

and despair; and between alienation in its double meaning of alienation from the world and alienation from God.[5]

Voegelin identifies these terms as *symbols* of man's quest for meaning in the universe, symbols which are 'intended to convey a truth experienced,' 'trails in the world of sense perception [where] meaning can be understood only if they evoke and through evocation reconstitute the engendered reality' at the heart of human existence.[6] Man is a creature who creates symbols to explain an existence in which he is pulled between order and chaos, truth and lie, and good and evil.

Given these fundamental human experiences, Voegelin can then describe political society: 'every society is burdened with the task, under its concrete conditions, of creating an order that will endow the fact of its existence with meaning . . . and attempts to find the symbolic forms that will adequately express that meaning.' 'The process of symbolization is the attempt at making the unknowable order of being intelligible as far as possible through the creation of symbols which interpret the unknown analogously with the really or supposedly known.'[7]

Human society thus develops as a 'cosmion, illuminated with meaning from within by the human beings who continuously create and bear it as the mode and condition of their self-realization. It is illuminated through an elaborate symbolism, in various degrees of compactness and differentiation (two more key Voegelinian terms to be explained shortly) from rite through myth to theory.'[8]

If society constitutes itself through representative symbols, history becomes 'the history of participation, and the symbols referring to the poles of participation are the indices of experience.'[9] 'What is permanent in the history of mankind is not the symbols' themselves, which evolve, 'but man himself in search of his humanity and its order. . . . The study of symbols is a reflective inquiry concerning the search for the truth of existential order, and will become, if fully developed, what is conventionally called a philosophy of history.'[10]

Voegelin devoted most of his life to elucidating and analyzing, as one of his articles is entitled, 'Equivalences of Experience and Symbolization in History.'[10] For 'the great societies, beginning with the civilizations of the ancient Near East, have created a sequence of orders, intellectually connected with one another as advances toward, or recessions from, an adequate symbolization of truth concerning the order of being of which the order of society is a part.'[12] In his many books and articles, Voegelin proceeded to trace the symbolisms of the cosmological empires, the 'leaps in being' which occurred with the Hebrews, Greeks, and Christianity, and what he terms the 'Gnostic' deformation or derailment typical of much modern social thought. The last of these, he argues, is characterized by the construction of dogmatic systems which reduce being, man, and society to derivatives of one element (psychology, biology, economics, utility, race, etc.) and seek to 'freeze history' in unattainable 'perfect' societies.

To begin at the beginning. In the empires of Egypt, China, and Mesopotamia, society is experienced 'compactly' as 'an analogue of the cosmos and its order.'[13]

> Rulership becomes the task of securing the order of society in harmony with cosmic order; the territory of the empire is an analogical representation of the world with its four quarters: the great ceremonies of the empire represent the rhythm of the cosmos; festivals and sacrifices are a cosmic liturgy, a symbolic participation of the cosmion in the cosmos; and the ruler himself represents the society, because on earth he represents the transcendent power which maintains cosmic order.[14]

Cosmic empires do not permit the development of alternative symbolizations which recognize the right of the individual conscience, appealing to an 'Unknown God' behind the pantheon, to judge their adequacy. Nor are politics, science, philosophy, and religion critically differentiated -- all are symbolized in compact myths which unify cosmos and empire.

However, no empire retains forever its self-proclaimed status as an adequate representation of an unchanging cosmos. 'Inevitably,' Voegelin writes, 'such an enterprise of representative order is exposed to resistance from enemies within and without: and the ruler is no more than a human being who may fail through circumstance or mismanagement, with the result of internal revolutions and external defeats. The experience of resistance, of possible or actual defeat now, is the occasion on which the meaning of truth comes into clearer view.'[15] In Peircean semiotic terms, it is doubt or catastrophe which compels thought: a cosmic empire may be regarded as a given 'first' which only understands itself in relation to a 'second' and which either clarifies, modifies, or loses its symbolism after each encounter with the other. Then the 'third,' critical judgment, is possible. Voegelin points to the incorporation of the lower-class cult of Osiris and the Underworld into Pharaonic sun-symbolism and the integration of Confucian philosophy into Chinese imperial symbolism as examples of how two ancient empires restored order following periods of trouble by stretching their symbolisms without breaking them.[16]

Israel marks a 'leap in being' from the cosmological empires. It 'alone constituted itself by recording its own genesis as a people as an event with a special meaning in history.' History becomes Israel's symbolic form of existence: 'Without Israel there would be no history, but only the eternal recurrence of societies in cosmological form.' Instead of adhering to a given cosmic symbolism, 'mankind creates history through its real approach to existence under God.' 'The divine creation of order is not finished . . . the process of world-history reaches its highest level with the divine choice of individuals and groups for special instruction and the trusting response of chosen individuals and groups. The special relationship between God and man is formalized through covenants':[17]

> The participation in being changes its structure when it becomes emphatically a partnership with God, while the participation in mundane being recedes to second rank. . . . And when this conversion befalls a society, the converted community will experience itself as qualitatively different from all other societies that have not taken the leap. . . . The community, as in the case of Israel, will be a chosen people.

Israel's historical existence is constituted by a new symbolism: Egypt is the Sheol or death out of which the Chosen People are brought by their representative Moses through the Wilderness to live in the Promised Land. God treats with man equitably according to covenants and through representative figures who leave history open to be created in partnership with God if man so chooses. Later, after Israel appeared to be on its way to becoming a cosmological kingdom through the monarchy of Saul, David, and Solomon and the divided kingdoms which followed, the Prophets' Revolt spiritualized this symbolism to equate the corrupt mundane kingdom of Israel with the Egyptian captivity and death.[18] They 'had to struggle for an understanding of Yahwism in opposition to the concrete social order of Israel . . . to make it clear that the political success of Israel was no substitute for a life in obedience to divine instructions . . . [and] that status in the social order of Israel did not confer spiritual status on a man before God.'[19] By differentiating the individual's responsibility to God, moral law, and the historical mission of his community from obedience to the powers that reigned on earth, the Prophets continued a process begun by Abraham and Moses, who constituted the Jews as

'Chosen' even before they had a homeland, and enabled them to remain so even when they had lost it. The Prophet, much as Christ later on, becomes the 'Suffering Servant' of a wayward but still chosen people who eventually become the collective suffering servant of mankind -- representative individuals and communities who seek to restore the symbols and reality of true order in the face of its worldly deformation.

If historical existence is the form that differentiation of the soul attuned to being took in Israel, the corresponding Greek leap is philosophical existence. If there is no history before Israel, there is no philosophy or political science before Greece. 'In their acts of resistance to the disorder of the age' of Pericles, which brought great wealth and cultural distinction but ultimately destruction to an unjust, imperialist Athenian polis, 'Socrates, Plato, and Aristotle experienced and explored the movements of a force that structured the psyche of man and enabled it to resist disorder. To this force, its movement, and the resulting structure, they gave the name of 'Nous' [Divine Ground, Reason].' 'The exploration of the 'metaleptic reality' [human-divine interaction] . . . as well as the articulation of the exploratory action through language symbols, in Plato's case of his myths, are the central concern of the philosopher's efforts,' which Voegelin terms an 'epochal feat.' The quest for right order is described through the symbols 'wondering,' 'searching,' and 'questioning'; 'justice' and 'injustice'; 'the good, the true, and the beautiful'; 'the philosopher,' loving searcher for and participant in the Nous as opposed to 'the philodoxer,' articulator of contemporary 'illusions'; the 'turning around' from 'ignorance' to 'truth,' and so forth. The philosopher is dead to the mundane world to be attuned to Nous, thereby to achieve Resurrection from the death of Hades in the myth of Er and liberation from the Cave of Illusion in Plato's *Republic*. Philosophy is the articulation of the symbols of the quest for right order, not, Voegelin insists, 'a doctrine of right order,' 'a body of ideas or opinions,' or 'information about the truth.' Like the mission of the Hebrew Prophets, philosophy is man's 'responsive pursuit of his questioning unrest to the divine source that has aroused it' culminating in *action*. The philosopher must articulate his 'arduous effort to locate the forces of evil and identify their nature,' then convey to his auditors through his life and teaching the experience of 'a philospher through whose psyche humanity has become luminous.' His goal is to institute a community of philosophers living according to 'right order' among themselves which 'relieves the pressure of the surrounding corrupt society.' Plato is thus 'the founder of a community of philosophy which lives through the ages' -- an indefinite community of inquiry much like Peirce's postulation of truth as an unattainable ideal only to be approached by a community of genuine truth-seekers.[20]

If Voegelin relies most heavily on Plato to convey the 'luminous essence' of philosophical experience, which includes the paradigmatic life and death of Socrates, it his distillation of Aristotle which provides philosophy's methodological guideposts and enables one to tell the philosophers from the philodoxers. He uses the following table to encapsulate the parameters of human experience in the natural, social, and divine worlds; a true philospher does not leave out any of the constituents of experience or explain away any element as derivative of any other. In other words, he must not dogmatize about existence by shrinking it or turning its constituents into autonomous facts or objects. To do so is to declare the philosophical quest at an end and destroy the openness of reality: to succumb to 'the temptation to fall from uncertain truth into certain untruth.'[21]

	Person	Society	History
Divine Nous			
Psyche - Noetic			
Psyche - Passions			
Animal Nature			
Vegetative Nature			
Inorganic Nature			
Apeiron - Depth			

Before turning to the ways in which modern philosophical systems have shrunk reality, it is important to show how Voegelin handles the oft-discussed manner in which Christianity fused the philosophical leap in being in Greece with the historical advance of Israel. Christ is 'the revelation of the unknown god in conscious continuity with the millennial process of revelation':

> The mystery of divine presence in existence had grown in consciousness . . . long before the drama of the Gospel started; and the symbols which the Evangelist uses for its expression -- the Son of God, the Messiah, the Son of Man, the Kingdom of God were historically at hand through the Egyptian Pharaonic, the Davidic royal, the prophetic and apocalyptic symbolisms, through Iranian traditions and Hellenic mysteries. Hence, the 'secret' of the Gospel is neither the mystery of divine presense in existence, nor its articulation through new symbols, but the event of its full

comprehension and enactment through the life and death of Jesus. The apparent contradictions dissolve into the same symbols at various levels of comprehension.[22]

Voegelin especially stresses the continuity of symbolism of light, darkness, death, Resurrection, and revelation of divine presence through a suffering representative in the lives of Christ and Socrates. The symbolism of Word (Logos) and Light at the beginning of the 'Greek' Gospel of John is one key linkage. For 'if the community of the Gospel had not entered the culture of the time by entering its life of reason, it would have remained an obscure sect and probably disappeared.' 'The Logos has been operative in the world from its creation; all men who have lived according to reason . . . have in a sense been Christians. Hence Christianity is not an alternative to philosophy . . . it is the history of the Logos come to its fulfillment.'[23]

Yet there is a definite advance with Christianity. The Unknown God 'who plays with man as a puppet' in Plato's *Laws* 'is not the God who becomes man to gain his life by suffering his death.'[24] The Unknown God has reached out to man, potentially to all men, explicitly and concretely, and no longer remains a mysterious presence sensed and articulated by philosophers through myths such as the Cave or by communities through notions such as Dike behind the Olympians. 'In the encounter with the Incarnation, we may say, history has become articulated down to the individual man, who through his faith participates in the constitution of history.'[25] 'The Gospel held out its promise not to Christians, but to the poor in spirit, that is to minds enquiring.'[26] Voegelin summarizes the differences between the 'saving tale of the Incarnation' and Greek philosophy as follows:

It is richer by missionary fervor of its spiritual universalism, poorer by its neglect of noetic control; broader by its appeal to the inarticulate humanity of the common man, more restricted by its bias against the articulate wisdom of the wise; more imposing through its imperial tone of divine authority, more imbalanced through its apocalyptic ferocity, which leads to conflicts with the conditions of man's existence in society; more compact through its generous absorption of earlier strata of mythical imagination, especially through the reception of Israelite historiogenesis and the exuberance of miracle-working; more differentiated through the intensely articulate experience of action in the illumination of existence with truth.[27]

If Christ's life and teachings marked a leap in being, development of Christian society and theology posed two problems. First, 'the *logia* of Jesus, and especially the Sermon on the Mount, had effectively disengaged the meaning of faith, as well as the life of the spirit, from the conditions of any particular civilizational order.' Christian statesmen 'had to make it clear that faith in Christ was no substitute for organized government,' that 'sacramental acceptance into the mystical Body did not touch the social status of a man,' and that 'Christianity in general was no insurance for individual or collective prosperity.'[28] The principal symbolization of the Christian order was St. Augustine's two cities, the City of God and the City of Man:

> This left the church as the universal spiritual organization of saints
> and sinners who professed faith in Christ, as the representative of the
> civitas Dei in history, as the flash of eternity into time, and
> correspondingly it left the power organization of society as a temporal
> representation of man in the specific sense of a representation of that
> part of human nature that will pass away with the transfiguration of
> time into eternity.[29]

By insuring 'there would be no divinization of society beyond the pneumatic presence of Christ in His church,' Augustine provided a basis for social order --

the state as necessary and good but not perfect and checked by the church and the divine law -- while forestalling the 'immanentization of the Christian eschaton'[30] -- that is, a particular society, existent or imagined, which identified the Supreme Good with a set of temporal institutions. By juxtaposing church and state, Pope and Emperor as symbols of dependent yet distinct realms, Augustine maintained a certain openness for political and philosophical questioning.

However, neither Augustine nor other Christian theologians were able to prevent the recasting of philosophy as theology, the reduction of the Gospel's spiritual relationship between God and man to a set of dogmatic propositions. Hence the 'critical function of noesis in radically freeing the areas of the world and history could not become fully effective.'[31] As a result, 'the older dogmatisms . . . provoked the ideological rebellion since the eighteenth century,' which in turn 'has freed socially effective areas of the world, society, and history that the social oppression of orthodoxy sought to keep under cover.' Today, 'orthodoxy's most important linguistic symbols are the 'traditions' and 'conservatisms.' We have the 'Judaeo-Christian and classical traditions, which, especially in English,' Voegelin remarks with some sarcasm, 'roll majestically off the tongue.'[32] In short, the prohibition of questioning and the proneness to identify Christianity with its mundane representation in particular churches and states could not help but raise obvious discrepancies between the message of Christ and the imperfect, not to say oppressive and depraved, behavior of priests and rulers.

But if Voegelin finds much to criticize in the historical development of professedly Christian societies, he reserves his greatest wrath for the 'gnostic' 'dream worlds' which have brought about, in the title of another article, 'The Eclipse of Reality.'[33] 'Wherever Gnostic movements spread they destroyed the truth of the open soul; a whole area of differentiated reality that had been gained by philosophy and Christianity was ruined.'[34] Voegelin describes a 'Gnostic' system as one using a network of symbols developed in the thirteenth century by a monk named Joachim of Flora. First, there is his 'conception of history as a sequence of three ages, of which the third age is intelligibly the final realm.' Symbolizations of this nature include the humanist and enlightenment periodization of history into ancient, medieval, and modern, in which the first serves as a retrospective Utopia to guide mankind from the darkness of the second to the light of the third; Comte's theological, metaphysical, and scientific eras; Marx's dialectic of primitive communism, class society, and post-capitalist communism; and the National Socialist symbolism of the Third Reich. Other characteristic Gnostic symbols are the 'leaders,' 'prophets,' and 'brotherhoods of autonomous persons' who will guide mankind to their worldly promised lands. The Marxist 'vanguard,' the Nazi Führer, the Superman, the Puritan community of saints, and the French Revolution's apostles of Reason all fell under this rubric. 'The new eschatology,' as Voegelin terms it, 'has produced a well-circumscribed symbolism by means of which Western political societies interpret the meaning of their existence.' Unfortunately, however, 'the symbolism has been accepted on the level of self-interpretation and described as a historical phenomenon.' It ought to be regarded instead as a deformation of Christian symbols of order and existence. It is easy to see in Führers and communities of revolutionaries symbolic equivalents of new Christs and apostles, find in their ideal states new Heavens on earth, and discover in opponents of the movements new devils.[35]

In order to postulate gnostic truth, it is necessary to 'destroy the order of being, which is experienced as defective and unjust, and through man's creative power to replace it with a just order.'[36] Furthermore, 'the truth' changes rapidly in the modern age: to argue in turn for the 'technical and planning intellect, the economic, psychological, and biological levels of human nature as the dominants in the image of man, is a strong contrast to the imposing stability of the Christian anthropology through eighteen centuries.'[37]   Man must be reduced to a 'nothing else but' and the experience of participation in the historically symbolized partnership with Being 'must be flattened and crushed until nothing but a rubble of doctrine is left.'   Excluding most of historically experienced reality from 'Reality' requires the doctrinaire 'to leave premises inarticulate, refuse to discuss them, invent devices to obscure them, and use fallacies.'[38]

Such intellectual feats destroy 'the world' in theory by reducing human experience to a fraction of itself.   They also destroy the world in practice: Voegelin terms his modern thinkers 'dangerous maniacs'[39] for the evil they and their disciples have done in trying to fit the world onto a variety of Procrustean beds.   But he is also careful to note that man cannot escape the true reality of existence differentiated and explicated by the Hebrew, Greeks, and Christian thinkers:

> As neither the man who engages in deforming himself to a self ceases to be a man; nor does the surrounding reality of God and man, world and society change its structure; nor can the relations between man and his surrounding reality be abolished; frictions between the shrunken self and reality are bound to develop. . . . He will deny his humanity and insist he is nothing but his shrunken self; he will deny ever having experienced the reality of common experience; he will deny that anybody could have a fuller perception of reality than he allows his self; in brief, he will set the contracted self as a model for himself as well as for everybody else.   Moreover, his insistence on conformity will be aggressive -- and in this aggressiveness there betrays itself the anxiety and alienation of the man who has lost contact with reality.[40]

To overcome the competing ideologies of respective shrunken humanities, Voegelin offers no panacea or system -- that would be a contradiction in terms -- but a return to true philosophy. 'In an hour of crisis, when the order of a society flounders and disintegrates, the fundamental problems of political existence are more apt to come into view,' he began *The New Science of Politics,*[41] pointing out that it is precisely at such times that possibilities for 'retheoreticization' occur. Voegelin argues that 'the quality of society depends on the degree to which the life of reason, actively carried out by a minority of its members, becomes a creative force in that society.'[42]

By a return to philosophy, Voegelin means the classic experience of reason: 'The justice of the human order depends on its participation in the Platonic Agathon, or the Aristotilean Nous, or the Stoic Logos, or the Thomistic ratio aeterna.'[43] The test of fidelity to their spirit 'will have to be: Do we have to ignore and eclipse a major part of the historical field, in order to maintain the truth of the propositions, as the fundamentalist adherents of this or that ideological doctrine must do; or are the propositions recognizably equivalent with the symbols created by our predecessors in the search of truth about human existence. The test of truth, to put it pointedly, will be the lack of originality in the propositions.'[44]

Voegelin's concepts of experience, reality, and philosophizing coincide to a large extent with the enterprise of modern semiotics. For semioticians 'Reality' is a field of symbols, arising in historical contexts, articulated in codes communicated to and then actively shaped by specific communities. Voegelin especially resonates with the Peircean semiotic in his insistence that signs are not merely linguistic symbols, but are based on man's efforts to explain and get in touch with an undefinable and inexplicable but still recognizable Reality. Voegelin's notion that a society's symbolization may attain greater clarity in a contest in which it is either denied or placed in opposition to rival symbolizations fits the process of firstness, secondness, and thirdness through which Peirce postulates we arrive at ideas. Voegelin's insistence that 'leaps in being' occur in times of crisis through representative men and nations parallels Peirce's notion of anancastic or cataclysmic evolution -- that history does not proceed in a straight line or have a definitive conclusion, but that when order has collapsed doubt is incited which stirs thought and enables individuals with new visions to persuade a troubled humanity that they have genuine insights into Being. Finally, for both Peirce and Voegelin, these representative men do not merely speak to their age, but are key participants in a potentially infinite community of inquirers into the nature of Being and existence. Both Peirce and Voegelin distinguish sincere thinkers operating according to correct methodologies who shape this community from 'philodoxers' who merely trumpet biased opinions.[45]

Such similarities between Peirce and Voegelin are not surprising given the latter's extensive studies of the American pragmatists, including Peirce, during the 1920s, which led to the publication of his first book, *Über die Form des Amerikanischen Geistes,* which contains a detailed treatment of Peirce. Voegelin later reminisced about the positive influence American philosophy had on his development:

These two years in America brought the great break in my intellectual development. . . . This English conception of common sense as a human attitude which incorporates a philospher's attitude toward life without the philosopher's technical apparatus, and inversely the understanding of Classic and the Stoic philosophy as a technical analytical elaboration of the common sense attitude, has remained a lasting influence. . . . There was strong background [in America] of Christianity and classical culture which was so signally fading out, if not missing, in the methodological debates in which I had grown up as a student. In brief, here was a world in which this other world I had known was intellectually, morally, and spiritually irrelevant.[46]

Voegelin's analysis of Peirce concentrates chiefly on three essays: 'The Law of Mind,' 'Man's Glassy Essence,' and 'Evolutionary Love.' He calls Peirce a 'seer,' and remarks that 'a prophetic will has formed his ideas, not the love of objectivity or of Works' (in the Biblical sense) characteristic of positivism. In short, like Voegelin himself, Peirce is a restorer of the openness to being characteristic of the true philosopher. First, Peirce agrees with Voegelin in refusing to treat ideas as facts or derivatives of sense experience, but rather as mystical entities beyond the self which only come into being through the dedication of men who love them. An idea, Peirce insists in 'Evolutionary Love,' as quoted by Voegelin, is 'a little person' and it can only develop 'if I will sink myself in perfecting it.' This demands love -- the 'philosophy we draw from John's Gospel' -- the high point of human elucidation of the mystery of Being for Voegelin. Peirce's insistence that the survival of ideas requires the self-sacrifice and lack of concern with worldly success which characterized the early Christians also clearly struck a responsive chord with Voegelin: 'The Christians have always been ready to risk their lives for the sake of having prayers in common.' Peirce's insistence that a person is 'the symbol of an idea' and that 'every general idea has the unified living feeling of a person' is thus, like Voegelin's detailed analysis of how ideas have in fact been personified and communicated throughout history, both a theory of knowledge and a philosophy of history. It is also a theory of how the 'representative man' in search of truth has been the force behind evolution in history rather than the mechanistic-materialistic evolution preached by the various pseudo-sciences of the nineteenth century. Peirce condemns these in passages cited by Voegelin, much as will Voegelin himself, maintaining that the ideologies of the past century have led to 'food in plenty and perfect comfort . . . for the greedy master of intelligence.' In conclusion, Voegelin pays the highest possible tribute to Peirce: following the darkness of Marxism, Social Darwinism, and Comtean positivism, he has reopened man's soul and restored to him the means of thinking seriously and correctly about the world and his place in it. With Peirce, 'the Gospel of Love and Growth of Goodness and Knowledge is hopefully held up through a God or gods who stand beside us in the overcoming of evil. . . . One can offer the philosophy of Peirce and [William] James under the name of *the Open Soul* [a phrase of Voegelin used often in his works], as opposed to *the closed Soul* [of the European dialecticians] as an answer to the problem of human consciousness.'[47]

My analysis of Voegelin's thought thus far has been thoroughly sympathetic. I believe he is correct that we must take the totality of human experience as men claim to have experienced it as the starting point of our inquiry into man and history: we cannot abstract elements we like and interpret everything in terms of them. The Unknown God, the Beyond, or what Kant termed the noumenal world is thus one of the most significant experiences in history. The fact that all political societies claim some divine -- or in the case of modern atheistic societies derivatively divine -- sanction compels the historian to investigate the symbolisms by which they have defined themselves. It is then possible to try to identify and account for continuity and change in history, and the development or influence of the critical symbols which constitute civilization's collective memory. I also agree with Voegelin that the closed soul which attempts to realize a vision of Paradise on Earth is not only denying history, but that if he proceeds politically and violently he is morally reprehensible. Such individuals, Voegelin insists, must take responsibility for their actions in the manner Max Weber has outlined in his discussion of 'the ethics of responsibility' in the great essay 'Politics as a Vocation.'[48]

Nevertheless, I find one huge omission in Voegelin's vision of history, the very shrinking of reality of which he rightly accuses his dogmatic opponents. Russians did not revolt in 1917 and Chinese in 1949 because they dreamed of a Marxist paradise: they did so because governments pretending to stand for civilizational and moral truths committed unspeakable atrocities on their own populations. And while this is more arguable, reigns of terror only indirectly arise out of a desire to achieve the millennium: more practically, they are instituted to protect revolutionary regimes from those who would restore the old order. In fact, looking at the Soviet Union and China from the perspective of 1988, their long-term tendency to behave like normal nation-states is becoming increasingly evident. But traumatized as he was by exile from Nazi-occupied Austria, Stalinism, and the politics of the early Cold War, Voegelin identified the political practices of anti-western regimes with the ideological content of theoretical writings which, save in the case of Hitler, had at best partial application. For example, Marxist revolutions occur neither in the nations predicted by Marx nor with the results he foretold. Moreover, while Voegelin admirably shows how the nature of man's partnership with God has evolved, he does not perform a similar analysis of the evolution of the quest for justice save through exegesis of Biblical and ancient philosophical texts. Justice and ideas such as equality and freedom have not been used historically primarily to realize false paradises on earth, but to hold up their own standards to governments in power and try to feed the hungry, educate the ignorant, and liberate the oppressed, from the very conservative, Christian nations Voegelin has been very reticent in criticizing. Creating justice through political action is a strain in Christian history at least as important as man's speculation about his relationship with God. And if we are to accept Peirce's insistence that one only believes in an idea when one gives one's love and entire being to its realization, then our models must not only be Christ and

Socrates the martyrs for truth but Christ and Socrates the preachers of justice and defiers of establishments. And demanding justice need have nothing to do with expecting paradise on earth, but rather with the amelioration of concrete evils.

But to conclude on so negative a note would be unjust to a thinker whose writings have inspired me for years. Voegelin's effort to locate the symbols by which men understand themselves in a world of experience and symbols provides a magnificent framework within which semioticians may locate the Ground of their signs. His elucidation of the development of equivalent symbols offers historians exciting new possibilities for comparative history. I can only hope my own work here, and on Peirce and historical semiotics, can further Voegelin's inquiry.

Author's Note: Another thinker, subject of a paper at the Semiotics Society of America[49], who deeply influenced Voegelin was his life-long friend Alfred Schütz. Schütz's philosophy of consciousness and experience resembled Voegelin's: for instance, Schütz began *Life Forms and Meaning Structures* by arguing that 'Philosophy, as developed during the last half-century, was unable to achieve anything for *Geisteswissenschaften*, Knowledge of the Soul.' The positivistic sciences had 'chopped up unitary objects of experience into the objects of uncounted special sciences' with the result that by the early twentieth century there was 'an ever-growing remoteness of social science from life, no attempt at exploring the most fundamental phenomena of our daily life with the help of these methods: awakeness-sleep, Eros, music, understanding, Thou, dualism, syncretism, etc. . . . Reality of life is totality.'[50]

ENDNOTES

(Except where noted, author is Eric Voegelin.)

1.   The 1991 issue, edited by Brooke Williams and William Pencak, is the first to include only articles by historians using semiotics rather than people from other disciplines theorizing about history.

2.   *Political Religions*, trans. T.J. DiNapoli and E.S. Easterly, Lewiston, NY: Edwin Mellen Press, 1986; originally published 1938, 10-11.

3.   *Order in History, Volume 1: Israel and Revelation*, Baton Rouge: Louisiana State University Press, 1956, 6.

4.   *Ibid.*, 1-4.

5.   'Equivalences of Experience and Symbolizations in History,' *Eternita è Storia*, Florence: Valecchi, 1970, 220.

6.   'Immortality: Experience and Symbol,' 60 *Harvard Theological Review*, 1967, 238.

7.   *Order in History, Volume 1*, ix, 5.

8.   *The New Science of Politics*, Chicago: University of Chicago Press, 1952, 27.

9.   *Anamnesis*, trans. Gerhart Niemeyer, Notre Dame and London: University of Notre Dame Press 1986; mostly published originally in 1966, 182.

10.   'Equivalences of Experience,' 216.

11.   *Ibid.*

12.   *Order in History, Volume 1*, 9.

13.   *Ibid.*, 6.

14.   *New Science of Politics*, 54.

15.   *Ibid.*, 54-55.

16.   *Order in History, Volume 1*, 6.

17.   *Ibid.*, 124, 128, 171.

18.   *Ibid.*, 10.

19.   *Ibid.*, 183.

20.   'Reason: The Classic Experience,' 10 *Southern Review*, 1974, 238-244; *Order in History, Volume 3: Plato and Aristotle*, Baton Rouge: Louisiana State University Press, 1957, 62-69, 213.

21.   *Science, Politics, and Gnosticism*, Chicago: Henry Regnery, 1968, 108; 'Reason,' 262.

22.   'The Gospel and Culture,' in D. Miller and D.G. Hadidian, eds., *Jesus and Man's Hope*, Pittsburgh: Pittsburgh Theological Seminary Press, 1:92-93.

23.   *Ibid.*, 60.

24.   *Ibid.*, 62.

25.   'History and Gnosis,' in Bernhard Anderson, ed., *The Old Testament and Christian Faith*, New York: Herder and Herder, 1969, 83.

26.   'Gospel and Culture,' 61.

27.   *Ibid.*, 77.

28.   *Order and History, Volume 1*, 182-183.

29.   *New Science of Politics*, 110.

30.   *Ibid.*, 77.

31.   *Anamnesis*, 186.

32.   *Ibid.*, 189.

33.   'History and Gnosis'; 'The Eclipse of Reality,' in Maurice Natanson, ed., *Phenomenology and Social Reality*, The Hague: Martinus Nijhoff, 1970.

34.   *New Science of Politics*, 163.

35.   *Ibid.*, 107-161.

36.   *Science, Politics, and Gnosticism*, 53.

37.   *From Enlightenment to Revolution*, John H. Hallowell, ed., Durham, NC: Duke University Press, 1975, 13.

38.   'Immortality,' 254.

39. 'World Empire and the Unity of Mankind,' 38 *International Affairs*, 1976, 182.

40. 'Eclipse of Reality,' 185-186.

41. *New Science of Politics*, 1.

42. 'Industrial Society in Search of Reason,' in Raymond Aron, ed., *World Technology and Human Destiny*, Ann Arbor: University of Michigan Press, 1963, 64.

43. *New Science of Politics*, 6.

44. 'Equivalences of Experience,' 222.

45. For Peirce, a good introduction may be found in R. Jackson Wilson, *In Search of Community: Social Philosophy in the United States, 1860-1920*, New York: Oxford University Press, 1968; see also William Pencak, 'Charles Sanders Peirce and Arisbe,' included in this volume.

46. Ellis Sandoz, *The Voegelinian Revolution: A Biographical Introduction*, Baton Rouge: Louisiana State University Press, 1981, 20-22; Sandoz has a fine bibliography of Voegelin's writings.

47. *Über die Form des Amerikanischen Geistes*, Tubingen: J.C.B. Mohr, 1928, discussion of Peirce on 32-41 and 51-52; translations are mine. Voegelin used the collection of essays by Peirce entitled *Chance, Love, and Logic*, Morris R. Cohen, ed., New York: Harcourt Brace, 1923 and concentrated especially on 202-203, 265-266, and 269-270, the source of the quotations here.

48. Voegelin's discussion is in *New Science of Politics*, 20-26.

49. Richard L. Lanigan, 'Semiotic Precis of Alfred Schütz on Semiotic Phenomenology,' John Deely, ed., *Semiotics 1984*, Lanham, MD: University Press of America, 1985, 393-399.

50. Alfred Schütz, *Life Forms and Meaning Structures*, trans. and ed., by Helmut Wagner, London: Routledge and Kegan Paul, 1982; originally written 1924-1928, 15.

Chapter 8

Thorstein Veblen's Semiotic
Analysis of American Capitalism

On December 30, 1911, no less a figure than William Howard Taft, President of the United States, travelled to Philadelphia to dedicate Wanamaker's House of Business, the now world-famous department store at Broad and Market Streets which boasted an Egyptian Hall seating two thousand, a Greek Hall with a capacity of six hundred, and a huge organ with three thousand pipes. Taft not only expressed the 'appreciation that the country at large has for the successful creation of an aid to the happiness of the people.' He also called attention to the ethical means by which 'one of the most important instrumentalities in modern life for the promotion of comfort' had flourished. 'With no adventitious aid, with no combinations in restraint of competition, but simply by a natural growth and aggregation of means to end, this great business was built up,' the President enthused, 'to form a model for all other stores of the same kind throughout the country and throughout the world.'[1]

Not only Wanamaker's, but Taft's speech dedicating it may indeed serve as a model for, well, a world. His defense of the methods and results accompanying American business concentration accurately represented both lay and academic thinking that capitalism had evolved naturally to stand at the apex of history for the betterment of the human race. John Wanamaker himself argued that 'the evolution in the mercantile business during the last quarter century has been wrought not by combinations of capital, corporations, or trusts, but by the natural

growth of individual mercantile enterprises.'   Charles Francis Adams, Jr.,
President of the Union Pacific Railroad, insisted that 'the principle of consolidation
. . . is a necessity -- a natural law of growth.'   John Moody, founder of the
nation's finest statistical information service, asserted that 'the modern trust is the
natural outcome of evolution of societary conditions and ethical standards which
are recognized and established among men today as being necessary elements in
the development of civilization.' As a corollary, theorist William Graham Sumner
wrote in the ironically entitled *What the Social Classes Owe to Each Other* -- that
is to say, nothing -- 'the great gains of a capitalist in a modern state must be put
under the head of wages of superintendence. . . . It was for the benefit of all.
. . . It is a necessary condition of many forms of social advance.'[2]

The old adage -- 'They protest too much!' -- comes to mind. The repeated
use of words such as natural, evolution, and necessary also recalls the observation
of historian Carl Becker concerning the 'magic words' shared by a community --
'certain unobtrusive words with uncertain meanings that are permitted to slip off
the tongue without fear and without research; words which, having from constant
repetition lost their metaphysical significance, are unconsciously mistaken for
objective realities.'[3]   Two Gilded Age Americans who did not mistake these
signifiers for that which was signified were Charles Peirce (1839-1914) and
Thorstein Veblen (1857-1929), arguably the foremost philosopher and economist
of their era. Not only did Veblen study briefly with Peirce in 1881 at the Johns
Hopkins University, but the two men shared amazingly similar biographies of
which their similar critical approaches to capitalism may serve as signs. Both
were outsiders. Peirce never obtained a regular academic appointment and Veblen
bounced from Yale to Hopkins to Cornell to Chicago to Stanford to the University
of Missouri to the New School for Social Research. Peirce and Veblen both
married highly intelligent women from prominent families who left them, in part

because of their philandering. Our sages then married much younger women who remained incredibly devoted to them despite their poverty and sloppy personal habits. Finally, both endured the slings and arrows of outrageous fortune at the hands of capitalism: Peirce raged in his essay 'Evolutionary Love,' his most detailed critique of 'The Economical Century,' against a nameless 'Millionaire Master in Gloomery' who stole an invention from him 'and who administers wholesome lessons to unwary scientific men by passing worthless checks upon them,' thereby 'bequeathing to your children something to boast about of their father.' Similarly, both Veblen's father and grandfather lost farms they had labored on for years, in Minnesota and Norway, respectively, through legal chicanery.[4] While Veblen nowhere explicitly cites Peirce, scholarly practice at that time was much less rigorous than today, and many of their ideas were shared by critics of contemporary economic theory and practice.

Now Peirce's and Veblen's economic pronouncements ought not to be dismissed as sour grapes, even if Peirce did not begin to write on economics until a catastrophe in 1892 turned him from a gentleman of means into a pauper. Just as apologists for capitalism are signs of their success, Peirce and Veblen represent the class of men whom no less an expert than John D. Rockefeller admitted were the buds which had to be clipped that the American Beauty Rose of Standard Oil could more gloriously bloom. Economics, like history, is frequently written by those subsidized by the winners; Peirce and Veblen give us the other side.

Peirce's critique of capitalist economics and its pseudo-scientific justification, Social Darwinism, is simple. Competition does not allow the 'fittest' to survive, but rather 'the greedy master of intelligence' who makes personal accumulation his primary goal. Peirce rather argues for 'The Gospel of Christ [which] says that progress comes from every individual merging his individuality in sympathy with his neighbor.' A true lover of humanity will thus exhibit a 'devotion to the pursuit of truth for truth's sake.' This truth must be 'UTTERLY USELESS,' Peirce once wrote in capital letters: to the extent that a discovery is novel and meaningful, the discoverer will find 'the whole moral weight of the community will be cast against' him, 'because science implies a desire to learn, and a desire to learn implies dissatisfaction with current opinions.' Men who are real agents of progress thus do not profit from it and are likely to be scorned: only their disinterested love of truth and humanity keep them going.   And far from 'evolving' 'necessarily' or 'naturally,' advances will be achieved 'by violent breaking up of habits': 'a habit of thought having been overthrown is supplanted by the next strongest. Now this next strongest is sure to be widely disparate from the first, and as often as not its direct contrary.' Thus Peirce could describe his work as 'an onslaught upon the doctrine of necessity,' and insist that Darwinism has made 'no figure at all, except in retrograde movements.'[5]

Veblen, unlike Peirce -- who confined his remarks on economics to a few essays -- spent his whole life analyzing contemporary capitalism. But not only are the main outlines of his theory similar to Peirce's, it can even be shown that Veblen's economics embodies the semiotic approach Peirce might have undertaken had he delved more deeply in that line. Veblen devoted his career to demolishing the notion that economic 'laws' are either natural, beneficent, or even 'laws' in any meaningful sense.   To put Veblen's argument in the language of modern semiotics, he regards the neoclassical economists of his day much as the semiotician treats the deductive or rationalist philosopher. They would propound laws -- free enterprise, invisible hand, supply and demand, marginal utility, equilibrium, etc. -- and judge economic phenomena in terms of their consonance with these laws.   Thus government interference with a 'natural' 'law' of competition can be pronounced harmful since it supposedly reduces the quantity of goods that would otherwise have been produced or raises their price. Veblen urges us to get rid of this whole way of thinking, to stop treating the signifiers which capitalists pay their academic lackeys to 'manufacture' as the reality of economic life. He directs us instead toward the signs by which what he calls 'the leisure class' actually presents itself to the world. Upon investigating these signs, we find that in many instances capitalist economic behavior is precisely the reverse of the justification claimed for it by capitalist economic theory. To the idea that men accumulate wealth to maximize pleasure and minimize pain, hence the traditional supply and demand curves where men seek the most and best goods at the lowest prices, Veblen says nonsense. Capitalist behavior is a residue of barbarian impulses by which men seek to dominate their fellows through 'invidious distinctions' signified by 'conspicuous waste' attained by means of 'pecuniary emulation.' Hence we find extravagant expenditure on useless 'prestige' items, addictive accumulation of more money than one can possibly spend and more things than one can possibly use, and numerous other 'signs' absolutely incomprehensible in terms of capitalism's self-justifying theory.

Before examining in more detail the signs of capitalism as Veblen discusses them in *The Theory of the Leisure Class* and *The Higher Learning in America*, let us turn to his theoretical deconstruction of capitalist economics, which echoes and elaborates on Peirce's. 'Christian Morals and the Competitive System,' written in 1910, is Veblen's equivalent of Peirce's 'Evolutionary Love.' Veblen draws a sharp distinction between religious principles of brotherly love and non-resistance and the 'individualism . . . worked out and incorporated in the modern institutional fabric.' Unlike Peirce, a Christian who belonged to the Episcopal Church, Veblen kept his religious opinions secret and was generally considered an atheist or an agnostic.[6] So while he begins by attributing the origins of Christian altruism to the self-justification of servile classes in Rome and the Middle Ages compelled to turn the other cheek, much as does Nietzsche in *The Genealogy of Morals*, he does not regard altruism as merely that:

> This spirit is forever reasserting itself in economic matters, in the impulsive approval of whatever conduct is serviceable to the common good and in the disapproval of disserviceable conduct even within the limits of legality and natural right. It seems, indeed, to be nothing else than a somewhat specialized manifestation of the instinct of workmanship, and as such it has the indefeasible vitality that belongs to the hereditary traits of human nature.

And workmanship is not, according to Veblen, undertaken for gain, but for its own sake and to please one's fellows. It thus resembles the raison d'etre of Peirce's pursuit of scientific truth and real progress.[7]

Like Peirce, Veblen argues that as time goes on, competitive individualism and the economic system accompanying it will disappear. To be sure, his analysis is more temperate than Peirce's great curse, which I cannot forbear quoting:

> The Reign of Terror was very bad; but now the Gradgrind banner has been this century long flaunting in the face of heaven, with an insolence to provoke the very skies to scowl and rumble. Soon a flash and quick peal will shake economists quite out of their complacency, too late. The twentieth century, in its latter half, shall surely see the deluge-tempest burst upon the social order -- to clean up a world as deep in ruin as that greed-philosophy has long plunged it into guilt.[8]

But the upshot is the same for Veblen. As long as 'the acquisition of property depended, in the main, on the workmanlike serviceability of the man who acquired it, and in which, on the whole, honesty was the best policy, under such conditions the principles of fair play and the inviolability of ownership would be somewhat closely in touch with the ancient human instinct of workmanship, which approves mutual aid and serviceability to the common good.'[9]

Interestingly, Veblen's argument is precisely that of the foremost late twentieth century historian of early American capitalism, Joyce Appleby. In the new republic, where economic opportunity (for white males, of course) was abundant and concentrations of great wealth non-existent, a rough correlation existed between the quantity and quality of one's efforts and one's economic status. However, the Jeffersonian ideology underlying this era persisted and was rewritten in Darwinist and economic jargon for the late nineteenth century world in which it no longer applied.[10] Veblen put it thus:

> With the revolutionary changes that have supervened in technology
> and in pecuniary relations, there is no longer such a close and visible
> touch between the workman and his product as would persuade men
> that the product belongs to him by force of an extension of his
> personality; nor is there a visible relationship between serviceability
> and acquisition; nor between the discretionary use of wealth and the
> common welfare. . . . Particularly is this true since business has
> taken on the character of an impersonal, dispassionate, not to say
> graceless, investment for profit. There is little in the current situation
> to keep the natural rights of pecuniary discretion in touch with the
> impulsive bias of brotherly love.

Hence, with capitalism's primary justification of tending toward the common good seeming less and less plausible, Veblen predicts that 'ancient racial bias embodied in the Christian principle of brotherhood should logically continue to gain ground at the expense of the pecuniary morals of competitive business.'[11]

Veblen also comes very close to Peirce in a 1906 essay, 'The Place of Science in Modern Civilization,' which draws a sharp distinction between science, born of 'idle curiosity' which 'creates nothing but theories,' as opposed to 'wisdom and proficiency of a pragmatic sort,' which 'has only an incidental bearing on scientific research.' And Veblen agrees with Peirce that this 'bearing is chiefly that of inhibition and misdirection' for much the same reason: 'wherever canons of expedience are intruded into or are attempted to be incorporated in the inquiry, the consequence is an unhappy one for science.' Much of what passes for science 'turns about questions of personal advantage' and boils down to 'a taxonomy of credenda' consisting of 'deductions from authentic tradition.'[12]

Veblen also agrees with Peirce that what distinguishes true scientific inquiry from ideology is its willingness to suspend belief. Peirce expressed his 'abhorrence of the doctrine that any proposition whatsoever is infallibly true' and that the best we could hope for was indefinitely approximating to truth in the long run.'[13] Similarly, Veblen insisted that 'modern scientific inquiry in any case comes to rest only provisionally, because its prime postulate is that of consecutive change, and consecutive change can, of course, not come to rest, except provisionally.' Hence in his 1898 essay, 'Why is Economics Not an Evolutionary Science?' Veblen has a lot of fun with 'this facile recourse to inscrutable figures of speech as the ultimate terms of theory that has saved the economists from being dragooned into the ranks of modern science.' Economics 'still shows too many reminiscences of the 'natural' and the 'normal,' of the 'verities' and 'tendencies,' of 'controlling principles' and 'disturbing causes'.' He regards these terms as signifying both a 'long and devious course of disintegrating animism' -- mechanistic residues of a belief that God ruled the univerise -- and also of the place of the economist in capitalist society trained and paid to praise his employer.[14] Veblen argues elsewhere -- in 'Economic Theory in the Calculable Future' (1925) -- that such 'archaic holdovers of knowledge' cannot describe economic reality because 'the facts current in this calculable future are presumably due to go on changing, in detail and at large, cumulatively and at an unexampled rate, as time goes on'; whereas the academic economist is tied to 'certain perfunctory antiquities out of the Victorian Age.'[15]   Not surprisingly, one of Veblen's former students recalled that he took the greatest delight 'when analysis led you into further problems in place of elucidations.'   'Where one problem bloomed before,' he would announce happily, 'Two are now blooming.'   This anecdote encapsulates Veblen's semiotic conception of knowledge as provisional and growing.[16]

For convenience, I will group Veblen's critique of the substance of academic theory into four categories: (1) wealth is not created individually but communally; (2) hedonism fails to define human nature; (3) economic theory does not distinguish between business and industry, the manipulation of money vs. the creation of wealth; and (4) most characteristics of capitalist civilization are degenerate residues of barbarian customs to dominate others and exhibit prowess and status rather than the glories of the modern world that they pretend to be.

(1)   Veblen writes: 'production takes place only in society -- only through the cooperation of an industrial community. . . . The isolated individual is not a productive agent. . . . Since there is no individual production and no individual productivity, the natural rights preconception that ownership rests on the individually productive labor of the owner reduces itself to absurdity, even under the logic of its own assumptions.'[17]

Veblen thus treats economic activity much as Peirce treats knowledge. According to Peirce 'the very origins of the concept of reality shows that this conception essentially involves the notion of a COMMUNITY, without definite limits, and capable of an indefinite increase in knowledge.'[18]   Veblen argued for the equal distribution of income on the grounds that wealth was created by the community and hence any unequal assignment was the result of social and political arrangements which accorded with neither justice nor communal well-being. To accomplish this end would of course require collective social and economic planning, which would produce the added bonus of eliminating excess work generated by the leisure class' demand for conspicuous waste and the seepage of comparable behavior into the lower classes. Veblen estimated people could live just as well using two-ninths of the labor currently expended.[19]

(2)   One of Veblen's most famous passages denounces: 'The hedonistic conception of man [which] is that of a lightning calculator of pleasures and pains, which oscillates like a homogeneous globule of desire of happiness under the impulse of stimuli that shift him about the area, but leave him intact. He has neither antecedent nor consequent. He is an isolated, definitive human datum, in stable equilibrium except for the buffets of impinging forces that displace him in one direction or another. Self-imposed in elemental space, he spins symmetrically about his own spiritual axis until the parallelogram of forces bears down upon him, whereupon he follows the line of the resultant. When the force of the impact is spent, he comes to rest, a self-contained globule of desire as before.'

If man is 'not simply a bundle of desires that are to be saturated by being placed in the path of the forces of the environment,' what is he? Veblen responds that he is 'a coherent structure of propensities and habits which seeks realization and expression in an unfolding activity.' Veblen frequently uses the words 'action' and 'activity' to emphasize 'change,' to stress that 'in all this flux there is no definitively adequate method of life and no definitive or absolutely worthy end of action, so far as concerns the science which sets out to formulate as a theory the process of economic life.' Hence, all talk of supply and demand, the greatest good of the greatest number, marginal utility, etc. as justifications for free enterprise fall by the wayside since people simply do not act that way. Their goals, habits, and means change over time -- the economists' task is historical rather than mathematical. Once again, Peirce comes to mind: for Peirce 'the irritation of doubt raises a struggle to attain a state of belief,' which then becomes a 'rule of action.' Similarly, for Veblen, the economy is in a constant state of change, as a result of 'a change in habits of thought,' which then 'affects the further growth of habits of thought -- habitual methods of procedure -- and so becomes a point of departure for further development of the methods of compassing the ends sought and for the further variation of ends that are to be compassed.' Like Peirce's community of inquirers searching for truth but never finding it, Veblen's economic man is searching for satisfaction, but its nature changes over time and is not primarily economic.[20]

(3)   For Veblen, the key development of nineteenth century economic life was the separation of ownership from actual creation of wealth or direction of economic activity, which he sometimes terms the divorce between business (what creates income) and industry (what creates production), or alternatively, the imperatives of business vs. those of technology. Veblen explains: 'Business traffic seeks a differential gain in terms of price; technological enterprise perforce seeks a gain in productive efficiency at large. Any given business concern may profit by the disabilities of its competitors. . . . [But] the technical efficiency of any given industrial plant and of its personnel is furthered by efficient work on the part of other concerns in the same or related lines of production.' Veblen also attributes social tensions and waste to enterprise which competes rather than cooperates.[21]

(4)   Veblen's most famous critique of modern capitalism is his catalogue of the unnecessary, conspicuous consumption generated by a parasitic leisure class which nevertheless dominates the world at the expense of the general community. Veblen takes as his starting point 'barbarian' or 'predatory' culture which is essentially masculine and displaces 'savage' or 'peaceful' civilization which is

essentially feminine at the dawn of history. Veblen then reverses all the standard legitimation fantasies of the contemporary social order. 'The ancient tradition of the predatory culture is that productive labor is to be shunned as unworthy of able-bodied men,' in part because 'the whole range of industrial employments is an outgrowth of what is classed as women's work in the primitive barbarian community.' Woman is the provider, the force for order, man the dependent. Far from justifying themselves through productivity, the people who have benefitted most from contemporary capitalism glory in their lack of productivity, in fact in their ability to waste production. And modern industrial civilization is basically a degenerate form of barbarian predation. Veblen, by the way, was a great supporter of women's equality, and found it no mystery that wealthy, well-educated women, relegated to useless ornaments of their husbands and forbidden from either exercising power or their instinct of workmanship, took the lead in the women's rights movement rather than poor working women who had the satisfaction, at least, of doing something useful.[22]

Veblen then gives us a semiotic of capitalism. I can only offer a few illustrations here which also exemplify Veblen's sardonic wit:[23]

(a)　Good Manners -- 'Refined tastes, manners, and habits of life are a useful evidence of gentility, because good breeding requires time, application, and expense and therefore cannot be compassed by those whose time is taken up by work.' 'The pervading principle and abiding test of good breeding is the requirement of a substantial and patent waste of time.'

(b)　Servants with Good Manners -- 'it is not enough that he [a servant] knows how to effect certain desired mechanical results; he must, above all, know how to effect these results with good form. Domestic service might be said to be a spiritual rather than a mechanical function' because it implies 'ability to pay for the consumption of time, effort, and instruction required to fit a trained servant for special service under an exacting code of forms.' Veblen terms this process 'vicarious leisure'; the upper class not only demonstrates power and status through its own uselessness, but by the extent to which it can compel uselessness in others. Hence, Veblen remarks, 'men, especially lusty, personable fellows, such as footmen and other menials should be,' are to be preferred to women, 'as showing a larger waste of time and human energy.'

(c)   'The ceremonial differentiation of the dietary' -- Veblen writes, 'is best seen in the use of intoxicating beverages and narcotics. If these articles of consumption are costly, they are felt to be noble and honorific.' One need only think of the popularity of cocaine or absurdly expensive wines and restaurants among those who can afford these in our own time.

(d)   Make-Believe Work --   Veblen argues that both the 'instinct of workmanship' and social respectability require the leisure class to do something to justify its own existence. The tension with demonstrating wealth and power is resolved by 'make-believe' work such as 'social duties' and in 'quasi-artistic or quasi-scholarly accomplishments, in the care and decoration of the house, in sewing circle activity, in proficiency at dress, cards, yachting, golf, and various sports.' Such activity satisfies the 'instinct of workmanship' and also 'the more immediately constraining incentive to a reputable leisure and an avoidance of indecorous usefulness.'

(e)   Devout Consumption -- 'of sacred edifices, vestments, and other goods of the same class.' The 'priestly caste' is an ideal field for the wealthy to display 'vicarious leisure,' as 'priestly demeanor at its best is aloof, leisurely, perfunctory.' 'Priestly vestments are notoriously expensive, ornate, and inconvenient, for the end of vicarious consumption is to enhance, not the fullness of life of the consumer, but the pecuniary repute of the master for whose behoof the consumption takes place.' The leisure class even projects its search for repute onto God himself, for 'beyond the priestly class, and ranged into an ascending order, ordinarily comes a superhuman vicarious leisure class of saints, angels, etc.' And the fact the poor immigrants of turn-of-the-century America were religious and spent a great deal of money on beautiful churches shows the ability of the leisure class to convey its values down the social hierarchy: 'There are few persons of delicate tastes in the matter of devout consumption to whom this austerely wasteful discomfort does not appeal as intrinsically right and good.'

(f)   Belief in superiority of hand-made, exotic articles -- 'A hand-wrought silver spoon, of a commercial value of some ten to twenty dollars, is not ordinarily more serviceable. . . . than a machine-made spoon of some 'base' metal, such as aluminum, the value of which may be no more than some ten to twenty cents. However, we prefer the hand-made silver spoon because the superior gratification derived from the use and contemplation of costly and supposedly beautiful products is, commonly, in great measure a gratification of our sense of costliness masquerading under the name of beauty.'

(g)   Fashion -- 'The high gloss of a gentleman's hat or of a patent leather shoe has no more of intrinsic beauty than a similarly high gloss on a threadbare sleeve, and yet there is no question but that all well-bred people (in the Occidental civilized community) instinctively and unaffectedly cleave to the one as a phenomenon of great beauty, and eschew the other as offensive to every sense to which it can appeal. It is extremely doubtful if anyone could be induced to wear such a contrivance as the high hat of civilized society, except for some urgent reason, based on other than aesthetic grounds.' Of course, this is especially true of women's dress, and Veblen makes much of high-heeled shoes and corsets as 'indices,' equivalent to Chinese footbinding, 'in the way of demonstrating the wearer's abstinence from productive employment.' Somewhat paradoxically, 'tasteful' clothing is preferred to 'loud' dress because the latter 'evinced an undue desire to reach and impress the untrained sensitivities of the vulgar,' rather than 'a sufficiently large wealthy class . . . who have leisure for acquiring skill in interpreting the subtler signs of expenditure.'   The bearded Veblen similarly regarded shaving as proof a man had time to waste. He also wore comfortable old clothes, kept his books in boxes, never made his bed, and built furniture out of old crates. At the University of Missouri, he lived for a while in a tent in a friend's basement; at Stanford, he chose a log cabin surrounded by weeds.

(h) 'Domestic animals which ordinarily serve no industrial end: such as pigeons, parrots and other cage-birds, cats, dogs, and fast horses' -- Dogs are preferred to cats because where the latter 'lives with man on terms of equality,' the former 'is man's servant and has the gift of an unquestioning subservience and a slave's quickness in guessing his master's mood.' The dog is thus preferable to all save the most exotic cat even though 'he is the filthiest in his habits.' As for horses, they win in races: 'it gratifies the owner's sense of aggression and dominance to have his own horse outstrip his neighbors'.'

(i)   Architecture -- 'The endless variety of fronts presented by the better class of tenements and apartment houses in our cities is an endless variety of architectural distress and of suggestions of expensive discomfort.' Of course in Veblen's day, the tendency was to construct imitation Renaissance and Gothic buildings, another sign that beneficiaries of capitalism took solace in an idealized version of a different civilization than the one they urged so effusively on the masses.

(j)   The Law -- 'The profession of the law does not imply large ownership; but since no taint of usefulness, for other than competitive purposes, attaches to the lawyer's trade, it grades high in the conventional scheme. The lawyer is exclusively occupied with details of predatory fraud, either in achieving or checkmating chicane, and success in the profession is therefore accepted as marking a large endowment of that barbarian astuteness which has always commanded men's respect and fear.'

(k)   The Higher Learning -- Veblen regarded the contemporary American university as a travesty of its true mission: the pursuit of knowledge. He explains that 'instruction that falls legitimately under the hand of the university man is necessarily subsidiary and incidental to the work of inquiry, and it can effectually be carried on only by such a teacher as is himself occupied with the scrutiny of what knowledge is already in hand and with pushing the inquiry to further goals.' Unfortunately, with the state universities run by politicians obliged to demonstrate usefulness to constituents and the private ones serving as ornaments for the leisure class, universities degenerated into models of the contemporary business enterprise. Veblen sarcastically noted that: 'In the business-like view of the captain of erudition, taken from the standpoint of the counting-house, learning and university instruction are a species of skilled labor, to be hired at competitive wages and to turn out the largest merchantable output that can be obtained by shrewd bargain with their employees.' 'Perfunctory work and mechanical accountancy' was demanded of underpaid and overworked faculty while universities lavished expenditure on 'the plant' as their most visible attribute and wasted time with cap and gown ceremonies Veblen compared to 'circus and operatic entertainments.' State schools turned out drones for the leisure class, private colleges cultivated 'the graces of gentility and a suitable place of residence for young men of spendthrift habits . . . in which scholarship is advisedly made subordinate to genteel dissipation, to a grounding in those methods of conspicuous consumption that should engage the thought and energies of the well-to-do man of the world.'[24] Veblen also found college athletics at least equal to the 'acquisition of the dead languages' as a badge of 'talismanic virtue.' 'This latter branch of learning -- if athletics may be freely classified as learning -- was becoming [the] rival of the classics for the primacy of leisure-class education in American and English schools.' The reason? 'Success as an athlete presumes not only a waste of time, but also a waste of money, as well as the possession of certain highly unindustrial archaic traits of character and temperment.'[25] Peirce felt the same way:

> Our American universities have, one and all, a narrowly and rigidly
> prescribed end, that of education for the individual advantage of the
> students. And what [is that?]. . . . That they should lead luxurious
> lives. Wretched business. [Wonderful double entendre.][26]

Conclusion

One pithy observation concerning Veblen came from Stanford President David Starr Jordan: 'What he cannot reverse and make appear the opposite of what it purports to be isn't worth reversing.'[27] One of Veblen's most amusing essays, 'An Early Experiment in Trusts,' suggests Viking plundering and slave raiding was the ancestor and prototype of the modern business conglomerate. Veblen here takes a swipe at those who would uphold the blond Nordic 'racial' type as a model for the modern world by pointing out this 'Aryan' contribution to 'civilization.'[28] Other delectable Veblenian reversals referred to the Russian Soviet as analogous to the New England town-meeting and to the United States government as the Supreme Soviet of big business.[29] Demolishing the myths and 'laws' through which his society justified its existence, Veblen basically insisted that we judge people and societies by the signs through which they present themselves to the world; capitalist economic ideology was 'animistic,' much like the gods of primitive people, with an invisible hand substituting for the hands of Wotan and Zeus to explain phenomena and compel obedience.[30]

Veblen began to publish precisely at the time -- the late 1890's -- when American businesses combined in hundreds of trusts producing vaster concentrations of wealth than ever before (Andrew Carnegie made $300 million from selling Carnegie Steel to J. P. Morgan, more than he ever made from selling steel).[31] His works are also, John Taylor has suggested in *Circus of Ambition: The Culture of Wealth and Power in the Eighties*, appropriate in criticizing the world of yuppie culture, Donald Trump, Ivan Boesky, Leona Helmsley, and Michael Jackson, an America where real estate deals, sales of junk bonds, leveraged buyouts, hostile takeovers, and show business and professional sports have displaced industrial production as the path to the greatest prosperity.[32] This in a nation where the real income of most people has been declining since the early 1970's.[33]

Of course, capitalists would remark that the collectivism favored by Veblen has worked even more poorly in practice. I would submit that such a judgment ignores the phenomenal increase in real income in the Communist world since World War II (solving the subsistence problem in China for the first time in history being the most spectacular example), and this in spite of internal corruption and enormous defense expenditures forced on these nations by the West. A capitalist apologist must ignore the fact that Czechoslovakia, East Germany, Hungary, Poland, and Bulgaria enjoyed in the 1980's higher average standards of living than the wealthiest large nation in Latin America (Venezuela) and that the same five nations enjoyed the most equal income distribution of any nations in the world.[34]

We can, if we wish, tag along with our present-day leisure class and confuse Eastern Europeans' laudable desire for freedom with their supposed desire to imitate the declining economy of the world's largest debtor nation instead of the far more productive and centrally planned economies of Western Europe and

Japan. Or, if we wish, we may be semioticians along with Veblen and Peirce. However, if we prefer, we can retain our traditional role as signifiers of their insight that the theory of the leisure class and the leisure of the theoried class coincide in reinforcing injustice and inequality. With capitalist waste now taking the form of incipient environmental catastrophe, such as the destruction of the Amazon and greenhouse effect, military spending being predicated explicitly on the possibility of 'wasting' the entire planet, and economic decline plaguing the United States, I suggest that we start taking Peirce, Veblen, and semiotics, seriously.

ENDNOTES

1. William Howard Taft, 'Dedication of Wanamaker's, 1911,' in *Golden Book of the Wanamaker Store, Jubilee Year, 1861-1911*, Philadelphia, 1911, vol. 2, 3-5. For a description of the store, *ibid.*, 150-152. Excerpted in David and Sheila Rothman, *Sources of the American Social Tradition, II*, New York, 1975.

2. John Wanamaker, 'The Evolution of Mercantile Business, 1900,' in *Corporations and Public Welfare*, Philadelphia, 1900, 126. Excerpted in Rothman, *Sources*; Charles Francis Adams, Jr., *Speech Before the Joint Standing Committee on Railroads*, Boston, 1873, 35, and John Moody, *The Truth about Trusts*, New York, 1904, 494, quoted in Gabriel Kolko, *The Triumph of Conservatism: A Reinterpretation of American History, 1900-1916*, New York, 1963, 14, 15. William Graham Sumner, *What the Social Classes Owe to Each Other*, New York, 1883, 47. Excerpted in Rothman, *Sources*.

3. Carl Becker, *The Heavenly City of the Eighteenth Century Philosophers*, New Haven, 1932, 47.

4. Biographical information on Peirce in William Pencak, 'Charles Sanders Peirce and Arisbe,' included in this volume. For Veblen, see Joseph Dorfman, *Thorstein Veblen and His America*, New York, 1934; reprinted 1961. The Peirce quotation is from 'Evolutionary Love,' in Charles Hartshorne et al., eds., *Collected Papers of Charles Sanders Peirce*, Cambridge, 1931-1958, vol. 6, paragraph 292.

5. Peirce, 'Evolutionary Love' in *Collected Papers*, vol. 6, paragraph 294; see also vol. 1, paragraph 76; 'Lectures on the History of Science,' in Carolyn Eisele, ed. *Historical Perspectives on Peirce's Logic of Science*, Berlin and New York, 1985, 287.

6.   Thorstein Veblen, in Leon Ardzrooni, ed., *Essays in Our Changing Order,* New York, 1934, 212. Peirce's Anglicanism noted in his diary for 1887; he joined the Episcopal Church in Milford, PA; Ms. 1623, in Peirce Papers, Houghton Library, Harvard University, as catalogued in Richard S. Robin, *Annotated Catalogue of the Papers of Charles S. Peirce,* Amherst, 1967.

7.   Veblen, *Essays,* 216.

8.   Peirce, 'Evolutionary Love,' in *Collected Papers*, vol. 6, paragraph 292.

9.   Veblen, *Essays*, 217.

10.   Among her many works, *Capitalism and a New Social Order: The Republican Vision of the 1790s,* New York, 1984.

11.   Veblen, *Essays*, 218.

12.   Veblen, *The Place of Science in Modern Civilization and Other Essays,* New York, 1946, 9, 20-21, 23.

13.   Peirce, 'Letters to Lady Welby,' in Philip P. Weiner, ed., *Values in a University of Chance: Selected Writings of Charles S. Peirce,* Garden City, 1958, 398; Peirce, 'The General Theory of Probable Inference,' in Justus Buchler, ed. *Philosophical Writings of Peirce,* London, 1940, 217.

14.   Veblen, 'The Evolution of the Scientific Point of View, 1908,' in *The Place of Science*, 33; 'Why is Economics Not an Evolutionary Science?,' *ibid.*, 66, 64.

15.   Veblen, 'Economic Theory in the Calculable Future,' in *Essays,* 5-15.

16.   Dorfman, *Veblen*, 318, citing Winifred Sabine.

17.   Veblen, 'The Beginnings of Ownership,' 1898, in *Essays*, 34.

18.   Peirce, 'Some Consequences of the Four Incapacities,' 1868, in *Philosophical Writings*, 247.

19.   Dorfman, *Veblen*, 387-388.

20.   Veblen, 'Why is Economics Not an Evolutionary Science?' in *The Place of Science*, 73-76; Peirce, 'How To Make our Ideas Clear,' 1878, in *Philosophical Writings*, 11, 29.

21.   Veblen, 'Economic Theory in the Calculable Future,' in *Essays*, 13-15.

22. Veblen, *The Theory of the Leisure Class,* New York, 1899, 30, 9. On 281, Veblen writes, 'So long as woman's place is consistently that of a drudge, she is, in the average of cases, fairly contented with her lot. She not only has something tangible and purposeful to do, but she has also no time or thought to spare for a rebellious assertion of such human propensity to self-direction as she has inherited.'

23. *Ibid.*, letters (a) through (j) as follows: a) 38-40; b) 44-47; c) 54-55; d) 72-73; e) 92-93, 248; f) 98-99; g) 102, 133-136, 146: for Veblen's personal habits, see Dorfman, Veblen, *passim*; h) 109-110; i) 119 -- Veblen also mocks the use of candles rather than electric light as an example of conspicuous waste, 121; j) 181; k) Veblen, *The Higher Learning in America,* New York, 1918, 12-13; 85; 80; 98; 78; 88.

24. Veblen, *The Higher Learning in America,* New York, 1918, 12-13; 85; 80; 98; 78; 88.

25. Veblen, *Leisure Class*, 309-310; Veblen also criticized 'classic' in general as a sign of the 'wasteful and archaic,' and extended its scope to 'classic' English polite speech: 'a facile use of it lends dignity to even the most commonplace and trivial string of talk'; English spelling, 'satisfies all the requirements of the canons of respectability under the law of conspicuous waste. It is archaic, cumbrous, and ineffective; its acquisition consumes much time and effort.'

26. Ms. 1329, 27, 1892, unpublished manuscripts of Charles S. Peirce at Harvard University, Houghton Library, as catalogued by Richard S. Robin, *Annotated Catalogue of the Papers of Charles S. Peirce.*

27. Dorfman, *Veblen*, 269.

28. Veblen, 'An Early Experiment in Trusts,' 1904, in *The Place of Science*, 494-507.

29. Article in *The Freeman*, 1921, cited in David Riesman, *Thorstein Veblen*, New York, 1953, 32; Veblen, *Absentee Ownership and Business Enterprise in Recent Times: The Case of America,* New York, 1923; see Dorfman, *Veblen*, 469-470 for a description.

30. Veblen's discussion of the Adam Smith's 'invisible hand' as 'animistic' appears in 'The Preconceptions of Economic Science, II,' 1899, in *The Place of Science*, 114-117. Animism is alive and well in the scholarly world of economics today. See, for example, Milton Friedman, 'Adam Smith's Relevance for 1976,' in Fred R. Glahe, ed. *Adam Smith and the Wealth of Nations,* Boulder, 1978: 'The invisible hand in politics is as potent a force for harm as the invisible hand in economics is for good.' (19).

31. Kolko, *Triumph of Conservatism*, ch. 2.

32. John Taylor, *Circus of Ambition*, New York, 1989. My favorite Veblenesque example here is the rental of art museums for private parties. Taylor writes of the 1980's leisure class: 'Their world resembled Rome in the days before Christianity introduced the idea

of compassion for the unfortunate.' (127) Further contemporary insight may be obtained from Nicolaus Mills, ed., 'Culture in an Age of Money,' *Dissent,* Winter, 1990, which includes illuminating and amusing discussions of movies, novels, architecture, televangelism, and selling admission to presidential inaugurations.

33. Frank S. Levy and Richard C. Michel, 'The Economic Future of the Baby Boom,' report for the Joint Economic Committee of the U.S. Congress,' December 5, 1985, cited in Sidney Blumenthal and Thomas Edsall, eds., *The Reagan Legacy,* New York, 1988, 44-47.

34. *World Bank Atlas* and *World Handbook of Political and Social Indicators,* nos. 65 and 67, cited by Facts on File, *The New Book of World Rankings,* New York, 1984.

Chapter 9

The Declaration of Independence:
Changing Interpretations and a New Hypothesis

'Nothing important merely happens -- it develops,' wrote Albert Beveridge in 1926 when he discussed the Declaration of Independence on its 150th anniversary.[1] Few documents in history have indeed developed in so many directions as the Declaration.   Americans over the past two centuries have argued over it as a sacred text, much as believers and doubters debate the correct interpretation and authoritative status of the Bible. The Declaration's interpreters may be grouped into four categories: (1) the Founding Fathers and the Revolutionary generation; (2) the radical/reform tradition; (3) the conservative critique; and (4) the scholarly debate over origins and the meaning of terms such as equality, liberty, and natural rights.   The logical semiotic conclusion is that there is no Declaration of Independence but only a symbol representing the aspirations of the various interpreters.   In fact, almost everything popularly accepted as true about the Declaration is a myth -- that it was adopted unanimously (John Dickinson refused to sign and the New York delegates were forbidden by instruction to vote); that it was either signed or promulgated on July 4 (independence was approved July 2, proclaimed on July 8, and the document signed by everyone except John Hancock after July 4); and even that it is a 'Declaration of Independence' -- the real title is 'A Declaration By the Representatives of the United States in General Congress Assembled.'[2]

Nevertheless, I argue that only the radical/reform tradition reads the Declaration at all: the other interpreters have respectively celebrated, denied, or dissected it. Only those who have sought to use the Declaration to change society in the direction of greater liberty and equality have considered *both* parts of the document -- not merely the philosophical introduction or the list of practical grievances -- and situated in it a context which gives both sections meaning.

First, consider what the Declaration meant to the generation of the American Revolution. Congress contemplated a Declaration of Independence for two practical military reasons: to enlist foreign support and to increase enthusiasm for the struggle at home. Not only is the Declaration addressed to 'a candid world,' but Jefferson's notes on Congress' deliberations stress that 'a declaration of independence alone could render it consistent with European delicacy, for European powers to treat with us . . . and receive our vessels,' therefore enabling the new nation 'to enter into alliance with France.'[3] Within the newly proclaimed nation, the Declaration provoked official and unofficial demonstrations and 'had a glorious effect.' It 'has made these colonies all alive' in the words of New Hampshire signer William Whipple. In Sussex County, New Jersey, Joseph Barton noted that 'we have had great numbers who could do nothing until we were declared a free state, who are now ready to spend their lives and fortunes in defense of our country.' It also spurred George Washington's hopes 'that this important event will act as a fresh incentive to every officer and soldier to act with fidelity and courage.'[4]

In terms of stimulating support for the American cause at home and abroad, the Declaration was a success. Its aim was to promote patriotic loyalty, not philosophical inquiry. As such, most Americans then and subsequently celebrated the Fourth of July rather than the Declaration itself as John Adams hoped they would celebrate the Second, the day Congress voted for independence, 'as the

Great Anniversary Festival . . . as the day of deliverance, by solemn acts of devotion to God Almighty, solemnized with pomp and parade, shows, games, sports, balls, bonfires, and illuminations, from one end of the continent to the other.'[5] When the people learned of the Declaration, they immediately burned, buried, or otherwise destroyed effigies or statues of King George or British coats of arms, illuminated their houses, drank numerous toasts, and otherwise celebrated the great event uncritically.[6]

Such joyous displays of public spirit troubled more thoughtful souls as time went on.[7] Preparing for the fiftieth anniversary celebrations in 1826, the *National Intelligencer* asked 'whether we are to have [the celebration] in the usual way, that is, by frying chickens, firing away damaged powder, or fuddling our noses over tavern wine? Or shall we do something, of which we may say in the language of the father of the poets, 'Let future ages hear it and admire'.'[8] Three decades later, Abraham Lincoln voiced the same thought -- that to be true to the greatness and spirit of the Founders required further effort on behalf of their ideals rather than mindless praise of what they had accomplished:

> When we were the political slaves of King George, and wanted to be free, we called the maxim that 'all men are created equal' a self-evident truth, but now when we have grown fat, and have lost all dread of becoming slaves ourselves, we have become so greedy to be masters that we call the same maxim a self-evident lie. The Fourth of July is not quite dwindled away: it is still a great day -- for burning firecrackers![9]

Even during the debates over the Declaration, the delegates were troubled by the awareness that the new republic could only justify its existence to a 'candid world' if it promised more than the tyranny it denounced. Jefferson's famous denunciation of the slave trade, omitted from the final draft, termed it a 'cruel war

against human nature itself, violating it's [sic] most sacred rights of life & liberty
. . . .'[10]   Tories were quick to pounce on the inconsistency between the
Americans' loud insistence on human equality and the fact that they held slaves --
a practice declared unconstitutional in the British Isles in Somerset's Case in 1772.
As exiled Massachusetts Governor Thomas Hutchinson asked the delegates in his
critique of the Declaration, 'how [do] their constituents justify the deprivation of
more than a hundred thousand of their rights to liberty, the pursuit of happiness,
and in some degree of their lives, if these rights were absolutely inalienable?'[11]
One sign the Founding Fathers were troubled by this inconsistency is that the
beginnings of the abolitionist movement in the United States date from the time of
the Revolution.   This culminated in gradual emancipation in the North and
numerous individual manumissions in the South, and indicates that while
Americans did not always subordinate economics to idealism, contradictions
between the two seriously troubled the Revolutionary generation.[12]

Nor did contemporaries limit their concern with domestic inequalities to
slavery. Remarking on his hopes for the Declaration, the document's only Roman
Catholic signer, Charles Carroll of Maryland, 'had in view not only our
independence of England, but the toleration of all equal rights.'[13]   The late
eighteenth century in fact witnessed the disestablishment of churches and the
provision for equal political rights regardless of religion in most states.[14]
Similarly, the new states rectified complaints in the second half of the Declaration
that royal policy denied newly settled regions proper representation in colonial
legislatures. State assemblies increased in size, voting qualifications were lowered,
and state capitals shifted westward to permit easier access for frontiersmen.[15]

The revolutionary generation thus clearly intended the rights of life, liberty,
and the pursuit of happiness to be more than either mere rhetoric, or the minimal
statement that America possessed the same right of self-government as other

nations. Efforts to reform internal institutions show that the revolutionaries were sufficiently moved by their own principles, their opponents' jibes, the need to recruit as many people for the Revolution as possible, or some combination of all three, to support Abraham Lincoln's interpretation of their intentions:

> They meant to set up a standard maxim for a free society, which should be familiar to all and revered by all, constantly looked to, constantly labored for, and even though never perfectly attained, constantly approximated, and thereby constantly spreading and deepening its influence and augmenting the happiness and value of life to all people of all colors everywhere. . . . Its authors meant it to be a stumbling block to all those who in after times might seek to turn a free people back into the hateful paths of despotism. They knew the proneness of prosperity to breed tyrants, and they meant when such should appear in this fair land and commence their vocation, they should find left for them at least one hard nut to crack.[16]

Hence, one reaches the radical/reform view of the Declaration. Throughout American history, groups claiming that the United States has denied equal rights to 'life, liberty, and the pursuit of happiness,' have held up the Declaration as a standard. As did Lincoln and the Founding Fathers themselves, they regard 'the United States' as a community testing the workability of the hypotheses of equality and freedom rather than its identification with the economic and political arrangements prevailing at any given time. Frequently they have penned alternative Declarations of Independence, incorporating much of the original phraseology while substituting different instances where violations of principles have occurred. Not surprisingly, alternative declarations have emanated from three main sources: the labor movement, beginning with Robert Owen's fiftieth anniversary manifesto in 1826; the black civil rights movement, which issued manifestos in 1870 and 1966; and the women's rights' movement, notably the Seneca Falls Declaration of 1848.[17] Even though not writing counter-declarations, individuals including Abigail Adams (in her 1776 rebuke to John to 'remember the ladies'), David Walker (who appealed for black revolution in 1829), Abraham Lincoln in 1865, and Martin Luther King, Jr. at Washington in 1963 have based their arguments on the contradiction between America's principles as stated in the Declaration and its practices.[18]

In addition to prodding a community to live up to its own principles in the United States, the Declaration has served as a model for revolutionaries in other nations. Thomas Jefferson's fiftieth anniversary testimonial, penned two weeks before his death on July 4, 1826, regarded the Declaration as an inspiration to the world:

> May it be to the world, what I believe it will be (to some parts sooner, to others later, but finally to all), the signal of arousing men to burst their chains, under which monkish ignorance and superstition had persuaded them to bind themselves, and to assume the blessings of the security of self-government. The form which we have substituted restores the free right to the unbounded exercise of reason and freedom of opinion. All eyes are opened or opening to the rights of man. The general spread of the light of science has already laid open to every view the palpable truth, that the mass of mankind has not been born with saddles on their backs, nor a favored few, booted and spurred, ready to ride them legitimately, by the Grace of God. These are grounds for hope for others; for ourselves, let the annual return of this day forever refresh our recollections of these rights, and an undiminished devotion to them. [19]

Thoughts similar to Jefferson's have inspired emerging nations since 1776 to 'declare' independence from imperial powers, using the same format of principles followed by grievances. Perhaps most ironically, in 1946 Ho Chi Minh declared the independence of Vietnam from the French, using as a model copies of the Declaration flown in by United States military intelligence.[20]   The Declaration has also been used to criticize United States foreign policy by those upset with American expansionism. Three such examples include Abraham Lincoln's opposition to the Mexican War,[21] William Graham Sumner's memorable 1899 pamphlet 'The Conquest of the United States by Spain' (which insisted American greatness lay in providing for the domestic happiness of its people rather than in acquiring power overseas)[22] and contemporary Central American peace activists' insistence that revolutionaries against United States-supported tyrannies are following the Declaration's principles.[23] Also noteworthy is the 'Declaration of Interdependence' framed by historian Henry Steele Commager in 1976. It proclaims that 'all peoples and nations of the globe should acknowledge their interdependence and join together . . . to establish a new world order of compassion, peace, justice, and security.'[24] Commager thus explicitly articulated the logical conclusion of a Declaration intended as a universal example.

The third group of interpreters consists of critics of the Declaration's principles.   If the Declaration has inspired a tradition of dedication to its principles of correcting injustices and inequalities throughout the world, it has also generated a counter-tradition denying its validity. Supporters of England during the Revolution articulated the three crucial points at the outset. First, the ideas of human equality and that men have inalienable rights are false: 'All men, they tell us, are created equal.   This is surely a new discovery; now, for the first time we learn, that a child, at the moment of his birth, has the same quantity of natural power as the parent, and the same quantity of political power as the magistrate,'

John Lind wrote in his 'Answer to the Declaration.' As for 'life, liberty, and the pursuit of happiness' being rights, Lind argued that 'nothing which can be called government ever was, or ever could be, in any instance, exercised, but at the expense of one or the other of those rights.'[25]   Second, even assuming such principles were valid, the Americans violated them themselves, not only through owning slaves, as Thomas Hutchinson noted, but by invading Canada in the hopes of conquering ethnically French subjects of England who had no desire to exchange masters.[26] Hutchinson provided the third critique: the Declaration put the cart before the horse. Far from being goaded to arms by British oppression, the colonists brought on themselves 'the acts of a justly incensed sovereign, for suppression of a most unnatural, unprovoked rebellion.'[27] Revolutions are the products of propaganda put out by disgruntled minorities, usually of intellectuals, not of tyranny. So Thomas Hutchinson believed.

At the very beginning of the 'Age of Democratic Revolution' which Alexis de Tocqueville predicted would become the dominant force of the modern world,[28] the Tories presented the essentials of all future critiques of revolution and democracy.   Since human equality is impossible, and all governments (revolutionary ones more than most) must abridge some 'inalienable' rights to guarantee others, it is best each nation works things out in accordance with its own needs and traditions. Revolutions are efforts to realize a false Utopia -- or would be were revolutionaries sincere rather than power-hungry.

American conservatives' felt need to deny or modify the Declaration led to two different responses. First, some have insisted that the Declaration's principles do not apply at all. John C. Calhoun, speaking for a South committed to both slavery and its extension, termed human equality 'the most false and dangerous of all political errors' and insisted that men acquired rights not naturally, but as they became civilized. The American Revolution was 'formed of old materials and on practical and well-established principles, borrowed for the most part from our experience and that of the country from which we sprang.'[29] The refusal of many Southerners to celebrate July 4 as the Civil War approached and in its aftermath confirmed this denial.[30] On the other hand, some conservatives have maintained that the Declaration primarily argued for limited government and the rights of individuals to 'pursue happiness' in an unregulated environment. In the words of Woodrow Wilson, the Declaration proclaimed 'there can be no liberty if the individual is not free; there is no such thing as corporate liberty. There is no other possible formula for a free government than this: that the law must deal with individuals, allowing them to choose their own lives . . . and that government must regulate not as a superintendent does, but as a judge does.'[31]

I would argue that the conservative denial of the Declaration represents a serious distortion. Also, I submit that the conservative revision ignores both the list of grievances appended to the preamble and historical evidence of what government actually did in early America. First, it is unrealistic to suppose Jefferson and his co-conspirators ever entertained the idea men were equal in every conceivable respect, such as wealth or ability. If we plausibly assume 'all men are created equal' is explained by what follows immediately -- that is to say, equal with respect to the right to 'life, liberty, and the pursuit of happiness' -- the absurdity vanishes. Furthermore, unlike those who have used the Declaration as a model to advocate social change, conservatives stop reading with the preamble. But it is the list of grievances which explains the manner in which government may in fact trespass on man's inalienable rights. No scholar I know of has tried to use the grievances to help explain the principles' political theory.

Four general points underlie the grievances against George III: a) 'he has refused to assent to laws, the most wholesome and necessary for the public good,' for the most part denying representation to newly settled regions or forbidding further settlement; b) through denial of representation he has abridged the popular right of self-government; c) he has corrupted justice by interfering with fair trials; and d) he has made war against the people, both directly and by inflicting upon them 'swarms of new officers to harass them' and 'eat out their substance.'

The Declaration therefore implies there are four conditions any government must fulfill to guarantee to the populace their equal rights to life, liberty, and the pursuit of happiness: a) pass laws necessary for the public good. This I should stress is a positive injunction, not one insisting on non-interference with states rights or private property, for example. Government in colonial America did not hesitate to regulate prices, distribute charity, or foster economic development as it perceived the public welfare dictated;[32] b) no group of people within a polity ought to be denied adequate representation of its collective interest -- reference to frontier settlements again makes clear the Founders were not thinking only in terms of individual rights. They were thinking of the collective rights of underprivileged minorities to gain access to equal individual rights; c) justice must be administered impartially (one of the Intolerable Acts had created trials for Americans before unrepresentative British juries) and therefore by true representatives of the real community to which an individual belongs; and d) people should not be robbed, murdered, or harassed by their government. The Declaration's insistence that George III has denied frontier settlement and representation is especially significant. It indicates the signers envisioned an expanding polity in which the same rights enjoyed by the original settlers would be opened to new groups of people. As their own reforms in the direction of greater equality (such as extending the franchise and disestablishing the churches) indicate, they cared deeply that the new nation live up to its principles domestically in order that its international example not strike a hollow note. In light of the foregoing analysis, two auxiliary criticisms -- that at any given time the United

States has realized a fairly optimal equality ('under the law') or that the Declaration was never intended to apply to 'unfit' people -- fall by the wayside.[33]

Finally, the scholar-explicators. Strangely, the scholarly approach to the Declaration is subject to the same criticism as the conservative misreading. Scholars have been primarily concerned with the Declaration's 'origins.' Concepts of equality and happiness have been traced to sources as diverse as classical antiquity,[34] British constitutional law,[35] John Locke,[36] the Scottish Enlightenment,[37] and Protestant-Puritan Christianity.[38] More immediate suggested antecedents include Thomas Paine,[39] some farmers in Mecklenburg County, North Carolina,[40] and most important colonial documents of the 1760's.[41] Like the conservatives, the scholars deal with the preamble rather than with the grievances. In this case, however, I guess the reason is the grievances are either extremely obvious or extremely controversial. Superficial knowledge of the events from 1760-1776 is all that is required to know what Jefferson is talking about. On the other hand, to inquire into the validity of the grievances is to ask who is to blame for the Revolution. This is the sort of value-judgment modern scholarship shuns, at least explicitly. But doing so renders it impossible to do justice to the whole Declaration. Only Peter Hoffer, to my knowledge, who has imaginatively interpreted the entire document as an adaptation of the form of the traditional Bill in Equity -- which justified an appeal to higher law when specific grievances could not be subsumed under statute -- has regarded the grievances as equally 'real' with the philosophy preceding them.[42]

Ironically, public opinion in the late twentieth century both denies the Declaration's principles and yet celebrates the document itself. A *Miami Herald* reporter nearly found himself arrested for suggesting fifty people randomly selected affix their signatures to a copy of the Declaration. Only one would. The rest not only failed to recognize it, but dismissed it as 'rubbish' or 'Commie junk,' and its author as 'a hippie,' a 'raver,' or a 'red-neck revolutionist.'[43] The public which celebrated a Bicentennial rather than a Revolution is thus paradoxically true to the public of 1776 in its uncritical patriotism.

However, my guess is that the Founding Fathers would be less than pleased with the conservative and scholarly interpretations of the Declaration which also hold current sway. The former dissects the principles which begin the Declaration while ignoring the text which explains them. The latter tends to derive rights from an intellectual tradition rather than from a life-or-death revolutionary struggle. The Founding Fathers and their radical heirs, by writing and reading the Declaration as an expression of concrete grievances and of the minimal courtesies a government owes its population as well as a statement of political theory, interpreted it as an action intended to initiate an ongoing, world-wide community striving for equality, justice, and freedom. To be sure, in differing degrees the Fathers disagreed over specific institutional arrangements which would prevent this striving from deteriorating into social disorder. Nor could they anticipate the various contexts in which their ideas would prove relevant over the ensuing two centuries. But the internal reform accompanying the War for Independence demonstrates that only reformers and radicals have read the document correctly -- as a continuing inspiration in the United States and throughout the world to eliminate oppression and to insure that all groups of people enjoy adequate self government and representation of both their collective interests and their personal freedom.

ENDNOTES

1.   Albert J. Beveridge, 'Sources of the Declaration of Independence,' *Pennsylvania Magazine of History and Biography*, 50, 1926, 289-315, quotation on 289.

2. Charles Warren, 'Fourth of July Myths,' *William and Mary Quarterly*, 3rd ser. 2, 1945, 237-272, esp. 247-248.

3. Thomas Jefferson, 'Notes and Proceedings of the Continental Congress,' reprinted in Robert Ginsberg, ed. *A Casebook on the Declaration of Independence*, New York: Thomas Crowell, 1967, 16-17.

4. Charles D. Deshler, 'How the Declaration Was Received in the Old Thirteen,' *Harper's New Monthly Magazine*, 85, 1892, 165-187, esp. 169-170.

5. M.M. Baldwin, 'The Declaration of Independence,' *Magazine of American History*, 20, 1888, 479-484, esp. 480-481.

6. Deshler as cited in number 4.

7. Philip F. Detweiler, 'The Changing Reputation of the Declaration of Independence: The First Fifty Years,' *William and Mary Quarterly*, 3rd ser. 19, 1962, 557-574.

8. Lyman H. Butterfield, 'The Jubilee of Independence, July 4, 1826,' *Virginia Magazine of History and Biography*, 61, 1953, 119-140, quotation on 121.

9. Quoted in Daniel L. Marsh, 'The Second Gospel of Americanism: The Declaration of Independence,' *Methodist Review*, 5th ser. 42, 1926, 512-530, quotation on 528.

10. Quoted in Carl Becker, *The Declaration of Independence*, New York: Harcourt Brace, 1922, 180.

11. Thomas Hutchinson, 'Strictures Upon the Declaration of the Congress at Philadelphia . . .,' *Remembrancer*, 4, 1776, 25-42, quotation on 26.

12. Ira Berlin and Ronald Hoffman, eds., *Slavery and Freedom in the Age of the American Revolution*, Charlottesville: University Press of Virginia, 1983.

13. Marsh, 'Second Gospel,' 527.

14. J. Franklin Jameson, *The American Revolution Considered as a Social Movement*, Princeton: Princeton University Press, 1926.

15. Chilton Williamson, *American Suffrage from Property to Democracy, 1760-1860*, Princeton: Princeton University Press, 1960; Jackson T. Main, 'Government By the People: The American Revolution and the Democratization of the Legislatures,' *William and Mary Quarterly*, 3rd ser. 23, 1966, 391-407.

16. Quoted in Henry Steele Commager, 'The Declaration Is For Today!' *New York Times Magazine*, July 1, 1951, 5, 29.

17. Philip S. Foner, ed., *We The Other People*, Urbana: University of Illinois Press, 1976.

18. Albert Matthews, 'Thomas Paine and the Declaration of Independence,' *Proceedings of the Massachusetts Historical Society*, 43, 1910, 247 for Abigail Adams; David Walker, *Appeal to the Colored Citizens of the World*, Boston: David Walker, 1830; Roy P. Basler, 'As One Southerner to Another: Concerning Lincoln and the Declaration of Independence,' *South Atlantic Quarterly*, 42, 1943, 45-53.

19. Butterfield, 'Jubilee of Independence,' 124.

20. Archimedes Patti, *Why Vietnam? Prelude to America's Albatross*, Berkeley: University of California Press, 1980, 250-252.

21. Basler, 'One Southerner to Another,' 45-47.

22. William Graham Sumner, 'The Conquest of the United States by Spain,' *Yale Law Journal*, 8, 1899, 168-193.

23. Cited by Ed Asner in Obie Benz, director, *Americas in Transition*, ICARUS films 1981.

24. Foner, *We the Other People*, 202-206.

25. John Lind, *An Answer to the Declaration of the American Congress*, London: T. Cadell, 1776, 119.

26. *Ibid.*, 120.

27. Hutchinson, 'Strictures,' 41.

28. Alexis de Tocqueville, *Democracy in America*; first published 1835-1840, numerous editions and translations.

29. John C. Calhoun, 'Speech on the Oregon Bill, June 27, 1848,' *Appendix to the Congressional Globe*, 30th Congress, 1st Session, Washington: Blair and Rives, 1848, 872.

30. Michael Kammen, *A Season of Youth: The American Revolution and the Historical Imagination*, New York: Oxford University Press, 1978, 57-58.

31. Woodrow Wilson, 'The Author and Signers of the Declaration of Independence,' *North American Review*, 186, 1907, 32-33; Beveridge, 'Sources of the Declaration'; R. Carter Pittman, 'Equality v. Liberty: The Eternal Conflict,' *American Bar Association Journal*, 46, 1960, 873-880.

32.   Curtis P. Nettels, *The Emergence of a National Economy, 1775-1815*, New York: Harper and Row, 1962.

33.   L. Bradford Prince, 'The Declaration of Independence: Its Principle and Its Power,' *Journal of American History*, 11, 1917, 108-112, 129-132 and Amos Fiske, 'Some Consecrated Fallacies,' *North American Review*, 169, 1899, 821-828, respectively argue these interpretations.

34.   Thomas C. Grey, 'Origins of the Unwritten Constitution: Fundamental Law in American Revolutionary Thought,' *Stanford Law Review*, 30, 1978, 843-893.

35.   Beveridge, 'Sources of the Declaration.'

36.   Ronald Hamowy, 'Jefferson and the Scottish Enlightenment: A Critique of Garry Wills' *Inventing America: Jefferson's Declaration of Independence,'* *William and Mary Quarterly,* 3rd ser. 36, 1979, 503-523.

37.   Garry Wills, *Inventing America: Jefferson's Declaration of Independence*, Garden City: Doubleday, 1978.

38.   George W. Richards, 'The Declaration of Independence,' *Reformed Church Review*, 4th ser., 1911, 204-230.

39.   Joseph Lewis, 'Thomas Paine: Author of the Declaration of Independence,' *The Age of Reason Magazine*, 34, 1965, 1-16.

40.   Nellie Morris Hess, 'The Birth of the American Republic,' *Potter's American Monthly*, 5, 1875, 491-504.

41.   Beveridge, 'Sources of the Declaration.'

42.   Peter Hoffer, 'The Declaration of Independence as a Bill in Equity,' in William Pencak and Wythe Holt, Jr., eds., *The Law in America, 1607-1861*, New York: The New-York Historical Society, 1989.

43.   Jules Siegel and Bernard Garfinkel, *The Journal of the Absurd*, New York: Workman Publishing, 1980; Michael Kammen, in *A Machine that Would Go of Itself: The Constitution in American Culture*, New York: Knopf, 1986, has many examples of Americans' appalling ignorance of the fundamentals of their government; for instance, in a 1943 survey only 23 percent of citizens polled could identify the Bill of Rights, 340; see also xvii, 3-4, 83-84, 217, 222, 230, 309, 383-384.

Chapter 10

The United States Constitution:
A Semiotic Interpretation

One problem which legal semiotics addresses is the manner in which legal systems 'represent' social institutions and, conversely, the manner in which societies reflect their legal structures (Kevelson 1986: 191-198). The creation and preservation of the United States Constitution is an ideal topic for the legal semiotician, as it offers us a chance to view statesmen as semioticians. At few times in history have men had the opportunity to construct a nation from the beginning, to frame a new fundamental legal code in accordance with experience and reason largely unencumbered by existing institutions. The United States was not a political entity until 1776, and possessed no established church, aristocracy, standing army, or concentrations of economic power. 'We exhibit,' George Washington informed an English correspondent, 'the novel and astonishing spectacle of a whole people deliberating calmly on what form of government will be most conducive to their happiness' (Farrand 3:339). Because America's source of nationhood was political -- arising out of revolutionary unification -- the Constitution was framed specifically to represent the needs of its culturally diverse society.

A semiotic approach to the Constitution is no 'unconstitutional' innovation. The Founders themselves realized only too well that in framing a government, 'the greatest difficulty lies in the affair of representation, and if this could be adjusted, all others would be surmountable,' in James Madison's words (Farrand 1:321). Madison was here referring to a specific problem under debate: balancing the interests of the large and the small states.   But the same issue underlay every major issue discussed at the Convention.   Who would be represented in the Senate?   Who in the House?   Who would elect the President?   What about the respective rights of the states and people, the respective powers of branches of government selected in different ways?   'A representation is the sign of the reality,' Charles Pinckney observed, and James Wilson compared the manner in which America's constituent elements would be represented in its government to a medical 'concoction': 'a vice in the representation, like an error in the first concoction, must be followed by disease, convulsion, and finally death itself' (Farrand 1:109; 2:10).

To the extent that the Constitution accurately represented the nation's social reality, the republic would survive.   To the extent the representation failed, America would join 'the petty republics of Greece and Italy,' of which 'it is impossible to read the history . . . without feeling sensations of horror and disgust,' and provide further ammunition for those 'advocates of despotism' who 'have decried all free government as inconsistent with the order of society, and have indulged themselves in malicious exaltation over its friends and partisans' (*Federalist* 9).   The legal semiotician may therefore ask: First, how did the Founding Fathers seek to represent their nation through the Constitution?   Second, were they successful both in their time and for the following centuries?

A third question evolves out of these two.   Scholars searching for the roots of Charles Peirce's semiotic method have concentrated on philosophical influences. But the similarities between Peirce's thought, the Founding Fathers' notion of a political community, and the key linkage of the community of intellectuals at Cambridge, Massachusetts with whom he grew up cannot be ignored.   Peircean semiotics extends the Constitution's notion that in a republic of virtuous citizens interests could be reconciled to the methodological reconciliation of the arts, humanities, and sciences given a republic of thinkers dedicated to the truth.

The context in which the Founders drafted the Constitution may be elaborated indefinitely, but at least three key elements stand out. First, a last-ditch effort was needed to save an infant republic already plagued by rebellion, unpayable debts, and 'imbecility' in foreign affairs. In 1776, the United States had proclaimed itself, 'an asylum for mankind' in 'an old world . . . overrun with oppression' in the words of Thomas Paine's *Common Sense* (Paine 1776: 120). By 1787, George Washington wrote of 'a general government shaken to its foundation, and liable to be overturned at a blast. In a word it is at an end . . . unless a remedy be found' (Farrand 3:31).

Second, the Founders realized with Madison that the Constitution which emerged, whatever it may be, 'must have a material influence on our own destiny, and in that on republican liberty in the world' (Farrand 3:37). Not only was the fate of free government in America at stake, but also throughout the world. Gouverneur Morris realized full well that he attended Philadelphia 'as a representative of [not just his constituents or] America; he flattered himself he came here in some degree as a representative of the whole human race; for the whole human race will be affected by the proceedings of this convention' (Farrand 1:529). The Constitution was to be more than a representation of the republican government America needed to survive: it was to show the world how, for the first time, a republic could work and thereby provide an inspiration and model for future generations at home and abroad.

But if the context of their historic responsibility and the specter of a host of shattered republics formed part of the context in which the Framers wrote the Constitution, so did the decade of experience they had acquired in waging war against the world's most powerful nation. Of the 55 delegates at Philadelphia, 30 had served in the military and 42 in Congress. These men had functioned as the *national* government to the extent America had one, not only fighting the English, but struggling to overcome the jealousies, parochialisms, and ineptitude of the state governments and inhabitants less committed to the Revolution than they. For a decade, the men of Philadelphia had been reconciling, cajoling, threatening, and pleading, somehow energizing and stabilizing the affairs of a diverse population in the common cause (Rossiter 1966: 138-158). Charles Pinckney noted that when Congressmen came to the national capital, 'an esprit de corps. . . has made heretofore every anti-federalist member of Congress, after his election become strictly federalist' (Farrand 1:365). In short, the Founders hoped the Constitution would institutionalize and represent the experience whereby 'men who possessed the confidence of the people, and many of whom had become highly distinguished by their patriotism, virtue, and wisdom, in times which tried the hearts and minds of men' (*Federalist 2*) managed to bury the differences among themselves and unite in a patriotic spirit.

The Founding Fathers were also 'the young men of the revolution' as Stanley Elkins and Eric McKitrick have noted (1961: 181-216). The Framers averaged 43 years of age in 1787, or 32 when the Declaration was signed. Even the relatively few elder statesmen on hand, such as 81 year-old Benjamin Franklin and 55 year-old George Washington, shared with their younger colleagues the experience of placing the creation of a major nation at the center of their existence for much of their adult lives. As Douglass Adair has so eloquently argued, 'the greatest and the most effective leaders of 1787 -- no angels they, but passionately selfish and self-interested men -- were giants in part because the Revolution had led them to redefine their notions of interest and had given them, through the concept of fame, a personal stake in creating a national system dedicated to liberty, to justice, and to the general welfare' (Adair 1974: 24). Alexander Hamilton found 'the situation of a member of Congress . . . the most illustrious and important of any I am able to conceive. He is to be regarded not only as a legislator, but as a FOUNDER OF AN EMPIRE!' (Hamilton 1778). The Founders heeded Thomas Paine's eloquent plea not to 'shrink back at a time, when a little more, a little further, would have rendered this continent the glory of the earth' (Paine 1776: 94).

The context the Constitution represented, then, involved at least three elements: the Founders' fear their dreams of a free government would be shattered; their desperate yet still living hope that it could not only be saved, but erected into a model for the world; and the experience of revolution which taught them that it was possible for a diverse people to unite and accomplish the unprecedented: a 'union of sovereign states, preserving their civil liberties and connected together by such ties as to preserve their permanent and effective governments, is a system not described, it is a circumstance that has not occurred in the history of men' (Farrand 3:46).

Broadly and properly understood, the Constitution may be viewed as an icon (a framework of national government for practical purposes, providing guidelines for legislation and its enforcement), an index (of the Founders' perception of the new nation's problems, and their collective vision of a good society and the extent to which the United States could practically implement it) and a symbol (of the possibilities republicanism offered the future and the world for a better society). The Constitution was addressed simultaneously to several audiences: the voters of 1787 (who had to institutionalize it); legislators and citizens of the future republic (who had to preserve it); and the oppressed peoples of the world (who had the option to be inspired by it). The Constitution thus created an ongoing community of inquirers into the good society, potentially extending to all of human history and to the entire human race. How did the Framers hope to implement this? Did they hope to succeed?

Perhaps the most telling sign of what the Founders were trying to do with the Constitution appears in the series of speeches which closed the Convention. Many of the delegates would never see each other again, and the leave-taking may be regarded as the symbolic confirmation of the consensus politics which had made the Revolution possible. The delegates paradoxically vied with each other in expressing reservations about an instrument they then urged their colleagues to support as wholeheartedly and unanimously as possible. Benjamin Franklin, who himself served as the primary agent of reconciliation at the Convention, began the proceedings. It was he who had urged a three-day recess, where 'opposite parties mixed with each other' for 'a free and frank exchange of sentiments,' when the small states seemed on the verge of bolting. He admitted 'that there are several parts of this Constitution which I do not at all approve, but I am not sure I shall never approve them.' Summoning all the prestige his eight decades brought him, Franklin lectured his younger brethren that 'the older I grow the more apt I am to doubt my own judgment, and to pay more respect to the judgment of others. . . . I doubt too whether any other Convention we can obtain may be able to make a better Constitution.' Many others did the same. Alexander Hamilton had earlier posed the basic problem for the delegates. They had better come close to unanimous agreement, for a document the people would not endorse would be useless: 'if there had not been a unanimity, nothing could have been done; for the Convention had not power to establish, but only to recommend' a government to thirteen state conventions (Farrand 2:524, 641-645; 3:333).

Both the manner in which the Founders conducted the Constitutional Convention and the document itself may be understood as an elaborate code of reconciliation. Consensus, not majority rule, was the order of the day. As

Franklin noted when four small states threatened to walk out unless they obtained equal representation in at least one house: 'Our strength and prosperity will depend on our unity; and the secession of even four of our smallest states, interspersed as they are, would, in my mind, paralyze and render useless, any plan which the majority could devise' (Farrand 3:467-473). The Constitution-framing *process*, like the document itself, was to be a representation of the sort of compromises for the common good the republic required to survive.

The Founders drew up an informal code to govern their deliberations, which may serve as an index of the spirit they hoped the Constitution itself would embody. Those present had to pay attention to the speaker: 'whilst he shall be speaking, none shall hold discourse with another, or pass between them, or read a book, pamphlet, or paper, printed or manuscript.' The citizens of Philadelphia's republic of 55 had to keep their attention focused on the public realm, respect each other's opinions, and not occupy themselves with private matters. No member could speak more than twice to a point without special permission (Farrand 1:8), insuring all interests could be represented and all points of view aired. Delegates would have to subordinate their desire to launch flights of oratorical fancy or dominate the proceedings to a collective search for wisdom. The delegates were sworn to secrecy concerning the proceedings, 'a necessary precaution to prevent misrepresentations or mistakes,' George Mason noted, 'there being a material difference between the appearance of a subject in its first crude and undigested shape, and after it shall have been properly matured and arranged' (Farrand 3:28). The Founders wished no external pressures to interfere with their deliberations and did not wish to commit themselves to publicly announced dogmatic positions in the course of the debates. (Had Madison not taken notes, in fact, there would be almost no record of what was said at the Convention at all.) Within the hall itself, compromise and willingness to consider the subject from different angles would prevail. With the exception of anti-federalists Luther Martin and Robert Yates, who left the Convention to organize opposition, the delegates limited their outside communications concerning the Convention to stressing its amazing consensus: as the *Pennsylvania Packet* reported on July 19, 'so great is the unanimity . . . that it has been proposed to call the room in which they assemble -- Unanimity Hall' (Farrand 3:60).

The Framers thus practiced at the Convention a miniature of the truly representative republic they hoped to launch. This appears in the remarkable civility of the debates themselves. There was only one unpleasant incident. When Delaware's Gunning Bedford found the large states too insistent that representation be proportional to population, only he warned that 'the small ones will find some foreign ally of more honor and good faith, who will take them by the hand and do them justice.' At once Rufus King rebuked such 'vehemence unprecedented in that house,' causing Bedford to apologize: 'he could only excuse it to himself on the score of passion.' At this juncture, when 'there was much warm feeling exhibited' and 'a rupture seemed almost inevitable,' Franklin -- 'who exhibited daily a spectacle of transcendent benevolence' -- spoke extemporaneously, the only time James Wilson did not read a speech for him, and calmed everyone down (Farrand 1:492-493; 3:467-473). Franklin's dramatic speech set the tone for the rest of the Convention. The other great issues vexing the delegates -- the 'three-fifths' compromise, the continuation of the slave trade desired by South Carolina and Georgia, and the northern states' preference for a majority (rather than two-thirds) vote for commercial legislation -- were decided by general agreement.

In fact, if we are to look at 'the intention of the Founding Fathers' as a guide for interpreting the Constitution as an icon -- a framework of government -- most of the document reduces itself to a code for reconciliation: of the large states and the small, the slave and the free, those who feared aristocracy, democracy, or monarchy, or too much or too little federal or state power. The institution of such reconciliation -- that the federal government truly represent the diverse interests of the nation on a continuing basis -- became for the Founders the achievement of 1787.

What the Founders did not compromise, they left vague. Where did the powers of the states end and that of the federal government begin? What was to be the role of the Senate in consulting with the executive when treaties were made? What were the powers of the Supreme Court? What were those ambiguous rights 'reserved to the states and the people' in the Tenth Amendment? Hamilton argued in *Federalist* 73 on the 'insufficiency of a mere parchment delineation of the boundaries' between 'legislative and executive power.' As William Paterson realized 'if the power now proposed be not enough, the people hereafter will make additions to it' (Farrand 1:251). Madison advocated a flexible, developing conception of liberty in opposition to anti-federalists who urged the people to be protected on paper from the excesses of government: 'Liberty is not . . . confined to any single point of time, but lies within extremes, which afford sufficient latitude for all the variations which may be required by the various situations and and circumstances of civil society' (*Federalist* 53).

Two principles then emerge from the Founding Fathers' solution to the nation's crisis. First, major interests on the state and local level ought to be respected, reconciled, and adequately represented in the national government. Second, given disagreements among the delegates themselves as to the optimal division of powers among the state and federal governments, among the branches of the latter, and how these ought to be chosen, the division of powers ought to be left open to be decided by the people in accordance with their needs in the course of time.

The harmonizing of interests established at the Convention thus became the precedent the Founders hoped would be adhered to in Constitutional interpretation as both desirable and essential for the republic's preservation.   As early as July, 1787, Nicholas Gilman praised his colleagues' 'great wisdom and prudence as well as liberality of sentiment and a readiness to surrender natural rights and privileges for the good of the nation.'   He then 'devoutly wished that the same spirit may pervade the whole country'   (Farrand 3:66).   Nearly a decade later, James Madison addressed the House of Representatives to argue that the Founders intended the Constitution to guide an ongoing process of reconciliation for the general good rather than to stipulate particular laws or administrative arrangements as 'unconstitutional':

> Whatever veneration might be entertained for the body of men who formed our Constitution, the sense of that body could never be regarded as the oracular guide in expounding the Constitution. As the instrument came from them it was nothing more than the draft of a plan, nothing but a dead letter, until life and validity were breathed into it by the voice of the people.

'If we were to look, therefore, for the meaning of the instrument beyond the face of the instrument,' Madison suggested we look at the spirit of amity and mutual concession from which the Constitution resulted.   In the case he was discussing, 'that construction ought to be favored which would preserve the mutual control between the Senate and House of Representatives, rather than that which gave powers to the Senate not controllable by, and paramount over those of the House' (Farrand 3:374).   Where balance of interests was possible, it should take precedence over the claims of one party.

On different occasions, other Framers backed up Madison's contention that it was nonsense to appeal to the 'sense of the Fathers' on specific issues in interpreting the Constitution. This not only amounted to selective quotation to prove a predetermined point, but in fact went against the true 'sense of the Fathers' that the Constitution was a living document, a process initiated rather than a fiat handed down from on high. Already in 1791, Elbridge Gerry succinctly exposed the absurdity of the contrary position: 'The memories of different gentlemen would probably vary as they had already done with respect to those facts, and if not, the opinions of the individual members who debated are not to be considered as opinions of the Convention' (Farrand 3:362-363). Abraham Baldwin, discussing the respective treaty-making powers of the President and Senate said, 'it was not to disparage the instrument, to say that it had not definitely, and with precision, absolutely settled everything on which it had spoken. . . . Some subjects were left a little ambiguous and uncertain' (Farrand 3:369-370).

On many occasions, the Founding Fathers argued for constitutional interpretation as a dynamic process, undertaken by the citizens and their representatives, to best achieve the common good. Thomas Jefferson maintained that 'laws and institutions must go hand-in-hand with the progress of the human mind' (Jefferson 1816: 291), and George Washington, so discouraged before the Convention began, in fact trusted the people to improve on the Constitution's deficiencies:

> I think the people (for it is with them to judge) can, as they will have the advantage of experience on their side, decide with as much propriety on the alterations and amendments which are necessary as ourselves. I do not think we are more inspired, have more wisdom, or possess more virtue than those who will come after us (Washington 1787:164).

In their confidential debates at the Convention, the Framers sang the praises of the people and put their faith in the republic's future squarely in their hands. Franklin took the lead in emphasizing the 'virtue and public spirit of our common people, of which they displayed a great deal during the war.' In urging that the Constitution establish no property qualifications for voting, he called attention to the unwillingness of American prisoners of war to defect to the British even when subjected to the most horrible conditions. Hessian troops, on the other hand, changed sides in large numbers, demonstrating the international republican spirit upon which the nation could safely depend (Farrand 2:204). On the only occasion he spoke up at the Convention, at the very end, George Washington also stressed maximizing the popular input: 'the smallness of the proportion of representatives had been considered by many members of the Convention, an insufficient security for rights and interests of the people' (Farrand 2:644). The writings of the Founders at the time of the Convention contain many remarks such as James Wilson's 'that the supreme power should be vested in the people, is in my judgment the great panacea of human politics' (Farrand 3:142) and 'the streams of national power ought to flow immediately from that pure, original fountain of all legislative authority -- THE PEOPLE' (*Federalist* 22).

It was in their discussion of opening the privileges of citizenship and public office to immigrants that the full extent of the Founders' willingness to trust the people with the future of republican government became evident. Both Hamilton and Madison 'wished to invite foreigners of merit and republican principles among us.' James Wilson pointed to his home state of Pennsylvania as a proof of the advantage of encouraging emigrations:

> It was perhaps the youngest (except Georgia) settlement on the
> Atlantic; yet it was at least among the foremost in population and
> prosperity. He remarked that almost all the general officers of the

Pennsylvania line (of the late army) were foreigners. And no complaint had ever been made against their fidelity or merit. Three of her deputies to the convention (Mr. Morris, Mr. Fitzsimmons, and himself) were also not natives (Farrand 2:268-269).

As a sign to the world, then, the Founders intended America to be a society where the civic debate was not only open to those born in America. The republican-minded throughout the world were invited to participate. The Founders not only trusted the 'experiment' to their own posterity, but put its fate and their faith in the people of the world.

If we are to consider the Founders' intention, the silence of the Constitution on immigration, their stated opinions on citizenship, admission of naturalized citizens to all offices save the Presidency, and the equality of admission for western states all point to their vision of America as a community open to all people willing to join and conduct themselves lawfully within a republican community. Even as the Founders were debating, they were extending the political community and reconciling the discontented. Property requirements for the franchise, vestiges of established churches, and slavery in the northern states were disappearing. Readmission was offered to many Loyalists, the Shays rebels in Massachusetts received wholesale pardons, and the first ten amendments wooed the anti-federalists. If the Founders could not envision blacks, Native Americans, and women as full citizens, the logic of their ideas and actions welcomed rather than precluded such inclusiveness.

The Founding Fathers, then, intended no specific representation of a social order in the Constitution. They looked forward with anticipation to a growing republic, incorporating more and more citizens into the union, trusting to their public-spirited patriotism to abide by the rules of the game -- to work for their interests lawfully within the Constitution.

But the Framers did not expect their republic to endure forever. If they demonstrated to the world that a large republic would have too many minority interests to prevent an unchecked majority from destroying majority rights (*Federalist* 10), they retained the classical ideal that a republic is only possible in a relatively egalitarian society. Once the gap between rich and poor began to define the social order, either the rich would oppress the poor or the poor would plunder the rich. They could see no alternative. The representation of diverse but reconcilable interests by diverse but reconcilable federal, state, and local legal entities would no longer be possible.

Still, if the Constitution was ultimately doomed, the Founders wished, with North Carolina's delegates, that: 'no precaution [ought] to be omitted that might postpone the event as long as possible' (Farrand 2:101). John Adams predicted that when the nation became 'rich, powerful and luxurious' it would be 'good sense' to 'make transitions to a nearer resemblance of the British constitution' (Adams 1787: 358-359). Franklin was slightly more optimistic, confessing himself 'apprehensive -- perhaps too apprehensive -- that the government of these states may in future times end in monarchy.' But he expressed the general consensus that this 'catastrophe' be 'long delayed' (Farrand 1:83).

Contrary to historians who have argued that the Founders intended to replace the democratic government of the Articles of Confederation with an aristocracy (Beard 1913; Main 1961; Wood 1969: 562), the Convention collectively understood the new republic as a relatively classless society which it ought to preserve as long as possible. As might have been expected, Franklin took the lead in expressing 'his dislike of every thing that tended to debase the spirit of the common people':

If honesty was often the companion of wealth, and if poverty was exposed to peculiar temptation, it was not less true that the possession

of property increased the desire of more property. Some of the
greatest rogues he was ever acquainted with, were the richest rogues.
. . . This Constitution will be much read and attended to in Europe,
and if it should betray a great partiality to the rich -- will not only
hurt us in the esteem of the most liberal and enlightened men there,
but discourage the common people from removing to this country
(Farrand 2:249).

At the Convention, the delegates devoted much thought to constructing a
framework which would prevent the formation of a two-class society. Three well
developed positions were argued: Charles Pinckney's (that such a danger was too
remote to worry about); James Madison's (that it was a long-range possibility that
would lead to levelling and class war); and Gouverneur Morris's (that in the long
run America would be dominated by oligarchs).

Pinckney insisted 'equality is the leading feature of the United States,' and
believed the other Founders failed to appreciate that 'the people of this country are
not only very different from the inhabitants of any state we are acquainted with in
the modern world, but . . . distinct from . . . any state we are acquainted with
among the ancients.' Other delegates erred, he thought, in 'having unwisely
considered ourselves as the inhabitants of an old instead of a new country' by
concerning themselves with divisions among commercial, manufacturing, and
landed interests (Farrand 1:398-400).

Madison offered a trenchant critique of Pinckney's view of America 'as one
homogeneous mass.' Even in the America of 1787 there were 'creditors and
debtors, farmers, merchants, and manufacturers' and 'particularly the distinction
of rich and poor.' In an argument he developed more extensively in the famous
Federalist 10, Madison feared 'the majority interest might under sudden impulses
be tempted to commit injustice on the minority.' And while in the short run class

warfare posed little danger, Madison thought that in a system which 'we wish to last for ages, we should not lose sight of the changes which ages will produce':

> An increase of population will of necessity increase the proportion of those who will labor under all the hardships of life, and secretly sigh for a more equal distribution of its blessings. These may in time outnumber those who are placed above the feelings of indigence. According to equal laws of suffrage, the power will slide into the hands of the former. No agrarian attempts have yet been made in this country, but the symptoms of a levelling spirit, as we have understood, have sufficiently appeared in certain quarters, [i.e., Shays' Rebellion] to give notice of future danger (Farrand 1:421-423).

Gouverneur Morris, usually regarded as one of the most high-toned of the Framers, in fact offered the Convention's most potent argument that oligarchy, rather than anarchy and levelling, threatened the nation in the very long run. Morris offered a fascinating argument for limiting suffrage to those who possessed freeholds or a moderate amount of property. He did so in the interest of preserving, rather than limiting, popular government:

> Aristocracy will grow out of the House of Representatives. Give the votes to people who have no property and they will sell them to the rich who will be able to buy them. We should not confine our attention to the present moment. The time is not distant when this country will abound with mechanics and manufacturers who will receive their bread from their employers. Will such men be the secure and faithful guardians of liberty? Will they be the impregnable barrier against aristocracy?' (Farrand 2:202-203)

Reading the debates of the Convention, it is possible to imagine at times that the Founding Fathers possessed clairvoyance. In discussing the interests which would need to be represented and reconciled were the republic to survive, Madison argued that the quarrel between large and small states which took up so much of the debate was a theoretical rather than a practical concern: 'The great danger to our general government' he underscored in the copy of the debates subsequently published, 'is the great northern and southern interests of the Continent. . . . Look to the votes in Congress, and the most of them stand divided by the geography of the country, and not according to the size of the states' (Farrand 1:476). Here was yet a third threat to the republic's survival, which in this case in fact split the nation and led to a peace imposed by force.

To postpone the inevitable, the Fathers realized that they had to 'draw forth a good representation' (*Federalist* 35). Much of what is criticized as anti-democratic in the Constitution can more sensibly be understood as precisely the reverse: *not* an effort to achieve maximum *imaginable* representation (the government closest to the people) but maximum *feasible* representation -- the sort of republican government which would successfully avoid the disastrous precedents of which history was full, elect men concerned with the public welfare, and provide the most popular government consistent with 'the stability and energy' *Federalist* 37 argued so eloquently it required to survive.

Federalist 36 goes on to insist that left to their own devices, the people would elect as their 'natural representatives' landholders, merchants, and members of the learned professions. (However, 'the door ought to be equally open to all.') Nor was a large number of representatives necessarily good; in vital matters such as taxation, 'nations in general, even under governments of the most popular kind, usually commit the administration of their finances to single men or to boards composed of a few individuals . . . inquisitive and enlightened statesmen.' Similarly, James Wilson argued that in 'large districts' as opposed to the small ones of the state legislatures, congressional candidates of 'intelligence and uprightness' would be more likely (Farrand 1:154). Hamilton even defended the most 'monarchical' aspect of his 'personal, experimental propositions' -- a President for life, holding office unless removed -- as the most 'representative' of the public good.   He predicted 'incalculable mischiefs' from 'too frequent' elections and predicted with chilling accuracy: 'You and I, my friend, may not live to see the day, but most assuredly it will come, when every vital interest of the state will be merged in the all-absorbing question of *who shall be the next* PRESIDENT?' (Farrand 3:409).

In short, the Founding Fathers trusted the people as a whole to agree with Hamilton's analysis of their virtues and limitations in *Federalist* 71:

It is a just observation that the people commonly *intend* the PUBLIC GOOD. This often applies to their very errors. But their good sense would despise the adulator who should pretend that they always *reason right* about the *means* of promoting it. They know from experience that they sometimes err; and the wonder is that they so seldom err as they do.

Or, as Madison put it in *Federalist* 57, 'the aim of every political constitution is or ought to be, first to obtain for rulers men who possess the most wisdom to discern, and most virtue to pursue, the common good of the society.' Why did Madison favor large representative districts: 'in so great a number (of voters) a fit representative would be most likely to be found, so the choice would be less likely to be diverted from him by the intrigues of the ambitious or the bribes of the *rich*' (my emphasis).

In the final analysis, the Founders pinned their hopes for the survival of the republic on the gamble that they provided a framework wherein public-spirited citizens would choose representatives who would reflect the 'general will' rather than the will of all (to use the not inappropriate Rousseauian terminology) and be willing to compromise particularistic interests for the common good. On the last day of the Convention, Franklin summed it up: 'there is no form of government but what may be a blessing to the people if well administered, and [I] believe further that this is likely to be well-administered for a course of years, and can only end in despotism, as other forms have done before it, when the people shall become so corrupted as to need despotic government, being incapable of any other' (Farrand 2:642). More succinctly, as he is supposed to have remarked to a woman who asked if the Convention created a monarchy or a republic, Franklin replied: 'A republic if you can keep it' (Farrand 3:85).

Having discussed what the Founders intended the Constitution to be, we may ask to what extent has it continued to represent adequately a changing republic? Has it successfully guided an open society, where different interests can be reconciled without the stronger overpowering the weaker, where different levels of law can conflict and compete without destroying each other, where public-spirited citizens are still concerned with the perpetuation of such an experiment? Or has the Constitution become a sham, as have so many modelled upon it either cynically or with the greatest of hope, masking a system of repression? Evidence has been presented forcefully on both sides for two hundred years: the strongest case I can make for both follows, with my own effort toward reaching a 'constitutional' synthesis.

The three dangers feared by the Founders -- the dominance of a majority faction, the division of North and South, and the tyranny of an oligarchy -- have all been noted by some of the most powerful observers of the American scene. As early as 1835, echoing the sentiments of the eastern elite with whom he spent much time, French traveller Alexis de Tocqueville coined the phrase 'tyranny of the majority' to describe the most baneful effect of *Democracy in America*. Instead of diverse interests being reconciled politically at the national level, they were suppressed socially at the local level. As modern political parties developed in the 1830's, their first great theorist and organizer, Martin Van Buren, in fact praised them for reconciling diversity within themselves, thereby keeping potentially destabilizing issues out of the national arena (Van Buren 1867).

Such compromises led to the second catastrophe feared by the Framers, a collision between the North and the South. Because the sections could not adjust their differences in the legal spirit the Fathers intended, the Civil War ensued. Dominance not of the northern majority, but of industrial capitalists who profited greatly from the war, resulted. This led to the third of the three tragedies the Founders predicted.

Since the Civil War, social theorists (Lloyd 1894; George 1905; Mills 1956; Domhoff 1967) have called attention to 'robber barons' or a 'power elite' ruling the nation. So have national leaders in their speeches (as in Eisenhower's warning on the 'military-industrial complex'). At the same time, critics of the 'lonely crowd' (Riesman 1953) and 'one dimensional man' (Marcuse 1964) produced by modern society have warned that the oligarchy maintains its rule not merely because opposing interests have difficulty finding a hearing, but because people are cowed by so-called 'public opinion' into not even seeking representation.

One could even argue that modern America has turned into all three of the Fathers' nightmares simultaneously. As mass society cajoles and threatens us to go along with oligarchic leadership and mores, new territories have been added (without representation) to America's empire, not formally, but through economic penetration of underdeveloped countries. These are ruled through local oligarchs who are either directly (CIA, foreign aid) or indirectly (by benefiting from economic dependence) paid off to represent 'North' rather than 'South' America. America measures its greatness in terms of empire, conquest, military power, and wealth vis-a-vis the European systems the republic had rejected, rather than by fidelity to its original goals. So William Graham Sumner argued most eloquently in 'The Conquest of the United States by Spain' (1899) written to protest the Spanish-American War.

Yet there is the other side. Throughout American history, extremes beget reactions which achieve non-revolutionary change. The Progressive and New Deal reforms, the civil rights movement, and anti-war protests in the 1960s were not always met with tolerance, but the sort of repression which would have closed off political debate was neither attempted nor probably even imagined by mainstream political leaders. Of course, this raises a further question: does meaningful change occur in favor of unrepresented groups, or is an elite of the hitherto unrepresented co-opted into the system, forestalling, rather than promoting a wider representation and reconciliation?

Is it possible to reconcile these two visions of America, the elitist and the pluralist, as political scientists call them? Perhaps. The Constitution does not offer representation to any group. It offers the *opportunity* (not an equal opportunity) for groups to be represented, in a evolving political configuration in which those who care about obtaining benefits or achieving the public good are directed to appropriate means of action. Historically, one of the most important of these have been disobedience and protest where laws are perceived to be unjust. The need for extra-legal protest may seem to be an argument that the Constitution has failed. Yet the retrospective validation of protests as diverse as the Civil Rights Movement and the South's 'Lost Cause' by granting representation to excluded groups argues otherwise. Furthermore, the fact that it is even possible to raise these questions, and to find evidence that something like the Constitution intended by the Framers still functions (to be more dogmatic than that and than they would be to contradict oneself) is a presumptive argument that a second 'miracle' has occurred. Not only was the United States able to create a workable republic where diverse interests could be represented, but it has maintained one even when the social structure (an agrarian society of small property holders) upon which it rested has disappeared. In fact, one may postulate that respect for the Constitution itself (however diversely interpreted) has served as a major force in American political development, imposing limits on how far most individuals and groups will go either to seek change or to preserve the status quo. Law not only reflects society -- society may reflect and be molded by law (Wigmore 1928).

Law not only shapes society: it effects a nation's intellectual heritage. This may be observed in the relationship between the philosophy of Charles S. Peirce and the Constitution set up by the Founders. For decades, Peirce was known as the founder of a 'pragmatism' popularized and changed by William James and John Dewey. He is now becoming known as a pioneer theorist in semiotics, the study of how we perceive signs to arrive at interpretations of reality. It is probably not possible to distinguish completely the pragmatic and semiotic aspects of Peirce's complex thinking. However, several features resemble the process of searching for political truth undertaken by the Founding Fathers at the Convention and framed into a methodology by the Constitution. Peirce may in fact have been indirectly influenced by the Founders to coin an 'American' philosophy:

1. Thought is only undertaken to relieve doubt -- 'There must be a real and living doubt and without this all discussion is idle.' 'The irritation of doubt causes a struggle to attain a state of belief' (CP 5.373, 397). Historically, Peirce interpreted this to mean that in periods of catastrophe, such as the state of the infant republic in 1787, 'cataclasmine' or 'anancastic' evolution is possible (CP 6.312-314). Real thinking, new ideas, progress comes out of an effort to solve overwhelming problems.

2. Thought is only undertaken by a community -- Even the loneliest thinker in his study addresses a community of inquirers -- that is, he projects his thought

into the future -- and uses a community-inspired body of signs (words, ways of thinking). And thinking is seldom performed by such isolated people. Peirce writes that 'the very origin of the concept of reality shows that this conception essentially involves the notion of a COMMUNITY' (CP 5.313). 'Unless truth be recognized as public -- as that of which any person would come to be convinced if he carried his inquiry, his sincere search for immovable belief, far enough -- then there will be nothing to prevent each of us from adopting an utterly futile belief of his own which all the rest will disbelieve' (Peirce 1903-1911:26). The Founding Fathers were exactly such a community -- people engaged in a 'sincere search' for the principles which would establish political truth and enable a workable republic to survive. They too realized that future Americans would have to continue the quest for political truth upon pain of dissolving the community.

3. Thought proceeds by the testing of hypotheses -- Peirce termed these 'abductions,' which came from surprising facts or guesses. He was not very interested in where they came from (CP 6.469). What was important was that an agreed-upon methodology to test the workability of the hypothesis evolved. The United States may be regarded as a (politically) philosophical guess, to be tested over time by a community through a methodology (the Constitution) which is dependent on the inquirers (citizens) retaining an interest in the truth (public welfare) -- at least to the extent of preserving the methodology or Constitution. If the republic 'works' pragmatically, political decision-making will be a true 'sign' and a real representation of the nation's social diversity. The Founders themselves interpreted their work in this manner, and frequently referred to the Constitution as an 'experiment' made in accordance with the latest knowledge of 'political science' (Farrand 2:284; 3:37, 303).

From whence came Peirce's own philosophy? In his autobiographical writings, he describes two communities which most influenced his thought.

Peirce's father, Benjamin, American's foremost mathematician of the early nineteenth century, was a Harvard professor who lived right in the yard. At his father's house in the 1850s, the younger Peirce 'was forced to think hard and continuously' by the assemblage of intellectuals who visited. In personal distinction, diversity of backgrounds, ideas, interests, and concern with representing American ideals and culture to the world, they may truly be considered an intellectual community similar to the Founding Fathers. There was one major difference: not only were distinguished men of politics present (Daniel Webster, Rufus Choate, and Charles Sumner -- the last of whom Peirce considered 'absurd', by the way) -- but a judge (Joseph Story), two poets (Henry Wadsworth Longfellow, James Russell Lowell), a historian (George Bancroft), a philosopher (Ralph Waldo Emerson), and even a 'liberated' woman (Margaret Fuller). Later in the 1870s, Peirce and his generation set up a 'Metaphysical Club' in Cambridge to consider great issues: a discussion group formed including philosophers William James and Chauncey Wright, John Fiske, and jurist Oliver Wendell Holmes in addition to Peirce himself (CP 5.12-13; 6.12).

The parallel between the Founders and these self-constituted communities goes further. Historians of nineteenth century America frequently note the 'status anxiety' of the New England intelligentsia, manifested most acutely in the Adams family from John Quincy to Henry and Brooks, in the public education, peace, and women's movements, and in the abolitionist crusade. As power and wealth moved away from the guardians of New England's and the nation's conscience, the spiritual sons and daughters of the Fathers depicted a republic in peril, under the dominion of greed, conformity, and stupidity, in need of intellectual, moral, and political redemption (Rothman 1971; Hofstadter 1955).

In short, the community at Benjamin Peirce's house, the community Charles and his generation re-created in the 1870s, the community he hoped to establish at Arisbe in the 1890s (Pencak 1985), and the disinterested philosophical community of truth-seekers he postulated in his writings may all be regarded as heirs of the Founders' community at Philadelphia in 1787. Unwilling to succumb to the forces of self-interest prevalent at the time, men believing themselves possessed of superior wisdom and virtue undertook the salvation of America and through it, of the human race. In Emerson's words, they were the 'Representative Men' who periodically regenerate the world (Emerson 1849).

Peirce stressed the ideas of community, disinterestedness, and evolution of thought out of doubt and catastrophe throughout his life. The reconciliation of differences -- that a methodology can be established to bring order out of disorder in knowledge (semiotics) while preserving the sciences and humanities in their respective realms -- is the philosophical application of the political solution invented by the Founders of the American Republic: that unity and order are possible without destroying freedom and diversity. Peirce makes the political roots of his ideas explicit in one of his earliest essays, 'The Place of Our Age in the History of Civilization' (Peirce 1863: 101-114).

Much as the Founding Fathers saw a republic in peril, Peirce identifies a crisis in western civilization based upon his philosophy of history. He constructs six ages of about 325 years each: the rise of Christianity (0-325 A.D.); the age of migration (barbarian invasions from 325-650); the establishment of modern nations (650-975); the Crusades (975-1300); the age of Reformation (1300-1650); and the age of Reason (1650-2000).

Peirce's chronology is more than slightly off. The Crusades did not begin until 1095, the Reformation until 1519. However, he is really interested in demonstrating serious failings in the age of progress and reason, much like the problems which brought about the fall of Rome and the rise of Christianity. He thereby hoped to show his own civilization's potential for regeneration. Peirce would continue to write on history and civilization in this vein for the rest of his life, most notably in 'Evolutionary Love' (CP 6.290-314).

Peirce's description of conditions in the late Roman Empire becomes especially interesting when contrasted with his analysis of flaws in the age of Reason:

> The age of the rise of Christianity presents no other event which has had any influence upon the destinies of mankind. The whole era must be interpreted according to that central fact. For what do we see? A complete centralization of power in the Emperor, so that subjects had no rights whatever. Here is a very remarkable thing, that Rome, so distinguished for her ethical ideas, should have lost sight of the reciprocity of right and duty, altogether.

The nineteenth century is the new Rome:

> Are we then to go on forever toying with electricity and steam, whether in the laboratory or in business, and never use these means in the broad field of humanity and social destiny? I seem, perhaps, to sneer at what you respect. And I confess we have utilized a little surplus energy in the business of philanthropy on our triumphant road to wooing things. But I agree with the man [Emerson] who says of this age that. . . . Things are in the saddle, and ride mankind.

Peirce is here making good use of his own intellectual community, especially the great Emerson. Just as the lions of law could sit down with the lambs of poetry at the Peirce manse in Cambridge, so could a new age come out of the old, where poetry and religion, science and philosophy, materialism and idealism, man and nature, could be reconciled in a community pivoted on 'the fulcrum [which] has yet to be found that shall enable the lever of love to move the world.'

To return to the parallel with the Founding Fathers: they 'abducted' a republic from the ruins of history. With a government addressed to a potentially infinite community of inquirers after the public good, they devised the Constitution as a model within which this inquiry could take place. Peirce, influenced by an intellectual community similar to the Philadelphia Convention, 'abducted' a philosophy from the ruins of 'progress' and 'experimented' with a new methodology, capable of uniting spheres of knowledge in an open-ended quest for truth which he offered to the future as a means of spiritual, intellectual, and moral salvation. He thereby hoped to start a republic of seekers after truth, lovers of the unified harmony and love hidden behind the universe's multi-layered signs, comprised of 'representatives' of the arts and sciences, a symbolic extension of the reconciliation at Philadelphia to all realms of logic and life:

> When the conclusion of our age comes, and skepticism and materialism have done their perfect work we shall have a far greater faith than ever before. . . . Ah! What a heavenly harmony will that be when all the sciences, one as viol, another as flute, another as trump, shall peal forth in that majestic symphony of which the noble organ of astronomy forever sounds the theme.

REFERENCES

Adair, Douglas, 1974, *Fame and the Founding Fathers*, New York: Norton.

Adams, John, 1787, *A Defense of the Constitutions of the United States of America,* ed. Charles F. Adams, Boston: Little, Brown, 1850-1856, vol. 4.

Beard, Charles A., 1913, *An Economic Interpretation of the Constitution,* New York, Macmillan.

DeTocqueville, Alexis, 1835, *Democracy in America,* trans. Henry Reeve, New York: The Colonial Press, c. 1900.

Domhoff, G. William, 1967, *Who Rules America?* Englewood Cliffs: Prentice-Hall.

Elkins, Stanley and McKitrick, Eric, 'The Founding Fathers: Young Men of the American Revolution,' *Political Science Quarterly*, 1961, 181-216.

Emerson, Ralph Waldo, 1849, *Representative Men,* Boston: Philips, Sampson.

Farrand, Max, 1911, *The Records of the Federal Convention of 1787,* 4 volumes, New Haven: Yale University Press. A collection of several hundred documents including James Madison's notes of the Convention.

Federalist, The, 1788, Numerous editions usually cited, as here, by number. Authors Alexander Hamilton, John Jay, James Madison.

George, Henry, 1905, *The Menace of Privilege,* New York: Grosset & Dunlap.

Hamilton, Alexander, 1778, Letter of Hamilton, in *The Papers of Alexander Hamilton,* eds. Harold C. Syrett and Jacob E. Cooke, New York: Columbia University Press, 1961, 1, 580.

Hofstadter, Richard, 1955, *The Age of Reform,* New York: Knopf.

Jefferson, Thomas, 1816, Letter to Samuel Kercheval in *The Complete Jefferson,* ed. Saul K. Padover, New York: Duel, Sloan & Pierce, 1943, 291.

Kevelson, Roberta, 1986, 'Prologomena to a Comparative Legal Semiotic,' in *Frontiers in Semiotics,* eds. John Deely, Brooke Williams, and Felicia E. Kruse, Bloomington: Indiana University Press, 191-198.

Lloyd, Henry Demarest, 1894, *Wealth Against Commonwealth,* New York: Harper Brothers.

Main, Jackson Turner, 1961, *The Anti-Federalists,* Chapel Hill: University of North Carolina Press.

Marcuse, Herbert, 1964, *One-Dimensional Man,* Boston: Beacon Press.

Mills, C. Wright, 1956, *The Power Elite,* New York: Oxford University Press.

Paine, Thomas, 1776, *Common Sense,* in *Writings of Thomas Paine,* ed. M. D. Conway, New York: 1894-1896, vol. 1.

Peirce, Charles Sanders. The abbreviation *CP* followed by volume number(s) separated from paragraph number(s) by a period, is to the eight volume *Collected Papers of Charles Sanders Peirce,* vols. I-VI, ed. Charles Hartshorne and Paul Weiss, Cambridge, MA: Harvard University Press, 1931-1935; vols. VII and VIII, ed. Arthur W. Burks, Cambridge, MA: Harvard University Press, 1958.

_____, 1863, 'The Place of Our Age in the History of Civilization,' in *Writings of Charles S. Peirce,* ed. Max H. Fisch, et al., Bloomington: Indiana University Press, 1982, vol. 1, 101-114.

_____, 1903-1911, *Charles S. Peirce's Letters to Lady Welby,* ed. I.C. Leib, New Haven: Whitlock's, 1953.

Pencak, William, 1985, 'Charles Sanders Perice and Arisbe,' included in this volume.

Riesman, David, 1953, *The Lonely Crowd,* Garden City: Doubleday.

Rossiter, Clinton, 1966, *1787: The Grand Convention,* New York: Macmillan.

Rothman, David J., 1971, *The Discovery of the Asylum,* Boston: Beacon Press.

Sumner, William Graham, 1899, 'The Conquest of the United States by Spain,' *Yale Law Journal,* 8, 168-193.

Van Buren, Martin, 1867, *Inquiry into the Origin and Course of Political Parties in the United States,* New York: Augustus M. Kelley.

Washington, George, 1787, Letter to Bushrod Washington in Carl Van Doren, *The Great Rehearsal,* New York: The Viking Press, 1948, 164.

Wigmore, John H., 1928, *A Panorama of the World's Legal Systems,* 3 volumes, St. Paul: West.

Wood, Gordon S., 1969, *The Creation of the American Republic, 1776-1787,* Chapel Hill: University of North Carolina Press.

Chapter 11

The Sign of Francis Lieber

In April 1863, the very month the United States government adopted his code of war, political theorist and Columbia University Professor Francis Lieber (1798-1873) decided to construct a personal symbol. At first he thought of an eagle, resting on the words 'Our Country' which appeared on a globe.[1] Such a sign would show the German immigrant's gratitude toward the land that had been his home since 1826, when his native Prussia found his support for representative government too threatening.[2] He wanted the eagle, a traditional symbol for the United States, to be at rest, for during the turbulent years of the Civil War 'we ought to bring back the American eagle to its original nature of repose.' However, Lieber soon rejected the globe, preferring to perch the bird on a simple pedestal engraved 'Our Country.' The superimposition of a symbol of the United States over the entire planet was too imperialistic for so fervent a republican, even one who advised President Lincoln on legal matters.

The symbol Lieber finally adopted, which adorned his stationery and which he asked to have carved on his grave, was quite different. Gone was 'Our Country' as well as the globe. What remained might be considered an abstract bird in flight. One wing read 'No Right without its Duty'; the other, 'No Duty without its Right.' Much as he loved his adopted country, Lieber worked his way beyond patriotism to symbolize the international, universal matters his writings considered and the impact he (correctly) hoped they would have.[3] As he wrote in a letter the year before his death, 'From early youth I have had a peculiar love for these formulations of great truths.' Yet as he continued, he had 'formed and fashioned this maxim against all absolutism private or public, monarchical or democratic, political or purely social, ecclesiastical, in private law or public.'[4] As one who loved 'great truths' but despised absolutism in every form, Lieber's balanced sign thus explains his attraction for a semiotic legal philosophy. The rejections of reference to the United States in the symbol suggest that for all his genuine nationalism, Lieber was too intelligent to believe any one nation could possess an ideal political or legal system.

Of all legal theorists, it is logical that Lieber put so much thought into creating a personal motto and symbol. In his *Legal and Political Hermeneutics* (1839) he advanced a system of legal interpretation based on semiotic principles. His ethical theory, although it relied heavily on Kant and natural law, still introduced a semiotic element by using historical examples as signs to search for moral laws. Finally, it is quite possible that Lieber influenced Peirce given similarities in their thought and the fact that they had important friends in common.

Lieber begins with the idea that 'there is no direct communication between the minds of men' (p. 13).[5] We only communicate through 'signs,' that is, 'manifestations of the inward man' (pp. 13-14). Lieber puts forth the interesting idea that we act (put out signs) first and ask questions (interpret them) later: 'There is a primeval principle in man which ever urges him with irresistible power to represent outwardly what moves him strongly within' (p. 14). By extension, 'in no case are words, originally, produced in a finished state by the reflective intellect . . . but on the contrary, things, actions (rather activities), in short phenomena, present themselves as a whole, with a number of adjuncts, a mass of adhesion, and become in the course of time only, enlarged in their meaning to generic terms' (p. 26). Lieber thus set up his theory in direct opposition to the utilitarianism of Jeremy Bentham: man's 'anxious desire of utterance is independent of any principle of utility' and in fact arises from man's 'innate love of the beautiful' (p. 15). Man is the animal who puts forth signs *and then* interprets them.

Nevertheless, although signs are simply givens whether consciously intended or not, interpretation 'in its widest meaning is the discovery and representation of the true meaning of any signs, used to convey ideas.' And that 'true meaning' is that which 'those who used them were desirous of expressing' (p. 17). Now before we get our semiotic hackles up and start telling Lieber there is no 'true' meaning, let us remember his symbol and explanation for it: he loves great truths but detests any system which claims to have found 'the truth.' No sooner has Lieber told us that 'good faith in interpretation means that we conscientiously desire to arrive at the truth, that we honestly use all means to do so, and that we strive to adhere to it, when known to us' (p. 93), than he spends most of his book explaining why true meaning will forever elude us. He takes the simplest of cases: a man says to his servant 'Bring me some soup.' These four little words require a sophisticated if largely understood interpretation if their 'true' meaning would be discovered: what sort of soup? how much? served in what manner? at what time? (p. 28) If even a simple command like this is problematic, then laws and legal codes are infinitely more so. Lieber writes that to 'truly' understand a speech we 'must seek in the whole life and experience of the speaker for a key' (p. 155), clearly a bottomless pit. In short, Lieber concludes, 'all law codes are doubtful cases' and 'it would indeed be a subject greatly to be deplored -- happily it is not -- to produce a code so constructed as to be closed forever' (p. 43).

But because we cannot discover the truth definitively does not mean we should strive to do so whimsically. It is essential that 'we proceed in doing so, on safe ground, according to rules established by reason and not arbitrarily' (p. 28). Lieber spends most of his book outlining what these rules are. First, in a notion all Peirceans would instantly recognize -- that truth is provisionally held and constantly changing among a community of inquirers one hopes are dedicated to discovering truth -- Lieber insists that legal interpretation is a matter of civic life and national quest, toward which treatises and statutes are means rather than definitive statements: 'It is one of the most efficacious agents in the civil progress of a nation, that certain principles being established, they should be left to unfold themselves gradually, and to be expanded, modified, and limited by the civil action of the nation itself, by the practical political intercourse of society' (p. 43).

Much of what Lieber suggests is common sense: legal 'words are to be taken according to their customary, not their original or classical significance' (p. 167). 'The same rules which common sense teaches everyone to use, in order to understand his neighbor . . . are necessary likewise, *although not sufficient*, for the interpretation of texts or documents of the highest importance' (p. 28 -- my emphasis). Although not sufficient? What is?

Paradoxically, the clearest and best laws are those which leave room for doubt, that is, construction, or semiotic interpretation. Lieber writes that 'construction signifies the representation of an entire whole from given elements' (p. 61), or when reading law 'the drawing of conclusions respecting subjects, that are beyond the direct experience of the text, from elements known from and given in the text' (p. 56). Laws are like the man asking for soup: 'If we strive to go beyond plain clearness and perspicacity, the more do we increase, in fact, the chances of sinister interpretation' (p. 32). Lieber argues that the greatest men in political life have tended to express themselves with 'the few essential points, upon which the action depends' (p. 159).

Lieber then assesses strengths and weaknesses of different forms of construction. The best, most useful, and necessary forms of construction are also the most dangerous, he argues, because they cannot lay claim to a spurious absolute authority: 'Many things are dangerous, yet we cannot dispense with them nevertheless' (p. 64). To take an example from Lieber's *Political Ethics*,[6] he applauded English Chief Justice Mansfield's decision to charge a prisoner guilty of stealing a valuable article with a theft of under twenty shillings to avoid the death penalty:

> What then did this verdict mean, disagreeing as it did, according to the letter, with the facts? It meant that the prisoner ought not to die according to eternal justice; according to the truth of the law, which is to punish crime, not commit enormity; . . . It is the spirit of words, not that which I arbitrarily or fraudulently supply, but which they ought to have in the spirit of truth, which decides their truth, and real meaning, not their form.

In other words, laws are signs of human striving for justice, security, peace, and well-being, and must be so interpreted. In fact, the worst ways to interpret legal texts are in what Lieber terms 'literal' and 'predestined' manners. 'Literal interpretation is a most deceptive term, [as] under the guise of strict adherence to words it wrenches them from their sense' (p. 68). And to haul in an authoritative text such as *The Bible* to give meaning to other texts or contexts is to make interpretation 'subservient to dogmas. . . . It is not genuine interpretation . . . it corresponds to what might be called in ratiocination ex post facto reasoning (p. 72).

In keeping with his symbol, Lieber's other rules of interpretation stress balancing social and political forces to prevent any party from gaining undue power and thereby a monopoly of the right to interpret the law. Texts should be interpreted to favor the non-privileged over the privileged (p. 129), the weak over the powerful (p. 141), and the rights of citizens and the legislature over the executive: 'The Constitution of the United States bestows prerogatives upon the President, which might deprive the people of all liberty, the moment they should become indifferent enough to allow it' (p. 181, 211). Lieber especially warned of 'necessity' (p. 185), 'precedent' (p. 194 -- 'the most absolute chiefs of semi-civilized tribes are pleased to find real or pretended rules for their actions in the examples of their forefathers'), and 'transcendent construction' (p. 185 -- e.g. this and not that is what God wants) as threats to liberty and legal interpretation evolving within a community in its historical complexity. He concluded:

> In short let, with a manly nation, everything that is in favor of power, be closely construed. Everything in favor of the security of the citizen, the protection of the individual, comprehensively [construed] for the simple reason that power is power, and therefore able to take care of itself as well as tending, by its nature, to increase, while the citizen wants protection. (p. 188)

Therefore, the community which preserves human freedom also preserves flexible, evolving standards of legal interpretation. These are paradoxically the best when they avoid fixing the truth at a particular point in text or time.

Lieber's hermeneutics may strike some at first as inconsistent with his ethics, which are heavily based on natural law and the idea that all human beings possess rights as human beings.[7] But Lieber unlike Kant does not regard morality as a priori.   He undertakes an elaborate historical study to ground ethics in empirical fact: he demonstrates to his satisfaction that all nations have basically the same moral code.   Even among the cruelest barbarians, and gangs of thieves, members of the community may not be murdered.   Conversely civilized nations have been known to practice cruelty barbarians could not match, as in the conquest of empires.   Hypocrisy, the tribute vice pays to virtue, is also a symbol of morality.   The most despicable tyrants in history (Louis XIV seems to win that dubious honor -- Lieber disliked the French and never let anyone forget he fought at the Battle of Waterloo) tried to cloak their most evil actions using ethical justifications to appeal to the general moral sense.   Morality is known to us through our feelings, but it is confirmed by historical 'signs.'[8]

Lieber offers a criticism of Kant near the end of his *Political Ethics* which opens the path for reconciliation of his two great works (pp. 451-454).   Kant would argue that we must tell a man who would murder our friend that the friend is in our house, as lying is morally wrong under any circumstances: if we willed our action a universal law and people lied all the time, then life would be impossible.   But Lieber responds: 'The whole essay seems to me inconsistent, from a desire for consistency.'   We also need to consider 'the right which he who asks has to ask, and the wickedness of his purpose.'   The decision not to tell the truth, Lieber admits, is dangerous,' but 'no more so than a thousand other truths.' In other words, ethical action depends not on the inflexible and automatic application of a principle, but on semiotic reflection: judgment of a speech act (request for information about the friend) based on the speaker, context, code (the tone of the request, for instance), and audience.   'We have in no case moral rules which for each practical case are absolute,' Lieber continues.   'We have always to judge and weigh.   Yet, although dangerous, it is infinitely better boldly to approach the truth and state its precise character, than to give abstract rules which cannot, and every one feels ought not, to be applied.' The word 'dangerous' here appears twice, as it did in Lieber's discussion of judicial construction: freedom and action are dangerous if we would abandon automatic obedience to authority. They are also necessary.

By realizing speech is an action performed in a context, Lieber is able to offer a second criticism of Kant: he 'restricts his remarks upon speaking to words only.' Offering a parallel argument to his idea that we know morality through signs appearing in history, Lieber shows cases of both speech and action where deception is 'the unanimous voice of mankind': a physician lies about his patient's condition when he knows the truth will aggravate the disease; parents hide delicate facts from children; victims of persecution escape under false identities; and writers use pseudonyms in times of persecution. Lieber then states explicitly that he has 'not found the precise truth.' What he has done is to initiate the correct line of questioning: 'let others state their views, but let us not either pass over the subject in silence, or state rules with an absoluteness which no one does or can carry them out, which necessarily produces therefore that evil which invariably follows the acknowledgement of a moral rule in theory and its frequent disregard in practice.' As in legal construction, the best 'laws' in morality are flexible ones created through community discourse. They do not attempt to fix absolute rules for the application of moral standards once and for all.

Let us therefore judge Lieber by the spirit of his remarks rather than the letter, a standard he himself applied to the law. He clearly used natural rights and natural law in so different a context from Kant and the Enlightenment theorists that in their sense he was not using them at all.

Lieber's sense of how rights came about appears most vividly in his philosophy of history. Lieber believed, like a good nineteenth century liberal, that more nations were becoming civilized and that civility and representative government went hand in hand. 'To speak of civilized nations, that government ought to be called good which only protects and in which every man can obtain justice . . . that government which has in itself the peculiar expansiveness as well as the organization which not only allows, but necessarily leads to, farther and farther political development, and goes on raising the individual as a human being' (pp. 317-318). By extension, 'no greater bane can befall society' than the existence of 'knowledge, industry, and civilization' in a nation 'in which a large class is nevertheless excluded from them. They then become the very incentives and hot-beds of vice and crime' (p. 457). To go one step further, 'the multiplicity of civilized nations, their distinct independence (without which there would be enslaving Universal Monarchy), and their increasing resemblance and agreement, are some of the great safeguards of our civilization.' From a common alphabet, clothes, even children's toys, music, literature, science, visions of government, and international law, the spread of civilization could be demonstrably proven through such 'signs.'[9] Thus, nations, like people, excluded from civilization's benefits were likely to resort to 'vice and crime' on the international level. It is no wonder Lieber concludes his *Political Ethics* with a discussion of 'Wealth', on the grounds that 'a generally diffused desire of independence is an absolute requisite for a free and moral action' (p. 460). Such independence could not be obtained, either for a nation or an individual, without a modicum of wealth to secure leisure for mental and moral development. Hence, Lieber envisions civilization as an expanding community of nations and individuals within nations, empowered to participate in the discussion and (provisional) definition of law. If he insists that all individuals ought to enjoy liberty, justice, and safety, his symbol tells us that 'right' is contingent upon duty -- that is, involvement in a specific community as an active inquirer honestly seeking an always elusive yet always inspiring perfection. To put it somewhat paradoxically, we don't have rights, (natural or otherwise) we develop them. We aren't subject to law, natural or otherwise. As civilization develops, we create law.

Peirce scholars will be familiar with the idea of truth as provisionally held, inquiry as an action occurring in a particular social context to solve real doubts and problems, and the need for a community of inquirers to hone methods of investigation to insure real progress in knowledge. They will also recognize from Lieber's work Peirce's contention that we can only get at 'what is out there' through signs. Even the simplest experience or most obvious case requires interpretation of signs according to codes and contexts which are both communally based and yet, through the actions of the interpreter, continually changing in new directions. What may not be known is that Peirce was probably familiar with Lieber's work: the latter acquired great fame as the author of the Union's Code of War during the Civil War. Two members of Peirce's circle in Cambridge during these years were Justice Joseph Story and Senator Charles Sumner, both of whom were regular correspondents of Lieber. And there is one tantalizing passage in Peirce's 1863 essay 'The Place of Our Age in the History of Civilization,' which remarks that 'Rome, so distinguished for her ethical ideas, should have lost sight of the reciprocity of right and duty, altogether.'[10]   This was the sign of Francis Lieber.

Lieber's sensitivity to signs as the means by which we experience reality is most notable in his perceptions of the American Civil War. He especially cared about the symbolic aspects of nationalism. Symbols hold nations together. 'The more roads and means of communications. . . the more it becomes one country,' he noted, realizing that the United States' greatest 'road' was the Mississippi River. He described it as 'the permanent idea in the union fervor of the West . . . their symbol of Union.'[11]   Another important symbol was the President, especially President Lincoln. Anticipating the Republicans' wartime decision to recast themselves as a 'Union' party, which nominated Tennessee Democrat Andrew Johnson for Vice-President in 1864, Lieber observed that 'in proportion as the President is an honest and truthful man,' he will be 'conscious of being the symbol of the nation and not of a particular party.' This would make his practical administration more difficult by requiring him to reconcile Union Democrats as well as the factions within his own party, but Lieber believed the effort worth the incalculable payoffs.[12]

For Lieber, Lincoln's death also served as a symbol to remind the North of the great purpose it acquired while fighting the Civil War: the abolition of slavery. The martyred President, according to Lieber, became 'that representative of our imperilled nationality, of the national end to extirpate the evil and deadly institution which has imperilled it.' Lieber suggested to Senator Charles Sumner that the nation erect a bronze statue of Lincoln in front of the Capitol. This was 'politically necessary in practically every way,' to teach 'every Southern member [of Congress] while he loiters along Pennsylvania Avenue all the South has done.' Lieber incidentally pleaded that the design be 'different from the wretched Washington and Jackson disgracing now the public places of the city.'[13] He would undoubtedly have applauded the Lincoln Memorial, and its magnificent symbolic use by the civil rights and anti-Vietnam war movements.

Lieber also placed great stock in parades and ceremonies, especially those which elevated the estimation of black Americans in the eyes of whites. He regarded the march through the streets of Boston of the Fifty-Fourth Massachusetts regiment, the North's first comprised of black soldiers, as demonstrating 'the manly bearing of the men and the serious character of the bystanders.' The parade stood as a 'symbol of a most important historic turn of events and thoughts.' When even New York, which had witnessed the horrendous anti-black and draft riots of 1863, honored one of its own black regiments the following year, Lieber regarded it as 'one of the greatest days in our history.' Such events confirmed the sacrifice of black troops and the worthiness of blacks for freedom.[14]

If the character of its symbols showed the North's elevated purpose and cemented the union, the degenerate symbols of the South conveyed the opposite impression. In his capacity as curator of the captured Confederate archives at the end of the war, Lieber came across entries from a contest to design a new Confederate flag. He found 'no elevation of thought, no high-mindedness, no culture, not even the elements of these qualities,' in the submitted designs. They displayed instead, 'crudeness, coarseness, and puerility.' He especially noted one effort 'which stands forth, almost sublimely, in absurdity.' It proposed 'as a symbol of the Southern Confederacy a Negro carrying a globe with the motto Deus ordinat illud. . . . The grotesqueness, the stupendous stupidity of the fellow, the rascally Latin, which shows that he had in mind the delicate phrase 'God ordains that' all combine to make one acknowledge that it is an unfortunately fit symbolism of the South.' Other submissions included stars arranged in the Southern Cross and seven stars resting on a golden cotton bag.[15]

Another symbol of the South was the massacre of captured black Union troops at Fort Pillow. It showed the South's decline into barbarism. 'In political economy, in morals, in science, in culture, in civilization, destruction and dilapidation are quick,' Lieber noted. 'Growth and development are slow.'[16] The South, he believed, destroyed its overrated chivalry in addition to its economic foundations by undertaking the war.

Lieber considered one of the most important symbols of the Civil War to be the Code of War he drew up. The Union army adopted it in 1863. The first such code in history, it covered treatment of prisoners of war, spies, guerrillas, and runaway slaves, and prohibited plundering and atrocities. Lieber also attempted to define military necessity so as to protect civilian rights while adjusting to the 'total war' against Southern society waged by Grant and Sherman. Lieber applauded his friend, Union Chief of Staff General Henry W. Halleck, who authorized the code, as a proof of 'scientific zeal and earnestness . . . in the development and stability of the public conditions and relations of your country.' The Code itself was 'a symbol of the Law of Nations spreading its wings wider and wider over the globe.'[17]

Lieber was right. The French and Germans adopted his Code just in time for the Franco-Prussian War. It subsequently became the basis of the Hague and Geneva Conventions and remains the core of the United States armed forces' code of conduct to this day. It provides a splendid illustration of Peirce's notion that a community of inquirers sincerely devoted to perfecting a field of knowledge can seize upon an 'abduction' or hypothesis and make a difference in the world. If war has become more terrible in the twentieth century, it has at the same time engendered a body of law which holds up the perpetrators of the atrocities to world-wide execration and punishment. In some unmeasurable way, it has lessened human suffering.[18]

One example of how Lieber applied the Code of War in an especially semiotic manner was his rejection of the idea that the North assassinate Confederate leaders, particularly Jefferson Davis. He argued:

> Although he represents the state to us, in his hostility to ours, more than any one else, being the visible representation of the executive, he is also the concentrated representative of all that is not hostile in the state, of all that remains removed beyond the just act of the war, e.g. women, children, private property, etc. and we could not assassinate the representative of hostility without at the same time

killing the representative of the more general humanity in the hostile state.

Furthermore, assassination 'would lead to deplorable evils which would greatly impede the ultimate end of the war' -- 'qui est Paix.'[19] By placing mutual restraints on the manner in which they fought, civilized nations not only reduced destruction and suffering but prevented initiating an indefinitely expanding circle of escalated atrocities. Limitations also rendered peaceful reconciliation at the close of hostilities between victor and vanquished easier, and thus contributed in the long run to a peaceful climate. In historical perspective, Lieber may be criticized for overestimating men's ability to restrain themselves in war, but he cannot be faulted for his acute diagnosis of the consequences resulting from their failure to do so.

Lieber had a typical nineteenth century liberal's faith in the progress of civilization as represented by the western European nations. However, it was Lieber's special insight to formulate a list of signs which demonstrated how such nations were developing common laws and acquiring a common history. These 'outward signs' included the same alphabet, mathematical and musical notation, dress and fashion, systems of economics and manners, the gold/silver currency standard, jury trials, rights of citizens, division of government powers into executive, legislative, and judicial, monogamy, arts and sciences, and educational systems. For Lieber, the western world was what Peirce would have called a community inquiring not just into the truth of scientific problems, but into the truth of a good society, and realizing it increasingly through common cooperative effort. Looking at the situation from 1991, where western institutions are spreading now to the Third World through adoption of capitalist economics and political democracy, can we say that Lieber was wrong? Were the World Wars and

Communist interlude refutations of his thesis, or merely tragic interruptions of a general process?[20]

If civilization was progressing, even through the greatest war of the nineteenth century, Lieber's view of life was by no means entirely optimistic. He used the Civil War itself as a sign of human existence: 'We are all on a battlefield. Those that drop, drop; and those that cannot drop must fight until they too drop. Blessed are those who fight and fall in a righteous cause, but all must fight and fall in this life which is life only as far as it is struggle.'[21] By devoting his entire life to his inquiries into philosophical issues and their social application, culminating with his epoch-making code of war, Lieber proved himself worthy of a remark he made in his 1861 lectures at Columbia University:

> It would be a noble topic for a prize essay to discuss the influence of philosophical jurists and historians on the intercourse between nations in war as well as peace and to show how ideas of justice, honor, and mercy, far in advance of practice when first uttered by the lonely intellect of the jurist, have gradually worked themselves into acknowledgment.[22]

ENDNOTES

1.   Francis Lieber to Samuel B. Ruggles, April 14, 1863 and April 20, 1863, Lieber Papers, Library of Congress, Washington, DC.

2.   The best source of biographical information on Lieber is Frank Freidel, *Francis Lieber*, Baton Rouge: Louisiana State University Press, 1947.

3.   For Lieber's impact on international law -- his code of war became the basis of all future codes and conventions, see Freidel, *Lieber,* 338-341; for his impact on semiotics and legal theory, see Roberta Kevelson, *The Law as a System of Signs*, New York: Plenum, 1988, 205-212.

4.   Lieber to Benson Lossing, August 20, 1872, Lieber Papers, Library of Congress.

5.   Francis Lieber, *Legal and Political Hermeneutics*, Boston: Little, Brown, 1839, is the source for all references in this section of the paper except as noted in n. 6.

6.   Francis Lieber, *Manual of Politics Ethics, Volume 1*, 2nd ed.; Philadelphia: Lippincott, 1888, 452.

7.   *Ibid.* is the source for all quotations in the next few pages except as noted in n. 9.

8.   *Ibid.*, 42-48, 74-89.

9.   Francis Lieber, *Miscellaneous Writings, Volume 2*, Philadelphia: Lippincott, 1881, 240-243.

10. Charles S. Peirce, 'The Place of Our Age in the History of Civilization,' in *Writings of Charles S. Peirce*, ed. Max H. Fisch, et al., Bloomington: Indiana University Press, 1982, vol. 1, 101-114. See also Kevelson as cited in n. 3.

11. Francis Lieber to Samuel B. Ruggles, September 22, 1862, Lieber Papers, Library of Congress.

12. Francis Lieber to Edward Bates, June 13, 1862, Lieber Papers, Huntington Library, San Marino, California.

13. Francis Lieber to Charles Sumner, April 26, 1865 and October 20, 1865, Lieber Papers, Huntington Library.

14. Francis Lieber to Charles Sumner, June 8, 1863 and May 6, 1864, Lieber Papers, Huntington Library.

15. Francis Lieber to Henry Drisler, October 18, 1865, Lieber Papers, Huntington Library.

16. Francis Lieber to Martin Russell Thayer, March 23, 1864, Lieber Papers, Huntington Library.

17. Francis Lieber to Henry Halleck, October 4, 1863 and March 20, 1866, Lieber Papers, Huntington Library.

18. Good general discussions of the code include, Frank Freidel, 'General Orders 100 and Military Government,' *Mississippi Valley Historical Review*, 32, 1946, 541-556 and James F. Childless, 'Francis Lieber's Interpretation of the Laws of War: General Orders No. 100 in the Context of His Life and Thought,' *American Journal of Jurisprudence*, 21, 1976, 34-70.

19. Francis Lieber, 'Notes and Clippings on the Law of War from 1840 to 1866,' Lieber Papers, Huntington Library.

20. Francis Lieber, Lectures, 'Introduction to the Law of Nations,' November 23, 1863, Lieber Papers, Huntington Library.

21. Francis Lieber to Charles Sumner, December 24, 1864, Lieber Papers, Huntington Library.

22. Francis Lieber, Columbia University Lectures on War, 1861-1862, Booklet 2, Lieber Papers, Johns Hopkins University.

Chapter 12

Legality, Legitimacy and the American Middle Class

This paper considers a problem in legal history which the semiotic method of Charles Sanders Peirce may help address. Throughout American history, middle class communities (hereafter MCC) have committed, justified, and escaped punishment for technically illegal acts of violence committed against dissenters from their values. (For convenience, I will call these dissenters the 'counter-culture' or CC.) Examples include frontier vigilantes, the Ku Klux Klan, and colonials tarring and feathering Tories during the Revolution. In this paper, I will investigate three episodes of middle class-violence -- anti-abolitionist riots of the 1830s, the 'Red Scare' following World War I, and the 'white backlash' of the 1960s. (Principal information for these eras in this paper from Richards [1970]; Murray [1955]; and M. Friedman [1971] and Rogin [1971]).

Semiotically, I hope to show that as a 'sign' of the MCC, crowd violence reveals a whole system of signs which point to the fundamental moral and behavioral code of the MCC which in turn governs its perceptions of law and lawlessness. Performing the same operation for the CCs which have opposed the MCC, it can be shown that throughout American history, two notions of law have coexisted and competed side-by-side, embodying the life experiences of these two groups. Localized MCCs have espoused a customary law (or 'legitimacy') which consists of those practices which enable them to resist challenges to their way of life. These challenges often appear in the name of formal law (or 'legality'), where groups or individuals not anchored in a traditional, iocal community have used appeals to fundamental principles and documents such as the Constitution to try to impose their will on middle class America, which in turn reacts in customary although sometimes illegal ways to oppose the threat. The paper concludes by discussing briefly some of the legal issues contested between the MCC and CC, and argues than *an* American legal system based on a shared moral consensus is, and always has been, impossible.

At the outset, I should explain what this paper is *not*. It is not: a) An investigation of Peirce's semiotics or opinions on American law and history, which I have discussed elsewhere; b) a semiotic investigation of 'Law' or laws; c) a semiotic inquiry into the reality of the events described -- the details of these crowd actions are fairly well agreed upon according to 'common sense' perceptions even if the interpretation is not. But the paper does hope to show: a) how similar sign systems have characterized middle class violence over the course of American history, which makes talking about the persistence and importance of MCCs possible; b) how these signs point to consistent underlying moral codes of behavior for both the MCCs which commit the violence and the CCs which challenge them; c) how legal issues which arise from these crowd actions embody fundamental disagreements over the nature of American society, and are not reconcilable short of catastrophic change or one community's annihilating the other. One further caveat: I am not concerned with judging, on either technical legal grounds or moral grounds, the behavior of either the MCC or the CC. Such judgments have been, as mine would be, partial and a reflection on what law ought to be. I am concerned with describing what two consistent competitors for the right to define 'America' and 'Americanism' have in fact regarded as 'lawful' or 'just.'

The usefulness of a semiotic approach may be seen if the two schools of interpretation American historians have traditionally applied to crowd violence are examined. Neither is entirely without insight, but neither comes to grips with the key issue of why the MCC relinquishes its usual law-abiding habits to repel its opponents -- in the name of 'law and order.'

First, as Murray (1955) does with the post-World War I 'Red Scare,' it is possible to argue that elite or communications media manipulation stimulates the MCC to violence. Politicians seeking to ride hysterical waves to greater power (Attorney General A. Mitchell Palmer in 1919, Senator Joe McCarthy in the 1950s, James Buchanan and John Tyler in the 1830s) create the illusion that dissenters are tools of an international conspiracy to destroy the nation. They have hidden too long under the cloak of the First Amendment freedoms to assembly and press, and constitute a serious threat to the MCCs and, by extension, the nation's existence. This interpretation focusses on an important point: the MCCs violence is supported, or egged on, by prominent politicians, editors, and businessmen.

But there are two flaws. First, detailed investigation shows that the MCC is usually ahead of its 'leaders': World War I suppression of radicals by government authorities followed in the wake of numerous, more brutal local incidents; anti-abolitionist mobs preceded and paved the way for 'Northern politicians with Southern hearts'; McCarthyism and the Nixon/Agnew denunciations of 'effete snobs' followed local Red hunts and demonstrations. Second, even were the MCC 'manipulated' this begs the question of why the manipulation is effective. One could not manipulate the MCC into attacking the church, the home, the armed forces, or even the police, whose local, universal corruption is notorious. The 'manipulators' must be able to depict dissidents as 'signs' -- symbols which threaten something the MCC cares so deeply about that it is willing to use lawlessness in the cause of law. It is this something, this code, at which a semiotic analysis hopes to get.

Second, Lipset and Raab (1970), Hofstadter (1962), and Marcuse (1964) found a 'one dimensionality' or 'anti-intellectualism in American life' (to use the title of Marcuse's and Hofstadter's books) of which middle class violence may be regarded as one manifestation. The theories of these writers are essentially similar. The MCC fears freedom. It has been socialized from birth to be orderly, obedient, and patriotic. It therefore 'resents' the 'other' -- those with the freedom to move, to think, to be autonomous. But then these writers go on to label the MCC as psychologically disturbed and sociologically maladjusted -- it does not possess the openness and toleration which modern society and American principles demand.

But modern society here is simply a reification of those liberal values the writer assumes it ought to cherish. Like it or not (for what it's worth, I don't) lynch mobs, 'hardhats,' and the KKK attacking people are structurally similar occurrences which have not died away as 'modernity' progresses. The Presidential elections of the 1980s indicate that the MCC is as strong as ever, of equal importance with the reformers who attract far more scholarly attention. When the scholar of middle class violence assumes he is giving an adequate explanation by labelling them the 'other' or misfits of various sorts, he is echoing not only the conservative analysis of radicals made by Feuer (1975), Bettelheim (1970), and Hoffer (1951), to give three examples, but even that of the MCC and its spokesmen in their critique of 'ivory tower eggheads' in a perverse way.

Legal historians, such as Gilmore (1971), Hurst (1960) and even L. Friedman (1973) -- who is far more sensitive to popular challenges to elite legal institutions -- do not deal much with the informal 'legitimacy' of the MCC because 'law' means something different for the scholar and the MCC. The scholar looks at statutes and decisions and how they change over time; even sociological jurisprudence ('realism') directs its inquiry at how judges can seek to shape law in accordance with what *they* perceive as social needs and realities, which have usually been progressive. This tendency not to examine 'legitimate' community-made law is reinforced by the two finest treatments of the transformation of American law from the Revolution to the Civil War -- Nelson's (1975) and Horwitz's (1977). Both writers stress the *transition* from custom to codification, from legitimacy to legality, in the interest of orderly government in an expanding society (Nelson) or of facilitating a national market for capitalist enterprise (Horwitz). The persistence of the MCC is thus regarded as a constant, a vestige, an obstacle, or -- when it is active -- a dupe. The large number of historical studies of lower-class communities and dissenters, on the one hand, which complement the traditional 'high' history of statesmen and diplomacy, on the other, both leave out the MCC as a serious object of historical study in its own right. The MCC is squeezed out of existence historiographically much as its idea of 'legitimacy' has also been historically squeezed from below and above, as both the lower and upper class find the 'legality' imposed nationally more to their respective advantages. (Civil rights and welfare legislation, on the one hand; tax breaks, commercial subsidies, creation and protection of a world market on the other.)

Semiotics can aid in the study of the MCC by describing its behavior and its view of law as a series of signs. Beginning with an 'icon' -- say, an act of middle class violence -- we can then extrapolate an interpretation of the MCC by listening to what they say they are doing, and then observing what they are doing. The MCC and its view of law can be regarded as 'texts' containing logical arguments which are interpretants for icons such as crowd violence. The MCCs values can then be shown to be neither irrelevant nor anachronistic, but a reasonable (not hysterical or manipulated), persistent code of behavior, as conversely, can the mores and activities of the CCs which have opposed the MCC. Hence the impossibility of a consensual, morally based American legal system -- although there are some pragmatically possible alternatives.

We could begin with any single act of crowd violence, but the most illuminating material I have found is in an interview *The New York Times* published on June 28, 1970, with Joe Kelly, a Staten Island construction worker (Rogin, 1971). Kelly was one of the leaders of the lower Manhattan riot of that May 8, where 'hardhats' joined by Wall Street clerks and business people confronted anti-Vietnam protestors. How did Kelly justify the riot? Searching for a sign of what he thought worth breaking the law for -- which he did with the greatest reluctance, since he stated that 'physical violence doesn't solve a damn thing' -- it can be discovered that much of the confrontation with the anti-war group took place over the American flag: the riot began when a construction worker assaulted a demonstrator who spit on the flag; the 'hardhats' and their allies seized flags from the marchers and decorated their buildings with them; the middle class marchers went to City Hall, where they raised flags lowered to half mast by the order of Mayor John Lindsay in honor of four students recently killed in a peace demonstration at Kent State University; and on May 20, 100,000 construction workers and others marched in a loyalty parade with Joe Kelly in the lead, carrying an American flag.

In the course of the interview, Kelly turned twice to the theme that the 'flag represents the country.' He described himself and his colleagues as 'flag wavers -- you can call me a flag waver any day of the week.' He then went on to explain what 'the country' -- America -- represents: 'I think of all the people that died for that flag. And somebody's gonna spit on it, it's like spitting on their grave. So they better not spit on it in front of me. You think you could get it better someplace else -- well then, don't hang around, go there.'

Both the struggle over the flag and Kelly's explanation of it indicates that both the construction workers and the peace marchers indeed considered the riot part of a symbolic struggle for the right to possess, define, and speak for the nation, which the flag stands in place of. But for Kelly, what or who constitutes 'the nation'? He points to sacrifice -- 'I think of all the people that died for that flag.' Kelly is defining citizenship as the willingness to surrender one's life on the nation's behalf, and to appreciate the sacrifices of others. This sacrifice in turn has produced 'something to be proud of,' and those unwilling to appreciate it are urged to go somewhere else. The ultimate reason he became involved in the riot, he states, is that when the students began chanting '____ no, we won't go' (that is, they flaunted their unwillingness to sacrifice themselves), he and his co-workers went on the 'disperse' them and 'break up this chant because it just seemed so un-American.'

Sacrifice -- or on a less exalted level, the willingness to surrender one's self-gratification for the benefit of a community -- permeates Kelly's interview. He labels the peace demonstrators 'unAmerican' at another point for similar reasons: 'If they don't want to educate themselves or go out and work hard for a living and save a few dollars for a rainy day, that's their prerogative. But . . . this is not the American way.' Participation in the United States involves diligence, thrift, and the willingness to forego immediate satisfaction while planning for the 'long run' -- all virtues of the MCC.

It should come as no surprise that the 'signs' of 'the American way' Kelly describes represent a generalization of his own biography and, by extension, that of the MCC. He worked hard at a succession of jobs after having served in the army, and now works hard (he and his wife don't travel or go out much) because

'I wanted something nice for the wife and kids, some place where the kids could grow up and have their own back yard. They wouldn't have to be running in the street.' He uses his days off to build the children a swimming pool. He donates his time to coach boys' basketball and baseball teams. Similarly, Kelly's job as a construction worker demands the same virtues of cooperation and self-sacrifice as his life in the family and community. The job is dangerous: 'Like if anybody drops anything they immediately scream 'Look out below' and you got to get under something just as quick as you possibly can.' The men raise substantial funds for dependents if anyone is killed or injured at work. Work, home, and community, for Kelly and other members of the MCC, mutually reinforce the need for discipline, regularity, and subordination of the individual's impulses to a greater good.

Precisely this lack of control bothers Kelly most about the student protestors. Not only are they unwilling to sacrifice their lives for the country, but they lack the discipline essential to the existence of the MCC which the latter defines as the 'American way.' Kelly complains that 'these kids think they can do as they feel like. I mean burn, loot, steal, do anything they feel like in the name of social reform. But can the average Joe Blow citizen go out and do this?' The emphasis is on people who are not subject to the same restraints as 'the average Joe Blow citizen' (e.g., the MCC), people who 'feel' and act on their feelings as 'they like' -- Kelly uses each of these phrases twice.

In the aftermath of the riot, Kelly admits he would have preferred a less violent response: 'I would much rather prefer grabbing them by the hair of the head and taking a scissors and cutting their hair off, something that was much less violent but you still would have gotten your message across.' 'Long hair' for Kelly, as for defenders of traditional society in the sixties in general, symbolizes this same lack of self-control and unwillingness to conform to the standards of a

MCC which identifies itself with the nation. 'Long hair' thus serves as a 'sign' of the counter-culture just as the 'hardhat' or construction worker is a sign of the MCC. Kelly is quite aware of this: 'The construction worker is only an image that's being used. The hardhat is being used to represent all of the silent majority.' (As, we might add, was President Nixon, who identified himself with *that* sign by receiving his own hardhat from the construction workers at about this time. Nixon's action also reflected his approval of their sort of 'lawlessness.')

Using this riot and Kelly's interview as a starting point, it becomes possible to list a whole set of signs of a behavioral code, which describes the MCC to which Kelly and the construction workers belong. The MCC also develops a demonology -- a reverse set of 'unAmerican' signs which describe its adversaries. One can perform the reverse operation for the counter-culture:

Middle Class Community

Code		Symbols
1.	Regular, hard work.	Silent majority
		Construction worker
2.	Self-control.	American flag
		Archie Bunker
3.	Obedience to authority.	Middle America
		Main Street USA
4.	Respect for tradition.	Violence to defend MCC from threats to existence at home and abroad.
5.	Importance of family.	'Law and order' -- harsh punishment of those who threaten MCC.

6.   Importance of religion.

Reading matter -- <u>Reader's Digest</u>.

Short haircuts.

7.   Sexual monogamy, restraint.

Neat, unostentatious dress.

Music -- patroitic songs, Lawrence Welk, etc.

8.   Participation in local 'voluntary associations.'

Medium -- TV, newspapers.

Release -- alcohol.

9.   Mistrust of outsiders, those not rooted in similar communities.

<u>Demons</u>

Hippies

Limousine liberals

10.   Sacrifices self for MCC and nation which should act like MCC writ language.

Effete snobs

Long hair

Welfare bums

11.   Passion for security -- fear of Communinism, depression.

'Niggers'

Outside agitators

12.   Respect for property.

Counter-Culture

<u>Code</u>

1.   Primacy of self-expression.

2.   Question authority.

<u>Symbols</u>

Students

Blacks

Marchers, demonstrators.

Abbie Hoffman, Bob Dylan, etc.

3.   Freedom from tradtional restraints.

Violence to produce social change.

Radical literature.

Sympathy with underpriviledged.

4. Repudiation of family for peer group.	Dress -- army jackets, blue jeans, or extravagantly colorful attire.
	Music -- rock, folk.
5. Respect for egalitarian, universalist ideology.	Media -- films, pamphlets, books.
	Release -- drugs.
6. Sexual promiscuity.	Demons
7. Participation in trans-local and trans-national movements.	'Fascists'
	'Pigs' (police)
	Military-Industrial complex
8. Lack of attachment to locality, personal mobility (geographic, social).	Establishment
	'Uptight' people
	Mayor Daley, Nixon, etc.
9. Openness to alternatives to 'American way.'	
10. De-emphasis of property.	

Three notes: These, of course, are oversimplifications. Nearly as many middle Americans voted for Humphrey as for Nixon in 1968, and probably more students opposed than supported the Vietnam protests, in 1968 if not 1970. But given the adversary mentality of the two opposing cultures, the validity of the sign was accepted without question. Also, another sort of sign could be created, the 'idol': each side's demons, may, with a few obvious exceptions and substitutions of terminology, be regarded as the other's role models, or heroes.

So far, I have tried to classify semiotically events and characteristics generally familiar to late twentieth century Americans. What further historical insights can semiotics provide? It is possible to look for 'equivalent' sets of signs, and examine confrontations in the American past to ascertain change and continuity in history. For example, the anti-abolitionist mobs of the mid-1830's and the post-World War I 'Red Scare' generated similar signs and styles of middle class violence against 'counter-cultures' of abolitionists and radicals. In the 1830's, abolitionists were disproportionately seminarians, college graduates, preachers, and women (the presence of women in untraditionally activist roles is another index of all three challenges to the MCC) -- 'outsiders' 'invading' the turf of MCCs much as the students invaded Wall Street in 1970. They represented a trans-national organization which members of MCCs were quick to read as 'unAmerican.' A fair number of American abolitionists were recent British immigrants. The British had recently abolished slavery as a result of similar agitation, and Britain conveyed 'aristocratic' connotations left over from the American Revolution. Many were also blacks, and anti-abolitionists frequently travelled to England. The agitators thus represented an insidious combination of the upper class (much of the American Anti-Slavery Society's support came from a syndicate of New York merchants headed by Arthur and Lewis Tappan) inciting the lower orders (blacks) to 'revolution,' squeezing the MCC in the middle much as in the 1960s (Richards, 1970).

Similarly, during and in the years immediately following World War I, the Industrial Workers of the World, the Socialist Party, and as of 1920 the American Communist Party sent 'organizers' all over the country to oppose the war, call attention to injustices, and promote fundamental changes in the nation's life. They were supported by upper class 'parlor Bolsheviks' -- again, ministers and intellectuals -- who defended their right to agitate if not always their methods and ideas. The 'unAmerican' character of the radicals was confirmed for the MCC by the large number of radical immigrants, many of whom did not speak English. Not only were the radicals outsiders, but they regarded the soldiers who had risked their lives in the war as foolish dupes of the capitalist profiteers. As with

Vietnam, protestors denied the ennobling value of sacrifice and respect for authority, and preached the virtues of questioning accepted values in the name of a higher law or alternative ideology (Murray, 1955).

The following elements, therefore, appear in each of the three major instances of middle class violence: a) a union is perceived between upper class elements and lower class 'unAmericans' against the MCC; b) both enemies of the MCC are distinguished by similar codes of behavior despite their class differences: neither appears to the MCC rooted in a traditional, law-abiding community. The upper class doesn't have to control itself or work hard, the lower class is dissatisfied because work and self-discipline do not pay off as for the MCC; c) the usual middle class response to outside agitation is to expel the agitator from its midst -- only in protracted and exceptional cases does the middle class inflict murder or extreme physical violence; (e.g. Elijah Lovejoy's murder following his repeated efforts to install an abolitionist press in Alton, Illinois in 1837 after his resistance to a crowd); d) middle class violence is provoked by the appearance of outsiders who represent a national or world-wide movement which challenges the MCC's right to exist -- its legitimacy; e) the conflicting attitudes of the MCC and 'others' -- CCs, intellectuals -- on legal problems can also be deduced from their 'codes'.

To give a few examples: a) Freedom of Speech and the Press -- while held 'abstractly' by the MCC, is clearly defined in a limited manner as the right to debate change *within* the limits of existing society as they perceive it, rather than the right to advocate fundamental changes. Opinion polls demonstrate most Americans would not have let Communists speak in their communities if given the choice, and opposed permitting demonstrations against the Vietnam War (Simon, 1974). The CCs very existence depends upon questioning authority.

b) Punishment of Criminals -- in the interest of security, the MCC has supported harsh penalties for crimes against property and violence, whereas the CC has de-emphasized secure possession of property as 'materialistic' and sought to rehabilitate rather than punish criminals as victims of society, not the reverse. By contrast, the MCC has been more tolerant of 'police crimes' such as illegal searches and seizures and interrogations, as necessary to preserve the security of 'law-abiding' citizens.

c) Civil rights legislation -- the MCC has opposed school busing, affirmative action, housing integration, and poverty programs on the grounds others are being given unfair advantages they did not earn. The CC regards such measures as necessary to alleviate injustice.

d) Foreign Policy -- the MCC supports a strong defense policy, even if international law is violated in the support of pro-American 'authoritarian' governments. Since the MCC regards the nation as the MCC writ large, it demonstrates the same passion for national security that it does for the security of the person and the community. The more open CC is willing to tolerate Communism and diversity, and views overseas threats as less important than adjusting social differences at home in accordance with abstract principles.

e) Use of federal power -- The CC has come to view it as beneficial and necessary to protect itself from the MCC, especially in the form of judicial overruling of local ordinances, protection for civil rights, and welfare programs. The MCC regards it as an intrusion -- costly and inefficient -- except where guaranteeing 'law and order' at home and security abroad.

Throughout American history, the MCC and various CCs have argued over the nature of 'Americanism' and the legal system. Given the two communities and lifestyles involved, a common legal system based on a common moral code is clearly impossible. This, however, is not necessarily a tragedy. The historical alternatives have been three: --

a) The acceptance of the MCCs definition of 'Americanism.' This is still practically true in many local communities. It has been the consensus throughout American history. Kraditor (1981) has argued that challenges to the MCC from 1890 to 1917 were the work of marginal elements, and the perusal of any text on the Supreme Court and civil liberties (such as Oddo, 1979) demonstrates that only from the 1950s to 1970s did the 'Warren Court' support to a significant degree the CC's definitions of law. More restrictive definitions of the First, Fourth, and Fourteenth Amendments have usually prevailed.

b) The acceptance of the CCs definition of 'Americanism.' This is true in certain cosmopolitan areas (San Francisco, universities) and has sometimes been accepted in part (the New Deal) by the MCC. Vidich and Bensman (1968) have argued persuasively that dependent economically as it is on a mass, cosmopolitan society in modern times, the MCCs ideology of insularity is unrealistic in a pluralist society.

c) Uneasy coexistence -- has been the pattern for much of American history. Individuals unhappy with traditional communities have moved to areas where their lifestyles are tolerated. The exodus of blacks to the North is perhaps the greatest example, as are the numerous utopian communes ranging from the Oneida and Shaker communities of the early nineteenth century to the 'hippie' communes of modern times. The key to American political stability has not been the 'melting pot,' but the room for the 'mutually exclusive' communities based on ethnicity, religion, race, and ideas to coexist without stepping too drastically on each other's toes. In fact, each of the three periods of violence studied in this paper followed not only increased activity by CCs, but also a revolution in communications which forced the MCC and CC closer together. The anti-abolitionist riots were preceded by the invention of new printing processes which permitted the mass publication of cheap tracts, and by the development of a formal organization of abolitionist lecturers who blanketed the country. The invention of film and newsreels, the latter sponsored by the Committee on Public Information in World War I, brought the radical menace home to millions. And television news programs brought student and civil rights agitation into millions of homes in the 1960's. Law thus becomes a matter of public consensus on the local level, of political adjustment (or repression) on the national. But it cannot, given a pluralist society with two basically conflicting moral codes, stand for a common good or transcendent purpose.

REFERENCES

Bettelheim, Bruno, 1970, *Obsolete Youth and the Psychograph of Adolescent Rebellion*, San Francisco: San Francisco Press.

Feuer, Lewis, 1975, *Ideology and the Ideologues*, Oxford: Blackwell.

Friedman, Lawrence, 1973, *A History of American Law*, New York: Simon and Schuster.

Friedman, Murray, 1971, 'Introduction: Middle America and the 'New Pluralism', *Overcoming Middle Class Rage*, ed., M. Friedman, Philadelphia: The Westminster Press, 15-55.

Gilmore, Grant, 1971, *The Ages of American Law*, New Haven: Yale University Press.

Hoffer, Eric, 1951, *The True Believer: Thoughts on the Nature of Mass Movements*, New York: Harper and Row.

Hofstadter, Richard, 1962, *Anti-Intellectualism in American Life*, New York: Random House.

Horwitz, Morton, 1977, *The Transformation of American Law*, Cambridge, Mass.: Harvard University Press.

Hurst, Willard, 1960, *Law and Social Process in United States History*, Ann Arbor: University of Michigan Press.

Kraditor, Aileen, 1981, *The Radical Persuasion, 1890-1919*, Baton Rouge: Louisiana State University Press.

Lipset, Seymour Martin, and Earl Raab, 1970, *The Politics of Unreason: Right Wing Extremism in America, 1790-1970*, New York: Harper and Row.

Marcuse, Herbert, 1964, *One Dimensional Man: Studies in the Ideology of Advanced Industrial Society*, Boston: Beacon Press.

Murray, Robert, 1955, *Red Scare: A Study in National Hysteria 1919-1920*, Minneapolis: University of Minnesota Press.

Nelson, William E., 1975, *The Americanization of the Common Law*, Cambridge, Mass.: Harvard University Press.

Oddo, Gilbert, 1979, *Freedom and Equality: Civil Liberties and the Supreme Court*, Santa Monica, Cal.:Goodyear.

Richards, Leonard, 1970, *'Gentlemen of Property and Standing': Anti-Abolition Mobs in Jacksonian America*, New York and London: Oxford University Press.

Rogin, Richard, 1971, 'Joe Kelly Has Reached His Boiling Point,' in M. Friedman, ed., *Overcoming Middle-Class Rage*, 66-85.

Simon, Rita James, 1974, *Public Opinion in America: 1936-1970*, Chicago: Rand-McNally.

Vidich, Arthur, and Joseph Bensman, 1968, *Small Town in Mass Society*, Princeton: Princeton University Press.

Chapter 13

Thucydides as Semiotician

I

Thucydides and Peircean Semiotics

Modern semiotics raises to the level of theory a mode of thinking implicit throughout western history. It stands opposed to the 'dogmatic' belief that reality is either knowable or unknowable, provable and unprovable, according to deductive or inductive logic.   In this paper, I will not advance any new contributions to semiotic theory or to the study of its founder, Charles S. Peirce. Rather, as a historian, I hope to show that in his history of *The Peloponnesian War*, the Greek historian Thucydides used a mode of thought similar in several ways to that advocated by Peirce, much as Max Fisch has demonstrated (1971) that both the word 'semeiosis' and a manner of thinking in terms of signs were known to Greek Epicurean philosophers.

Thucydides and Peircean semiotics may be compared on at least seven points: (1) the 'sign' as the only means of experiencing and thinking about reality; (2) the Peircean categories of 'firstness,' 'secondness,' and 'thirdness' as equivalents for Thucydides' antitheses; (3) knowledge as provisional and always subject to revision; (4) a community of inquirers must exist for thought to occur; (5), (6), and (7) thought as *action*, taken to relieve *doubt*, usually undertaken as a *self-sacrificing* activity by a persecuted inquirer. I will briefly explain each of these before integrating them into a general analysis of *The Peloponnesian War*.

1. The 'Sign' as the means of experiencing reality -- Peirce writes that 'whenever we think, we have present to the consciousness some feeling, image, conception, or other representation, which serves as a sign.' (Peirce: 1868, 233) 'Man can only think by means of words or other external symbols . . . Every thought is a sign.' (Peirce: 1868, 249) Similarly, Thucydides treats the material of *The Peloponnesian War* as interlocking series of signs. Athens and Sparta signify certain codes of justice and ways of life; different speakers 'signify' attitudes or arguments which represent those used at the time. Thucydides admits that he may not remember, or even know, the exact words used in each speech, but writes what was 'called for' by each situation. (1:22) The war itself is a sign of the sort of 'great war' Thucydides predicts will occur when two competing civilizations struggle for hegemony. (1:24)

2. 'First,' 'Second' and 'Third' -- For Peirce, every experience requires three elements. 'First' is the immediate appearance or presentation of something; 'second' the juxtaposition of 'something it is not' which enables, 'third,' a judgment or perception on someone's part to occur. (Peirce: 1893-1910; 1903-1911, 381-393) Thucydides, too, presents his actions, actors, and ideas through 'antitheses' which invite judgments by the reader. Athens is opposed to and unintelligible without Sparta; Pericles, at different times, is opposed to Archidamus, Alcibiades, Cleon, and Nicias -- we cannot understand the relevance of his vision of Athens apart from alternative visions and the realities of Athenian history; the Athenian debate over Mytilene only makes sense after the Spartan debate at Potidaea, and it requires the Melian debate for its full significance to appear. Numerous antitheses within the speeches are discussed by Edmunds (1975: 143-204), who summarizes the literature on this subject. After setting up these 'firsts' and 'seconds,' Thucydides does not explicitly draw conclusions. *We,* like the audiences in the book, must judge the truth of the 'signs' for ourselves in

light of the historical evidence and the coherence, relevance, and consistency of the arguments used.

3. Knowledge as provisional and subject to revision -- Writing to Lady Welby in 1908, Peirce 'returned to the expression of my abhorrence of the doctrine that any proposition whatsoever is infallibly true.' (Peirce: 1903-1911, 398) Earlier, he had argued that the best we could attain through scientific and logical investigation was 'indefinitely approximating to the truth in the long run.' (Peirce: 1883, 217) Similarly, there are no absolutes for Thucydides. Does Athens live up to its Periclean ideals? Does Sparta approximate Archidamus' description of it? Does democracy work, and what happens when it becomes expansionist? When is a war justifiable? When is a disastrous policy reversible? Is an open society, with open political debate, desirable? We then must judge, comparing contrasting hypotheses, all the while remaining aware that the problems of the ancient Greeks were no more amenable to definitive solutions than our own.

4. Community of disinterested inquirers -- For truth-seeking to occur as described in (3), there must be people willing to test hypotheses systematically, and honestly try to arrive at a knowledge of reality. As Peirce wrote to Lady Welby (1903-1911, 398): 'unless truth be recognized as *public* -- as that of which any person would come to be convinced if he carried his inquiry, his sincere search for immovable belief, far enough -- then there will be nothing to prevent each one of us from adopting an utterly futile belief of his own which all the rest will disbelieve.' Earlier, he had maintained that 'the very origin of the concept of reality shows that this conception essentially involves the notion of a COMMUNITY, without definite limits, and capable of an indefinite increase of knowledge.' (Peirce: 1868, 247) Thucydides, too, regarding the Peloponnesian War as a 'sign' of great civilizational clashes, addresses his hypotheses concerning the good state and its proper conduct to 'those who want to understand' (1.23).

He invites, therefore, the reader to join a Peircean community of believers who sincerely care about war and peace, democracy and authoritarianism, imperialism, etc. to try to put their prejudices behind them and inquire as to the causes and effects of certain patterns of thought and conduct.

5, 6, 7. Thought as *action,* taken to relieve *doubt,* by a *self-sacrificing* inquirer -- Peirce considers thought 'essentially an action.' (Peirce: 1878, 29) Why does man think? 'There must be a real and *living* doubt and without this all discussion is idle.' 'The irritation of doubt causes a *struggle* to attain a state of belief.' And belief then becomes a 'rule of action.' (Peirce: 1878, 11; 1878, 29; my emphases) Thucydides presents his thought through a combination of actions -- speeches and descriptions of historical events. As for Peirce, speechmaking (inquiry) occurs when there is doubt as to what should be done -- it *is* action and causes action to take place. But hence arise three great paradoxes of Peircean, Thucydidean, and human existence. First, we think to attain a state of belief, and yet knowledge of truth is unattainable: 'Since belief is a rule for action, the application of which involves further doubt and further thought, at the same time that it is a stopping-place, it is also a new starting-place for thought.' (Peirce: 1878, 28) Even if the Spartans or Athenians decide on an action, or it seems at the time they have acted correctly, all speeches and actions have to be reassessed based on the future progress of the war. Second, to be truly thinking, we must try to be disinterested, logical and 'scientific.' And yet we only think in the first place because of a 'struggle,' a 'real,' 'living' concern with vital human problems. Is it possible to be both disinterested and yet interested? Thucydides' effort to deal both sympathetically and critically with Athenian civilization demonstrates the tightrope a genuine inquirer into human issues must walk. Which brings us to paradox three. Disinterested inquiry is self-sacrificial. Not only will it fail to attain absolute truth and provide a final resting point for doubt, it will frequently be carried on in the face of a majority which prefers to have its doubts assuaged and its prejudices praised. In 'The Fixation of Belief,' Peirce wrote (1877, 20):

> Following the method of authority is the path of peace. Certain non-conformities are permitted; certain others (considered unsafe) are forbidden. These are different in different countries and in different ages; but wherever you are, let it be known that you seriously hold a tabooed belief, and you may be perfectly sure of being treated with a cruelty less brutal but more refined than hunting you like a wolf.

Over thirty years later, he would define the 'true man of science' as 'every man belonging to a social group all members of which *sacrifice* all the ordinary motives of their life to their desire to make their beliefs concerning one subject conform to verified judgments of perception concerning sound reasoning.' (Peirce 1903-1911, 400)

Thucydides, like Peirce, reasoned to relieve doubt. Faced with military disaster and internal political revolution, Thucydides, like many Athenians of his age, was compelled to doubt whether the traditional pronouncements of Athenian superiority and freedom were 'really true.' Athens of the fourth century demonstrates Peirce's dictum that we think to relieve doubt on perhaps the grandest scale in human history: given a political catastrophe which undermined faith in traditional legal and political institutions, Thucydides, along with Socrates, Plato, Euripides, Aristophanes, and others, undertook a tremendous intellectual re-evaluation of the nature of the good state and of human nature and conduct. Again paradoxically, it is their collective meditation on the strengths, failures, and problems of Athens that we remember today as the capstone of Athenian civilization. But we need only remember the fate of Thucydides, who died in exile (much as Peirce spent the last twenty-seven years of his life in Milford, Pennsylvania, and never held a regular academic appointment) to recall that

Peirce's insistence on the sacrificial character of true inquiry has been the fate of many of our most profound thinkers.

II

Thucydides' Purpose

Having presented a general sketch of similarities between Thucydides' thought and Peirce's semiotics, I will now analyze some aspects of *The Peloponnesian War* to demonstrate that thinking about semiotics can indeed enrich our understanding of this inexhaustible masterpiece.

'My work is not a piece of writing designed to meet the taste of an immediate public, but was done to last forever,' Thucydides proclaims immodestly if accurately in his introduction. 'It will be enough for me, however, if these words of mine are judged useful by those who want to understand clearly the events which happened in the past and which (human nature being what it is) will, at some time or other and in much the same ways, be repeated in the future.' (1.22) The Peloponnesian War -- a historical fiction Thucydides constructed out of two separate wars between Athens and Sparta, a war between Athens and Sicily, and a number of peripheral skirmishes (Finley: 1942, 73-77) -- is thus a 'sign' presented to a Peircean community of 'those who want to understand' extending 'forever.'

But of what is the Peloponnesian War a sign? Thucydides stresses in his introduction that 'this was the greatest war of all' (1.21), 'more worth writing about than any of those which had taken place in the past' (1.1); 'the greatest disturbance in the history of the Hellenes, affecting also a large part of the non-Hellenic world, and indeed, I might almost say, the whole of mankind.' (1.1) This protracted struggle between Athens and Sparta that Thucydides has molded into 'the greatest war' thus becomes a sign of 'greatest wars.' We need only think superficially about the recent contest between the United States and Soviet Union to discern all sorts of parallels: larger clashes evolve out of those between client states; mutual claims are made for the moral superiority of respective systems; hard-liners confront negotiators; partisans of both sides are found in small, unstable states; emotional, unsound rhetoric is used to persuade citizens to identify with their leaders' crusades; and spheres of influence are overextended. Indeed, similar patterns may be discerned in every clash of civilizations in the intervening two millennia: the World Wars, the thousand-year struggle between Islam and the West, and the wars of religion in early modern Europe. Thucydides has indeed given us, before the fact, a semiotics of history and civilization, and a terrifying one at that.

Yet each of these major struggles was not only 'great' because of the numbers of people involved or the duration of the conflict. Each of the actors stood for a code of laws, an ideal of civilization, a vision of justice and right action.

The claim of this paper is that after presenting Spartan and Athenian systems and ideas of law, *The Peloponnesian War* then proceeds to test, about as rigorously, logically, and searchingly as possible, the civilizational 'hypotheses' of Athens and Sparta -- or rather, Thucydides presents the evidence so we are forced to undertake the inquiry as members of a 'community of inquirers' for ourselves. Can a civilization live up to its ideals under the strain of protracted, apparently endless conflict? Do ideals of law correspond to reality, or are they so much self-mystification for self-interest? Is there no *moral* difference between Sparta and Athens? And how does total war transform our ability to be faithful to our laws and institutions? I will argue that, at least after I have tried to perform the inquiry Thucydides invites, there does seem to be a difference between the deep-grey of Athens and the blackness of Sparta. But by Book VIII, the Athenians seem to have reduced themselves to the level of the Spartans and totally abandoned any resemblance to the people described in Pericles' Funeral Oration. However, a spectacular surprise ending (in what I believe is erroneously considered an incomplete book) shakes us out of our despair and once again makes us proud to be Athenians -- although a new sort of Athenian who, having performed the Thucydidean inquiry, is possessed of greater powers of self-criticism and less hubris.

III

Athens vs. Sparta -- The Ideals

We first encounter the Spartan and Athenian notions of law in the debate at Sparta over whether that city-state should declare war on Athens. (1. 65-87) The Corinthian, Athenian, and Spartan speakers all agree that caution, prudence, moderation, obedience, and anti-intellectualism define the Spartan character. The Corinthian envoy begins: 'Spartans, what makes you somewhat *reluctant to listen* to us others, if we have ideas to put forward, is the great trust and confidence which you have in your own constitution and in your own way of life. This is a quality which makes you moderate in your judgments.' In fact, the Corinthian complains that it was difficult even to set up a meeting with the Spartans. He castigates them as 'the only people in Hellas who wait calmly on events.' Unlike the Athenian, who 'is always an innovator,' the Spartan is 'good at keeping things as they are; you never originate an idea, and your action tends to stop short of its aim.' Archidamus, who opposes the Corinthian's effort to goad the Spartans into war, and represents the 'best' of Sparta as Pericles does the 'best' of Athens, praises these same qualities:

The city in which we live has always been free [unconquered] and always famous. 'Slow' and 'cautious' can equally well be 'wise and sensible.' . . . We are not carried away by the pleasure of hearing ourselves praised when people are urging us towards dangers that seem to us unnecessary; and we are no more likely to give in shamefacedly to other people's views when they try to spur us on by their accusations. [Or, Spartans have a dim view of intellectual discourse as genuine or helpful in decision making.] Because of our well-ordered life we are both brave in war and wise in council. Brave, because self-control is based upon a sense of honour, and honour is based on courage. And we are wise because we are not so highly educated as to look down upon our laws and customs, and we are too rigorously trained in self-control *to be able to disobey them*. We are trained to avoid being too clever in matters that are of no use -- such as being too able to produce an excellent theoretical criticism of one's enemies' dispositions, and then failing in practice to do quite so well against them. [Thought, in other words, leads to failure.] . . . Instead *we are taught* that there is not a great deal of difference between the way we think and the way others think [he has previously denied this for Athens]. . . . There is no need to suppose that human beings differ very much from one another; but it is true that the ones who come out on top are the ones who have been trained in the hardest school. . . . Let us never give up this discipline which our fathers have handed down to us and which we still preserve and which has always done us the greatest good. (My emphases)

In a few brief pages, Thucydides thus establishes the Spartan character and constitution well-known to history. They obey their laws and traditions unquestioningly and deny the value of independent thought.   Their behavior is taught to them; they only reluctantly even listen to outsiders.   As if to clinch the argument of a closed, totalitarian society, the Spartans ignore the three elaborately reasoned speeches by the Corinthian, the Athenian, and Archidamus.   They vote for war by a 'great majority' following a brief jingoistic exhortation by Sthenelaides which denies the value of the intellectual discourse:

> I do not understand these long speeches which the Athenians make.
> . . . All this is not a matter to be settled by law-suits and words; it
> is not because of words that our own interests are suffering. . . .
> And let no one try to tell us that when we are being attacked we
> should sit down and discuss matters. [The irony is Sparta is *not* being
> attacked; Athenian ships have taken part in a war involving Athenian
> and Spartan allies.]   These long discussions are rather for those who
> are meditating aggression themselves.   Therefore, Spartans, cast your
> votes for the honour of Sparta and for war!   Do not allow the
> Athenians to grow still stronger!   Do not betray your allies!   Instead,
> let us, with the help of heaven, go forward to meet the aggressor!

As if to make sure we were not asleep during the speeches, Thucydides notes that the Spartans do not *vote* as do the Athenians; they shout.   When the shouts for war and peace seem equal, they line up, and then a 'great majority' is for war. Spartans do not make up their own minds.   They are bullied into war by not wanting to appear cowardly.

In contrast to the traditional and unthinking if courageous and well-disciplined Spartans, the Athenians who emerge in their own and their enemies' descriptions (and in Pericles' speech which follows soon -- the 'Funeral Oration' -- 2.34-46) really confound the Spartan claim that people are very much alike. (Most of *The Peloponnesian War* tests this claim, and Athens' degeneration by the end indicates the Spartans have a point.) The Corinthian quite rightly asserts that 'you have never tried to imagine what sort of people these Athenians are against whom you will have to fight -- how much, indeed, how completely different from you.' Athenians are innovators, 'they outrun their resources'; 'as for their bodies, they regard them as expendable for their city's sake, as though they were not their own; but each man cultivates his intelligence with a view of doing something notable for his city. . . . Their view of a holiday is to do what needs doing; they prefer hardship and activity to peace and quiet. In a word, they are incapable of either living a quiet life themselves or of allowing anyone else to do so.' Pericles will shortly raise Athens to even greater heights:

> What I want to do, is in the first place, to discuss the spirit in which we faced our trials and also our constitution and the way of life which has made us great. [He makes this speech to an assembly of citizens *and* foreigners -- as the Spartans would not.] Let me say that our system of government does not copy the institutions of our neighbors. It is more the case with our being a model to others, than of our imitating anyone else. Our constitution is called a democracy because power is in the hands not of a minority but of the whole people. When it is a question of settling private disputes, everyone is equal before the law. And just as our political life is free and open, so is our day-to-day life in our relations with each other. We do not get into a state with our next-door neighbor if he enjoys himself in his own way, nor do we give him the kind of black looks which, though they do no real harm, still do hurt people's feelings. We are free and tolerant in our private lives; but in public affairs we keep to the law. This is because it commands our deep respect.

We give obedience to those whom we put in positions of authority, and we obey the laws themselves, especially those which are for the protection of the oppressed, and those unwritten laws which it is an acknowledged shame to break. . . . Taking everything together, then, I declare that our city is an education to Greece, and I declare that in my opinion each single one of our citizens, in all the manifold aspects of life, is able to show himself the rightful lord and owner of his own person, and do this, moreover, with exceptional grace and exceptional versatility.

The Athenians admit they have an empire, but as their envoys at Sparta argue: 'Those who really deserve praise are the people who, while human enough to enjoy power, nevertheless pay more attention to justice than they are compelled to do by their situation.' Here then, are people who claim to belong to a unique state, possessed of laws and customs to which they give internal assent, dedicated to their city and to their own self-improvement as inseparable, opening themselves up to learn from and teach each other and the world, and placing a higher emphasis on intelligence, equality, justice, individualism, and culture than any previous society in history. Or so they say.

Early in his book, then, Thucydides presents competing visions of law, justice, human nature, and international politics. The Athenians and the Spartans then act in the context of the war, which enables observers (both the audience within the book and its readers) to pass judgment on both the applicability of the Athenian and Spartan 'hypotheses' and the veracity and consistency of those who serve as 'signs' of each code.

IV

Athens vs. Sparta -- Practice

What actually occurs? Does Athens live up to its code? Does Sparta? Or are ideals a smokescreen for raw power and blatant self-interest as the Athenian delegate argues in the Melian debate. (5.85-115) 'The standard of justice depends on the equality of power to compel and that in fact the strong do what they have the power to do and the weak accept what they have to accept.' To trace the decline of Athens, and the moral bankruptcy of Sparta from the very beginning, would require a book in itself. So let me all too briefly run through some examples: the debates concerning the Mytileneans (3.36-50), the Plateans (3.51-67), and Melians, and Athens in the last days of the war.

The Athenians decide impulsively to massacre the Mytileneans, a free people who treacherously broke their alliance even though the Athenians had treated them better than any other client state. But they reconsider this 'cruel and unprecedented decision' after one day, and a great debate ensued. Cleon, 'remarkable among the Athenians for the violence of his character,' begins by criticizing everything about the laws of Athens Pericles had earlier praised: 'A democracy is incapable of governing others'; 'your empire is a dictatorship exercised over subjects who do not like it'; 'your leadership depends on superior strength and not on any goodwill of theirs. And this is the very worst thing -- to pass measures and then not to abide by them. We should realize that a city is better off with bad laws, so long as they remain fixed, than with good laws that are constantly being altered, that lack of learning combined with sound common sense is more helpful than the kind of cleverness which gets out of hand, and that as a general rule states are better governed by the man in the street than by intellectuals.' Cleon goes on to describe extended rational discourse over public affairs as 'stupid . . . competitive displays' which favor 'novelty in an argument' over 'what is tried and proved.' Cleon argues that the bottom line is power, which he equates with the authority of tradition and common sense as opposed to Periclean flexible reasoning: 'whatever the rights or wrongs of it may be, you propose to hold power all the same; then your interest demands that these, too, rightly or wrongly, must be punished. The only alternative is to surrender your empire, so that you can afford to go in for philanthropy.'

Now before we totally dismiss Cleon, only the most idealistic among us would not find his description of 'the way the world really works' at least as realistic as Pericles'. In fact, the Spartans are known as the 'liberators of Hellas' and nearly all the other Greek states side with them, rather than with the supposed exemplars of a just and open society. Does the Athenians' superiority, in short, rest on the exploitation of others or on the development of their own capabilities? And did the Athenians ever measure up to Pericles' description of their formal and informal constitution? One test was their behavior during the plague, which caused the great man's death, and follows as an antithesis ('second' in Peircean terminology) immediately after the Funeral Oration. (2.50-53) Here, in condensed form, the ultimate debasement of Athens caused by that other plague -- the war itself -- appears early in the work:

> Athens owed to the plague the beginnings of a state of unprecedented
> lawlessness. . . . People now began openly to venture on acts of self-
> indulgence which before they used to keep dark. Thus they resolved
> to spend their money quickly and to spend it on pleasure, since money
> and life seemed equally ephemeral. As for what is called honour, no
> one showed himself willing to abide by its laws, so doubtful it was
> whether one would survive to enjoy the name for it. . . . No fear of
> god or law of man had a restraining influence. As for the gods, it

seemed to be the same thing whether one worshipped them or not when one saw the good and the bad dying indiscriminately. As for offenses against human law, no one expected to live long enough to be brought to trail and punished.

Note well: it seems the Athenians, like all mortals, as the Spartans noted, need *fear* to compel obedience. Security for the future is crucial, too, not just voluntary assent, civic pride, and their much-vaunted love of change and novelty. Athenian exceptionalism is denied in fact as soon as it is presented in theory by Pericles. There are two ways to interpret the plague as a 'sign' of the moral decline which will be manifested through the war: (1) Athens never measured up to Pericles' ideology in the first place; or (2) it took this kind of calamity to upset such a great society. Thucydides leaves the answer open, and gives us the entire book to read and make up our own minds.

Cleon, however, is refuted by Diodotus. Where Cleon hopes to put an end to speechmaking, Diodotus argues both reasonably and passionately for reason and for Athens' traditionally untraditional laws: 'The good citizen, instead of trying to terrify the opposition, ought to prove his case in fair argument.' It does not follow that the Mytileneans ought to die even if 'they are the most guilty people in the world.' 'We should recognize that the proper basis of our security is in good administration rather than in the fear of legal penalties. [Has he forgotten the plague? Or has Athens recovered?] The right way to deal with a free people is this -- not to inflict tremendous punishments on them after they have revolted, but to take tremendous care of them before this point is reached, to prevent them from even contemplating the idea of revolt.'

The Diodotus vs. Cleon debate raises and encapsulates some of the most important issues in the book: how should an imperial state treat its allies; is large scale massacre a deterrent -- Diodotus even brings up the analogy with capital punishment; does reasoned debate and a reasonable attitude make a difference? Diodotus wins -- by a whisker -- after the hands are counted. Athens is still on the side of Pericles.

Sparta, in the very next scene of the book, has no problem deciding whether to massacre the Plataeans. They have only one question to ask: 'Have you done anything to help the Spartans and their allies in the present war?' In vain do the Plataeans protest that they had formerly been Sparta's allies, but that more recently the large state had rejected an alliance and told them to seek Athens' help against Thebes. The Plataeans add that Sparta will lose its reputation 'as an example of faith and honour,' and that 'Hellenic law forbids killing under these circumstances.' To the tradition-minded Spartans, who claim to learn their morals from their ancestors, the Plataeans urge them to 'look at the tombs of your fathers, who were killed by the Persians and are buried in our country.' (Indeed, Plataea may be a 'sign' which buries Spartan morality as the plague which kills Pericles may be for Athens.) Instead, Sparta either listens to or does not (would it make a difference?) the contrary Theban argument, since in the last analysis it keeps to the same position and question with which it began -- 'Have you done anything to help the Spartans?' Still, neither is the Theban analysis totally worthless. Nothing forced Plataea to enter an offensive alliance with Athens, and the Thebans tell the supplicants that 'it was a much more disgraceful and wicked thing utterly to betray all the Hellenic states, your allies who were liberating Hellas, than merely the Athenians who were enslaving it.' Tracing the tangled course of Plataean history back through the war, we also discover that Plataea, like so many of these cities, was divided into an Athenian and a Spartan party, so it was difficult to determine the legitimate government. Still, Sparta remains unmoved.

Several years later, the Athenians have no problem behaving like Spartans. At issue is whether to massacre the population of Melos, a Spartan colony which had tried to remain neutral and only fought back when Athens attacked it. So Thucydides tells us in (for him) unusually uncertain terms without presenting a complicated study of two sides. The Athenians now all think like Cleon -- there is no division of voices. When the Melians urge 'putting forward our own views in a calm atmosphere,' the Athenians abruptly rule out of court all considerations of reason and justice. They deny what they had asserted at the beginning of the war in Sparta -- that they had a right to their empire because of their role in the Persian Wars and benevolent administration -- as 'a great mass of words that nobody would believe.' And they admit Melos had never done them any harm. Then they put forward the famous theory of human nature which may (or may not) be Thucydides' own:

> We recommend that you should try to get what it is possible for you
> to get, taking into consideration what we both really do think; since
> you know as well as we do that, when these matters are discussed by
> practical people [have the Athenians been practical people?] the
> standard of justice depends on the equality of power to compel and
> that in fact the strong do what they have the power to do and the
> weak accept what they have to accept.

All laws, human or divine, are reduced to this:

> It is a general and necessary law of nature to rule wherever one can.
> This is not a law that we made ourselves, nor were we the first to act
> upon it. [The Athenians here deny their uniqueness.] We found it
> already in existence, and we shall leave it to exist forever among
> those who come after us.

Does Thucydides really believe this? Or has a noble if flawed heroic nation degraded itself through pursuit of unbounded self-aggrandizement to repudiate all that made it admirable? Is Athens delusion or tragedy? Through the evidence of the book, *we*, the supposedly disinterested community 'who want to understand,' must judge.

V

Thucydides' Conclusion

I could end here, and talk about how great nations repudiate their own ideals and redefine law to mean 'necessity' in their pursuit of an indefinite 'security' indistinguishable from empire. But Thucydides ends, I believe, on a hopeful note. Book VIII of *The Peloponnesian War* has no speeches. Is this because the book is unfinished? Perhaps, but it makes sense to have no speeches at this stage in Athenian history because the rational discourse associated with the democracy, which has been overthrown, has ceased. Domestic law and order has broken down, and various elements are intriguing to betray the country to the Spartans. But then a 'miracle' happens: (8.92)

> There was great confusion and a general state of panic, since the
> people in Athens thought the Piraeus had already been seized and
> Alexicles put to death, and the people in the Piraeus were expecting
> the troops from Athens to be upon them at any moment. The elder
> men did what they could to stop those who were running wildly
> through the city to the places where the arms were kept, and
> Thucydides the Pharsalian, the representative of Athenian interests at
> Pharsalus, who was in Athens, threw himself resolutely in their way,
> crying out to them not to destroy their country.

Then 'in spite of everything' the Athenians man twenty ships, (8.97) rout the Spartans, and as the book ends the Persians and Spartans are quarrelling. After the Sicilian fiasco, after having to be stopped from tearing down their own defenses, after fighting Sicily, Sparta, Persia, and Egypt at the same time, Athens could still win a victory. Thucydides ends with an open-ended situation favorable to Athens, not with the ultimate catastrophe.

A Thucydides (the author himself was in exile for his role in the Athenian defeat at Amphipolis) can save his country, or at least give it the chance of saving itself. In the final pages, he symbolically throws himself right into the war. The man of ideas, the life of the mind, intelligent inquiry into law, justice, right action, and the realization of the tragic fragility of these ideals under the best circumstances can, with the 'old men' left over from the days of Pericles, recall the Athens that was a possibility, if not a reality. This Athens had taken as its mission the practical task which was Thucydides' intellectual task -- the testing and rational discussion of the possibilities and problems of a just, egalitarian, and free society. By opening the discussion for itself and for future generations, the civilization of Periclean Athens forever remains a hypothesis to be tested by a community of inquirers concerned with justice, freedom, and law.

Point of curiosity. Why did a Pharsalian Thucydides stand in for our author? It is well known that Thucydides sometimes emphasized events unimportant for the historical course of war (Mytilene and Melos for example; see Stadter: 1973, 22) because they illustrated moral or political trends he wished to stress. He also (1.22) admits that not all of the speeches he records are accurate -- 'my method has been, while keeping as closely as possible to the general sense of the words that were actually used, to make the speakers say what, in my opinion, was called for by each situation.' In short, Thucydides was willing to invent suitable events. There may or may not have been a Pharsalian Thucydides. But given the secret messages placed in ancient texts (Gordon: 1974), we can look back in the book and see that Pharsalia, an ally of Athens, is mentioned significantly only once (1.110-111):

Orestes, the son of the King of Thessaly Echecratides, was exiled from his country and persuaded the Athenians to restore him. The Athenians took with them a force of Boetians and Phocians, who were not their allies, and marched to Pharsalus in Thessaly. Here they dominated the country -- though without being able to go far from their camp -- but they failed to capture the town or to secure any of the objects of the expedition, and they returned home again with Orestes, not having achieved any results.

Whether these events actually occurred or not, they too summarize the entire book. The Athenians could dominate the country, but came to grief when they try to expand too far. They failed to secure the objects of war, but 'returned home again with Orestes.' Any Athenian would know from Aeschylus' *Oresteia* that Orestes is given safe-conduct in Athens, having been hounded by the Furies. In Athens, justice is no longer a matter of the traditional eye-for-an-eye revenge manifested by the curse of the House of Atreus. It has become subject to the rational deliberation of free citizens in a court of law. If the Peloponnesian War achieved no military success, it at least brought Thucydides and Orestes to Athens. The war thus offered to what Peirce would term an infinite community of disinterested inquirers the opportunity to think rationally and test pragmatically whether a society dedicated to the coexistence of order and freedom, individuality and civic virtue, economic betterment and justice, can come into being and be saved from the Furies of history.

Final Point: Yet *The Peloponnesian War* still does not end. Tissaphernes, the Persian general, must yet go to the Hellespont and attempt to straighten out a bewildering pattern of alliances and double-crosses which Thucydides quickly describes in the last paragraphs of the book (8.106-109). Before he goes, he stops at Ephesus to make a sacrifice to Artemis. Again, every Greek would know the symbolic significance of the ending. The Hellespont was the site of the Trojan War, which began with Agamemnon's sacrifice of Iphigenia to Artemis. By linking the Peloponnesian War with the great founding legend and war of Greek society, Thucydides reconfirms his original contention that history repeats itself, and that the signs of the great wars will show themselves until the end of time.

REFERENCES

Edmunds, Lowell, 1975, *Chance and Intelligence in Thucydides*, Cambridge, Mass.: Harvard University Press.

Fisch, Max, 1971, 'Peirce's Arisbe: The Greek Influence in His Later Philosophy,' *Transactions of the Charles S. Peirce Society: Volume 7*, 187-210.

Finley, John H., Jr., 1942, *Thucydides,* Cambridge, Mass.: Harvard University Press.

Gordon, Cyrus, 1974, *Riddles in History*, New York: Crown.

Peirce, Charles, S., 1868, 'Some Consequences of the Four Incapacities,' reprinted in Justus Buchler, ed., *Philosophical Writings of Peirce*, London: Routledge and Kegan Paul, 1940, 228-250.

_____, 1877, 'The Fixation of Belief,' reprinted in Buchler, *op. cit.*, 5-22.

_____, 1878, 'How to Make Our Ideas Clear,' reprinted in Buchler, *op. cit.,* 23-41.

_____, 1883, 'The General Theory of Probable Inference,' reprinted in Buchler, *op. cit.,* 190-217.

_____, 1893-1910, 'Logic as Semiotic: The Theory of Signs,' reprinted in Buchler, *op. cit.,*98-119, from various manuscripts.

_____, 1903-1911, 'Letters to Lady Welby,' reprinted in *Values in A Universe of Chance: Selected Writings of Charles S. Peirce*, ed. Philip P. Wiener, Garden City, NY: Doubleday, 1958, 380-432.

Stadter, Philip, A., editor, 1973, *The Speeches in Thucydides*, Chapel Hill: University of North Carolina Press.

Thucydides, c.403 B.C., *The Peloponnesian War*, trans. Rex Warner, Harmondsworth, England: Penguin, 1954. Note: Pagination to book and paragraph, to enable readers of any edition to locate the passages cited.

Chapter 14

Peirce-suing Plato:
The Republic as a Semiotic Society

One of the annoyances of doing intellectual history is that thinkers are frequently branded with brief, superficial labels which distort their work unrecognizably. Poor Plato: 'Totalitarian or Democrat?' is the question posed by one collection of essays devoted to *The Republic* (Thorson 1963). There is also the famous Rafael fresco 'The School of Athens' in which Plato points one finger to the sky (idealist, truth is one) while Aristotle points a spread-out hand to the ground (materialist, truth is multi-faceted), with history's most prominent minds arrayed on one side or the other, while Michelangelo sits dejectedly in a corner.

Plato was none of these things, as Charles S. Peirce well knew. 'The rivulets at the head of the river of pragmatism are easily traced back to almost any desired antiquity. Socrates bathed in these waters,' he claimed. (Peirce c. 1910: 5. 11) On another occasion, he stated that pragmatism 'appears to have been virtually the philosophy of Socrates.' (Peirce c. 1906: 6. 490) On yet a third he found Socrates's most praiseworthy characteristic to be his open mind: 'The real spirit of Socrates . . . would have been delighted to have been overcome in argument, because he would have learned something by it.' (Peirce 1878: 5. 406)

Peirce's understanding that Socrates/Plato believed that we held our truths provisionally and ought to act on them in full awareness of their and our limitations is correct if we adopt what seems to me the only way to read a book written by a serious thinker. We cannot read a text in such a way that important parts of it are ignored or contradicted. If Socrates's message was to go forth and create a society without money or families and with sexual equality he would not say that 'the best and quickest way to establish our society and constitution' is to have philosophers start with a group of ten-year-olds separated from their parents' influence -- a manifest impossibility unless the philosophers held power in the first place. (Plato c.410 B.C.:   541a)[1]   Notice when Glaucon observes that the philosopher will only enter politics in the Republic, Socrates responds that 'I doubt if it will ever exist on earth. . . . Perhaps it is laid up as a pattern in heaven. . . . But it doesn't matter whether it exists or ever will exist.' (592b)

Similarly, if Socrates were telling us that the good, the true, and the beautiful were one and knowable and should be our guiding stars to practical action, then why would he present the simile of the Cave with the qualification that 'the truth of the matter is, after all, known only to god.' (517e) Elsewhere, he notes that 'to produce a . . . type of character, educated for excellence on standards different from those held by public opinion, is not, never has been, and never will be possible -- in terms of human possibility, and short of a miracle.' (492e) The existence of Socrates himself -- the man uninterested in popularity or possessions who lives only for philosophy -- is itself a miracle outside the (impossible) context of the Republic: 'My own divine sign, I think, hardly counts' as proof that corrupted societies can produce real philosophers, 'as hardly anyone before me has had it.' (496e)

In fact, *The Republic* explicitly warns that one should *not* go out and try to create a perfect society. Even to speak truthfully about important things means being prepared to suffer. Plato was writing both after Socrates had been executed for his preaching and after Plato's own efforts to found an ideal society in Sicily had come to grief. Socrates makes his famous pronouncement that 'the society we have described can never grow into a reality or see the light of day . . . till philosophers become kings in this world, or till those we now call kings and rulers truly become philosophers.' (That is, never: Socrates insists that you need the true society to create philosopher-rulers, and it is circular to argue they can set up the true society.) Glaucon replies: 'My dear Socrates, if you make pronouncements of that sort, you can't be surprised if a large number of decent people take their coats off, pick up the nearest weapon, and come after you in their shirt sleeves to do something terrible to you.' (473d) In a corrupt society, the true philosophers 'are likely to perish like a man thrown among wild beasts, without profit to themselves or others, before they can do any good to their friends or to society. When they reckon this up, they live quietly and keep to themselves, like a man who stands under the shelter of a wall during a driving storm of dust and hail.' (496e)

So what is *The Republic* about once we realize Plato has warned us against using it as a blueprint for action? Ironically, the fact that philosophers who enjoy a high degree of reputation have championed these misreadings powerfully illustrates Plato's argument that in imperfect societies where philosophers are improperly educated, pseudo-philosophers will arise mirroring the commonly held falsehoods on which the society is based. And we may thus take as our starting point the fact that *The Republic* begins and ends with discussions of what passes for justice in imperfect societies. At the beginning, Socrates is forced by his friends, rather comically but compelled nevertheless, to return to Athens to participate in the dialogue about justice. He doesn't want to: the philosopher wants to escape the dust and hail storm. 'We might persuade you that you ought to let us go,' says Socrates. 'You can't persuade people who won't listen,' replies Polemarchus. (327e) In other words, representatives of a corrupted order have forced the philosopher to turn political, and won't listen to reason -- that is, the impossibility of a sensible discussion under these conditions -- from the very start.

Socrates confronts in order Cephalus, Polemarchus, and Thrasymachus, representatives of timarchic, oligarchic, and tyrannical perversions of justice as will be outlined at the end of *The Republic*. Cephalus drives home the point that real discussion cannot take place in this context, for after claiming that in old age 'one's desire for rational conversation and one's enjoyment of it increase correspondingly' (328e) he quits the conversation after it has hardly begun! He goes off to worship the gods, signifying that the traditional, aristocratic society he represents values honor and is cemented by religion, but rejects critical thinking. (331d) Polemarchus then presents justice as a financial exchange: giving 'every man his due' (331d) involves business transactions (332d, 333a, 333c) and justice becomes a question of utility. Socrates dismisses this argument with some facile, unconvincing rhetoric, demonstrating the impossibility of discussing justice if people are not really interested in justice itself, but only in its usefulness in rationalizing the injustices of a particular corrupted society.

Things get interesting when Thrasymachus jumps in. He is a multi-faceted sign, representing the rejection of a reasonable search for justice and the tyrannical personality -- he 'had often tried to interrupt, but had been prevented' (336e) -- as well as the way other corrupt societies evolve into tyranny as *The Republic* describes near its end. But in this context, it is Thrasymachus who is in fact closest to the truth: in *all* corrupt societies, justice *is* the interest of the stronger, which is his definition, and efforts to disguise this are less insightful than calling hypocrisy what it is. When Thrasymachus at various points replies to Socrates: 'That's not a fair parallel' (337b), 'You must have your joke' (337d), 'I'm doing it to please you' (351b), 'Enjoy your argument. I won't annoy the company by contradicting you' (351b), and 'This is your holiday treat' (354b), he is pointing out fallacious arguments. Socrates himself later supports this interpretation: 'You have been most agreeable since you stopped being cross with me. . . . But I'm not enjoying it all the same. . . . I still know nothing.' (354b) That Thrasymachus's objections and Socrates's early replies are exemplars of how not to argue about justice (or anything else) is evidenced by the juxtaposition of two statements. Right after Socrates advances the point that 'there's no existing society good enough for the philosophic nature. . . . If only it could find a social structure whose excellence matched its own, then its truly divine nature would appear clearly' (497b), he warns the others: 'Now don't start a quarrel between me and Thrasymachus, when we've just become friends -- not that we were ever really enemies.' (499d)

In what sort of society, therefore, can justice be achieved? As a prelude, in what sort of society is it even possible to think and talk about justice -- that is, do real philosophy? The just society is impossible unless philosophers sit down and discuss things rationally -- that is, they are truly searching after truth and justice rather than doing what was done in the early part of the dialogue -- disguising various selfish interests with the mask of justice. Therefore, for true philosophers to exist, you need a society where they will not be tempted by values other than the pursuit of wisdom. If they can get their hands on money and luxuries, they will be tempted by them. If they have easy access to sexual indulgence, they will be drawn toward that. If they have families and can pass on wealth through inheritance, they will find ways of being partial to their children, keeping down other people's offspring, and explaining wealth, poverty, and hedonism as just.

Glaucon protests that the society without such pleasures and class divisions is 'just the fodder you would provide if you were founding a community of pigs.' (372d) So Socrates replies: 'I understand. We are to study . . . society when it enjoys the luxuries of civilization. Not a bad idea, perhaps, for in the process we may discover how justice and injustice are bred in a community. For though the [simple] society we have described seems to me to be the true one, like a man in health, there's nothing to prevent us, if you wish, studying one in a fever.' (372e) Once again, Socrates is telling us: you don't want justice. You want 'couches and tables and other furniture, and a variety of delicacies, scents, perfumes, call-girls, and confectionery.' (373a) In fact, he tells us 'a democracy is the most attractive of all societies. The diversity of its characters, like the different colors in a patterned dress, make it look very attractive. . . . Perhaps most people would, for this reason, judge it to be the best form of society, like women and children when they see gaily colored things.' (557d) However, democracy is not the just society which encourages philosophy, but 'a wonderfully pleasant way of carrying on in the short run.' (557e) If you want that, fine; but please don't pretend you are a philosopher seeking justice.

Plato gives two conditions for a just society or man to exist: absence of material or familial concerns, and a rigorous training program: two years of military service, ten years of mathematical study, five years of dialectic, and fifteen years in subordinate offices before, at age fifty, one can become a philosopher-ruler. In other words, you can't learn philosophy or become just by taking Philosophy 101 or, the Athenian equivalent, spending some time with a sophist. Socrates would find nothing more absurd than professors without military experience and knowledge of mathematics under the age of fifty teaching anyone sent in by the admissions office. Plato's arduous societal conditions and educational process as prerequisites to seeking truth and justice are the only ways, he thinks, to eliminate ulterior motives and ensure philosophers possess a genuine love of both community and knowledge.

That is crucial. Discussion about justice can only occur when people are truly 'well educated, and become reasonable', that is, they function in a context 'all of which ought so far as possible to be dealt with on the proverbial basis of 'all things in common between friends'.' (423e)   What Plato says about the Guardians is even more true of the philosopher-rulers: they must be 'gentle towards their fellow citizens and dangerous only to their enemies; otherwise, they will destroy each other before others can destroy them' (375e); they must be men 'who are free and fear slavery more than death.' (387b)   Further, unlike the soldiers of the state, they have progressed to be 'under the control of divine wisdom.   That wisdom and control should, if possible, come from within; failing that, it must be imposed from without, in order that, being under the same guidance, we may all be friends and equals.' (590e)

Inquiry into justice is only possible by legitimate inquirers: if we treat each other as friends and equals and do not have influences at work enabling us to present selfish interests as the good and true.   Now this is Charles Peirce's ideal community of inquirers.   They cannot *know* 'the' truth; they can only have a vision of it like the light in the Cave or the city laid up in Heaven.   They have to communicate their vision through signs -- similes and metaphors.   One reason Plato mistrusts poets and artists is that it is so much easier for them to represent the ideals treasured by imperfect societies and hedonistic men than it is for the philosopher to translate his vision into signs: 'the reasonable element and its unvarying calm are difficult to represent, and difficult to understand if represented, particularly by the motley audience gathered in a theater, to whose experience it is quite foreign.' (604e)[2]

The perfect philosopher, like the perfect state, is an impossibility.   But if we cannot know the truth, we have an obligation to test our visions or hypotheses continually in the context of the communities of inquirers where we find ourselves. This means we must be sensitive to the biases of the context shaping the discussion, and therefore make an effort to correct these biases by reference to other contexts and audiences real and hypothetical.   This is what Plato did in *The*

Republic. Through dramatic representation of societies and the types of personality they engendered, he hoped to educate those who want, like Thrasymachus, to find out what is really going on, to penetrate the prejudices behind our philosophies. Only a Socrates with a divine sign is contextually free, and perhaps not even he is.

Why does Peirce consider Socrates a pragmatist? Because the ideal context which will enable us to know the truth, do justice, or create the perfect society cannot exist. We test our imperfect approximations and learn of their relative value by their fruits or signs, namely the sort of men and results they produce. By acknowledging the limitations of upbringing, audience, self-interest, and intelligence shaping our thought we are *perhaps* able to move a bit closer to the elusive ideals that Peirce, like Plato, realized would only be grasped by a community of unbiased inquirers -- an impossibility -- in the long run -- that is, never. We shall never know the truth, and it is this that sets us free. But only if we know that we do not know it.

ENDNOTES

1. I have used the standard paragraph numbers for *The Republic* which will enable the readers of any edition to locate the ideas found here; the edition and translation used is cited below.

2. Professor David Savan of the University of Toronto quite properly informed me that Peirce's community of inquirers, unlike Plato's, was primarily concerned with acquisition of knowledge and only incidentally with questions of justice and social order. Although the communities have similar goals and constraints, the difference of emphasis is well worth noting.

REFERENCES

Peirce, Charles S., 1878, 'How to Make Our Ideas Clear,' *Popular Science Monthly* 12, 1878, 286-302; reprinted in *Collected Papers*, Charles Hartshorne, Paul Weiss, and Arthus Burks, eds., 8 vols.: Harvard University Press, 1931-1958; reference in text to volume and paragraph in this collection.

_____, c.1906, 'Pragmatism,' manuscript, reprinted in *Collected Papers*, reference in text to volume and paragraph.

_____, c.1910, Manuscript fragment, reprinted in *Collected Papers*, reference in text to volume and paragraph.

_____, c.410 B.C., *The Republic*, translated by Desmond Lee, Harmondsworth, England: Penguin Books, 2nd ed., 1974.

Thorson, Thomas L., 1963, *Plato: Totalitarian or Democrat?*, Englewood Cliffs, New Jersey: Prentice-Hall, 1963.

Chapter 15

Christian Symbolism and Political Unity in the English Reformation: A Historical Interpretation of the Semiotics of Anglican Doctrine.

When Henry VIII declared himself head of the Church of England, he could not help but open an acrimonious debate concerning the nature of the new church. As the anonymous 'Homilist' wrote in his 'Sermon Against Contention and Brawling' (Anonymous: 1535):

> Too many there be which, upon the ale-house benches or other places, delight to set forth certain questions, not so much pertaining to edification, as to vain-glory, and showing forth of their cunning; and so unsoberly to reason and dispute, that when neither part will give place to other, they fall to chiding and contention, and sometimes from hot words to further inconvenience.

These disputations went on for at least a century and a half, and to them we owe the Puritan settlement of North America, the English Civil War, the subsequent Restoration, and the Glorious Revolution. Nevertheless, if the 'Articles Devised by the Kings Highes Majestie' in 1536 and subsequently amended until standardized as the 'Thirty-Nine' Articles of Religion of 1571 did not succeed in their purpose 'to stablyshe Christen quietnes and unitie amonge us and to avoyde contentious opinions,' (Articles of 1536) it was not for lack of trying.* As historian G.J. Cuming (1969: 81) remarked of the efforts of Thomas Cranmer,

Anglicanism's first great theorist and author of most of the early formulations of faith and Prayer Books, 'the more doctrinal positions that could be read [into them] . . . the better.' Cranmer consciously sought 'the assistance of learned men who, having compared their opinions together with us, may do away with all doctrinal controversies' (Cranmer 1548: 65). Despite civil war and mutual animosity among Anglicans, Roman Catholics, and Dissenters of various denominations, the Anglican settlement achieved sufficiently durable support that England by the eighteenth century emerged as a unified nation and world power second to none.

It can plausibly be argued that what political stability England did enjoy owed much to the unusual nature of the Anglican Church and its doctrines. Every other Reformation church began as a principled objection to Roman Catholicism and sought to restore Christianity to its original state. The Roman Catholics, equally, asserted that they embodied the true spirit of Christianity because Christ and the Apostles had delegated their authority to the Popes and Councils who could authoritatively develop it. To translate this into philosophical language: the Reformers proceeded to deduce the correct interpretation of (a) the sacraments; (b) especially the Eucharist; (c) the service of worship; (d) man's (in)ability to aid in his own salvation; (e) the extent of human depravity; (f) the merits of the primitive as opposed to the historically developed church; and (g) the relationship of religion to political authority.

For example, Calvinists believed there were two sacraments, Communion and Baptism, which served as symbols of the faith rather than means of salvation; that a specific form of church and civil government (the Congregational) was mandated in the New Testament, and that man was totally depraved and saved through faith alone.

Lutherans also accepted two sacraments, total depravity, and justification through faith alone (although they downplayed the last two compared to Calvinists). But they preached that Christ's body and blood were present at Communion along with the bread and wine, kept the Mass but translated it into the vernacular, and insisted that the true Christian would be indifferent, and hence absolutely obedient, to whatever political authority existed. Where the State mandated violation of Christian ethics passive disobedience and suffering the consequences were the only options.

Other Protestant sects introduced a wide variety of practices: sixteenth century Europeans tended to group as 'Anabaptists' groups as diverse as those denying either infant baptism, or the possibility of sin once one is saved, millennarians, and those who denied civil authority and private property.

Roman Catholics adhered to the traditional positions that there were seven sacraments; that bread and wine of the Eucharist were miraculously transformed into the body and blood of Christ; that salvation was a complicated formula which could involve purgatory, saintly intercession and retrospective indulgence; and that the historical Papacy retained a legitimate role in both civil and religious affairs.

Anglicanism, unlike all of these, stressed that the above issues were 'adiaphora,' or things indifferent. At Thomas Cranmer's final examination for heresy under Roman Catholic Queen 'Bloody' Mary, he offered a defense that only an Anglican or semiotician would understand. Accused of maintaining all three (Roman, Lutheran, Calvinist) doctrines of communion, he responded, 'Nay, I taught but two contrary doctrines [not the Calvinist]' (Cranmer 1555: 12). As Henry VIII warned the clergy when the first Anglican credo, the Ten Articles of 1536, was promulgated, they should 'in no wise contentiously . . . treat of matters indifferent, which be neither necessary to our salvation . . . nor yet to be in any wise contemned.' The Ten Articles of 1536, the Forty-Two of 1553, and the

Thirty-Nine of 1571 were masterpieces adiaphoric equivocation. While maintaining that acceptance of the Holy Trinity and the Sacraments of Baptism and Holy Communion were 'necessary to our salvation,' other controversial matters dividing Christians were resolved through permitting a variety of beliefs. With the exception of 'certain Anabaptists,' any Christian could swear allegiance to the Church of England, even, I will argue, a Roman Catholic had the Pope allowed it.

The Articles themselves were adiaphoric. 'We do not suffer any man to reject the Thirty-Nine Articles of the Church of England at his pleasure,' wrote John Branhull (1654: 186). 'Yet neither do we look upon them as essentials of saving faith or legacies of Christ and of His Apostles, but . . . as pious opinions fitted for the preservation of unity. Neither do we oblige any man to believe them, but only not to contradict them.' Public refutation would disturb the civic peace, but the Church would not judge men's souls or consciences. Let us look at seven important religious issues and notice the development of the three declarations of faith in such a way as to avoid offending either Catholics or Calvinists, in the hopes of bringing them into the broad church.

A) Sacraments -- In 1536 only three are mentioned, Baptism, Communion and Penance. The other Roman Catholic sacraments are neither affirmed nor denied. Penance, however, is not quite the same as the Roman Catholic sort which requires auricular confession to a priest. The Anglican articles permit such confession, but leave open the possibility that not all Christians will use it. After over a page on the necessity of sincere feelings of shamefulness and repentance for the confession, the issue is equivocated as follows:

> In no wise do they contemn this auricular confession which is made
> unto the ministers of the Church, but that they ought to repute the
> same as a very expedient and necessary mean, whereby they may

require and seek this absolution at the priest's hands, at such time as
they shall find their consciences grieved with mortal sin, and have
occasion so to do, to the intent they may thereby attain certain
comfort and consolation of their consciences.

A Roman Catholic could read the passage stressing the words 'ought' and
'necessary.' A Reformer could privately confess his sins to God by noting
auricular confession as 'a' (not 'the') means of attaining forgiveness, and note the
purpose of such a confession is not to obtain a more certain forgiveness than
private confession, but to attain 'certain' (definite? to a degree?) 'comfort and
consolation.' As Francis White argued in 1624 (514), 'the difference between the
Papals and us in this question is not about the thing itself, considered without
abuses, but concerning the manner and also the necessity thereof.'

The Common Prayer Book and the Forty-Two Articles of 1553 are generally
thought to lean more toward Calvinism than either of the other two sets of
Articles. Article XXVI 'Of the Sacraments' begins with a preface that would be
removed in 1571 defining them as 'most few in number, most excellent in
signification, as is Baptism, and the Lord's Supper.' Sharp readers will note the
special pride of place given to the two sacraments on which all Christians agree,
and the only two the Calvinists accepted as genuine. Another genuflection toward
Calvinism is the stress on signification. The other five sacraments are not
mentioned, but neither are they denied. The Article goes out of its way *not* to say
that 'there are only two sacraments.'

The clarification, or, for Anglican unification purposes, the equivocation as
to how many sacraments there are, is perfected in the 1571 Article XXV:

Those five, commonly called Sacraments, that is to say Confirmation,
Penance, Orders, Matrimony, and extreme Unction, are not to be
compted for Sacraments of the Gospel, being such as have grown

partly of the corrupt following of the Apostles, partly are states of life allowed in the Scriptures; but yet have, not like nature of Sacraments with Baptism and the Lord's Supper, for that they have not any visible sign of ceremony ordained of God.

Nowhere are these sacraments either affirmed or denied. If they grew out of the 'corrupt following of the Apostles,' does this mean the sacraments are corrupt and hence not genuine, or simply that Christians who followed the apostles were of course not perfect. If they are not 'sacraments of the gospel,' does that not mean they could be sacraments of a different sort, 'states of life allowed in the scriptures'? One could also belabor the obvious and speculate on the significance of 'visible sign of ceremony' as well. They could also possess an 'invisible' signification.

B) Holy Communion -- Here there are two issues. First, are we actually eating the body and blood of Christ (Transubstantiation -- Roman Catholic doctrine), are they present along with the bread and wine (Consubstantiation -- Lutheran doctrine), or is the ritual a symbolic remembrance of the Last Supper entailing no real presence (Calvinist doctrine)? Second, is taking Communion itself a good work which aided in Salvation, as only the Roman Catholics maintained, a 'means of grace,' or rather a reflection of spiritual proclivity as the reformers insisted? The Articles of 1536 espoused the Catholic position, as the transition to Anglicanism was still incomplete (Henry VIII still forbade priests to marry). In 1553, the first two paragraphs of Article XXIX 'Of the Lord's Supper' respectively veer perilously close to the Roman Catholic and Calvinist positions without directly espousing either. On the one hand, the Sacrament 'is not only a sign' but also 'a sacrament of our redemption,' 'a Communion of the body [and blood] of Christ.' On the other:

Transubstantiation, or the change of the substance of bread and wine into the substance of Christ's body and blood cannot be proved by holy writ, but is repugnant to the plain words of Scripture, and hath given occasion to many superstitions.

The Article goes on to note that a body cannot be in two places at one time and that Christ's body was taken up into Heaven. Therefore, 'a faithful man ought not, either to believe, or openly confess the real and bodily presence [of Christ's flesh and blood], in the Sacrament of the Lord's Supper.' Of course, truth might be 'repugnant to the *plain* words of Scripture' and yet deducible from their contextual or logical interpretation. Also, one could argue that a distinction existed between the Sacrament and the physical bread and wine, thereby enabling a believer in transubstantiation to stress the first part of the Article rather than the second. But it should be noted that 1553 was the creed closest to Calvinism.

By 1571, the church is more subtle. The pro-Roman Catholic part of the article (now Article XXVIII) substitutes 'partaking' for 'Communion,' which strengthens the case for transubstantiation without quite saying 'physical eating' or insisting that a miracle has taken place. On the other hand, the clause about a body's inability to be in two different places at once is dropped. Six words are substituted for it: transubstantiation 'overthroweth the nature of a Sacrament' -- which could mean either it denies its efficacy, or that it removes the 'natural,' the presence of the bread and wine (thereby substituting Christ's divine body). People espousing either view could then look to support in a new final clause: 'The body of Christ is given, taken, and eaten in the Supper only after an heavenly or Spiritual manner; and the means whereby the body of Christ is received and eaten in the Supper is faith.' Note 'blood' is here omitted: either to avoid obvious repetition, if one believes with the Reformers that Communion should be taken by the Congregation in both kinds; or to stress that only the bread should be eaten by the people, as the Roman Catholics preach.

Also at issue is whether Communion is a real means to salvation (the Roman Catholic position) or rather a sign of one's willingness to be faithful (Reformed position). Both the 1553 and 1571 Articles are identical (Numbers XXVI and XXV respectively) in asserting that the bread and wine 'be not only badges or tokens of Christian men's profession: but rather they be certain sure witnesses and effectual signs of grace and God's good will toward us, by which he doth work invisibly in us, and doth not only quicken, but also strengthen and confirm our faith in him.' One could interpret 'sign' in the second part of the sentence either as 'symbol' or as 'indication of real presence.' Either a Roman Catholic or a Reformer could interpret this article as consonant with his conscience. As apologist Jeremy Taylor (1646: 176) wrote:

> The wisdom of the church thought it expedient to join both clauses; the first, lest the church should be suspected to be of the Sacramentary opinion; the latter, lest she should be mistaken as a patroness of Transubstantiation; and both these with so much temper and sweetness, that by her care she rather prevented all mistakes taken by any and by declaration in her prayers engaged herself on either side, that she might pray to God without strife and contention with her brethren.

C) The Service of Worship -- The Articles of 1536, Numbers VI and VIII, are 'First of Images' and 'Of Rites and Ceremonies.' They are included with Articles VI, IX and X under the general rubric 'Articles Concerning the Laudable Ceremonies Used in the Church.' These Articles praise these practices as useful, but not required for salvation. In the first Anglican commentary to stress the 'middle way,' Thomas Cranmer (1538) defended his position that too many ceremonies were wrong, but some were helpful; therefore 'some be abolished and some retained.' The people must remember and should be instructed not to worship the images but the God they signify, and also that 'none of these ceremonies have power to remit sin, but only to stir and lift our minds unto God.' By 1553 and 1571, the Church learned the wisdom of not mentioning a variety of specific ceremonies (use of Holy Water, the ceremony of palms on Palm Sunday, etc.) as it had in 1536. Now a wedge existed for people to accept or deny specific ceremonies. At the same time, however, the 1553 and 1571 Articles stressed the desirability of uniform ceremonies in matters of 'adiaphora' -- that is, things 'neither evil nor forbidden' (Verkamp 1977: 36,61) yet not commanded:

> Whosoever through his private judgment willingly, and purposely doth
> openly break the traditions and ceremonies of the Church which be
> not repugnant to the word of God, and be ordained, and approved by
> common authority, ought to be rebuked openly (that others may fear
> to do the like) as one that offendeth against the common order of the
> church, and hurteth the authority of the magistrate, and woundeth the
> consciences of weak brethren.

The Puritans could, and did, consider themselves the true church of England largely because they insisted that 'common authority' had in fact ordained ceremonies 'repugnant to the word of God.' On the other hand, mainstream Anglicans castigated them for lack of charity toward the 'weak brethren' who found the Mass, elaborately robed priests, and aesthetically pleasing churches aids to faith. Both sides could cite Article XXXIV of 1571 or XXXIII of 1553 to support their cases. But note that these articles regard non-observance of church customs not as a sin, but as a breach of civil order. Richard Hooker, Anglicanism's greatest apologist, nicely caught the mean between the extremes:

Two opinions therefore there are concerning sufficiency of Holy
Scripture, each extremely opposite unto the other, and both repugnant
unto truth. The schools of Rome teach Scripture to be so insufficient,
as if excellent traditions were not added, it did not contain all
revealed and perpetual truth, which absolutely is necessary for the
children of men in this life to know that they may in the next be
saved. Others justly condemning this opinion grow likewise unto a
dangerous extremity, as if Scripture did not only contain all things in
that kind necessary, but all things simply, and in such sort that to do
anything according to any other law were not only unnecessary but
even opposite unto salvation unlawful and sinful. (Hooker 1594-
1597: Book II, Ch. 8.7)

Hooker concluded that reason was required to interpret Scripture or it simply made
no sense, and that for all its faults the historical church had given much valuable
aid on that score.

D) Man's ability to aid in his own salvation -- The Anglican Church (Article XVII
in both 1553 and 1571) defends predestination as strongly as any Calvinist. But
it also contains qualifiers suggesting man can indeed aid in his salvation. In 1553,
the qualification is rather weak, and occurs in Article XIX: 'No man, (be he
never so perfect a Christian) is exempt and loose from the obedience of those
commandments which are called moral.' But in 1571, this article is removed and
a far stronger one (XII) 'Of Good Works' substituted:

Albeit that good works, which are the fruits of faith, and follow after
justification, cannot put away our sins, and endure the severity of
God's judgment: yet they are pleasing and acceptable to God in
Christ, and do spring out necessarily of a true and lively faith, in so

much that by them, a lively faith may evidently be known, as a tree is discerned by its fruit.

While no Christian would argue that good works alone could save anybody, the 1571 Article can be interpreted to allow them a major role as a contributing factor in a Christian's life. John Selden considered the division between faith and works 'unhappy', and as fatuous as arguing whether a candle provided light *or* heat. 'Put out the candle, they are both gone . . . in a right conception fides est opus' (Selden c.1654: section 42).

E) The extent of human depravity -- Is taken up in Article VIII (1553) and IX (1571). The latter states that man is 'very far gone from original righteousness,' which could encompass a variety of theories ranging from total depravity to merely somewhat perverted. George Bull (1669: 312) articulated the Anglican mean:

Whilst we avoid Pelagianism by acknowledging the necessity of grace, let us take care, on the other hand that we fall not into the abyss of Manichean folly, by taking away free will and the cooperation of human industry. The middle, the royal way must be chosen, so as to turn neither to the left hand nor to the right, which will be done if we suppose that with grace, but in subjection to it, the freedom of the will amicably unites.

F) The merits of the primitive vs. the historical church -- That observance of the five non-Scriptural sacraments is partly laudable and partly corrupt (see (a) above) is the model for other developments beyond the Apostles' time. The most significant Article here is XXXIII (1553) or XXXIV (1571) which explicitly endorses adiaphoric liberty:

It is not necessary that traditions and ceremonies be in all places, or utterly like, for at all times they have been diverse, and may be changed according to the diversity of countries, times, and men's manners, so that nothing be ordained against God's will.

This article imposes a dual obligation. National churches may ordain nothing repugnant to the will of God. But individuals must accept local religious customs for the sake of civil and ecclesiastical peace on matters of which they may disapprove, except where these are contrary to scripture. The Church of England could thus with a clear conscience enforce conformity on matters it considered indifferent, thereby angering Dissenters who considered vestments, images, the Mass, etc. repugnant to the faith. Yet this article also paved the way for English toleration following the Civil War: differences in liturgy could be tolerated if they did not threaten the civic peace. The 1661 Prayer Book's Preface explicitly articulated 'the wisdom of the Church of England, ever since the first compiling of the public liturgy, to keep the mean between the two extremes of too much stiffness in refusing; and of too much easiness in admitting, any variation from it.' 'Changes should occur,' but under 'mighty and important considerations according to the various exigency of existing occasions.' The main end: 'the preservation of peace and unity in the church.'

G) The relationship of Civil and Religious Authority -- Amazingly, the clause in Article XXVI in 1553 (XXVII in 1571) concerning the Papacy could in theory allow Roman Catholics to take the oath of allegiance and belong to the Church of England! 'The Bishop of Rome hath no jurisdiction in this Realm of England' could easily be equivocally interpreted to mean that the Pope in his *spiritual* capacity *does* have authority over Roman Catholics in England, for 'realm' is a political entity, and of course the Pope's authority outside Rome comes from the Papacy rather than from the bishopric of Rome. Of course, no Pope would permit such an interpretation. Pope Paul IV had previously offered Elizabeth I papal authorization for the English liturgy and the Prayer Book containing the Thirty-

Nine Articles, which Roman Catholics in England found consistent with their faith. (Taylor 1646: 173). Similarly, sixteenth century Puritans (Ramsey 1963: 42-48) and many eighteenth century Evangelicals, including some who rejected Anglicanism (Brown 1975) continued to use the Prayer Book and the Articles. Still, it is worth noting that James II, a Roman Catholic, was head of the Church of England from 1685 to 1688, and would have remained so had he not proselytized on his Church's behalf so vigorously.

The other most revealing clause on church and state is found in the 1571 Article XXXVII, which maintains that Queen Elizabeth possesses:

> That only prerogative which we see to have been given always to all godly Princes in Holy Scripture by God himself, that is, that they should rule all estates and degrees committed to their charge by God, whether they be Ecclesiastical or Temporal, and restrain with the civil sword the stubborn and evil doers.

In the time of Elizabeth (1558-1603), Parliament was already debating the limits of royal authority. Therefore, Article XXXVII does not define the scope of the Queen's powers. When in 1801 the Protestant Episcopal Church of the United States revised the Thirty-Nine Articles, the principal revision concerned Article XXXVII. Now, it omitted any reference to the Bishop of Rome, or the monarch of England, and instead mandated people 'to pay respectful obedience to the civil authority, regularly and legitimately constituted' (Protestant Episcopal Church 1801:610). Thus, an Episcopalian could in conscience either oppose an improperly constituted government, or on the contrary, put down a rebellion. At the Lambeth Conference of 1988, the world's Anglican bishops resolved (No. 27) to 'understand all those who, after exhausting all other ways, choose the way of armed struggle as the only way to justice, whilst drawing attention to the dangers and injustices possible in such action itself.' At the same meeting, however, all violence was condemned in the particular case of Northern Ireland (No. 73). (Garrett 1989: 313-315). The American version of the Articles also drops the English clauses that both the death penalty for 'heinous and grievous offences' 'may' (not must) be inflicted, and that 'it is lawful for Christian men, at the commandment of the magistrate, to wear weapons, and to serve in war.' The next article (XXXVII, 1553; XXXVIII, 1571) condemns the notion that Christians ought to hold their goods in common, 'as certain anabaptists do falsely boast.' Yet it permits men who are so inclined to give away all they possess: 'every man ought of such things as he possesseth, liberally to give alms to the poor, according to his ability.'

Similar compromises and equivocations in the interest of church and national unity appear in other important documents of the English Reformation. The Prayer Book of 1559 -- the basis for Anglican worship over the next four centuries -- remedied two passages needlessly provocative of Roman Catholics: the 'Black Rubric,' added at the request of John Knox and other Calvinists, asserting that kneeling for communion only implied gratitude rather than 'any real or essential presence' of Christ's blood and body. Nor did the latter book retain the section begging 'deliverance from the Pope and all his detestable enormities.'

Anglican theology takes a semiotic approach to the Christian faith in place of the attempt to fix the truth of doctrinal points as espoused by other religions. Instead, it creates the possibility for a spectrum of interpretation, limited only by belief in the Holy Trinity and the necessity for civil order. The Anglican creed institutes a community of interpreters which, by distinguishing between things indifferent and things necessary for salvation, permits freedom of conscience within wide boundaries but mandates outward conformity as far as the civil authorities deem necessary in the interests of Christian charity and domestic peace. John Locke's *Letter Concerning Toleration* (1689), which makes exactly this point, presents a quintessentially Anglican argument. Various Anglican thinkers had anticipated him: 'it is a hard case we should think all Papists and Anabaptists and Sacramentals to be fools and wicked persons. Certainly, among all these sects, there are very many wise men and good men' (Taylor 1647: 187). Thus, the diverse interpretations of doctrine debated furiously by other religions will be accepted by Anglicans as signs of Christian faith and practice rather than as truths.

The Anglican Church has continued in the spirit of the Thirty-Nine Articles and the early Prayer Books and apologists. Archbishop of Canterbury Ramsey spoke of 'a church never learning from its mistakes unless it is ready to risk making some,' when he opened the Lambeth Conference in 1988. In short, a semiotic church in which a community advances hypotheses and tests them provisionally. Various national churches have their own prayer books and liturgies. Unlike Vatican Councils and Papal Encyclicals, Lambeth Conferences cannot order anyone to do anything, but 'suggest' and 'advise' based on the sense of the church. Other Protestant, Roman Catholic, Greek Orthodox, and Jewish representatives also take part in the dialogue: 1988 gave special attention to women's rights and Third World issues, symbolized through major addresses presented by a black American woman priest and Peruvian Liberation Theologian Gustavo Guttierez. Examples of Angelican toleration of diversity amid unity were resolutions allowing, but not compelling, dioceses to accept women priests and bishops, and 'understanding' homosexual behavior while granting procreation is the purpose of intercourse (Garrett 1989).

Anglicanism is poorly understood, not only by non-Anglicans, but even by church members. For instance, E.R. Norman criticized Lambeth for 'fudging up some compromise that will allow people of enormously divergent opinion and commitment to continue to reside within the same organization.' Finding the resolutions, 'imprecise and diaphanous,' he thought the Archbishop of Canterbury played to every constituency by mentioning Mother Teresa, Bishop Tutu, Chernobyl, AIDS, and the problems of Australian aborigines in his opening address. When the Archbishop 'defined' 'unity' in terms of the cooperation of diverse elements, Norman predicted 'the provisional character . . . will make the Catholic officials in Rome, when they see it, shudder with disbelief' (1989: 372-375).

But it is precisely this imprecision, questing, and encompassing nature that has distinguished Anglicanism from the beginning. T.S. Eliot, in his *Thoughts After Lambeth* (1930: 332), commenting on a conference six decades earlier, rebutted Norman in advance. 'The admission of inconsistencies, sometimes ridiculed as indifference to logic and coherence, of which the English mind is often accused, may be largely the admission of inconsistencies inherent in life itself, and of the impossibility of overcoming them by the imposition of a uniformity greater than life will bear.' Or, as Archbishop Desmond Tutu described the 1988 Conference, 'We all left Canterbury possessed of a deepened unity precisely because of our diversity.' He summed up his church as 'totally untidy, but very, very lovable' (Tutu: 1989). Contrary to popular misconceptions, Anglicanism is not 'one step from Rome' or 'Catholicism without the Pope.' That *some* Anglicans love pomp and circumstance ignores the fact that simple ceremonies close to Calvinism also flourish, and that Puritans existed comfortably in the Elizabethan Church. People in the United States, too enamored of their 'persecuted' Pilgrim and Puritan ancestors, seem to forget that they were a small minority of Englishmen who were far more intolerant of general Anglican practices -- for instance, they sought to stamp out the Mass and fix the symbolic nature of the Eucharist -- than the Church was of them. Second, nothing could be further from the Roman Catholic insistence on sharp definition of matters including the Eucharist, Mass, historical validity of Papal and Conciliar decisions, and the role of good works and purgatory in salvation then the Anglican refusal to fix any of these points.   Heavily influenced by Renaissance Humanism in general and Erasmus in particular (Booty 1976: 327-366; Verkamp 1977: chs. 2 and 3), it is no accident that Anglicanism pioneered in religious toleration, or that two of the modern founders of semiotics -- John Locke and Charles Peirce -- were Anglicans. Links between the Anglican 'broad church' consensus, 'common sense' philosophy, and the survival of representative government and debate in the Anglo-Saxon world can all thus be interpreted as signs of a fundamental mind-set and approach to reality.   The American Constitution, for instance, is in many ways the Anglican compromise applied to politics.   It is therefore interesting, although ultimately inconclusive, to speculate as to how Anglicanism preceded and in many ways produced modern notions of civil, religious, and philosophical (that is, semiotic) liberty.

For convenience, all articles and Prayer Books will be referrred to by year and number. The Convocation of Bishops of the Church of England is the author in each case.

REFERENCES

_____, 1535, *Sermon Against Contention and Brawling*, no publication data, reprinted in part in Charles Hardwick, *A History of the Articles of Religion*, London: George Bell and Sons, 1884, 33-34.

Booty, John, 1976, 'History of the 1559 Book of Common Prayer,' in John Booty, ed., *The Book of Common Prayer*, Washington: Folger Books, 1976, 327-384.

Branhull, John, 1654, *Schism Guarded*, in More and Cross, eds., *Anglicanism*, 186.

Brown, C.J., 1975, 'Divided Loyalties? The Evangelicals, The Prayer-Book, And The Articles,' *Historical Magazine of the Protestant Episcopal Church*, 44, 1975, 189-209.

Bull, George, 1669, *Harmonia Apostolica: or Two Dissertations of which The Doctrine of St. James on Justification by Works is Explained and Defined*, in More and Cross, eds., *Anglicanism*, 312.

Church of England, Convocation of Bishops, 1536, *Articles Devised by the Kinges Highnes Majestie, To Stablyshe Christen Quietnes and Unitie*, no publication data, reprinted in Hardwick, *A History of the Articles of Religion*, Appendices, 237-258.

_____, 1552, *The Book of Common Prayer*, reprinted in *The First and Second Prayer Books of King Edward the Seventh*, London and Toronto: Everyman, 1910.

_____, 1553, *Articles of Religion*, no publication data, reprinted in Hardwick, *A History of the Articles of Religion*, Appendices, 289-353.

_____, 1559, *The Book of Common Prayer*, reprinted and edited by John E. Booty, Washington: Folger Books, 1976.

_____, 1571, *Articles of Religion*, no publication data, reprinted in Hardwick, *A History of the Articles of Religion*, Appendices, 289-353.

_____, 1661, *The Book of Common Prayer*, preface, reprinted in More and Cross, eds., *Anglicanism*, 167-168.

Cranmer, Thomas, 1538, 'Of Ceremonies,' quoted in Cuming, *A History of Anglican Liturgy*, 92.

_____, 1548, 'Original Letters,' quoted in Cuming, *A History of Anglican Liturgy*, 65.

_____, 1555, 'Final Examination of Thomas Cranmer,' quoted in Ramsey et al., *The English Prayer Books*, 12.

Cuming, G.J., 1969, *A History of Anglican Liturgy*, New York: St. Martin's, 1969.

Eliot, T.S., 1930, 'Thoughts After Lambeth,' reprinted in *Selected Essays: New Edition*, New York: Harcourt, Brace, and World.

Garrett, Samuel M., 1989, 'Three Weeks in Canterbury: An Interpretive Chronicle of the Twelfth Lambeth Conference,' *Anglican and Episcopal History*, 3, 1989, 291-332.

Hooker, Richard, 1594-1597, *Lawes of Ecclesiastical Politie*, numerous editions: first published London, references to volume, chapter, and paragraph.

Locke, John, 1689, *A Letter Concerning Toleration*, first published as *Epistola de Tolerantia*, Gouda, Holland, and reprinted that year in London, numerous editions.

More, Paul Elmer and Cross, Frank Leslie, eds., 1957, *Anglicanism*, New York: Macmillan.

Norman, E.R., 1989, 'Anglicanism and the Lambeth Conference of 1988,' *Anglican and Episcopal History*, 3, 1989, 370-378.

Protestant Episcopal Church in the United States of America, Bishops, Clergy, and Laity, 1801, 'Articles of Religion,' in *The Book of Common Prayer*, New York: Church Pension Fund, 1945, 603-611.

Ramsey, Michael, Archbishop of Canterbury, et al., 1963, *The English Prayer Book, 1549-1662*, London: Society for the Propagation of Christian Knowledge.

Selden, John, c.1654, *Table Talk*, first published London 1689, numerous editions, referred to usually by section.

Taylor, Jeremy, 1646, *An Apology for the Authorized and Set Forms of Liturgy*, in More and Cross, eds., *Anglicanism*, 169-175.

_____, 1647, A Discourse of the Liberty of Prophesying, in More and Cross, eds., *Anglicanism*, 187-190.

Tutu, Desmond, 1989, Address to Provincial Synod, Durban, South Africa, cited in Guy Fitch Lytle, 'Concluding Thoughts After Lambeth,' *Anglican and Episcopal History*, 3, 1989, 406-408.

Verkamp, Bernard J., 1977, *The Indifferent Mean: Adiaphorism in the English Reformation to 1554*, Athens, OH: Ohio University Press.

White, Francis, 1624, *A Reply to Jesuit Fisher's Answer to Certain Questions Propounded By His Most Gracious Majesty King James*, in More and Cross, eds., *Anglicanism*, 514.

Chapter 16

Of What is Music a Sign?:
Toscanini, Fürtwangler, and Walter on
Musical Interpretation and the
Philosophy of History

Of what is music a sign? And how may the signs of music -- notes, scores, instruments, communities of interpreters, audiences, composers -- be classified? Early work in musical semiotics (Nattiez 1975) was concerned largely with comparing the internal constituents of compositions to linguistic structures. Recently, Hatten (1980), Henrotte (1985, 1986), and Foell (1986) have expanded the semiotics of music to deal with 'three distinct roles in the semiotic experience of music: those of the composer, the performer, and the listener' (Henrotte 1985: 164). This paper hopes to alert semioticians to the fascinating grist they may find for their mills in the writings, performances, and personalities of three great orchestra conductors of the first half of the twentieth century: Arturo Toscanini (1867-1957), Wilhelm Fürtwangler (1886-1954), and Bruno Walter (1876-1962). Each of these titans looked at music as a complex sign system though they did not, of course, utilize semiotic terminology. They constructed towering personae for themselves and their styles of conducting, developed theories of communication and culture, and searched for the meaning of music in the progress of history, the nature of man, and the essence of the universe. To make music was to communicate a sign of one's being and of Being itself, to take a stand on the issues philosophers, mystics, and peoples have debated in other ways throughout the course of history.

I will begin with a few well-known and not so well-known biographical anecdotes about each conductor and treat these as signs themselves of their approaches to musical interpretation.   Second, I look at the role perceived for composer, interpreter, and audience by each of the three.   I then consider how each conductor justified his interpretive paradigm as a sign of a philosophy of music, life, and history, and relate their respective stands on fascism to this.   One caveat: unlike Walter and Fürtwangler, Toscanini never wrote a treatise explaining his notion of music.   Nevertheless, his silence on some issues and his conversational remarks on others speak most eloquently.

Toscanini's most famous interpretive attribute was his reverence for the score as the *only* available index of the composer's intention.   He condemned performance tradition ('The tradition is to be found in only one place -- in the music') and once replied to the famous Dutch conductor Willem Mengelberg's tale that he had learned to conduct Beethoven's 'Coriolan Overture' from someone who had known the composer: 'Bah! I told him I got it straight from Beethoven himself, from the score (Schonberg 1967: 254).   Once he exclaimed in delight when listening to his own recording of Debussy's 'La Mer': 'Is like reading the score!' (Haggin 1979: 25).   Indeed, Toscanini's adherents praised his interpretations much as one would the restorer of a severely tarnished painting. In the words of fellow-conductor George Szell, he 'wiped out the arbitrariness of the postromantic interpreters.   He did away with the meretricious tricks and the thick encrustation of the interpretive nuances that had been piling up for decades' (Schonberg 1967: 252).

What 'the score' as a thing in itself meant to Toscanini can be seen in the remarks he made while conducting rehearsals, when listening to records, and in discussing his colleagues' work. Two items stand out: obsession with perfection of details (such as the clear articulation of inner voices) and tempo -- nearly everyone else played too slowly. B.H. Haggin (1979: 84) describes a typical Toscanini rehearsal. He would begin by singling out some detail, as in Tchaikovsky's 'Pathetique' on March 2, 1950:

> [He] found the fourth measure after letter M in the third movement, explained to the flutes and clarinets that in this measure he wanted them to break off the held G-sharp in order to attack the subsequent descending scale with an accent, and had them do this for him several times, then found the similar measure at letter Z, and had the strings and woodwinds play it in the same way; then began to conduct the movement from the beginning, but stopped after the second measure because the strings had not been precisely together, began again, stopped again and -- the violas now being precisely together with the violins -- went on, but stopped after the third measure to tell the oboes and bassoons they were not playing an accurate two against the other woodwinds' three, and got this measure played correctly, and so on thereafter.

On more than one occasion, Toscanini corrected playing that was correct in the first place because his supposedly perfect memory failed him (Haggin 1979: 84) or because he simply did not hear what the orchestra had played (Craft 1989: 22). He worried: 'Even when I listen to record I am afraid horn will not play correct, clarinet will make mistake -- sempre, sempre' (Haggin 1979: 62).

Toscanini's criticisms of other conductors were both predictable and scathing: they played everything too slowly. 'Germans play everything too slowly,' he complained. He once programmed the Mozart Divertimento K. 287 explicitly to correct a performance by Serge Koussevitzky he found both inaccurate and lethargic (Haggin 1979: 38, 47). Yehudi Menuhin recalled a dinner in which Toscanini 'tore to shreds' no fewer than sixteen colleagues while 'the table sycophantically gobbled up his malice.' Unable to restrain himself, Menuhin put in a good word for Bruno Walter. 'A sentimental fool!' Toscanini retorted (Menuhin 1977: 172).

Indeed, Toscanini's rages and cruelty are part of his legend his admirers can only excuse by explaining that he was even harder on himself. He would tell the Metropolitan Opera Orchestra they 'play like pig' and once praised, if that is the word, his NBC Symphony by stating 'we're beginning to sound like a symphony orchestra.' He insulted the Philadelphians when their strings failed to play a passage to his satisfaction: 'you are not so wonderful -- no! NO!' (Haggin 1979: 64, 85, 34). According to critic Winthrop Sargent, he made each performance and rehearsal 'a continuous psychology of crisis.' So great was his reputation that musical parents in New York would warn their misbehaving children that Toscanini would get them (Schonberg 1967: 259).

Toscanini's hatred even extended to composers. He called Gustav Mahler 'crazy' and his Fourth Symphony 'terrible'; he never programmed Mahler. He only played the third of Schumann's four symphonies, dropped all Mendelssohn from his repertoire except for the 'Reformation' Symphony (because he found anticipations of Wagner's 'Parsifal'!), and on one occasion remarked how Donizetti's 'La Favorita' pleased him more than Wagner's 'Tristan and Isolde' (Haggin 1979: 76-77, 88-89).

Toscanini was, Virgil Thompson wrote, a man of 'elementary' culture (Schonberg 1967: 263). His opinions on music and musicians were terse -- usually one-liners. In semiotic terms, he approached both music and the score iconically. It was absolute, a thing unto itself. Played properly, it lacked an indexical dimension -- tradition or historical performance context -- or any 'symbolic' relation to philosophy or civilization. 'Some say this is Napoleon, some Hitler, some Mussolini. For me it is simply *allegro con brio*,' he remarked of Beethoven's 'Eroica' Symphony, encapsulating his view of his craft (Schonberg 1967: 254). Toscanini had no idea of musicians as collaborators creating a performance that reflected their ideas as well as his: on the podium, he paradoxically resembled the fascist dictators he despised and under whose regimes he would not perform. He also seemed unconcerned with an audience -- he acknowledged applause with the briefest of nods and spent the last years of his life conducting a radio broadcast orchestra for the most part. In fact, Toscanini regarded the making of music as 'great suffering for me. At home, with score, when I play piano, is great happiness. But with orchestra is great suffering -- sempre, sempre!' (Haggin 1979: 62).

In his superb biography, *Understanding Toscanini* (1987), Joseph Horowitz delineates how media hype, generated in part by RCA records and the NBC network with which Toscanini was associated in the United States, in part by American critics anxious to flaunt the superiority of 'their' conductor (read 'civilization') over the hidebound traditionalists of Europe, made Toscanini the standard to which a generation of young conductors aspired. His 'hard-driven, rushed through, landscape-level readings' (Craft 1987: 20) obtained the brilliance, precision, and drive desired by an America seething with Nietzschean *ressentiment* against post-World War I Germany and anxious to flaunt its technical prowess against the moribund culture it had supposedly 'saved.'

Paradoxically, Toscanini too was working in a tradition. The blazing power, intense drive, and clean melodic lines of his performances are characteristic of Italian opera, where the voices rarely cease to sing and the clear presentation of line is all-important. In the German operatic school in which Walter and Fürtwangler served their apprenticeships, the voice is but one element among chorus, ensemble, and the long orchestral interludes. Toscanini's conducting tended toward polyphony, Walter and Fürtwangler more toward harmony. But if Toscanini was indeed a symphonic innovator, he received a firm training in the Italian school.

Wilhelm Fürtwangler stands at the opposite pole from Toscanini. If anecdotes about the Italian center on personal humiliations and smashed watches and batons, Fürtwangler stories stress the imprecision of his beat and the mystical aura generated by his spiritual, improvisatory performances. Jokes abounded about how orchestras, once they became used to working with him, managed to follow 'that curious, quivering, trembling baton.' They would start on the thirteenth wiggle, when they lost patience, or when the baton reached a certain button on his vest (Schonberg 1967: 272). But far from trying to correct his imprecisions, Fürtwangler gloried in them. Once he showed an orchestra he could beat time in a regular fashion for a few measures, remarked 'it has no quality,' and gave it up. On another occasion, he pleaded with an orchestra: 'Gentleman, this phrase must be -- it must be -- it must -- you know what I mean' only to remark (probably humorously) during a break: 'You see how important it is for a conductor to convey his ideas clearly?' (Schonberg 1967: 275, 277). To a young conductor who asked him what he did with his left hand when he conducted, the maestro replied: 'I had never asked myself that question before, although I had been a conductor for more than twenty years' (Fürtwangler 1953: 51).

Fürtwangler despised 'mere' precision. As Henry Holst, one of his Berlin Philharmonic musicians, noted: 'he wanted the precision that grew out of the orchestra, from the players' own initiative as in chamber music' (Schonberg 1967: 276). True 'technique' was the opposite of perfectionism with respect to technical details (Fürtwangler 1953: 24-27):

The kind of intelligence required of the performer who would master such technical difficulties is so common nowadays. It is readily acquired by anyone with a modicum of talent. The same kind of intelligence required for the servicing, dismantling, and repairing of motorcars . . . enables the musician of today to play from memory the most complicated harmonies and rhythms. . . . the task of the performer. . . . is of a spiritual rather than of a technical nature. . . . What was naively enough admired as technique in former times was not at all what we understand by the term today. It was not the 'technique' of a Mozart and Beethoven. . . . which impressed their contemporaries, but the voice of the man behind this technique, who made it the vehicle of his inner necessity. The problems of interpretation only arose when technique became something which could be divorced from the personality of the artist as a whole, to be attained at any time by training. These are not problems of 'technique' at all.

Music-making, rather than involving an attempt to realize a score, becomes instead for Fürtwangler a means of participation in the Great Chain of Being: 'Music even today supposes a community . . . a community among man, Nature, and God' (Fürtwangler 1918-1954: 8). Fürtwangler provides a beautiful illustration of the irrelevance of technique by explaining the larger context in which the opening of Beethoven's Ninth Symphony ought to be understood (Fürtwangler 1948: 10):

Beethoven is depicting chaos -- the primeval beginning of time, out of which everything evolved. That this fifth [chord] should be resolved into accurately measured triplets in three-five time is irrelevant for the rendering of the idea as a whole. I once came

across a conductor who spent a full ten minutes trying to get as clean
and clear a rendering as possible. . . .   Beethoven's idea just
vanished. . . .   Many conductors work, so to speak, with the
technique of Dürer or Ingres.   Will that do if your task is to render
a work that depends on color, like a picture by Rembrandt or Titian?
Fürtwangler regarded the triumph of the merely technical as a symbol of the most
cataclysmic development in modern times.   Only in the twentieth century did
humanity 'become alive to the full implications of that unparalleled revolution' of
Copernicus, in which the 'ptolemaic-Christian view, according to which the
universe in the true sense revolves around Man, whom God created in His image
and for whom Christ died' was replaced by one 'which considers Man as nothing
more than a speck of dust within a huge universe.'   The arts -- in music until the
advent of atonality and the cult of precision technique -- took 'for granted' the
'decisive importance of the human being' (Fürtwangler 1953: 91-92, 73):

> We are not mere dayflies, helpless under the passage of time: we are
> also eternal, indestructible beings made in the image of God. . . .
> every work of art has two aspects, one turned towards its own 'time'
> and one towards eternity.   Just as we can say that man is different,
> new, at every moment, that it is the task of the artist to record his
> mutability, dependence, and limitations, so we can say that the human
> soul has been the same since time immemorial, that the artist must
> record its eternal essence, its unique quality and indestructibility.

In modern times, it was the task of the musician to remind man of his
humanity, dignity, and freedom, that he did not exist as the tool of mechanical
forces (in music, the score and conductor) but as creator, interpreter, and
emotional being: 'We are always trying to be wiser with our heads than our
hearts,' he complained (Fürtwangler 1948: 13), and praised the artist as 'the man

of love' to whom 'individuals matter . . . only in so far as they are incomparable' over the historian, 'the man of discriminating intelligence,' to whom they matter 'only in so far as they are comparable' (Fürtwangler 1953: 74). Johannes Brahms, with whom Fürtwangler obviously identified his own mission, tried to preserve classical structures in the age of Wagner and was thus the first musician to view his task as the preservation of man in an alien world (Fürtwangler c.1931: 2):

> Brahms was the first who set himself against his time, merely to be able to do deliberately what had been commonplace to the preceding generations: to make man the center of any kind of art and artistic production. . . . The significance of a work of art is not measured by the degree of its boldness, of the 'newness' of its diction . . . but by the degree of its inner logic and necessity, its humanity and power of expression.

The preservation of humanity through music was signified practically in two ways: what compositions were played and the manner in which they were performed. Fürtwangler regarded the struggle of tonal vs. atonal music as nothing less then 'a battle of the worlds.' The former reflected 'the biological constitution of human nature,' based as it was on 'the alternation between tension and relaxation' to which 'all organic life existing in time was subject.' On the other hand (Fürtwangler 1953: 87, 90-91):

> If we let ourselves be guided by the atonal musician we walk as through a dense forest. The strangest flowers and plants attract our attention. But we do not know where we are going nor whence we have come. The listener is seized by a feeling of being lost, of being at the mercy of forces of primeval existence. . . . A type of music which dispenses with a device to regulate tension and relaxation . . . must be considered as *biologically inferior* . . . which is at the root

of the insuperable, stubborn opposition offered to this kind of music by the vast majority of the public.

Similarly, performances in the Toscanini vein took man out of the universe. They denied precisely (double entendre intended) the community of audience, performer, and composer, all of whom participated in the recreation of music as a living art.   Fürtwangler complained of a small orchestra's 'authentic' performance of Bach's 'St. Matthew Passion' in which 'Bach had nothing, absolutely nothing, to say to the famished heart' (Fürtwangler 1953: 72). *That* was an inauthentic performance!   Over and over again, he insisted: 'Music addresses itself to a public, and not to a group of specialists'; 'It is a *public* and not a group of individuals. It must above all be people who feel and react as a community.' 'It is not only the public's right, but its duty to judge' the music it hears.   And 'communion between the artist and public requires, like all communion, reciprocity' (Fürtwangler 1918-1954: 10). In the long run, only those 'works of art are effective because they set out to be effective' for the public. 'Those works alone succeed which turn an audience, if only for seconds, into a *genuine* community, that take hold of the individual in such a way that he is no longer a separate entity, but a part of his people, a part of humanity, a part of the Divine Nature operating through him' (Fürtwangler 1953: 14-15).

To create a community moved to the depths of its existence by music, it was necessary to have interpreters who gave the impression of creating a work afresh instead of 'putting in alcohol' every last detail. 'The great masterpieces of music are subject to the law of improvisation to a far high degree than is commonly thought,' Fürtwangler argued (Fürtwangler 1953: 47-48):

The interpreter gets to know them through the written version. His approach to them is the reverse of the creator's.   The latter experiences the real import of what he has to say before or while he commits it to paper; the improvisation on which the written version is based represents the core of the creative process. But as far as the interpreter is concerned, the work is the exact opposite of such improvisation: it is an outer shell of signs and forms which he must pierce if he would penetrate to the work he wishes to perform.

'Real form' and 'authentic' performances demand that the interpreter do justice to the act of creation, rather than to the 'outer shell' signifying that creation has taken place. 'Right through the whole musical life of today,' Fürtwangler lamented (1953: 49-50) 'a cleavage is distinguishable between those who still have an inkling of, a remembrance of this knowledge, and those who have already lost it.' Henry Pleasants makes the same point in explaining the popularity and superiority of modern jazz to the ossified contemporary performance of classical works we must endure: the former remain true to the improvisatory tradition of Beethoven and Mozart that the latter eschews (Pleasants 1969: 74-89).

For Fürtwangler, unlike Toscanini, music performance practice is a sign of civilizational health. In the modern world, it has become inauthentic by searching for a spurious authenticity, a sign of cultural perversion and declining human values. Music must be an interpretive act, presupposing and preserving a community bridging the worlds of composer and audience, transcending time and history.

Fürtwangler's response to fascism, as opposed to Toscanini's, also serves as a sign of his philosophy of music. Toscanini left Europe for the United States to rage against Mussolini. He absented himself from the relevant context just as his performances abstracted themselves from tradition. Fürtwangler remained in Germany, saving the lives of numerous Jewish musicians, daring Hitler and Goebbels to put him in a concentration camp, and finally fleeing to Switzerland to escape arrest early in 1945. That he could survive such behavior, and never offering the required Nazi salute at concerts, indicates that his arguments for a community of music transcending historical circumstances have some plausibility. He could not conceive of taking from the German people their greatest consolation and strongest link with universal humanity in their darkest hour. Anyone who has listened to his unbelievable wartime and post-war performances (Fürtwangler could not perform for two years because of allegations of Nazism) can understand only too well how the historical and symbolic context of a performance can enrich it. For instance, the Bruckner Ninth, recorded in December 1944, is a shattering depiction of the agony the war had caused (Menuhin 1977: 292-296; Fürtwangler 1944).

Bruno Walter stands between the hyperintellectualism of Toscanini and the mystical intuitionism of Fürtwangler. (Of course, were Toscanini's performances without heart and Fürtwangler's without control, they would be unlistenable. I am speaking of tendencies). Walter's testament, *Of Music and Music-Making* (1957), published just after his eightieth birthday is a reasonable, gentle attempt to reconcile tradition and modernity, reason and emotion, man and nature, accuracy and spontaneity in a neo-Hegelian unity.

Anecdotes about Walter always stress his personal warmth and kindness. 'When he accompanies me,' said the great soprano Lotte Lehmann, 'I have the feeling of the utmost well-being and security. The end of his baton is like a cradle in which he rocks me' (Schonberg 1967: 284). One of Toscanini's barbs makes the same point: 'When Walter comes to something beautiful he melts. I suffer!' (Haggin 1979: 81).

Walter shared most of Fürtwangler's philosophical attitudes on the correspondence of music with the supernatural and natural worlds. He begins his book with a discussion of the 'harmony of the spheres' and concludes (Walter 1957: 13-15):

All creative and interpretive activities of man point to an origin of
music in the spheres of the coursing stars. Our art of music,
pervaded as its temporal manifestations are by its essential, timeless
character, does not only exert a decisive influence on our culture but
is also a message from higher regions which exhorts us to be aware
of our higher origin.

Similarly, Walter finds music deeply rooted in physical Nature, a word he
capitalizes (Walter 1957: 106):

The proximity of music and Nature is evidenced by the fact that many
great musicians are intimately drawn to Nature and that their spiritual
life, and even their daily habits, are often considerably shaped by it;
there can scarcely be a great musician -- or a true poet -- who is not
charmed or shattered, inspired and uplifted by Nature.

Walter goes on to use natural metaphors to urge young musicians to explore not
only Nature but drama, philosophy, history, and all the arts, to empathize as
deeply as possible with humanity and the universe, and thereby become better
musicians (Walter 1957: 107):

One who is no more than a musician is half a musician. The idea of
growing, the striving for development, must embrace the whole inner
man, and not only his musical gifts; the crown of his tree of life, his
musicianship, will spread and grow in proportion as he sinks his roots
firmly and broadly into the soil of universal humanity.

Walter sees the same crisis in his time as Fürtwangler. Musicians in the full
sense of the word are becoming rarer (Walter 1957: 201-202):

Is the lofty source of all great art, creative inspiration, in abeyance,
and is it a declared *anachronism* to be replaced by laboratory methods
based on abstract principles, applied experimentally, and producing

art for the satisfaction of intellectual interests? Yes, it does indeed
look as if materialism and intellectualism have taken hold . . . and
allotted to the arts a lower place in the life of society than the exalted
sphere in which they have hitherto reigned . . . not a[s] heart-moving
experience, but only entertainment, stimulation of intellectual
interests, or even the satisfaction of an inherent sensationalism.

The decadence of music is only one of a series of equivalent signs of a
'world [which] becomes colder' (Walter 1957: 204):

> With the increasing perfection of the external conditions of life goes
> the impoverishment of its intrinsic conditions; cordiality becomes
> politeness; the desire for education a craving for sensationalism;
> conversation gives way to television; books to newspapers or
> illustrated journals; music-making to radio-listening; travelling to
> sport.

Unlike Fürtwangler, however, who refused to compromise with modernity
and flaunted his anachronistic conducting, the gentle Walter hoped to reconcile a
measure of tradition to a mass, scientifically-minded society. For example, should
music be performed in strict tempo? No -- but performers should avoid
'*noticeable* changes in speed, other than those marked by the composer unless
. . . a painstaking interpreter should have come to the conclusion that such a
change was indicated by the meaning of the work and the implied intentions of the
score' (Walter 1957: 31). Such balanced, carefully qualified judgments abound
in Walter's writings and are reflected in his music-making. Should music
emphasize the lyrical or energetic elements? 'This is not a case of total opposites:
my pronounced youthful leaning towards the singable never inhibited my joy in
rhythmic, energetic, or stormily agitated music' (Walter 1957: 60). Should a
composer stress technical perfection or expressive freedom? On the one hand,

'perfect precision in the playing of an orchestra . . . is an indispensable quality.'
On the other, it should not impede 'the liberties of a flexible, lively interpretation
such as is congruent with true musicality and real dramatic import.'
Paradoxically, 'the fewer the liberties, the easier the task of the conductor, but also
the more inflexible and lifeless the performance.' Walter describes a satisfactory
rendition of Handel's 'Messiah': 'The richness, the greatness, the beauty of the
music, the dramatic vitality and religious profundity of the work made their full
effect, and, of course, the performance was precise, or else its musical and
spiritual impact should have been impaired' (Walter 1957: 127-128).

Walter finds that young conductors have to achieve a comparable synthesis
in their own lives. At the start, the talented musician possesses an 'unaffected
assurance: he wills, he gives, he overflows, his instinct helps, the ego operates as
an undivided unity.' Missing in this state of 'overwrought activity' is 'the calm,
critical functioning of his ear.' Then comes a period of questioning, doubting,
obsession with details, 'in which we search, err, experiment, and alternate between
competence and incompetence' in making 'tyrannical demands on our conducting
technique.' Only in a third, synthetic stage, 'when the conductor matures toward
mastery, will he be able to devote his energies entirely to the higher problems of
musical interpretation untroubled by technical difficulties' (Walter 1957: 91-94).

For Walter humility and self-criticism were key elements in achieving
synthesis and balance in the course of one's life cycle and between expression and
technique. Walter described how important it was for him to moderate his
excesses and work on his weaknesses (Walter 1957: 36):

> In my early music-making, one kind of expression would follow
> another, one climax hand on to the next, without strict planning or
> subordination to the form of the entire work. My interpretations
> suffered, therefore, from a sort of softness, or even weakness, of

which I became painfully conscious. . . . I gained firm ground, at
last, when I realized that there is a method of interpretation higher,
nobler, more in accord with the greatness of the work, than is
indulgence in the sway of one's feelings . . . directing one's attention
to the entire design of the work, its general emotional content, and
never losing sight of these through the intensive cultivation of details.

In looking at the future of music in western civilization, Walter therefore did
not despair. He hoped the synthesis he and other musicians achieved in the course
of their lives could serve as a model for a sorely troubled culture: 'Though the
muses seem exhausted today; though a cold autumn of the soul has called a
temporary halt to the flowering and fruit-bearing; . . . my confidence tells me that
the genius of mankind shall survive this period of illness once it has realized the
spiritual and moral powers that are nourished by those lofty springs' (Walter 1957:
211).

Walter's response to fascism is also a sign of his philosophy of music.
Where Toscanini chose separation and denunciation, and Fürtwangler remained to
help his distressed compatriots, Walter, a Jew, had no choice. He had to emigrate
and accommodate to change to survive, even as he found he had to modify his
intense spiritualism and romanticism by a greater concern with precision and
structure. Like Toscanini, Walter too directed a broadcast orchestra in the United
States (the CBS Symphony), but lived out his final years in the milder atmosphere
of Los Angeles instead of the tense New York in which Toscanini flourished.

To return to our original question. Of what is music a sign? Although
Walter in some sense synthesized the Apollonian Toscanini and the Dionysian
Fürtwangler, he shared with the latter the sense that the composer, performer, and
listener -- all of whom create music -- declare their allegiance in a modern struggle
to save the life of the mind and spirit in a dehumanized world. How one plays,

composes, and listens to music, and the music to which one listens, composes, or plays, become signs of a person's moral nature and philosophy of life. To side with Fürtwangler and Walter is to express the determination -- in the words of Hölderlin with which Walter concludes his book -- that 'where there is danger, the saving forces increase' (Walter 1957: 211).

REFERENCES

Craft, Robert, 1987, 'The Maestro on the Market,' *New York Review of Books* 24, 9 April 1987, 20-23.

Foell, Kristie, 1986, 'Towards a Semiotic Understanding of Music: The Definition of the Musical Object,' *Semiotics 1985,* ed. John Deely, Lanham, MD: University Press of America, 649-658.

Fürtwangler, Wilhelm, 1918-1954, *Ton und Wort. Aufsätze and Vorträge*, Wiesbanden: F. A. Brockhaus, 1958, reprinted in album notes for 'Wilhelm Fürtwangler: In Memoriam,' Deutsche Grammophon Records KL 27/31. Excerpts. My translations.

_____, c.1931, 'Brahms and the Crisis of Our Time,' excerpt reprinted in Sigurd Schimpf, 'Fürtwangler Conducts Brahms,' album notes for 'Johannes Brahms: Samtliche Sinfonien,' DaCapo Records 147-50 336/39.

_____, 1944, Recording of Anton Bruckner, Symphony no. 9 with the Berlin Philharmonic, Deutsche Grammophon Records KL 27/31.

_____, 1948, BBC interview cited in Henry Fogel, 'The Art of Wilhelm Fürtwangler,' *Keynote* 10, November 1986, 9-13.

_____, 1953, *Concerning Music,* trans. L.J. Laurie, London: Boosey and Hawkes.

Haggin, B.H., 1979, *Conversations with Toscanini*, New York: Horizon Press, enlarged version of 1959 edition.

Hatten, Robert, 1980, 'Nattiez's Semiology of Music: Flaws in the New Science,' *Semiotica* 31-1/2, 139-155.

Henrotte, Gayle, 1985, 'Music as Language: A Semiotic Paradigm?' *Semiotics 1984,* ed. John Deely, Lanham, MD: University Press of America, 163-170.

_____, 1986, 'Music and Liguistics: The Semiotic Connection,' *Semiotics 1985,* ed.   John Deely, Lanham, MD: University Press of America, 659-668.

Horowitz, Joseph, 1987, *Understanding Toscanini: How He Became an American Culture-God and Helped Create a New Audience for Old Music,* New York: Knopf.

Menuhin, Yehudi, 1977, *Unfinished Journey,* London: MacDonald and Jane's Publishers.

Nattiez, Jean-Jacques, 1975, *Fondements d'une sémiologie de la musique,* Paris: Union générale d'éditions.

Pleasants, Henry, 1969, *Serious Music and All That Jazz,* New York: Simon and Schuster.

Schonberg, Harold C., 1967, *The Great Conductors,* New York: Simon and Schuster.

Walter, Bruno, 1957, *Of Music and Music Making,* trans. by Paul Hamburger as *Von der Music und vom Musizieren,* New York: Norton 1961.

Chapter 17

The Operatic *Ulysses*

James Joyce loved opera -- had a lifelong passion for it, in fact.[1] Not only are several of the characters in *Ulysses* opera singers, most notably Molly Bloom herself, but the work abounds in references to various operas. These allusions are far from literary window dressing; what fascinates in Joyce's employment of operatic examples is that whenever they appear in the text, the plot of the opera alluded to mirrors the particular situation that is at the moment occurring in the novel. Thus the operatic references clarify the narrative.

Not only is each use of opera important in itself, but all the operatic allusions, taken together, possess a unity that leads to a definite conclusion about the meaning of *Ulysses* as a whole. The most helpful, not to mention most organized, way to approach an understanding of 'the operatic *Ulysses*' is to deal with each opera individually.[2]

Il trovatore ('Proteus,' 39)[3]

The 'Proteus' episode of *Ulysses* relates the thoughts of Stephen Daedalus as he is wandering on the Sandymount strand. In the course of this silent monologue, Stephen's thoughts range over his entire life and the philosophical and artistic problems with which he is struggling. However, the drift of his thought reveals a preoccupation with his recently deceased mother: 'Like me, like Algy, coming down to our mighty mother' (37). 'Wombed in sin darkness I was too, made not begotten. By them, the man with my voice and my eyes and a ghost woman with ashes on her breath' (38). At this point, his mind begins to wander and he thinks of a visit to his uncle Richie Goulding, highlighted by the latter's rendition of the *scena* beginning 'All'erta,' from Verdi's *Trovatore*.

Here, it appears superficially that Stephen is no longer thinking of his mother. But a knowledge of *Il trovatore*, and especially of this scene, explains why Stephen's thoughts go from his mother to the opera and, through it, to Goulding's visit. The dominant color of this episode is green. The sea, 'our mighty mother,' is represented as green, and 'Algy,' not only short for Algernon Swinburne whom the text mentions, is also a green sea plant. 'Verdi' is the Italian word for green; by thinking of Verdi, Stephen really still has his mother in mind.

Joyce introduces *Il trovatore*, an opera about a mother-son relationship, to help define Stephen's own situation. There are several similarities between Stephen and Manrico, the opera's hero. Manrico deserts his mother, Azucena, to rescue his beloved, Leonora, who is about to enter a convent because she believes him to be dead. This plot recalls Stephen's experience in *A Portrait of the Artist as a Young Man*, where he leaves his mother to go to France. His mother dies. Azucena, while searching for *her* son, is discovered by his mortal enemy, the Count di Luna, and sentenced to be burned at the stake. Manrico, like Stephen, returns but cannot save his mother. He is captured, and the opera ends with his death and those of Leonora and Azucena. Stephen also suffers remorse over his mother; he refused to pray for her on her deathbed. Yet, as the dialogue with her ghost in 'Circe' (580-81) proves, he also looked to her for inspiration as a life-giving force:

Stephen

(Choking with fright, remorse, and horror.) They said I killed you, mother. He offended your memory. Cancer did it, not I. Destiny.

The Mother

(A green rill of bile trickling from the side of her mouth.) You sang that song to me. *Love's bitter mystery.*

Stephen

(Eagerly.) Tell me the word, mother, if you know now. The word known to all men.

This passage brings us back to the 'Proteus' episode by the reference to 'green.'

Just by mentioning 'All'erta,' Joyce has placed before those familiar with *Il trovatore* a parallel situation that encapsulates Stephen's past, present, and possible future. Subconsciously, Stephen's thoughts are constantly heading toward the green sea and the mother. Richie Goulding's singing of this particular excerpt is full of dramatic purpose to Joyce. At the beginning of the opera, Ferrando, di Luna's captain, presents all the background material necessary to comprehend *Trovatore's* convoluted plot. Part of this concerns an old witch who is burned at the stake, and whose spirit returns to haunt her murderers. She is 'the ghost woman with ashes on her breath,' who symbolizes Stephen's remorse and fear when he thinks of his own mother.

At this point in *Ulysses*, Stephen's future prospects are not promising. The unhappy conclusion of *Il trovatore* reflects this state of affairs.

Le nozze di Figaro ('Proteus,' 40)

Though Joyce does not explicitly mention *Figaro* in *Ulysses*, one passage, in which Stephen confesses his sins in his imagination, contains several allusions to the opera, and there is nothing that could be considered even remotely 'coincidental' in Joyce's work:

Cousin Stephen, you will never be a saint. Isle of saints. You were awfully holy, weren't you? You prayed to the Blessed Virgin that you might not have a red nose. You prayed to the devil in Serpentine Avenue that the fusby widow in front might lift her clothes still more from the street. O si certo! Sell your soul for that, do, *dyed rags pinned round a squaw*. More tell me, more still! On top of the Howth tramalone crying to the rain-naked women! What about that, eh! (Italics mine)

The words that recall *Le nozze di Figaro* are 'O si, certo!' (so punctuated in the libretto) and 'Serpentine.' Cherubino, a page to the Count Almaviva and a bit of a teenage Don Juan, at one point tells Susanna, the Countess Almaviva's chambermaid, that he loves the Countess:

Cherubino: Ei mi rammenta, che abbandon degg'io comare tanto buona

Susanna: E tanto bella . . .

Cherubino: Ah si, certo!

Susanna: Ah si, certo! Ipocritone!

Cherubino: It reminds me I must leave such a good godmother . . .

Susanna: And such a beautiful one . . .

Cherubino: Ah yes, certainly!

Susanna: Ah yes, certainly! Hypocrite![4]

Cherubino and Susanna also refer to a ribbon belonging to the Countess, which the sentimental boy is keeping: 'dyed rags pinned round a squaw.' Susanna later addresses Cherubino as 'Serpentello,' or little serpent.

Joyce here compares Stephen to Cherubino: both are dissolute young artists for the page has a talent for composing sentimental love songs. Stephen is being gently mocked by this identification with a charming though immature, occasionally even silly character. Both take their art so seriously yet devote so great a portion of their leisure to sex (or thoughts thereof) that they become comic. This comparison also calls attention to the fact that Stephen is *not* Joyce, and that we should take him less seriously than he takes himself. Stephen's predicament, which on the very preceding page appeared tragic *(Il trovatore)*, has now become comic *(Le nozze di Figaro)*.[5]

Don Giovanni (many references)

William York Tindall writes that 'Stephen is intellect, Mrs. Bloom, flesh, and central Mr. Bloom, uniting the extremes, is almost everybody.'[6] Tindall's opinion of Bloom is borne out: in the course of *Ulysses*, he is identified with each of *Don Giovanni's* five male characters and emerges as their composite. Joyce uses this opera's plot to clarify the Bloom's relationship to each other and to Blazes Boylan, Molly's lover and current manager.

The first reference to *Don Giovanni* appears during a dialogue between Leopold and Molly that occurs when she receives a letter from Boylan (63):

-Who is the letter from? he asked.

Bold hand. Marion.

-O, Boylan, she said. He's bringing the programme.

-What are you singing?

-*La ci darem* with J.C. Doyle, she said, and *Love's Old Sweet Song*.

'Là ci darem' is a duet between Don Giovanni and Zerlina. The Don has just met Zerlina and Masetto, a peasant couple who are about to be married. He soon convinces Masetto to leave Zerlina alone with him. Although Masetto knows just what is going on, he feels incapable of standing up to the Don:

Zerlina: Va, non temere; nelle mani son io d'un cavalier.

Masetto: E per questo? . . .

Zerlina: E per questo non c'è da dubitar . . .

Masetto: Ed io, cospetto!

Giovanni: Olà, finiam le dispute; se subito senz'altro replicar, non te ne
vai, Masetto, guarda ben, ti pentirai.

Masetto (ironically sings the following aria):

> Ho capito, signor si!
>
> Chino il capo e me ne vo;
>
> gia che piace a voi cosi
>
> Altre repliche non fo.
>
> Cavalier voi siete gia
>
> dubitar non posso affé:
>
> me lo dice le bontà
>
> che volete aver per me.
>
> (to Zerlina)
>
> Bricconaccia, malandrina,
>
> fosti ognor la mia ruina.

Zerlina: Go, don't be afraid; I'm in the hands of a gentleman.

Masetto: So what?

Zerlina: So you needn't have any doubts.

Masetto: Oh, sure!

Giovanni: Alright, let's end this argument; if you don't leave immediately
without a fuss, watch out, Masetto, you'll be sorry.

Masetto (ironically sings the following aria):

> Yes, I understand, sir!
>
> I bow my head and go.
>
> Exactly as it pleases you,

without any arguments.

You're a gentleman,

I can't doubt that at all.

Your goodness to me

shows me that.

(to Zerlina)

Hussy, bad girl,

you've been the cause of my ruin.

After Masetto's angry departure and a *recitativo* that is, on Giovanni's part, a masterpiece of seductive reasoning, the duet follows:

Giovanni:	Là ci darem la mano,
	Là me dirai di si;
	Vedi, non e lontano,
	partiam ben mio da qui.
Zerlina:	Vorrei, e non vorrei . . .
	Mi trema un poco il cor . . .
	Felice, è ver, sarei:
	Ma puo burlarmi ancor.
Giovanni:	Vieni, mio bel diletto!
Zerlina:	Mi fa pietà Masetto.
Giovanni:	Io cangerò tua sorte.
Zerlina:	Presto . . . non son piu forte.
Both:	Andiam, andiam, mio bene,
	A ristorar le pene
	d'un innocente amor!

Giovanni:	There we'll hold hands,

and you'll say yes to me;

see, it's not far,

Let's leave this place, my dear.

Zerlina: I would like to, and yet I wouldn't . . .

My heart is trembling a bit.

It's true, I would be happy

but he could still be joking with me.

Giovanni: Come, my beautiful delight!

Zerlina: I'm sorry for Masetto.

Giovanni: I will change your fate.

Zerlina: Quick, I'm no longer strong.

Both: Come, come my dear one

to ease the pain

of an innocent love.

Just when the Don and Zerlina are at the point of going off together, Donna Elvira, who considers herself Giovanni's lawful wife, enters in the nick of time and informs Zerlina of her 'husband's' exploits. Before the end of the opera, Zerlina and Masetto are reunited.

Joyce mentions this duet to show that the Blooms and Boylan have the same relationship as Zerlina, Masetto, and Don Giovanni. Zerlina and Molly are both perfectly willing to be seduced, but in the end they recognize the need for their husbands. In both instances, the callousness of their lovers helps this realization along. The Don's compulsion causes him to attempt to rape Zerlina during a party;[7] Boylan offends Molly when he slaps her on the derrière. Neither husband, Masetto or Leopold, can do anything until his wife decides to accept him again.

On the following page of the novel (64), Bloom again thinks of this duet: 'Voglio e non vorrei: Wonder if she pronounces that right: voglio.' Leopold is actually wondering whether his wife really wishes to have relations with Boylan ('voglio' means 'I wish'); the mental ploy about 'pronunciation,' of course, merely disguises the true issue.

However, Bloom has made a mistake; the correct word in this line is 'vorrei,' not 'voglio.' The two words mean the same thing, but just as 'vorrei' is associated with Zerlina in 'Là ci darem,' 'voglio' is the word with which Giovanni's servant Leporello opens the opera:

> Voglio far il gentiluomo,
>
> e non voglio più servir.
>
> O che caro galantuomo! . . .
>
> Vuol star dentro con la bella
>
> ed io far la sentinella!

> I want to be a gentleman
>
> and I don't want to serve anymore.
>
> O, what a fine gallant man.
>
> He likes to stay inside with the girl
>
> while I play the sentinel.

The substitution of 'voglio' for 'vorrei' identifies Bloom with Leporello, who would like to behave like his master but lacks the requisite nerve. Bloom too wants to be a lover, but the closest he can come to it is an exchange of love letters with a woman he never meets. As the quotation indicates, he also has to wait outside, in a manner of speaking. The likeness is enhanced by the homophony of the names Leopold and Leporello.

The third reference to 'Là ci darem' identifies Bloom with the Don himself, for this time he is singing the latter's lines (77):

He drew the letter from his pocket and folded it into the newspaper he carried. Might just walk into her [Martha Clifford, the object of his love affair] here. The lane is safer.

He passed the cabman's shelter. Curious the life of drifting cabbies, all weathers, all places, time or setdown, no will of their own. *Voglio e non.* Like to give them an odd cigarette. Sociable. Shout a few flying syllables as they pass. He hummed:

> La ci darem la mano
> La la lala la la.

Bloom pretends that he is Don Giovanni, but nothing ever comes of this affair. He only *thinks* he is playing the Don, for he is really Leporello.

In still other references to this duet, Leopold is either the jealous peasant or the hopeful servant. In 'Aeolus' (93), he is Masetto expressing love for Zerlina despite her faults:

> Doing her hair, humming: *voglio e non vorrei.* No: *vorrei e non.*
> Looking at the tips of her hairs to see if they are split. *Mi trema un*
> *poco il.* Beautiful on that *tre* her voice is: weeping tone.

Throughout the early part of *Ulysses,* Bloom is unsure of his marriage's future. Thus, when he thinks, 'I could ask him [Alexander Keyes] perhaps about how to pronounce that *voglio?*' ('Aeolus', 120), he is uncertain whether Molly will prefer Boylan to himself. And he is not sure whether, as Leopold/Leporello, he wishes to chase after other women.

By the 'Circe' episode, Bloom has resolved to be faithful to Molly. He dreams that she appears to him as an exotic Eastern woman. She mocks him: '*Ti trema un poco il cuore?*' to which Bloom replies, 'Are you sure about that *Voglio?* I mean the pronunciati . . .' (441). Then she goes off. Bloom's reply, literally, 'Are you sure about that 'I want'?' indicates that he would like to return to Molly if she'll have him. He hopes that she no longer wants to go off with her Don Giovanni, Boylan. He tries to say, 'I mean the pronunciation,' which would disguise the issue, but he cannot. Meekly tolerating Boylan as he has done until now is no longer possible. Bloom confirms his loyalty to Molly shortly thereafter (445), when his old lover, Mrs. Breen, tries to force herself on him. When she sings, 'Voglio e non,' Bloom answers firmly: 'When you made your present choice they said it was beauty and the beast. I can never forgive you for that. (His clenched fist at his brow).' His constancy is reaffirmed in 'Eumaeus' (622) when he tells Stephen: *'Belladonna voglio.'* Though this could mean that he seeks a poison, it definitely means that he wants a beautiful woman. By now, Molly is the only woman he thinks of.

Joyce uses 'Là ci darem' not only to indicate Bloom's desire to return to Molly; the same words indicate her acceptance of him. The final references to *Don Giovanni* in *Ulysses* (Molly's soliloquy: 780) are 'mi fa pietà Masetto' and 'presto non son più forte' ('I feel sorry for Masetto' and 'Quick, I am no longer strong'). Molly has recognized the triumph of Masetto over Giovanni. By stating 'I am no longer strong,' she predicts the restoration of Bloom as the masculine, dominant member of the family. Thus, the various elements in the Masetto/Zerlina relationship -- separation, jealousy, despair, and reconciliation -- reflect and parallel the behavior of Leopold and Molly.

Bloom is also identified with Don Ottavio. In 'Aeolus' (131), he recalls three words from Ottavio's aria 'Dalla sua pace.' He is thus connected with this polite but timid man, who is dominated by his volatile fiancée, Donna Anna. This reference sums up Leopold's position with respect to Molly.

Finally, Leopold Bloom acts the part of the Commandant, Donna Anna's father, who is killed by Don Giovanni in the opening scene while defending his daughter's honor. He returns from the dead in the finale to take revenge on the Don. The Commandant motif is mentioned briefly in 'Laestrygonians' (179). The music of his entrance in the final scene of the opera is hummed by Bloom, and then immediately dropped, just as the character appears for a few moments at the beginning of *Don Giovanni*, only to disappear until the end. But the motif, like the old man himself, returns resoundingly in 'Sirens,' at the very moment Bloom knows that Boylan is seducing Molly. The jealous husband would like to play the Commandant to Boylan's Giovanni, punish him, and thereby reinstate himself with his wife.

Like the reference to *Le nozze di Figaro* in 'Proteus,' the Commandant's presence is only implied, but it is equally obvious:

One rapped on the door, one tapped with a knock, did he knock Paul
de Kock, with a loud proud knocker, with a cock carracarracarra.
. . . Tap. (282)
Low sank the music, air and words. Then hastened. The false priest
rustling soldier from his cassock. A yeoman captain. They know it
all by heart. They thrill they itch for. Yeoman cap.
Tap. Tap. (285)
With a cock with a carra.
Tap. Tap. Tap.
I hold this house. Amen. He gnashed in fury. Traitors swing. (286)

The 'taps' recall a similar tapping rhythm in the strings and brass that underlies the entire death scene of *Don Giovanni*. Furthermore, when Leporello announces to his master that the Commandant's statue is outside, he imitates the knocking at the door with the syllables 'ta, ta, ta, ta.' The bold, unobscured sexual imagery surrounding the 'taps' equates seduction, knocking, penetration, and death. To Joyce, 'low music' refers to the sex act and the area of the body where it is performed, of course, but also to the fact that the role of the Commandant is sung by a basso profondo.

Through *Don Giovanni*, Joyce not only clarifies the relationship of Molly and Leopold, he shows that an ordinary man's inner life encompasses the thoughts and personalities of several people, and that ultimately his behavior is a composite of the interaction of these imagined roles.

Lucia di Lammermoor ('Hades,' 111)

In the 'Hades' chapter, Bloom is among a group of mourners who observe Paddy Dignam's burial. The following thoughts run through his mind:

> Last act of *Lucia*. *Shall I nevermore behold thee?*[8] Bam! expires.
> Gone at last. People talk about you a bit: forget you. Don't forget
> to pray for him. Remember him in your prayers.

The plot of *Lucia* is appropriate to Bloom's thoughts at this moment. Lucia loves Edgardo, the mortal enemy of her brother Enrico. Enrico wants her to marry Arturo, who has promised to advance his political career. Enrico shows Lucia what he claims is a love letter from Edgardo to another woman, which he himself has forged. Lucia, devastated, reluctantly agrees to marry Arutro. Edgardo appears at the wedding and denounces her as faithless. Lucia loses her mind (providing an excuse for the famous 'mad scene'), murders Arturo, and falls gravely ill. Edgardo, still believing her unfaithful, prepares to kill himself. He learns of the true situation just as funeral bells begin to toll for Lucia, at which time he goes through with his suicide.

Before his death, while still believing Lucia faithless, Edgardo sings the aria 'Fra poco a me ricovero,' in which he expresses the same thoughts about death as Bloom:

Fra poco a me ricovero

darà negletto avello . . .

Una pietosa lagrima

non scenderà su quello!

Ah! fin degli estinti, ahi misero!

Manca il conforto a me.

Tu pur, tu pur, dimentica

quel marmo dispregiato:

mai non passarvi, o barbara,

del tuo consorte a lato . . .

Ah! rispetta almen le ceneri

di chi moria per te.

Before long I will be sheltered

by a neglected grave.

No pitying tear

will descend on it.

I will even lack the comforts

of the dead.

You will also forget

the despised tomb.

Never pass it, cruel one,

with your husband at your side.

At least respect the ashes

of him who died for you.

Bloom's marital situation is also reflected in this allusion: 'Shall I nevermore behold thee?' of course refers to Molly. Like Edgardo, Leopold believes the woman he loves to be unfaithful, and wonders if she will ever love him again. Joyce thus shows Bloom preoccupied with Molly even at his friend's funeral.

Carmen ('Scylla and Charybdis,' 212; 'Circe,' 527)

During the discussion of Shakespeare in 'Scylla and Charybdis,' Stephen describes the Bard as follows:

> The boy of act one is the mature man of act five. All in all. In *Cymbeline*, in *Othello* he is bawd and cuckold. He acts and is acted on. Lover of an ideal or a perversion, like José he kills the real Carmen. His unremitting intellect is the hornmad Iago ceaselessly willing that the moor in him shall suffer.

The soldier Don José pursues an ideal of feminine beauty that he imagines in the gypsy girl Carmen. Yet Carmen is violent and crude; early in the opera she stabs a co-worker in a cigarette factory. She seduces José so that he will allow her to escape from custody following her arrest for the knifing. José sees none of this: thus, he cannot tolerate her later flirtations with the bullfighter Escamillo. As the opera ends, after he has stabbed her, José cries, 'Carmen, oh my adored Carmen.' But he has not loved her at all; 'he kills the real Carmen,' as Stephen says, because he only loved his fantasy of her.

In this instance, *Carmen* is used to clarify a point about Shakespeare. In 'Circe,' the opera is mentioned again as part of a whimsical description of the madam Bella Cohen, who carries 'a black horn fan, like Minnie Hauk in *Carmen*.'[9] The connection of *Carmen* with the word 'horn' ('hornmad Iago,' 'horn fan') in these two widely separated passages indicates a relationship. Since the Shakespeare passage was concerned with the concurrence of illusion and reality, it is logical that 'horn' symbolizes the horned gates of Morpheus, from whence, in Greek mythology, true visions emanate, in addition to its sexual connotations. The use of *Carmen*, where José confuses the real and the ideal, mirrors the confusion that occurs throughout 'Circe.'

Wagner and *Ulysses*[10]

Wagner was a major influence on the genre of the stream-of-consciousness novel. The basic unit of his 'music dramas,' as he called his stage works, is not the aria and ensemble, but the monologue. Whereas in traditional opera the words either carry the action ahead or express straightforward emotional responses to a situation, Wagner expanded the complexity of operatic characterization. His principals expound upon their thoughts and feelings in depth, often voicing what would be suppressed in ordinary speech. Wagner also uses musical leitmotifs to indicate the presence of other characters or events in the *unconscious* mind of whoever is singing. The device of the 'internal monologue,' which probes the character's psyche, is an innovation of Wagner imitated by many modern novelists. The Mime scenes of the *Ring* cycle impressed Joyce particularly in this respect.

Like Leopold Bloom ('Eumaeus,' 661), Joyce was not attracted to Wagner's music. They both preferred the more melodically accessible Italian repertoire. Joyce nevertheless knew a great deal about Wagner, and though I could find only two specific and two implicit references to the German composer in *Ulysses*, they are of such importance that they bespeak a considerable influence.

In the midst of the brothel scene (560), the prostitute Zoe asks Bloom whether Stephen is hungry. Stephen answers for himself:

(*Extends his hand to her smiling and chants to the air of the bloodoath in the* Dusk of the Gods.)

Hangende Hunger,

> Fragende Frau,
>
> Macht uns alle kaput.

This translates as, 'Gnawing hunger, questioning woman, kills us all.' Stephen is exhausted, drunk, and tired of the whole business at the bawdy house. Shortly thereafter he puts an end to his stay by smashing the light in the room with his 'ashplant,' an odd designation for a walking stick.

The blood-oath to which Joyce refers occurs in act 1 of *Götterdämmerung*, when Siegfried and Gunther swear eternal brotherhood. The words Joyce has changed are:

> Blehenden Lebens
>
> Labendes Blut
>
> Träufelt ich in der Trank.

> The invigorating blood
>
> of blossoming life
>
> I pour into the drink.

However, this oath does not last out the day, for Gunther allows Hagen (whose name may be implied by Joyce's use of 'hangende') to murder Siegfried after the latter has been tricked into betraying the oath.

Joyce's substitution of 'fragende Frau' in the second line recalls the conclusion of Siegmund's narration of his unhappy life to Sieglinde in *Die Walküre*, the second of the four operas of the *Ring*:

> Nun weisst, du, fragende Frau, warum ich Friedmund nicht heisse!
>
> Now you know, questioning woman, why I am not called Friedmund [joyous man].

These explicit references prepare the way for Stephen's demolition of the light by the '*ash*plant'-- an implicitly Wagnerian reference. The use of this unusual word instead of the more familiar 'walking stick' can only be explained by the appearance of ash trees in *Die Walküre* and *Götterdämmerung*, the two operas of the *Ring* that Joyce mentions. In the former work, Siegmund draws the sword, Nothung, from an ash tree, around which has been constructed the hut belonging to Hunding, Sieglinde's husband. Siegmund's behavior in *Die Walküre* resembles Stephen's in 'Circe.' He enters the hut in an exhausted condition, but has enough energy to explain his miserable existence to Sieglinde. Her husband recognizes him as an enemy, but abides by the rules of hospitality, postponing their fight until the morning. Siegmund has no weapon, but he sees the sword in the ash tree and pulls it out, a feat which many men had attempted but none had accomplished. With the sword in his possession, he recovers his strength. He and Sieglinde fall in love.

Siegmund's action, like Stephen's, marks the beginning of a new life -- not only for Siegmund, but for the world. Though Wotan kills Siegmund the next day for committing the crimes of adultery and incest (Sieglinde has revealed that she is his sister), the sword is used years later by Siegfried, their son, to smash Wotan's spear, which is cut from the 'Weltesche,' or 'world ash' tree. This occurs in *Siegfried*, the third of the *Ring* dramas. The old order of the Gods, which, as we learn in the prologue, *Das Rheingold*, is founded on lust, treachery, and greed, is thereby destroyed.

The other ash tree in the *Ring* cycle is the 'Weltesche' itself, which is mentioned in the first scene of *Götterdämmerung*. This tree, on which the Norns wound the rope that they used to spin the web of Fate, withered and died when Wotan broke off a branch to fashion his spear. After Siegfried shatters the spear, the Norns tell us that Wotan has had the remains of the tree cut in pieces and piled about Valhalla, where the Gods await their final destruction.

The full significance of Stephen's act of smashing the light at the brothel can now be appreciated. He has hitherto sought excitement and satisfaction in both intellectual and sexual pursuits. He will now go off with Leopold and find satisfaction in personal friendship. One possible message of Wagner's *Ring* is similar. The public world is founded on greed (which stole the gold from the Rhinemaidens), love of power (which caused Wotan to build Valhalla), treachery (he fails to pay the Giants who built it for him), and lust (the younger Wotan spent his time roaming the world in search of women). This world must be destroyed to make way for one based on love, which is symbolized by the loves of Sieglinde and Siegmund, Siegfried and Brünnhilde. Wotan himself attains a tragic grandeur when he realizes that the new world is better than the old, and then wills the latter's destruction.

Stephen thus symbolically destroys an entire way of life, a whole world, with his dramatic gesture. But destruction is not enough: a new world and new relationships must be created. By closing *Ulysses* with a gigantic monologue for Molly, comparable to and reminiscent of the equally stupendous 'Immolation Scene' of Brünnhilde that concludes *Götterdämmerung*, Joyce shows his message -- that the love of individuals is more important than the 'nightmare' of history -- as being ultimately the same as Wagner's. Molly's last word is 'Yes,' indicating that she will go to bed with Leopold and restore their love to its original state. Brünnhilde's last words are 'Siegfried!' Sieh! Selig grüsst dir dein Weib!' ('Siegfried! See! Your wife greets you joyfully!'). Siegfried is dead, and she rides her horse onto the funeral pyre to join him. She returns the ring, symbol of world-domination that Wotan had sought and Siegfried had actually possessed (but did not use), to the Rhinemaidens, from whom it had been stolen. The Rhine then rises up and covers the entire scene, while Valhalla is destroyed with the torch from Siegfried's pyre. Brünnhilde thus restores the world to its state of nature, just as Molly restores her marriage to *its* natural state. Molly's wish on the last page ('I'd love to have the whole place swimming in roses') is a clue that links the finale of Wagner's epic with that of Joyce's novel. At the end of the *Ring*, the whole place is literally flooded by the overflowing Rhine.

The theme of redemption through love, which obsessed Wagner throughout his life, dominates the operas *Lohengrin, Tannhäuser, Tristan und Isolde,* and *Der fliegende Holländer* (*The Flying Dutchman*). Bloom mentions this last opera in passing in the course of his long conversation with Stephen ('Eumaeus,' 636). In this work a Dutch sea captain is cursed to sail the oceans forever until he finds a faithful wife. (This, to elucidate the obvious, is also the quest of Homer's Ulysses.) The Dutchman finds that rare woman in Senta, but through a misunderstanding believes that she is preparing to wed another. He leaves her, and, proclaiming her fidelity, she jumps off a cliff. The curse is broken, and they ascend to heaven together.

Even though Joyce experienced Wagner's music as interminable and heavy, this concept of redemption through love was one aspect of the composer's philosophy that he found congenial. Although many of the symbolists and modern novelists were influenced by Wagner's method, Joyce actually followed him in asserting the primacy of personal relationships based upon love over the public world of politics, the debased life of sex *without* love, and the practice of pure intellectualism. (Wagner's Loge, a cynical, intellectual God, does not appear in the *Ring* after the prologue except, invisibly, as the force that starts the fire at the end of *Die Walküre*.)

Martha (throughout *Ulysses*; especially in 'Sirens')

Bloom first thinks of the opera *Martha* when he is roaming disconsolately through Dublin in the morning. He sees a man who looks like Jesus, but who also resembles the great tenor Giovanni Mario. After he thinks of Jesus, his thoughts turn to the biblical Martha and Mary, and Mario brings to mind the opera *Martha*. This is significant, for it shows that Martha Clifford, with whom Bloom is having a 'love affair' by mail, is definitely not the 'lost, dear one' whom he wants to come to him. Joyce seems to have gone out of his way *not* to have Bloom recall this opera when thinking of Martha Clifford

Martha's plot, like that of *Don Giovanni*, mirrors Bloom and Molly's relationship. Lionel, a young farmer, engages a servant girl named Martha, who is really Lady Harriet in disguise. Martha soon breaks her contract, runs away, and pretends never to have heard of Lionel. Meanwhile, Lionel has fallen in love with her. It is soon discovered that he is really the Earl of Derby, which causes Lady Harriet to try to make him renew his courtship. But he will have nothing to do with her; she then disguises herself again as Martha, whereupon Lionel's love is restored and they plight their troth.

Lionel sings the aria 'M'appari'[11] just before he decides to marry Harriet:

> M'appari tutt'amor,
>
> Il mio sguardo l'incontrò;
>
> Bella si, che il mio cor,
>
> Ansioso a lei volo, . . .
>
> mi ferì, m'invaghì
>
> quell' angelica beltà,
>
> sculta in cor dall'amor
>
> cancellar si non potrà;
>
> Il pensier di poter

palpitar con lei d'amor,

puo sopir il martir

che m'affano, e strazia il cor!

Marta, Marta tu sparisti

è il mio cor col tuo n'ando!

Tu la pace mi rapisti

di dolor io morirò!

She appeared to me, full of love,

my glance encountered hers.

She was so beautiful that my heart

instantly flew to hers.

I fell in love with

such angelic beauty

that such love can never be

cancelled in my heart;

the thought of being able

to sigh with love for her

can calm the pain

which afflicts and rends my heart.

Martha, Martha you appeared

and my heart flew to you.

You robbed me of my peace

and I will die of sadness!

In 'Sirens,' Simon Daedalus signs two arias: 'M'appari,' from *Martha* and 'Tutto è sciolto' from Bellini's *La sonnambula*: in both of these, an unhappy man longs for the return of the woman he loves. Bloom's real 'Martha' is Molly. He only decides to mail the letter to Martha Clifford as an afterthought, when he is desperate with jealousy and rage. As Simon sings the *Martha* aria, Bloom's thoughts are recorded by Joyce after each line. They all express his love for Molly; he recalls memories of her several times in the course of the song (275-76):

--*Each graceful look* . . .

First night when I saw her at Mat Dillon's in Terenure. . . .

--*Charmed my eye* . . .

Singing. *Waiting* she sang. I turned her music. . . . Ah, alluring. . . .

--*Co-me, thou lost one!*

Co-me thou dear one!

Alone. One love. One hope. One comfort me. Martha, chestnote, return.

--*Come!*

It soared, a bird, it held its flight, a swift pure cry, soar silver orb it leaped serene, speeding, sustained, to come, don't spin it out too long breath he breath long life, soaring high, high resplendent, aflame, crowned, high, in the effulgence symbolistic, high, of the ethereal bosom, high, of the high vast irradiation everywhere all soaring all around about the all, the endlessnessnessness . . .

--*To me!*

As Leopold himself realizes, the chest note is symbolic of his love for Molly. Throughout this section everything he sings and hears turns his thoughts to his wife.

The operatic Martha next appears in 'The Oxen of the Sun' (414):

And, lo, wonder of metempsychosis, it is she, the everlasting bride,

harbinger of the daystar, the bride, ever virgin. It is she, Martha,

thou lost one, Millicent, the young, the dear, the radiant.

Leopold here expresses his love both for Molly and for their deceased daughter. Like Lionel in Flotow's opera, he here recalls the happy beginning of his relationship with his wife.

When the real-life Martha (Clifford) appears in 'Circe' (456) and accuses Bloom, in so many words, of being a heartless flirt, he calls her a drunk. Clearly, she is not his idealized 'Martha.'

Finally, in 'Eumaeus' (661), Bloom symbolizes his increasing desire for acceptance and reconciliation with Molly by 'favouring preferably light opera of the *Don Giovanni* description, and *Martha*, a gem in its line' to Wagner's music dramas, which are 'heavy' and 'too hard to follow.' He prefers those operas that end happily, where all is forgiven and forgotten and a return is effected to the status quo that existed *before* any threat to the romance appeared. Focusing on *Martha* not only demonstrates that Bloom is looking forward to such a conclusion, but the fact of this opera's happy ending becomes a sign from Joyce that the desired denouement will in fact take place, that the fates of that homophonic pair, 'Lionel' and 'Leopold,' will be the same.

La sonnambula ('Sirens,' 269-70)

Amina, who is unaware that she sleepwalks, is to be married to Elvino. Unfortunately, she awakens in another man's bedroom one night. Elvino believes her unfaithful and sings the aria 'Tutto è sciolto,' which expresses his grief over her betrayal. In the finale, however, the truth is made known and the lovers are reunited.

Elvino's aria is sung by Simon Daedalus in 'Sirens,' and echoes Leopold's feelings toward Molly at the moment. He is extremely angry over her affair with Boylan, and is unhappy because he truly loves her. He deeply regrets the loss of the happiness they formerly shared, and like Elvino, he cannot bring himself to hate the woman he loves:

> Tutto è sciolto.
>
> Più per me non v'ha conforto
>
> Il mio cor per sempre è morto
>
> Alla gioia ed all'amor.
>
> Ah! perche non posso odiarti,
>
> Infedel, com'io vorrei!
>
> Ah! del tutto ancor non sei
>
> Cancellata dal mio cor.
>
> Possa un altro, ah! possa amarti
>
> Qual t'amò quest'infelice!
>
> Altro voto, o traditrice,
>
> Non temer del mio dolor!
>
>
>
> Everything is lost.
>
> There is no more comfort for me.
>
> My heart is forever dead
>
> to joy and love.
>
> Oh, why can't I hate you,
>
> faithless one, as I should?
>
> Oh, you are not entirely
>
> yet cancelled from my heart.
>
> May another be able to

love you as this unfortunate man has.

Do not fear another wish

from my grief, o traitress!

La sonnambula is one more indication that the Blooms' problems are going to be resolved. Like *Martha* and *Don Giovanni* (where Zerlina and Masetto are concerned), Bellini's opera ends happily for the lovers.

Les huguenots ('Eumaeus,' 661; 'Penelope,' 771)

Les huguenots concerns the Catholic-Protestant conflict in sixteenth-century France. Several important figures on each side, at the request of Queen Marguerite of Valois, meet to negotiate a peace, but their efforts fail. By identifying Molly with Marguerite, Joyce further establishes her character as a woman who loves the beauty of nature and earthly, simple things -- a universal mother figure who loves everybody. Molly thinks of Marguerite's aria 'O beau pays de la Touraine' (771), which expresses the Queen's love for the natural beauty of her native province:

O wasn't I the born fool to believe all his [Leopold's] blather about home rule and the land league sending me that long strool of a song out of the Huguenots to sing in French to be more classy O beau pays de la Touraine that I never even sang once explaining and rigmaroling about religion and persecution he wont let you enjoy anything naturally

Molly here summarizes all of her own traits. She (like Queen Marguerite) is uninterested in politics; she is not concerned with the opera's historical background or plot or with singing it in French. And though she has no use for Marguerite's music, she is very much like the Queen. She loves the natural pleasures of life, and has turned away from Leopold because he denies them to her. We are also reminded of her wish 'to have the whole place swimming in roses' (781) at the very end of the novel, for Meyerbeer's Marguerite sings her aria while her ladies-in-waiting are bathing and frolicking in a river.

Molly considers the intellectual subjects discussed by Stephen and Leopold meaningless. And she, representing the flesh and natural pleasures, wins out in the end, for however much the two men debate philosophy, they nevertheless devote considerable time and thought to sex. The chasm between theory and practice in the lives of Stephen and Leopold is painfully evident throughout the book. Their aspirations and behavior have to be reconciled, and this can only be done through Molly.

This interpretation is symbolized by a mistake Bloom makes in 'Eumaeus'(661). While discussing his favorite composers and compositions with Stephen, he mentions Mercadante's *Huguenots* and Meyerbeer's *Seven Last Words on the Cross*, thereby attributing to each composer a work he did not write. This is an error that Stephen ought to have caught, but when the men are tired and drunk, such mistakes are allowed to pass. Or, perhaps, Stephen does not wish to interrupt Bloom's enthusiastic discourse by raising such a point. This would reveal a definitely more mature Stephen than the smug intellectual of the earlier chapters. The accuracy of Bloom's musicology is not important; what matters is that the two men are united in friendship through their love of music. They are thereby also united with Molly, who, Bloom notes at the time, made a 'veritable sensation' with her singing of Rossini's *Stabat mater*. In addition, Leopold's mistaking the composer of *Huguenots* directly anticipates Molly's lack of concern, in her final monologue, with the nonmusical aspects of that opera. An appreciation of the spiritual essence of music, which she has always instinctively possessed, can become the common denominator of the relationship that we expect will develop between Molly, Stephen, and Leopold.

Like all the novel's intrinsic elements (psychological, literary, medical, figurative), Joyce's use of operatic references in *Ulysses* clarifies the plot and the behavior of the major characters. Knowledge of even a few of these allusions greatly increases our understanding, not to say enjoyment, of the novel: we learn that his wife's affair with Boylan prods Leopold into seeking a return to their original relationship, when he was the man of the family in fact as well as in name; that Molly has a lover because Leopold will not fulfill his marital duties; that she accepts her husband when at last she realizes that he will do so; and that Stephen, the young artist, obtains, in the persons of Leopold and Molly, both the parental affection and the contact with down-to-earth people that are needed to inspire his creative efforts. Moreover, taken together, the operas mentioned by Joyce reveal an important pattern. Most of their plots lead to the reconciliation of two lovers who are temporarily separated because of real or assumed infidelity -- usually on the part of the woman. Even in those where the cast is massacred (*Les huguenots or Götterdämmerung)*, the lovers die affirming their fidelity. Joyce uses operas whose endings predict Molly's ultimate 'Yes' at the end of *Ulysses*.

Among other things, the author of *Ulysses* attempts to incorporate into his novel a great deal of life and civilization in concentrated, symbolic form. The activities of three people during one day epitomize the human experience in general. Insofar as the world of opera is both a part of and a microcosmic reflection of man's culture, Joyce has successfully demonstrated its relevance to the lives of his characters. When Molly, Leopold, and Stephen reenact the great operatic roles, Joyce reveals the existence of heroism and romance in the daily activities of ordinary human beings.

ENDNOTES

1.   Richard Ellman, in *James Joyce*, New York: Oxford University Pres, 1959, discusses Joyce's lifelong passion for opera; pp. 47, 74, 116, etc.

2.   I have limited consideration to opera proper, excluding references to operetta, ballet, and song. Many of Joyce's allusions to operas are so subtle and indirect that some fleeting instances have been omitted. These include mentions of Donizetti's *Daughter of Regiment*, Gounod's *Faust*, and Wallace's *Maritana,* among others.

3.   Page numbers from and chapters of *Ulysses* cited in the text refer to the Vintage Books edition, New York, 1961.

4.   All translations are my own. They are intended to be as literal as possible within the limits of comprehensibility.

5.   Several times in *Ulysses*, Bloom mentions, with reference to some intoxicated person, that 'he's as bad as old Antonio' e.g., 97. This song is from 'Has Anybody Here Seen Kelly?' but there appears to be the subtlest reference to *Le nozze di Figaro* as well. Not only is Antonio the name of the drunken gardener in Mozart's opera, but an Irishman named Michael Kelly sang both character tenor roles, Don Basilio and Don Curzio, at the opera's Vienna premiere in 1786.

6.   William York Tindall, *A Reader's Guide to James Joyce*, New York: Noonday Press, 1959, p. 124.

7.   Bloom hears the Minuet from *Don Giovanni* played on the piano at the bar, 'Sirens,' 282, precisely when Boylan meets Molly. It is during the minuet that Giovanni takes Zerlina to a back room for several minutes. They emerge with the girl shrieking, 'Son morta' ('I'm dead'). Joyce thus uses opera (see also discussion of the Commandant that follows) to inform us exactly when the seduction of Molly takes place.

8.   'Shall I nevermore behold thee?' is probably from the Stephen Foster song 'Gentle Annie'; see Weldon Thornton, *Allusions in 'Ulysses,'* Chapel Hill: University of North Carolina Press, 1968, p. 103.

9.   Minnie Hauk, 1851-1929, American soprano, born New York City, who sang Carmen in Paris, London, Vienna, Berlin, and at the Metropolitan Opera, most often in Italian. On 23 October 1879, she was the first Carmen in the United States, at New York's Academy of Music.

10.   See references to Wagner in Ellman, *Joyce,* pp. 74, 116, 249, 393, 473-74, 632, etc.

11.   Although *Martha* is in fact a German opera (Lionel's aria begins 'Ach so fromm, ach so traut' in the original) and Simon sings the aria, in *Ulysses,* in English, the universally

known Italian text is given because that is the language in which Joyce is most likely to have heard performances of the opera.

Chapter 18

Cherubini Stages a Revolution

Four days before the thirty-one-year-old Luigi Cherubini's new opera *Lodoïska* premiered on 18 July 1791 at the Théâtre Feydeau in Paris, the French citizenry had celebrated the second anniversary of the storming of the Bastille. Moreover, less than a month before that *jour de fête*, Louis XVI and his family were brought back to the capital from Varennes following their ill-fated attempt to escape the Revolution. Set to a libretto by Claude-François Fillette-Loraux in which oppressed people storm a castle, liberate prisoners, and overthrow tyrants, *Lodoïska* was the ideal opera for revolutionary France.[1]

The work was performed more than two hundred times in one year, a first run seldom equalled in operatic history, and another two hundred during the remainder of the Revolution.[2] Standing ovations frequently greeted individual numbers, and the Parisian press supplied reviews that were the stuff of a composer's dreams. *Lodoïska* 'heralded a great master of infinite promise,' raved the *Journal de Paris:* 'One has never been more astonished than by the numerous brilliant effects found throughout this work.' Babault's *Dramatic Annals* found the music 'ravishing and sublime, with admirable choruses, profound orchestration, astonishing verve, and extraordinary originality.' Cherubini surpassed the great masters, recorded the *General Almanac of All Spectacles* for 1792: 'Never before have French ears heard more expressive music.' Even the *Moniteur Universel's* criticism was a form of praise: 'It is too beautiful, and that is a real problem. The pieces are composed with infinite care, and all equally so, which does not give the listener a chance to relax. . . . One would prefer simpler pieces from time to time, and a chance to rest.'[3]

Students of *Lodoïska* in succeeding generations have also praised it effusively. In 1890, when the opera was one year short of its centenary, Frederick Crowest linked it with *Don Giovanni* as a work possessed of 'great life-giving properties -- the deep-grounded musical purpose and intent, the profound learning combined with harmonic and melodic resource, the richness of fancy and idea, the command of vocal and instrumental forms, the grasp of happy periods and great dramatic situations -- all this, and more.'[4] Basil Deane has termed *Lodoïska* an 'entirely new departure in opera . . . entirely original in its depth of psychological insight, dramatic tension, and musical technique . . . *Lodoïska* opened a new path for opera composers, by demonstrating that areas of human experience outside the restricted fields of historical or mythological grand opera and comic opera could be treated seriously.'[5] (Cherubini and revolutionary France, it should be stressed, had no knowledge of Mozart's mature operas.)[6] Finally, in his biography of the composer, Vittorio Della Croce finds in *Lodoïska* 'a coherent and extraordinarily modern personal style.'[7]

And yet, up until its recent revival at La Scala (March 1991), *Lodoïska* seemed to have been buried with its composer. More than that, it has been completely overshadowed in the operagoing public's estimation, and unjustly so, by Cherubini's 1797 opera *Médée* in its Italian-language incarnation (*Medea*). *Lodoïska* bears investigating for other reasons besides its considerable musical merits. First, it is a wonderful example of the transmittal of revolutionary ideology to the populace through theater and spectacle and of one way in which Masonic and Enlightenment thought thereby spread among the people. Second, *Lodoïska* occupies an interesting place in the history of ideas. It develops the master/servant relationship, of which Cervantes's *Don Quixote* is the great model. Also, *Lodoïska* was an important inspiration for Beethoven's *Fidelio*. The argument that Beethoven might not have written an opera had he not known and admired Cherubini's isn't in the least far-fetched. *Lodoïska* also inspired two minor works: Rodolphe Kreutzer's opera of the same name, which directly capitalized on Cherubini's success and premiered in Paris later in 1791 (Beethoven dedicated what is now called the *Kreutzer* Sonata, op. 47 for violin and piano, to him); and a pastiche *Lodoïska* using music by Cherubini and others that was assembled by Stephen Storace and J.P. Kemble and first staged at the Theatre Royal in Drury Lane, London, on 9 July 1794. Examining Cherubini's *Lodoïska*, along with some of the works it inspired, provides insight into the reasons for the nineteenth-century rejection of the French Revolution's idealization of a heroic, freedom-loving populace in favor of the more conservative notion of a people following its 'betters.' This change had important consequences for operatic as well as political history.

Why did Cherubini write *Lodoïska?* In 1789, the young composer, fresh from a string of operatic successes in Italy, was invited by Marie Antoinette's hair dresser, Alexis Léonard, to take charge of a newly created opera house in Paris. The troupe that was to be resident in that house performed briefly at Versailles under the patronage of 'Monsieur,' the brother of Louis XVI who would become Louis XVIII in 1815. But then the Revolution erupted. Cherubini tried to maintain a low profile because of this association with the royal family, but doing so did not suffice to guarantee his safety. On one occasion, when accosted by a mob of sansculottes, he saved his life only by playing revolutionary tunes on a violin. He subsequently established his republican credentials by joining the National Guard and escorting unfortunates to the guillotine, by writing revolutionary hymns and cantatas, *and* by composing *Lodoïska*. Cherubini's plight during the Revolution presages those of musicians in our own times, forced to live under tyrannical regimes and to write music designed as political propaganda.[8]

The score of *Lodoïska* is so fervent and convincing that Cherubini seems to have believed every word of its simplistic, repetitive, and frequently bombastic libretto, a libretto that illustrates perfectly one French revolutionary legislator's belief that 'every occasion should be celebrated with the singing of hymns praising the fatherland, liberty, equality, and fraternity, because hymns have the power to endow the citizens with all manner of virtues.'[9] However, much of the opera's quality may stem from the fact that its composer was writing for his life as well as for his career in an uncertain political and musical world; the French Revolution censored works it considered ideologically suspect and subsidized those that extolled its values.[10] Cherubini may have been forced to act like a true revolutionary for a while, but his biography resembles no one's as much as that of the great French statesman Talleyrand (1754-1838). Both men managed to survive and prosper not only under the various revolutionary regimes but during the reign of Napoleon (with whom Cherubini quarreled over his poor taste in music) and in the Bourbon and Orleans restorations as well. The composer of the radical *Lodoïska* was accorded the honor of writing the coronation mass for the arch-reactionary Charles X (reigned 1824-30) more than three decades later![11]

Lodoïska opens with an overture comparable in power to and somewhat reminiscent of that to Mozart's *Don Giovanni*, with which Cherubini was not acquainted. Arturo Toscanini recorded it with the NBC Symphony, and Riccardo Muti, another champion of Cherubini's music, performed it with great success in Philadelphia in March 1990. (It was Muti who masterminded the La Scala revival of the opera the next year.) A brief, slow introduction relies heavily on the 'column of harmony.' This was a staple of Masonic ceremonial music of which

Mozart's, such as the *Trauermusik*, is the most famous. Here stately chords emphasizing the lower winds depict the harmonizing of classes and nations.[12] Similar chords abound in *Lodoïska*.

Cherubini prescribes, in his stage directions, a somewhat heavy-handed use of light and darkness to symbolize good and evil in the mise-en-scène, which one contemporary reviewer praised as alternatively 'frightening' and 'picturesque'.[13] The Masons made much use of these extremes as moral indicators in their rituals: the most famous musico-dramatic juxtaposition of the two by a Mason is Mozart's contrast of the Queen of the Night's realm to the sun-drenched kingdom of Sarastro in *Die Zauberflöte*. In one of musical history's more interesting coincidences, that work premiered on 30 September 1791, only two months after the first performance of *Lodoïska*. But whereas Mozart makes a case for how Masonic ideals can enter the world through Enlightened rulers such as Tamino and Sarastro (translation: Enlightened, Masonic monarchs such as Austrian emperors Josef II, who ruled 1780-90, and Leopold II, who ruled 1790-92), Cherubini's opera argues that violent revolution can also serve as a vehicle for the achievement of harmony, equality, and justice.

To return to the overture: After the flutes present a beautiful lyric theme (*adagio*, p.2), the first long section is a rousing *allegro vivace* that would not disgrace Beethoven (p.3ff.).[14] A more lyrical second theme (p.10), still in the *allegro* but creating a marked change of mood, is punctuated with unusual flute turns (p.11) before giving way to the fiery violin runs that are a Cherubini trademark (p. 12ff.) -- he later used them to underline Medea's fury. The powerful *allegro* is sustained for several minutes until an oboe solo reprises the initial theme (pp, 27-29), a slow respite (marked *moderato*) before the final, triumphant, *allegro vivace* conclusion (p.31).

In act 1, scene 1, the Tartars, led by their chief, Titzikan, gather just before dawn in a forest outside the castle of the Polish count Dourlinski. (Symbolically, the darkness of oppression is ready to yield to the dawn of liberty.) The Tartars are preparing an assault in order to free some of their number, whom Dourlinski holds as prisoners. Titzikan successfully urges his men to courageous action and leads them in a chorus modeled on the French Revolution's distinctive antiphonal 'crowd participation' type of hymn: a soloist makes an inspiring pronouncement, to which a chorus leader (in this case two Tartars) and then the people respond (p. 33ff.)[15]

Titzikan:

Approchez sans défiance,

Tout est calme en ce séjour;

Titzikan, then two Tartars and chorus *(the variants sung by Tartars and Chorus are in parentheses; lines sung only by Titzikan are noted by an asterisk; the remainder are sung by everyone)*:

Concertons notre vengeance,

Visitons chaque détour.

Tu connais notre courage;

(Quel sera notre partage?)

*Comme tu connais mon coeur--

C'est la Palme du vainqueur.

Secondez bien mon* (ses) desseins,

*Chers amis, quand je vous guide

(Notre chef est intrépide)

*Votre chef est intrépide

(Titzikan est notre guide)

La victoire est dans nos mains.

Titzikan

> Approach without fear;
>
> All is calm in this place.

Titzikan, then two Tartars and chorus:

> Let us plan our revenge
>
> And check out every obstacle.
>
> You know our courage
>
> (What will be our reward?)
>
> *As you know my heart--
>
> It is the Palm of the victor.
>
> Follow my* (his) plans well,
>
> *Dear friends, when I direct you
>
> (Our leader is intrepid)
>
> *Your leader is intrepid
>
> (Titzikan is our leader)
>
> Victory will be ours.

The dialogue following this opening chorus is nothing less than a primer for proper revolutionary behavior.   Titzikan orders his followers to detain any 'innocent bystanders' traveling to the castle to prevent their warning the count of the impending attack.   But he insists that they respect these people (p.51):

> Surtout, respectez les jours de ceux que le hasard vous liverera; il ne
> faut pas que l'innocent souffre pour le coupable. Et n'oubliez jamais,
> braves gens, qu'on ne doit point servir ses interêts aux dépens de la
> justice et de l'humanité! Allez!

Above all respect the lives of those whom fate places in your hands;
the innocent must not suffer for the guilty. And never forget, good
people, that you can never serve your own interests at the cost of
justice and humanity! Forward!

At this point, Titzikan's argument with a skeptical Tartar illustrates the
contention of the leaders of the French Revolution (among others) that rebellion
only begins when injustice has been borne for too long. Even though the
insurgents have yet to think through their plans for the future, their uprising is still
justified (p.51):

Tartar: Titzikan, quel est ton dessein sur ce Dourlinski?

Titzikan: Je n'en sais rien encore.

Tartar: Et tu viens de dire à tous nos Tartares de se tenir prêts, sans savoir
ce que tu veux entreprendre?

Titzikan: Sans doubte . . . je suis lent à me préparer, prompt a saisir
l'occasion, et courageux dans l'action.

Tartar: Mais encore, faudrait-il savoir . . .

Titzikan (*avec force*): Je sais que je veux me venger, et c'est assez pour
moi . . .

Tartar: Titzikan, what are your plans for this Dourlinski?

Titzikan: I don't know yet.

Tartar: You told us Tartars to be ready just now without knowing what you
were going to do? [Tenet: Revolutionary crowds should blindly trust
their leaders; rebellion is justified even if no one knows what they
hope to achieve!]

Titzikan: No doubt I'm slow to prepare, but I'm quick to seize a chance
and courageous in action.

Tartar: But still, shouldn't we know . . .

Titzikan (*forcefully*): I know I want to avenge myself, and that's enough for

me . . .

But our doubting Tartar still is not silenced. He calls attention to Dourlinski's great power, arms, and fortifications and suggests that it would be more prudent to ambush him when he leaves the castle. Titzikan explodes with wrath at this idea: 'Triompher d'un traître par la trahison, c'est l'imiter et non pas le vaincre. . . . Souviens-toi que tu conseilles Titzikan' (p.51). (To triumph over a traitor through treason is to imitate him and not to defeat him. . . . Remember that you are giving advice to Titzikan!) The Tartar thus represents all the popular fears that must be overcome in order for revolution to begin, and Titzikan explains why terrorism and assassination are no substitutes for a heroic popular uprising. He then bursts into a furious *allegro* (p. 52). Beethoven must have had it in the back, if not the front, of his mind when he penned Pizarro's aria in *Fidelio*, for they possess the same general tone:

Titzikan:

> Triomphons avec noblesse,
>
> De vous tout à la valeur;
>
> La ruse est une faiblesse,
>
> Elle flétrit le vainqueur.
>
>
> Si tu m'offres la victoire,
>
> Peins la digne de mon coeur:
>
> Titzikan chérit la gloire,
>
> Mais offerte par l'honneur.

Titzikan:

> Let us triumph with nobility
>
> You should owe everything to bravery;
>
> Trickery is weakness,
>
> It strikes down the victor.
>
> If you offer me victory,
>
> It must be worthy of my heart;
>
> Titzikan cherishes glory,
>
> But only with honor.

At the conclusion of this aria, the sun rises (p.65). Goodness is dawning, and the people are triumphing 'avec noblesse.' They are assuming the nobility of spirit that the nobility itself has desecrated. Scenes 1 and 2 thus establish the heroic character of the people and their revolutionary leaders and begin the legitimation of revolution, which is the opera's political agenda. There are also important reasons for which librettist Fillette-Loraux has *Tartars* attacking a *Polish* castle. Several of these can be linked with the thought of Jean-Jacques Rousseau (1712-78), the French philosopher whose ideas were arguably as influential as any during the Revolution. (Rosseau himself wrote a short opera, *Le devin du village* or *The Village Sorcerer*, which illustrated that true love flourishes best without the interference of a sorcerer and his potions. This glorification of natural life and the good, simple impulses of ordinary folk also served as the inspiration for a better opera, the twelve-year-old Mozart's singspiel *Bastien und Bastienne*.)

Eighteenth-century Poland showed only too well the results of permitting a corrupt nobility to govern. From its seventeenth-century glory -- King John Sobieski of Poland saved Vienna from the Turks in 1683 -- the nation had sunk to such depths that its kings were usually succeeded at death by the foreign bidders who could most effectively bribe the Seym, or Diet, of the Polish nobility. Poland

and its aristocracy had become symbols of degeneracy throughout Western civilization: one of the American Founding Fathers' greatest fears was that 'the corruption of Poland' would descend on the new republic.[16] And during the Enlightenment, 'corruption' meant not only greed, selfishness, and dishonesty but primarily a lack of disinterested love of country, the 'virtue' necessary for a nation to avoid Poland's fate. (At the time of *Lodoïska's* composition, Poland was but a few years away from the third partition, which effectively abolished its independence.)

Where does Rosseau come in? In 1771, in response to a plea from Polish patriots sensing their nation's desperate plight, he wrote *On the Government of Poland*, which called for the Poles to rekindle their patriotic ardor.[17] The Rousseau connection becomes more apparent in the use of Tartars as Poland's foes. One of the main themes of *The Social Contract*, Rosseau's most famous work, is the superiority of the uncorrupted 'savage' living close to nature over the effete civilized man, who 'is born free and everywhere is in chains,' as the opening line proclaims.[18] Or, as *Lodoïska* shows us, we need natural, unspoiled people to save those who are literally in chains thanks to a corrupt nobility.

Finally, the use of Tartars in Poland demonstrates an important element of French revolutionary 'spectacle' to which historian Mona Ozouf has recently called attention. Cherubini was setting to music a spectacle performed thousands of times in France following the fall of the Bastille. Cities and public officials would build mock Bastilles on a grand scale and reenact its destruction; theatrical troupes and puppeteers did the same in miniature, spreading revolutionary pride and consciousness throughout France. One element all of these spectacles had in common was the effort to strip the storming of the Bastille of its particularistic location in time and space. The destruction of tyranny was meant to be universal, applicable to all peoples at all times; hence the Tartars and the Poles circa 1600.

By rendering the Bastille spectacles abstract, the revolutionaries meant to show that their revolution could and should be extended to all mankind, including peoples of other races and continents as well as those who were victims of the worst tyranny in Europe. It is significant that *Lodoïska* dealt with freedom-loving Tartars at precisely the same time that the French National Assembly was debating the rights of blacks and the abolition of slavery in the French West Indies.[19]

In scene 3 of act 1 we meet Floreski, a young, idealistic, and utterly impractical Polish noble. He is searching for his beloved Lodoïska, who has been hidden by her father, a man deeply angry over Floreski's refusal to vote as he was told in the election for king (p. 82). Along with Floreski travels his cynical, down-to-earth squire, Varbel. Such master/squire pairs, in a number of guises, are standard in both literature and opera of the pre-Romantic period: one thinks of Belmonte and Pedrillo, Don Giovanni and Leporello, and Tamino and Papageno in the operas of Mozart alone. But the archetypes are Don Quixote and Sancho Panza, to whom Floreski and Varbel bear a marked resemblance. At one point Varbel even suggests this kinship: 'Nous sommes vous et moi dans le train des grands aventures' (We are, you and I, in the midst of great adventures) (p.136).

In their first dialogue, Varbel complains of the absurdity of wandering all over Poland looking for one particular woman, especially when they are hungry and thirsty, have lost their horses, and are surrounded by Tartars. Varbel plays up the quixotic nature of Floreski's quest in his first aria (p.66ff.):

> Voyez la belle besogne,
>
> Vraiment, j'en rougis pour vous;
>
> Courir toute la Pologne,
>
> On nous prendrait pour deux fous . . .
>
> Courtiser une femme jolie,
>
> C'est un plaisir de saison;

On peut aimer pour la vie,

Et conserver la raison.

Look at this fine quest.

I really blush for you,

Running all over Poland

They'll think we're a couple of lunatics . . .

Flirting with a beautiful woman

It's a momentary pleasure;

You could love for life

And keep your sanity.

The Varbel/Floreski coupling allows Fillette-Loraux the opportunity for yet another revolutionary lesson. In mid-1791 many nobles such as Mirabeau, Lafayette, and Condorcet still favored and functioned as leaders of the Revolution. However, *Lodoïska* points out through the character of Floreski that aristocratic idealism is impractical and requires a strong dose of the people's common sense. A reforming noble, whether a Floreski or a Quixote, becomes a lunatic or a comic figure when he exists under aristocratic rule. Even the nobility, implies the librettist, needs revolution to fulfill its greatness.

When Varbel's aria ends, Floreski further demonstrates his lack of prudence by becoming involved in a duel with Titzikan. The Tartar reappears and asks Floreski to lay down his arms and remain temporarily in his custody to prevent a possible warning to Dourlinski. But Floreski refuses to surrender and insists on fighting despite the fact that there are Tartars all around (p.82) and that Titzikan has guaranteed his safety. Then, to demonstrate *his* nobility, Titzikan, proclaiming, 'Nous ne sommes point inhumains' (We are in no way inhuman), duels Floreski single-handedly in the presence of his men. When he loses,

Floreski spares his life, and Titzikan returns the favor by preventing the enraged Tartars from wreaking vengeance. As he explains: 'Je suis Tartare, mais un coeur généreux peut naître en tous les climats' (I am a Tartar, but a generous soul can be born anywhere) (p.103). The two embrace, and then all join in an oath of brotherhood (p.104ff.). Public oath-swearing was an important feature of the French Revolution: those (notably the nonjuring clergy who remained loyal to the Roman Catholic church) who refused to place allegiance to the republic above all else were considered enemies and were dealt with harshly:[20]

>   All:
>
>   Jurons qu'il faille entreprendre,
>
>   Amis de nous, joindre à leur sort;
>
>   Oui, s'il le faut pour les défendre
>
>   Nous combattrons jusqu'à la mort.
>
>   All:
>
>   Let us swear to join
>
>   Our fate to our brothers'--
>
>   Yes, to defend them to the death
>
>   If need be.

Following this incorporation of yet another standard bit of revolutionary pageantry, Titzikan explains, as though he had to, that his war against Dourlinski has no sordid motive but is justified by the count's plunder of the land and imprisonment of the people (p.119). Floreski and Varbel marvel at the discovery that Tartars can be so high-minded; Fillette-Loraux is demonstrating the aristocrat's gradual recognition of the dignity and equality of men:

>   Floreski: Quel étonnant langage!
>
>   Varbel: Ma foi, Seigneur, je n'en reviens pas; être tout
>
>   ensemble, Tartare, honnête homme, sensible, franc, et

généreux! . . . Ce n'est qu'en voyageant beaucoup
qu'on peut rencontrer un tel prodige!

Floreski: What amazing language!

Varbel: My goodness, Lord, I have never seen the like -- a
           Tartar, honest, sensitive, forthright, and generous all in
           one! . . . You'd have to travel a great deal to find such
           a prodigy.

The Tartars disappear, and Floreski and Varbel sing consecutive couplets to
drive home further the Don Quixote/Sancho Panza parallel. Varbel cynically
remarks that when he was young, he too, burned with love, but that now he
prefers a good meal. Floreski, on the other hand, lives only for Lodoïska and
would gladly die for her (pp.120-35).

As they finish, two bricks fall from Dourlinski's castle (p.136). Varbel
pointedly attributes this to 'les fâcheux effets de la décadence de cette antique
fortresse' (the unfortunate effects of the decadence of this old fortress), a line that
undoubtedly provoked some cheering in the audience in revolutionary Paris. But
this time it is Floreski who is right. He senses some 'mystère.' Sure enough,
Lodoïska, imprisoned in a tower, has sent down two requests for help: 'Est-ce
vous, Floreski?' (Is it you Floreski?) and 'C'est toi . . . je te reconnais . . .
Délivre la malheureuse Lodoïska mais sois prudent' (It's you . . . I recognize you
. . . Save your unhappy Lodoïska, but be careful). She knows her man: despite
Varbel's advice that without the Tartars they should return to Warsaw for help,
Floreski orders his servant to ring the castle bell. He will obtain her freedom
through some as yet unknown strategem. The act ends as the two are admitted to
the castle by Dourlinski's right-hand man, Altamoras, amid numerous warnings
from the guards to be careful. As is also true of the finales to acts 2 and 3, this

is an elaborate, beautifully worked-out concerted piece, with many changes of mood, that lasts for more than ten minutes (pp.137-91).

Acts 2 and 3 illustrate the proof of Titzikan's statement that liberty cannot be obtained through ruses and plots but only through revolutionary action. As the second act begins, we see Lodoïska herself for the first time. She is in a large hall in Dourlinski's castle, in the center of which is an equestrian statue, emblematic of his tyranny, according to a note in the stage directions (p.192). Lodoïska is a tigress: her first words, spoken to Altamoras, are 'Quel nouveau crime médite ton maître et le détermine de nous tirer à l'horrible séjour où nous sommes confinées?' (What new crime is your master planning, that he should take us from the horrible place where we are confined?) (p.192). Dourlinski tells her that he is about to have her separated from her confidant, Lysinka, until she yields to his lust. Lodoïska then launches into the first of her two spirited arias, expressing her anxiety that Floreski is undertaking too perilous a task in trying to liberate her single-handedly (pp.193-207).

Lodoïska herself embodies a figure familiar to the French Revolution: 'Liberty' or 'Marianne,' the courageous feminine ideal who inspired men to fight for freedom. (Marianne remained a popular figure in French art and culture; we know her best in Eugène Delacroix's 1830 painting *Liberty Leading the People*.) Lodoïska also symbolizes the increasing political activism of women during the French Revolution. They attended trials, participated in demonstrations, and marched from Paris to Versailles to bring the royal family back to face the people. Somewhat less positively, she represents as well the fact that for all their heroism, revolutionary women were denied an independent role as agents of their own liberation. Like Lodoïska, they could inspire and assist men without achieving any political rights.[21]

Next, Dourlinski appears and offers Lodoïska a huge fortune, his noble lineage, and a chance to share in his power if she marries him (p. 208), all of which she declines. Then they sing a furious duet in which she terms his imprisonment of her 'une crime digne de toi' (a crime worthy of you), and he responds that neither her anger nor her beloved's efforts will free her (pp. 209-23). After a brief dialogue in which she reaffirms her 'implacable hatred' of the 'barbarian' (p.223), Dourlinski orders her locked up in the castle's deepest dungeon, to be 'forgotten forever.' An ensemble follows in which guards and female prisoners take part. Dourlinski and Lodoïska trade insults while even the count's own guards plead in vain for clemency (pp. 224-46).

After Lodoïska is led away, Floreski enters (his identity is unknown to Dourlinski) and asks that she be given to him. He is an emissary from her mother, he pretends, who seeks her company ostensibly because Lodoïska's father has died. Dourlinski's boorish reception of him further enhances the count's villainy (p.247):

Dourlinski: Faites-trêve a ces révérences. Que demandez-vous?

Floreski: Quel homme!

Varbel: Il est pressant.

Dourlinski: Vous auriez de prendre hors de chez moi le temps de vous concilier.

Floreski (*d'un ton déconcerté*): Seigneur, je ne prenais conseil de personne, mais j'observais à mon frère qu'avec moins de confiance, on pourrait être intimidé de votre ton.

Dourlinski (*avec humeur*): Épargnez-moi l'ennui de vous y faire et répondez.

Varbel (*a part*): Voici un aimable seigneur qui nous donnera, je crois, de la besogne.

Dourlinski: Stop these pleasantries. What do you want?

Floreski: The brute!

Varbel: He's in a hurry.

Dourlinski: You should have taken the time to confer before coming here.

Floreski (*in an injured tone*): Sir, I was not conferring: I was observing to my brother [Floreski now believes in equality and fraternity] that someone with less confidence would be intimidated by your tone.

Dourlinski (*angrily*): Spare me this tedium, and answer me.

Varbel (*aside*): An agreeable lord. He's sure to give us some trouble.

The dialogue concludes with Dourlinski telling them that Lodoïska is no longer in the castle and refusing to explain why, or where she is. A trio follows in which Floreski, Varbel, and Dourlinski all speculate *sotto voce* (pp. 249-60) as to what will happen next. Dourlinski permits the two men to remain one night at the castle but orders guards to be placed around them. Now it is Floreski's turn to denounce the tyrant the moment Dourlinski exits. The title of his aria, 'Rien n'égale sa barbarie' (Nothing equals his barbarity), summarizes its message. He swears, 'Dans mon courroux trop légitime, je punirai tes attentats' (In my *too* legitimate fury I will punish your offenses) (pp. 261-73). (If anything, death to tyrants is letting them off easy!)

At this point, the opera's longest set piece, the act 2 finale (pp. 275-338), begins. Observing that three of Dourlinski's men are planning to drug Floreski's and Varbel's wine with a sleeping potion, the pair put on a comic act, asking for pen and paper to write a letter, then confusing everything and managing to mix up the wine so that it is the guards who fall asleep. Floreski (p.313ff.) then urges a very reluctant Varbel to follow him in the search for Lodoïska. But Dourlinski appears with his soldiers and orders the two seized, and the act ends with an ensemble in which Dourlinski threatens frightful torments and Floreski voices his terrible anger.

Symbolically, act 2 of *Lodoïska* demonstrates the failure of aristocratic reform unsupported by the people. Floreski is repeatedly called imprudent by the other characters, even by Lodoïska herself. Good aristocrats playing within the system will have to descend to the lies and trickery of their enemies, and of course they are no match for the Dourlinskis of the world. In historical terms, this act represents the limits of the nobility's efforts to achieve liberty in 1788 and 1789 by transferring power from the monarch to themselves -- forgetting, in the meantime, the vast majority of the population.

The third act opens with the counterrevolution in triumph. Dourlinski gloats over his success in a second Pizarro-like aria (pp.339-48), to be answered by a defiant Lodoïska. She practically spits at him the words 'Tournez sur moi votre colère' (Turn your anger against me) (pp. 350-60) in a bravura number worthy or Verdi's Odabella or Abigaille, which has four high C's in the concluding measures (see ex. 1). Then Floreski is brought in. He and Lodoïska have a final shouting match with Dourlinski (pp. 361-81) and then resolve to die together.

But they are saved by the Tartars, which is to say, by the people. Poles and Tartars fight while a long, powerful orchestral passage is played. Cherubini's battle takes place onstage. He wants the revolution enacted before our eyes, whereas most operatic battles (such as Verdi's much later in *Macbeth* and *Forza del destino*) are relegated to the backstage area and end up consisting of feeble sound effects. Cherubini regards the popular struggle as the culmination of the action rather that an event to be perceived indirectly through the fates of the principal characters.

The light shines for the first time since act 1. The light is not the sun but rather the flames from the destruction of the tyrant's castle. Dourlinski is defeated; he insolently asks Titzikan what ransom is required for his freedom. The Tartar answers (pp. 408-9):

> Tu voudrais donc souiller ma gloire,
>
> Aux méchants va sers de leçon;
>
> Quand on étouffe dans son ame
>
> Tout sentiment d'humanité,
>
> Le prix d'une odieuse trame
>
> C'est l'affreuse captivité.

> You would sully my glory,
>
> So you will be an example for the wicked.
>
> When all traces of humanity
>
> Are stifled in the soul,
>
> The reward for such an odious plot
>
> Is frightful captivity.

The opera concludes with the characters, in effect, addressing the audience, justifying the action of the spectacle and, by extension, the Revolution itself (p. 416ff.):

Tartars:

> Notre fureur est légitime,
>
> Engloutissons ces lieux affreux.
>
> Ce spectacle sied à son crime;
>
> Nous pouvons l'offrir à ses yeux.

Poles:

> Dans la fureur qui les anime,

> Quel spectacle on offre à nos yeux.
>
> Ciel, faillait-il servir son crime
>
> Pour partager ce sort affreux?

Tartars:

> Our fury is legitimate;
>
> Let us destroy this hideous place.
>
> This spectacle came from his crime;
>
> We can offer it to his sight.

Poles:

> Through the fury inspiring them,
>
> What a spectacle we behold.
>
> Heavens, did we have to aid his crime
>
> To share his terrible fate?

The word *spectacle* as used here refers not only to the action of *Lodoïska* but to the fact that the entire opera fits the genre 'spectacle,' which we have seen is the term for pageants put on during the Revolution, especially those illustrating the Bastille's destruction. The opera ends with the triumph of the people, the destruction of their enemies, and a warning to counterrevolutionaries of the fate that awaits them.[22]

* * * * * * * *

Ludwig van Beethoven treated both Cherubini and *Lodoïska* with considerable respect. On different occasions he remarked that he considered Cherubini the finest living opera composer -- indeed, the finest living composer, period.[23] Until he encountered Cherubini's operas -- first in performances staged by Emmanuel Schikaneder, the librettist of *Die Zauberflöte*, in 1802, and then in 1805, when the older composer himself came to Vienna -- Beethoven had little interest in writing an opera. He even considered Mozart's masterpieces *Le nozze di Figaro* and *Don*

Giovanni 'frivolous and indeed repugnant,' according to Winton Dean.[24] But following Cherubini's visit, Beethoven began *Leonore*, whose plot and music were both influenced by *Lodoïska*. *Fidelio*, the form in which *Leonore* finally emerged after much revision, was based on a true incident written up in 1798 by J. N. Bouilly, a French revolutionary official-turned-playwright who had witnessed the dramatic rescue of a husband by his wife, with the dungeons in question being those of the Revolution.   (Dean even speculates that the real-life models for Florestan and Leonore may actually have witnessed one or more of their theatrical or operatic incarnations.)   Moreover, the most plausible explanation for the derivation of the name Florestan is that it was taken from that of the hero of Cherubini's oft-performed work. Dean has found musical connections as well:

[Beethoven] imitated Cherubini's practice with remarkable assiduity. The powerful overture presenting the kernel of the drama in symphonic form, the use of *Melodram* (spoken dialogue over music) and recitative as well as spoken dialogue, the very wide range of musical design -- simple quasi-strophic airs and duets alongside others of concentrated symphonic development, trios and quartets that look now backward to Italian tradition, now forward to romantic opera, enormous finales involving a succession of large-scale movements for chorus and principals -- are the regular ingredients of Cherubini's . . . style, [which] with its pounding rhythms, constant sforzandos, cross-accents and dynamic treatment of the orchestra, and still perceptible though partly transformed influence of the Neapolitan *opera buffa* left a palpable mark on *Fidelio*. . . . [Pizarro] was modelled on Dourlinski. . . . Their vengeful outbursts are expressed in strikingly similar terms. The rhetorical vocal line and the whole orchestral layout -- busy first violin figuration, tremolando second violins and violas, heavy wind chords and contrasted dynamics -- are common to several passages in both operas.[25]

There is at least one other striking example in *Fidelio* of Beethoven's having borrowed from *Lodoïska*. It is the famous trumpet call that announces the arrival of Don Fernando and that also introduces the final sections of the great *Leonore* overtures (see ex. 2), clearly a close relative of the trumpet call that greets Floreski and Varbel when they appear at Dourlinski's castle (see ex. 3). Such usage, by the way, was not considered plagarism: it was common for early nineteenth-century composers to honor admired colleagues by incorporating brief passages into their own works from those of others. Perhaps the most moving example of the practice is Haydn's quotation from Mozart's G minor Symphony in the final bass aria of *Die Jahreszeiten*, at the moment the soloist sings the words mourning the quick passing of youth. Basil Deane has pointed out that two of Beethoven's most famous themes -- that which introduces the 'Marcia Funèbre' of the Third Symphony and the famous four-note figure that opens the Fifth -- were respectively adapted from Cherubini's 'Hymne funèbre sur la mort du Général Hoche' and his 'Hymne du Panthéon.'[26] (Writing in counterrevolutionary Austria, Beethoven could have intended that his subtle use of Cherubini's revolutionary music serve as a secret code for his sympathies.) He also admired Cherubini's Requiem in C minor tremendously and once stated that 'if I should ever come to write one of my own, I shall borrow several passages *ad notam.*'[27] Cherubini, it should be noted, did not reciprocally admire Beethoven's only opera, although he liked the German's orchestral works. He believed that *Fidelio* showed little knowledge of the art of singing and found some of the modulations in the overture he heard (the *Leonore* No. 2) so confusing that he could not locate the main key.[28]

* * * * * * * *

The way *Lodoïska* 'became' *Fidelio* tells us a great deal about the interaction of political and operatic history.   Historians sometimes engage in counterfactual or what-if thinking to better understand what actually did happen.   Let us imagine a French Revolution whose principles took root in much of Europe, establishing popular governments.   Would we have had so many operas in which wealthy, royal, or noble ladies and gentlemen fall in love and plot against each other, with the people reduced to the role of confidants such as nurses and old retainers, or, as the chorus, merely passive commentators and observers of the dramatic situation?   Some of Verdi's operas are notable exceptions, of course, combining, as they do, elements of passion *and* politics, reflecting the fact that Verdi was passionately involved in the Italian struggle for independence.   But such is the conservative tone of the nineteenth century that even when ordinary people reappear in the *verismo* operas of Puccini, Mascagni, and Leoncavallo, the subject is rarely political.   They engage, rather, in the same love triangles and amorous deeds and misdeeds as their upper-class operatic predecessors had.

News of Cherubini's success reached London.   However, the *Lodoïska* prepared by Stephen Storace and J.P. Kemble, with Cherubini's music and that of other composers set to an English text, not only added some sentimental love songs but made of Dourlinski (whom they rechristened Lovinski) a somewhat sympathetic figure; he regrets his cruelty but excuses it as the only way he can realize his love for Lodoïska.[29]   He also becomes a 'humble baron' whom the heroine, who has been prompted to princess in this version, would never consider: the villain is now the lower ranked person (pp.30-31).   The Tartars take on a more negative cast: they lock up the Poles in their castle (p.21) and are out for plunder rather than justice, as one of the new choruses (in which one of Gilbert and Sullivan's jolly pirate songs can almost be heard) explains (p.50):

Tartars:

> When the darkened midnight sky,
>
> Howls with wild tempestuous cry,
>
> Then we quit the Tartar plain,
>
> Death and terror in our train.
>
> Where the sweeping vengeance drives,
>
> Hopeless man in horror flies;
>
> Worlds of wealth, and worlds of wives,
>
> Are the hardy Tartar's prize.

(The last two lines are an oft-repeated refrain.)

Dourlinski/Lovinski is killed in the final battle and the Tartars' revenge is legitimated not because they have stamped out his cruelty but because his death is sanctioned by Lodoïska's father, the prince. In this antirevolutionary *Lodoïska*, the masses are plunderers, and all the upper-class figures attract some sympathy.

Beethoven's *Leonore* and *Fidelio* represent a middle ground between Cherubini's and Storace/Kemble's operas. Since Florestan and Leonore are victims of revolutionary tyranny, Beethoven had no trouble with censors in depicting them as heroic and Pizarro as villainous. Here, liberation comes not from the people and revolution but from Leonore herself, seconded by Don Fernando, whose small part is but a shadow of Titzikan's. That people are essentially sympathetic and good hearted is demonstrated in the character of Rocco and in the jubilation of the final chorus, but their proper role is to applaud and support the action of magnanimous aristocrats.

Leonore is more populist in tone than *Fidelio* in two ways, however. First, the earlier Rocco sings a second strophe to the aria 'Hat man nicht auch Gold beineben,' one that reveals considerable resentment against those who are wealthy,

in addition to expressing (as the first strophe, retained in *Fidelio*, stresses) a desire
to be wealthy himself (p.21):[30]

Rocco:

> Das nur Gold in Beutel lache,
>
> jedes Erdenglück ist dein.
>
> Stolz und Übermut und Rache
>
> werden schnell befriedigt sein.
>
> Drum ist auch Fortuna den Reichen so hold,
>
> sie tuen ja nur, was sie wollen,
>
> verhüllen die Handlungen künstlich mit Gold,
>
> worüber sie schämen sich sollen.
>
> Das Gluck dient wie ein Knecht um Sold,
>
> es ist ein machtig, machtig Ding,
>
> das Gold, das Gold.

Rocco:

> If there's gold jingling in your purse,
>
> every earthly joy is yours.
>
> Pride, arrogance, and revenge
>
> are quickly gratified.
>
> Fortune, too, adores the rich;
>
> they do as they please,
>
> cleverly disguising in gold
>
> deeds they should be ashamed of.
>
> Luck serves at a price, like a servant.
>
> Gold is a powerful thing.

In the finale, Rocco tosses at Pizarro the purse with which the latter hoped
to buy the jailer's complicity in Florestan's murder, putting 'the curse of heaven'

upon it. He also explains, perhaps not truthfully (the libretto leaves it open to interpretation), that he himself would have saved Florestan had Don Fernando not arrived (p.91). In *Leonore* also, the crowd rushes into the prison along with Don Fernando, actively assisting in the liberation of the captives instead of just expressing their appreciation for the outcome after the fact.

Lodoïska represents a new departure in opera. Unlike the choruses in Gluck or Mozart operas, Cherubini's chorus is a major histrionic participant in the drama rather than a more or less static commentator (however emotional the commentary may be) in the manner of a Greek chorus. Even though certain later operas (*Guillaume Tell, Rienzi, Boris Godunov, Peter Grimes*) offer magnificent exceptions, the people or chorus as actor rather than spectator has not been a frequent operatic conceit. But the tremendous success and unprecedented first run of *Lodoïska* suggest that in a different political world, operatic history might have taken another turn. The titles of totally forgotten operas of the French Revolution -- *Sacrifice on the Altar of Liberty*; *The Siege of Lille; Republican Discipline: A Historical Picture in One Act; The Real Sansculotte or the Boatman; The Crimes of the Ancien Regime*; and *Hymn to the Supreme Being*[31] -- provide an idea of the direction of that turn. Given the glories of nineteenth century opera, we probably came out ahead, for nowhere does the law of diminishing returns set in faster than with art made to serve the political purpose of the moment. But as a unique, beautiful work and a significant document of both the French Revolution and operatic history, *Lodoïska* is more than worthy of its brief reemergence at La Scala.

The author wishes to thank his colleague, Professor Natalie Isser, for the references on the history of the French Revolution and for much useful advice, and Professor Pierre Cintas for his assistance with translations. An earlier version of this article was delivered at the 1990 meeting of the Western Society for French History, Santa Barbara, California.

Example 1. Lodoïska's act 3 aria "Tournez sur moi votre colère" (conclusion)

Example 2. Fidelio *trumpet call*

Example 3. Lodoïska *trumpet call*

ENDNOTES

1. Fillette-Loraux based his libretto on *La vie et les amours du Chevalier de Faublas* by Jean-Baptiste Louvet de Couvrai (1760-97), another active French revolutionary. Louvet's wife was the original Lodoïska. The several Chevalier de Faublas novels, published beginning in 1787, were enormously popular and appeared in translation in Germany, England, and the United States. The Lodoïska episode forms but a small part, the most overtly political, inserted into a series of romantic escapades. Louvet's Floreski is called 'Pulaski' and is a fictionalized representation of Count Casimir Pulaski, who went to the United States and died during the American Revolution. For a discussion of Louvet's life and work, see Kathryn Norberg, 'The Hero as Heroine: The Politics of Gender in the Novels of Louvet de Couvrai,' in Sara Maza and Leslie Rabine, eds., *Women and the French Revolution*, New York: Oxford University Press, 1991. It is also to be noted that Lodoïska is a much more passive, self-sacrificing character in Louvet than in the Cherubini/Fillette-Loraux opera.

2. Edward Bellasis, *Cherubini: Memorials Illustrative of His Life*, London: Burns and Oats, 1874, p. 58.

3. Reviews quoted in the original French in Vittorio Della Croce, *Cherubini: E i musicisti italiani del suo tempo*, Turin: Eda, 1983, pp. 233-34. The translations are mine, as are all those that appear in the article unless otherwise credited.

4. Frederick J. Crowest, *Cherubini*, New York: Scribner and Welford, 1890, p. 10.

5. Basil Deane, *Cherubini*, London: Oxford University Press, 1965, p. 5.

6. *Ibid.*

7. Della Croce, *Cherubini*, p. 232.

8. Bellasis, *Cherubini*, pp. 39-43.

9. Paul Henry Lang, 'French Opera and the Spirit of the Revolution,' in Harold E. Paligaro, ed., *Irrationalism in the Eighteenth Century*, Cleveland: Case Western Reserve University Press, 1972, 106.

10. Alexander L. Ringer, 'The Political Uses of Opera in Revolutionary France,' in Carl Dahlhaus et al., eds., *Bericht über den Internationalen Musikwissenschaftlichen Kongress Bonn, 1970*, Kassel: Bärenreiter, 1971, pp. 238-39.

11. There is a beautiful recording of this piece by Riccardo Muti with the New Philharmonia Orchestra on EMI (EL2702834).

12. Mona Ozouf, *Festivals and the French Revolution*, trans. Alan Sheridan, Cambridge, Mass.: Harvard University Press, 1988, pp. 277 and 346. For Mozart and Masonic symbols see Jacques Chailly, *'The Magic Flute,' Masonic Opera: An Interpretation of the Libretto and Music*, trans. Herbert Weinstock, New York: Alfred A. Knopf, 1971.

13. Quoted in Basil Deane, 'Cherubini and the Opéra-Comique,' *Opera*, vol. 40, November 1989, p. 1308.

14. References to pages in *Lodoïska* throughout the article are to the published facsimile score, New York and London: Garland, 1978, with an introduction by Charles Rosen. I have silently corrected a few minor typographical errors and added punctuation to clarify the verse, which is unpunctuated in the score.

15. Ozouf, *Festivals*, p. 346.

16. See especially the chapter entitled 'The Corruption of Poland' in Gordon S. Wood, *The Creation of the American Republic, 1776-1789*, New York: W. W. Norton, 1969.

17. Jean-Jacques Rousseau, *The Government of Poland,* trans. Willmoore Kendall, Indianapolis: Bobbs-Merrill, 1972.

18. Jean-Jacques Rousseau, *The Social Contract,* trans. G. D. H. Cole, Everyman's Library, London, J. M. Dent, 1913, p. 5.

19. Mona Ozouf, 'Space and Time in the Festivals of the French Revolution,' *Comparative Studies in Society and History*, no. 17, 1975, pp. 372-84; David Geggus, 'Racial

Equality, Slavery, and Colonial Secession during the Constituent Assembly,' *American Historical Review,* no. 94, 1989, pp. 1290-1304.

20. Timothy Tackett, 'The Meaning of the Oath,' chap. 12 of *Religion, Revolution, and Regional Culture in Eighteenth-Century France: The Ecclesiastical Oath of 1791,* Princeton, N.J.: Princeton University Press, 1986.

21. Maurice Agulhon, *Marianne into Battle: Republican Imagery and Symbolism in France,* trans. Janet Lloyd, Cambridge: Cambridge University Press, 1981, pp. 11-37; Lynn Hunt, *Politics, Culture, and Class in the French Revolution,* Ithaca, N.Y.: Cornell University Press, 1988.

22. For a long time, the only available recording that purported to be *Lodoïska* omitted many numbers, employed lengthy recitatives not written by Cherubini, inserted other music *not* in the score, and suffered from a good deal of miscasting in the leading roles. An RAI Rome 1967 performance, this hodgepodge is available on MRF Records C-02, 3 LPs. This company has enabled us to hear several of Cherubini's operas and choral works. As recordings of live performances, the discs simply document whatever version was put on stage. Fortunately, Muti recorded a powerful, accurate performance with La Scala (Ricoldi/SONY RSCD 2450) which appeared in 1991. Unfortunately, most of the singing is mediocre.

23. Michael Hamburger, ed., *Beethoven: Letters, Journals, and Conversations,* Garden City, N.Y.: Doubleday, Anchor Books, 1960, pp. 155 and 194.

24. Winton Dean, 'Beethoven and Opera.' in Dennis Arnold and Nigel Fortune, eds., *The Beethoven Reader,* New York: W. W. Norton, 1971, p. 335.

25. *Ibid.,* p. 374.

26. Basil Deane, 'The Symphonies and Overtures,' in Arnold and Fortune, *The Beethoven Reader,* pp. 291-92 and 297.

27. Hamburger, *Beethoven,* p. 98.

28. Dean, 'Beethoven and Opera,' p. 335.

29. The English libretto for Storace and Kemble's *Lodoïska* was published in London by G. G. and J. Robinson in 1794. Page numbers are references to this edition.

30. The libretto to Beethoven's *Leonore,* 1805, may be found in the Arabesque reissue of a 1977 EMI recording with Herbert Blomstedt conducting the Staatskapelle Dresden. Page references are to the booklet included in the cassette format, SBC9043 3 L.

31. Lang, 'French Opera,' p. 108.

Chapter 19

The Dead and John McCormack:
The Irish Tenor and the Irish Renaissance

In *The Dead*, the final story of James Joyce's *Dubliners*, Irish tenor Bartell D'Arcy gives just about the worst rendition possible of an Irish ballad, 'The Lass of Aughrim,' under the most unfavorable of circumstances. He is finally attempting a few lines after being importuned all night at a party; he is hoarse and unwilling. There is noise as the guests are leaving. He interrupts the song in the middle (pp. 210-211).[1] Nevertheless, of the three musical interludes at the Misses Morkan's soiree, this is the only one which touches the heart of Gabriel Conroy.

Now this should not be the case, for throughout the evening Gabriel is presented as the cosmopolitan. He summers on the continent, because he is sick of his country, earning the epithet 'West Briton' from the nationalistic Miss Ivors (p. 188). He makes his wife Gretta wear 'goloshes,' as they do on the continent, to protect herself from the elements. She would instead 'walk home in the snow if she were let,' he remarks, a nice symbolic hint of *The Dead's* conclusion: that is, its plunge into the depths of memory and emotion absent from the superficial festivities (pp. 180-181).

But just as the party, a friendly and pleasant affair as gatherings go, is only a prelude to Gretta's confession that she never loved her husband as she did Michael Furey, the classical music performed and discussed by the assembled revelers is set up by Joyce to demonstrate the emotional inferiority of classical music to the simple ballad, of the cosmopolitan to the Irish. The fancy show-piece performed by Mary Jane as the party begins 'had no melody for him [Gabriel] and he doubted whether it had any melody for the other listeners (p. 186).   Aunt Julia's 'old song' -- 'Arrayed for the Bridal' -- fares better.   It, too, is mostly filigree, being an English version of 'Son vergin vezzosa' from Vincenzo Bellini's opera *I Puritani*.   Gabriel is pleased at how 'her voice, strong and clear in tone, attacked with great spirit the runs which embellish the air and though she sang very rapidly she did not miss even the smallest of the grace notes.   To follow the voice, without looking at the singer's face, was to feel and share the excitement of swift and secure flight.' (p. 193).   But Aunt Julia is old, and only at the story's end do we learn that 'he had caught that haggard look upon her face' which suggested her forthcoming death (p.222).   That she is singing a young girl's bridal song turns a lively tune into a meditation on mortality, a very different emotion than the music conveys.

Between Julia's and D'Arcy's songs, around the dinner table the guests discuss great singers they have known.   Although D'Arcy puts in a brief for Caruso as the equal, at least, of past immortals, the honors go to a Negro chieftain currently performing at the local cabaret and to an English tenor named Parkinson whom only Aunt Kate remembers (pp. 198-200).   As music moves from classical to popular, from the continent closer to home, more genuine emotions, foreclosed by the need to maintain one's decorum for the party, seem to be touched although not yet expressed.

However, it is the Irish ballad which moves Gretta, and through his observation of her, Gabriel. He 'asked himself what is a woman standing on the stairs in the shadows, listening to distant music, a symbol of' (p.210).   The rest of *The Dead* provides the answer: that within us all are the 'might-have-beens,' the lost loves and hopes suppressed so that we can continue functioning in the everyday world without driving ourselves and others mad.   The subtext: a simple song such as an Irish ballad expresses these hopes and loves in a way that most classical music does not. A second subtext: as the world's oldest colony when Joyce published *Dubliners* in 1914, Ireland faced the dilemma whether to extol its autonomous tradition as morally and aesthetically superior, or to assimilate to the technically proficient world of the conqueror which subordinates national differences to a cosmopolitan high culture. Joyce had his problems with this: his later celebrations of ordinary Irish folk in *Ulysses* and *Finnegan's Wake* are perhaps the most virtuosic tour-de-forces in the English language. If their final message may be the inadequacy of hyperintellectualism when contrasted with the good-hearted Molly Bloom, Joyce is clearly relishing the shameless display of his knowledge and craft even as he is mocking it. Let us not forget that personally he preferred Paris to Dublin.

In 1913, the year before *Dubliners* appeared, John McCormack, already at twenty-nine the world's most famous Irish tenor, decided to stop singing opera and devote himself exclusively to concert tours. His reasons were mixed. He was no great actor; his voice was extraordinarily pure and beautiful but on the small side and lacking the raw force required by the standard repertory of the time; and his one-man concerts and the recording contracts they generated were already well on their way to making him the wealthiest 'serious' singer on the planet. In the course of a life of extravagance and indulgence, McCormack would eventually own homes on New York's Park Avenue, on Long Island Sound in Connecticut, in Hollywood, and the spacious Moore Abbey in Ireland, simultaneously. To the four homes may be added Old Masters by Hals, Rubens, Corot, etc., twelve Rolls Royces, and the string of race horses he bought in a futile effort to win the Ascot Derby.

Of course, McCormack had a more reasonable explanation for abandoning the opera house:

The minstrel sang to the people, and it is a certain thing that music is
not for the highbrow. It is for the simple people -- that is, sensitive
and not sophisticated ones. The best songs are simple. The right
simplicity is that of the traditional air, whose pure melody tugs at the
heart. . . . When I began I was frightened to the teeth by the name
of Brahms, and when I got to know him I found he was a charming,
simple fellow.[2]

In other words, classical music at its best approached the simplicity and sincerity
of the ballad. This was how he answered the highbrow music critics, who
bemoaned 'a man of genius wasting the sweetness of his art on the desert air of
inferior ballads. But why on earth should a man sacrifice the fortune he can make
by gratifying the public taste at the altar of an ideal that will bring him only the
gratitude of a few?'[3]

But McCormack sometimes took another tack. His concerts almost always
mixed four types of music: some Handel, Mozart, and Bach; some lieder by
Schubert, Brahms or more modern composers; some contemporary ballads; and
some traditional Irish songs. He therefore alternatively presented himself as the
educator of the masses who sugar-coated the 'higher things' of music by including
a healthy dose of the songs they loved:

I sing music, which for real artistic value, goes from one extreme to
another -- from the glories of Bach, Mozart, and Schubert and Hugo
Wolf to the most simple ballad. The popular ballad is as vital today
as it ever was, for the hearts of men and women do not change.
Little by little the masses who came to hear them learned to love the
higher things of music; and I have been able gradually to increase the
number of these at my concerts. I have realized with genuine
emotion the ever-increasing response Mozart, Schubert, Hugo Wolf,

and Rachmaninov have aroused among my hearers, hearers who would never have accepted them if their ears had not grown accustomed to them by my offering them only sparingly at first. I for one, however much I love and however well I may sing the songs of the classic repertory, will never be ashamed of the fact that I made my first success as a ballad singer.[4] (My emphasis.)

Who was the real John McCormack? It would be easy to say simply that he was the mediator between two worlds, an ambassador of Irish song to the world of classical music, on the one hand, an educator of popular taste on the other, and let it go at that. But in McCormack's own life, as in Joyce's and his writings, the dilemma was not easily solved.

The world's most famous Irishman made his name abroad. He studied in Italy (the unusual yet beautiful elongated vowels in his singing of Irish songs are Italianate, not Gaelic), made his first big success in England, and lived most of his life in England and America. He applied to become an American citizen in 1914 (to stay out of the war, critics charged), and only retired permanently to Ireland in 1942, four years before his death. He performed so many charity concerts for the Catholic Church that the Pope made him a Count: for two weeks every year for a decade from 1928 he served as the Papal Chamberlain in Rome, and it was in his papal uniform that he was buried.

Yet Ireland's ambassador of song to the world was not very charitable when it came to his homeland: after concerts, he refused to see boyhood acquaintances and refused ungraciously to sing upon revisiting his old school. Although he won first prize for tenors in the 1904 *Feis Ceoil*, Ireland's annual music competition, he did not receive the rave reviews in his early Irish appearances which later followed, probably because he had not yet acquired the Italian training which made a promising voice into a great one. And Irish nationalists objected to his refusal to sing songs critical of England, the land which first offered his art uncritical adulation and financial reward.

What mattered to McCormack and his wife, Lily Foley, herself a promising singer who gave up her career to shepherd her husband and children, can be learned from her memoir *I Hear You Calling Me*. Once the McCormacks were established, life became a world-wide parade among the rich and famous of the political, social, and artistic worlds, tales of how Popes and Presidents, Kings and movie stars, and the world's greatest musicians partied with and paid homage to the great McCormack. Also recounted with obvious glee are tales of McCormack's extravagant purchases and lifestyle, although Mrs. McCormack downplays the champagne parties until dawn which frequently followed his concerts. This self-indulgence undoubtedly shortened his career (his recordings began to decline precipitously in quality about 1932, when he was forty-six, an age when most singers are in their prime) and life (he weighed over 350 pounds when he died at sixty-one and could not even rise to greet visitors). Of McCormack the legendary conversationalist who read and talked widely about everything under the sun, or McCormack the fun-loving and doting parent who was like a child himself, there is almost nothing. How much more interesting an account of that would have been, or some explicit examples of McCormack's famous temper and occasionally violent tongue, instead of another account of a trip to such and such where we met so and so and they loved us.

The paradox of McCormack's career appears in the one feature film in which he was starred, the 1930 vehicle '*Song 'O My Heart*.' Like most films which portray opera singers as just folks like you and me -- one thinks of Robert Merrill's *Aaron Slick From Pumpkin Crick* and Pavarotti's *Yes! Giorgio* -- it is frequently unintentionally hilarious. In '*Song 'O My Heart's*' case the lunacy is compounded by the fact that McCormack sings a great deal, but except for half-a-dozen phrases of dialogue the rest of the film is silent. The story -- an Irish singing teacher reluctantly leaves home to make a fortune in America to support the children of his dead beloved -- is in fact a variation of McCormack's own. It might even serve as an idealization, or sentimentalization, of what McCormack wished for: that his leaving Ireland was in fact reluctant, and that he longed for the dear old homeland rather than the glitzy world of high society.

Another way to understand McCormack as a man torn between two worlds is to look at his two favorite operatic roles: Don Ottavio in Mozart's *Don Giovanni* and Rodolfo in Puccini's *La Bohème*. Ottavio appealed to him because he could sing the difficult, long-phrased arias with beauty and precision which has probably not been heard before or since. The elaborate scales between the aria 'Il Mio Tesoro's' first and second sections will be forever known as the 'McCormack phrase' because he unbelievably sings them on one breath, a feat only occasionally matched: 'If my reputation as a singer is to be judged in the future by any particular record of mine, I am willing to stand or fall by 'Il Mio Tesoro'.'[5] In Mozart, McCormack could demonstrate the hard work and technique he learned in Italy. Rodolfo, however, appealed to McCormack's common touch: 'He's a real fellow. I can sing him and still feel like a human being. I can pace up and down the stage, with my hands in my trouser pockets, and seem true to character.'[6]

McCormack never solved the contradiction of whether he was 'a real fellow,' touching the hearts of ordinary people with Irish ballads and classical melodies which served the same purpose, or one of the most perfect singers who ever lived who made his country's music known the world over. Strange that people cannot enjoy music because certain genres are considered appropriate for high or low culture! Today, 'Irish' tenor Frank Patterson can move easily from folksong to opera without having to apologize for one or the other.

But let us conclude with *Dubliners*, and its parable of the dilemmas of the Irish artist. When D'Arcy sings 'The Lass of Aughrim,' he omits the final line and a half of the stanza he delivers (p. 210):

O, the rain falls on my heavy locks

And the dew wets my skin,

My babe lies cold *within my arms*

And none will let me in. [italicized works omitted]

Michael Furey, like the babe in the song, dies in the rain because he cannot be admitted inside to see Gretta. He too is a singer. For all the adulation showered upon him, John McCormack was destined to remain outside, a visitor to two worlds, never wholly comfortable in either. But as with Joyce, it was precisely his embodiment of the paradoxes of high vs. popular culture, cosmopolitan vs. Irish art, which constituted the essence of his achievement. They needed both worlds, even as we need the party to appreciate Michael Furey. McCormack and Joyce thus help us understand the cultural and political dilemmas of early twentieth century Ireland, and join Yeats, Shaw, Synge, and O'Casey in representing one of those rare historical moments of creative splendor at which future ages can only marvel.

ENDNOTES

1.   All references to James Joyce's *Dubliners* in parenthesis, New York: The Viking Press, corrected edition of 1968; first published 1914.

2.   Raymond Foxall, *John McCormack*, Worcester and London, UK: Trinity Press, 1963, 59.

3.   *Ibid.*, 17.

4.   Lily McCormack, *I Hear You Calling Me*, Milwaukee: Bruce Publishing Co., 1949, 168.

5.   *Ibid.*, 60.

6.   Gordon T. Ledbetter, *The Great Irish Tenor*, New York: Scribners', 1977. The three biographies used contain much overlapping information and are in basic agreement on the tenor's musical attitudes and lifestyle; Foxall's is the most critical, Countess McCormack's the most appreciative and rich in detail, Ledbetter's best at placing him in his historical context.

Chapter 20

Napoleonic Semiosis:
'*Napoleon Vu Par Abel Gance*'

In an unpublished essay criticizing virtually the entire nineteenth century historical literature on Napoleon, the philosopher Charles S. Peirce concluded that 'Napoleon was veritably an epic hero, heroic in his greatness of heart and head, heroic in his brutality, heroic in his worship of his people, heroic in his subjective merging of destiny, of France, and of self' (Peirce c.1893). Napoleon, transcending the limits of historical analysis, was a 'theme for the lyre of an epic poet.' A decade after Peirce's death in 1914, the visionary French film director Abel Gance (1889-1981) began work on just such a scale, to render Napoleon 'as large as the imagination of the crowds that understand the *Chanson de Roland*' (Arroy 1927: 34). Upon his masterpiece's restoration in the 1970's, *The Washington Post* (April 10, 1973) ranked it with Tolstoy's *War and Peace* and Beethoven's 'Eroica' Symphony as works of genius inspired by the French general. *Time* (February 2, 1981: 84) compared it to Michelangelo's 'Last Judgment' come to life. The *Los Angeles Times* dubbed it 'the measure of all other films, forever' (Brownlow 1983: 250).

Napoleon demands semiotic analysis of a different sort than that usually applied to films. Gance's astonishing technique and idealistic conception require historical and philosophical as well as cinematic analysis. So do the film's tragic lapse into distortion and obscurity, its reconstruction and triumph after five decades, and the fierce debate over its ideological content. The truly Napoleonic

heroics associated with Gance's life and the film's history render *Napoleon* a sign
of great complexity.

To introduce my favorite film to those who have not seen it, and in the hope
of enhancing its appeal for those who have, I will look at *Napoleon* iconically (as
a film, stressing Gance's grandiose notion of cinema and the technique he
developed to realize it), indexically (as a statement about Gance's philosophy and
the cultural and political milieu in which he worked) and symbolically (as an
invitation to reflection on the role of genius in history). I also consider briefly the
history of *Napoleon's* filming and its reception over the past six decades, looking
at the entire process as an expanded test of Gance's crusade 'to make an actor of
[the spectator]. He must no longer watch, he must participate in the action and
then his critical powers will be stifled in favor of his emotions' (Gance 1927a: 35).
Napoleon -- vu par Abel Gance, to be sure, but also an act of communication
created and shaped by actors and subsequently audiences.

Gance described *Napoleon* as 'a symphony in time and a symphony in space
. . . a visual orchestra, as rich, complex, and monumental as those that play
concerts' (Gance 1929: 72). The description is apt, although *Napoleon* is also like
a grand opera in a prologue and three acts. It begins with a snowball fight where
the plebeian Napoleon, a twelve-year-old at the Brienne military academy, defeats
his aristocratic, inept schoolmates through superior strategy even though the latter
cheat by putting rocks in their missiles. The young Napoleon has only two friends
-- an eagle (symbol of France) and the genial cook (Tristan Fleuri -- symbol of the
average Frenchman) both of whom reappear throughout the film to certify
Napoleon's claim to glory. The prologue ends with the enraged boy taking on the
entire school in a pillow fight to avenge the release of his beloved eagle. The
bird, however, returns voluntarily that night.

From Brienne Gance plunges us into the center of the French Revolution. At the National Convention, the 'Marseillaise' is sung for the first time, the King is condemned to death, Antonin Artaud appears as Marat, and Gance himself takes the part of the idealistic Saint-Just. Napoleon is then chased out of Corsica by a pro-British faction. In one of the film's three sustained heroic climaxes, Napoleon's escape from the island in a skiff -- he uses a French flag for a sail -- is superimposed on the 'human waves' of the surging revolutionaries at the Convention, who seem to flow into the theater. Upon his return to France, Napoleon captures the supposedly impregnable British stronghold at Toulon through a surprise attack in a torrential, night rainfall.

The second of Gance's official three 'acts' is a lyric interlude. Napoleon courts the fickle Josephine in a Paris run mad with gaiety following the Revolution's excesses. They meet at the Bal des Victimes, where Parisians masquerade as the guillotined, symbolized by wearing ribbons around their necks. Napoleon is a fish out of water amid the frivolous and conventional -- he even forgets his own wedding as he plans the invasion of Italy.

The third part of the film is an extended sequence, employing three screens, where Napoleon reviews his army as it marches off to glory. Just before he leaves Paris, he visits the Convention, where he swears to the ghosts of the slain revolutionary leaders that he will not betray the Revolution, but rather extend it to all lands.

Even critics such as Pauline Kael (1981: 114-116) who find Gance's ideas 'schoolboy gush,' 'high-falutin', romantic, and foolish,' or even worse, his hero 'a Bonaparte for budding fascists' (Moussinac 1927: 35), still admire, in Kael's words, Gance's 'zingy virtuosity.' But for Gance and other French idealists of the cinema as the 'seventh art,' (silent) movies were to be a speechless, hence universal language to unify mankind, an artistic equivalent of the League of

Nations which also emerged in response to the horrors of the First World War. Gance hoped to 'create for the whole of humanity a unique memory, a kind of music of faith, of hope.' Not requiring language 'which has done so much to divide people,' he prayed: 'may cinema help us to realize that superior form of human civilization that is called peace. . . . May it go beyond the elitist spirit and enter into the hearts of all nations and peoples.' 'Cinema allows us to see or at least to glimpse aspects of the great and immortal enchantment that is the real life of nature.' In a properly made film, 'our sufferings, our loves, our hopes are multiplied, transposed, magnified, cast out beyond the tiny prison of our existence towards unknown worlds' (Gance 1929: 78,66). Peirceans will recognize similarities between Gance's hopes for cinema and Peirce's belief that a community of dedicated thinkers could pave the way for a triumphant 'Evolutionary Love' (1893: 6.287-317).

Gance used at least six new or freshly employed techniques to implement his grandiose visions:

1. The movable camera -- which now 'took its place in the dance.' Gance attached it to a horse's back to put the audience in the middle of the chase as Napoleon's enemies hounded him across Corsica. He had the French schoolboys throw snowballs into cameras and punch at cameras (protected with sponges) during the Brienne scene. He spun cameras from a ceiling to capture the giddy madness of the Bal des Victimes. He put a camera under water to seize the terror of a man adrift in a small boat in a storm. And a camera undulated from a giant pendulum to capture the frenzy of the Convention. 'I made it into a living person, a brain, and most of all, I tried to turn it into a heart,' Gance praised the tool of his medium. He described the snowball fight 'with its fifteen hundred juxtaposed shots' and asked his audience to 'understand that the camera was not a witness but an actor in the drama, that it took part in the battle, that it smiled, that it was

victorious alongside the young Napoleon, like an inquisitive archangel with a memory of fire' (Gance 1929: 71).

2. Superimpression -- images imposed on each other. Napoleon's heroic profile is superimposed on the Battle of Toulon, and, as a boy, on the snowball fight (King 1984: 69,70). When Napoleon confronts the ghosts of the Revolution, they are superimposed on shots of the Convention sequence which are in turn superimposed on the empty hall where Napoleon muses -- a double impression (Brownlow 1983: 149). He wrote that 'superimpression can itself evoke the secret and magical life of the immense space in which our bodies and our souls evolve and put a new face on the drama of human life' (Gance 1929: 68).

3. The triptych or Polyvision -- as the film nears its end, curtains around the single screen part to triple its width. (Gance also subdivides the screen -- into as many as 27 shots, if I counted correctly in the pillow fight -- to create an impression of frenetic activity (King 1984: 207). Richard Abel (1982: 13) also describes the triptych, though I quote here from King (1984: 147). As Napoleon

> Looks out over the mountains, the valley, three separate sequences
> erupt simultaneously onto the triple screen, images metamorphosing
> through superimpositions, dissolves, and iris masks that shift back and
> forth from panel to panel in a fugue-like movement of dizzying
> rhythms. Initially, they include a front shot of Napoleon, long shots
> of the army attacking across the plains, a long shot of his white horse,
> and a suspended close-up of Josephine. Soon, in addition, appear the
> revolving globe, long shots of the valleys and mountains, maps of
> Italy and England, insignia, cannon fire, and attacking cavalry.
> Finally, the sequences shift into rapid montage, drawing together
> closer and closer shots of the victorious marching soldiers, closeups
> of Napoleon as a boy and man, extreme close-ups of his eyes, blurred

shots of the Revolutionary leaders, a beating drum, flames, cloud drifts, streaming water, and waves exploding in sunlight.

Gance described the triptych as being less 'pictorial' than 'the creation of visual harmonies . . . the transporting of the spectator's imagination into a new and sublime world.'   For the tempest/Convention scene, he also prepared 'an apocalyptic fresco [unfortunately lost], a noble symphony in which, with eight superimpressions per frame, there were sometimes twenty-four interwined visions' (Gance 1929: 72).   Besides the underlying political and cinematic messages Gance hoped to convey through rapid juxtaposition -- there is one memorable triptych of Napoleon turning his back on Josephine as he gazes at a globe -- (King 1984: 40) it is not far-fetched to compare Gance's technique with the 'stream of consciousness' novel of Joyce and Proust. He takes us inside Napoleon's mind, revealing his unconscious and conscious thoughts as he marches off to glory.

4.   Rapid cutting -- from large crowd scenes -- the snowball fight, the Convention, the army -- to shots of individuals in them. Gance thus humanizes both the crowd and Napoleon, who is thereby presented not only through his imperturable scowl but softened through what King (1984: 194-196) terms the 'mediating vision' of the common folk.

5.   Color -- through the elaborate use of red, white, blue, brown, and green filters, Gance turns the black and white of his day into a richer canvas. The Convention ghosts emerge with an eerie greenish pallor. Blue and brown add dimension to the 'double tempest.' At the film's conclusion, the riotous orgy of images in the triptych ultimately reconcile themselves into the French tricolor, which prompted Charles de Gaulle at the Paris premiere to jump to his feet screaming 'Bravo, tremendous, magnificent' (Brownlow 1983: 153).

6. Historical and literary allusions -- Gance employs symbols of the national heritage, sometimes anachronistically, but always effectively. The assassination

of Marat is a mirror image of the David painting; the revolutionaries are the spitting images of their portraits in a well-known print by Herkomer; the female representation of 'Liberty' who appears to lead Napoleon's army into Italy is none other than Delacroix's, borrowed from the barricades of 1830 (Brownlow 1983: 105,39; Welsh and Kramer 1978: 102). Even more daring, Gance turns the female Parisian party-goers at the Bal des Victimes into twenties flappers, cavorting in semi-nude déshabillé, to call attention to the frivolity (and depravity) in both the post-Revolution and post-war eras. And Gance explicitly cites Victor Hugo's novel of the Revolution, *Ninety-Three*, as the inspiration for the double tempest: 'To be a member of the Convention was to be a wave of the ocean. . . . There was a will in the Convention which was that of all yet not that of any one person. This Will was an Idea, an idea indomitable and immeasurable, which swept from the summit of Heaven into the darkness below. We call this the Revolution' (Hugo 1874: 162).

But Gance went beyond even historical references which would resonate in the souls of French and western audiences. He predicted cinema would achieve the catharsis and unity for modern man which Greek tragedy did for the ancients: 'The 'tearing out' of our usual ways of thinking and seeing will cure the illness of our souls. I can predict for you delirious displays of enthusiasm as fantastic as those which perhaps the Greek tragedians experienced in their immense theaters in front of 20,000 breathless spectators' (Gance 1954: 80). At the age of eighty, Gance was still dreaming of an 'overwhelming Polyvision . . . virtual images without the support of screens, in stadiums of 50,000 where enraptured victims shall see the grand epics of all the continents projected in space, the ecumenism of religions which alone can lower the frontiers between peoples, with the new canons of new thaumaturgists and mythologists' (Gance 1972: 158). Ideally, cinema recapitulates the human experience, clarifies man's collective symbols (my deliberate reference to the title of Jung's book) and saves the world.

An examination of Gance's conception of cinema as the new church -- he referred to films as 'cathedrals of light' (Gance 1926: 164) -- with himself as the new savior gives the lie to those interpreters who have found *Napoleon* pro-fascist and its enthusiastic greeting by Americans from 1979 to 1981 a sign of their receptivity to Ronald Reagan's smiling neo-fascism (Grenier 1981: 65-70; Westerbeck 1981: 115-116). Such readings of *Napoleon* are untenable because they ignore the context of Gance's ideals and other works. But they even do violence to the film itself. As two critics of the American version of *Napoleon* noted, a subtitle terms Napoleon the 'tempter' and identifies him with Satan, directly after he has promised the ghosts of the Revolution that he will not betray them (*Newsweek* February 2, 1981: 78; *The Nation* February 18, 1981: 251). He then speaks to his soldiers and leads them into Italy not to create 'The Universal Republic . . . [where] anyone, wherever he travels, will always find himself in a common fatherland,' but to find 'honor, glory, and riches' (Brownlow 1983: 283-284). Gance planned no less than a six-part film series on Napoleon. The other films were to have been 'Arcole' (1792-1798); '18 Brumaire' (1798-1800); 'Austerlitz' (1804-1808); 'Retreat from Moscow' (1809-1813); and 'St. Helena' (1815-1821) (Brownlow 1983: 36-37). What remains is a torso of parts one and two, where Napoleon is taken to the point where he ceases to *be* the Revolution (as he proclaims during the film) and turns against it. Gance's Napoleon is in fact a tragic hero -- undone by his military genius, he makes conquest the end of his life rather than the means to the Universal Republic. Gance wrote:

> I conceive of a Napoleon who did not altogether detest warfare, but
> who was forced into it by an irresistible process which he was always
> trying vainly to halt. . . . He does all he can to avoid it, but he must

submit to it. That is his tragedy. Napoleon represents the perpetual conflict between the great revolutionary who wanted the Revolution and peace and a man of war, fighting in the mistaken belief that the war would bring peace forever. He was a man whose arms were not long enough to encompass something greater than himself: the Revolution.

Gance blamed Napoleon for establishing the Empire and 'turning his relatives into royalty.' He thus 'perverted his destiny partly by being the chief of his tribe, when he was born to be the great man of the Revolution.' Gance distinguished Bonaparte the general and revolutionary from Napoleon the Emperor: the former is 'lucid' and 'master of his fate'; the latter 'lies in the whirlpool and is dragged into it; he must go where fate leads him; that is his tragedy' (Gance 1927a: 35-36).

Putting Gance's image of Napoleon and his conception of cinema together, it becomes clear, as Emile Vuillermoz (1927: 44) wrote, that 'there is as much in this adventure story, and perhaps more, of Abel Gance as there is of Napoleon.' Gance hoped to create the 'Universal Republic' through cinema, to succeed through art where his predecessor had failed through war. During the course of filming 'Napoleon,' Gance began to assume with respect to his actors and crew characteristics of Napoleon leading his troops, thereby achieving the 'moral equivalent of war' of which William James found the world in dire need. Descriptions of his directorial charisma border on the unbelievable. 'You aren't film extras, you are taking part in the epic of the French Revolution,' he would tell them. He even posted a proclamation for his subordinates to read:

It is imperative that this film should allow us to enter once and for all into the temple of the arts by way of the huge portal of history. An unspeakable anguish grips me at the thought that my will and the gift of my life even are nothing if you do not give me your undivided loyalty and devotion. . . . The Revolution and its laugh of agony, the Empire and its giant shadows, the Grand Army and its suns; upon you falls the duty of recreating their immortal figures. My friends, all the screens of the world await you.

The extras responded in kind. Cheers of 'Vive Abel Gance' resounded on the sets as once had cheers of 'Vive L'Empéreur' on the battlefields (Brownlow 1983: 110-121). Although ill from the cold, the little boys at Brienne also cheered and worked additional days. Actors threw themselves into their parts with such vehemence that serious injuries occurred during the Convention and battle scenes. Most remarkable of all, though, was Albert Dieudonné, who went on a crash diet to get in shape for his great role. He managed to convince Gance's gatekeeper that he *was* Napoleon returned to life to get the part; during the filming in Corsica, the inhabitants insisted he attend their ceremonies and lead their parades. Being Napoleon spoiled every other role for Dieudonné: he retired from stage and screen to spend the rest of his life impersonating Napoleon (Brownlow 1983: 76-79, 83, 110-121, 61, 80, 158).

If Gance viewed himself as the heir of Napoleon, and film as the medium of international brotherhood, most of the other films he regarded as his masterpieces were pleas for international order and defenses of persecuted geniuses. I will only deal with two of the greatest: *J'Accuse* (1918-1919) and *Un Grand Amour de Beethoven* (1936).

J'Accuse is still one of the most powerful anti-war movies ever made. As Kael notes, it 'ends with a sequence so overpowering that it obliterates the rest of the film. In this finale, the war dead rise to confront the living; the mutilated, the crippled get up and march toward us. . . . It's a nightmare miracle, and awesome. The soldiers just keep marching toward us -- a vast army of the dead filling the screen' (Kael 1981: 119). What makes the film even more powerful is its context:

Gance's film army consisted of soldiers on leave from the Western Front who in fact came out of their graves (the trenches) to accuse the warmakers of betraying civilization (the title, of course, is adapted form Emile Zola's criticism of the 'respectable' society and military which betrayed Dreyfus). Most of the actors would, in fact, be killed in a very short time (Brownlow 1983: 26-29).

Beethoven, in which Gance pioneered stereophonic sound two decades before it was generally used, featured heart-rending sequences of sound fading in and out to enable the audience to participate in Beethoven's agony of intermittent deafness. Gance identified with Beethoven as a sign of the neglected genius:

> I share the distress and the sorrow of the great man who was unappreciated by his time. For me, it's sorrowful to think that life passed by such men as Beethoven, Dante, Michelangelo and the rest, without understanding their true value. . . . As Nietzsche [Gance's favorite philosopher] said: 'The edge of wisdom is always turned against the wise man.' Why? The great men have always . . . wanted to go too far on the road of sensibility, to explore too far, and life brings them back. The world is filled with vulgarity. And great men don't have the fate they deserve in life. Afterwards, they are given statues, concerts -- people can't speak enough of them. But they die unhappy -- the clenched fist of the dying Beethoven. That overwhelms me, and that's why I wanted to present the lives of certain great men to show that fate just wasn't with them. Columbus [about whom Gance planned an aborted film] that's the same thing; he was a great man, a veritable Don Quixote, an illuminé who transformed everything (Gance 1974: 131).

Gance's films thus resolve themselves into signs of his own neglect. He fictionalized history to get across his poetic message. Napoleon probably never had the idealism Gance attributed to him, and Beethoven for all his problems was the world's most highly regarded composer during his own lifetime. Gance was actually 'projecting,' in both senses, how his audience had betrayed him. Cinema was taken over by 'shopkeepers,' 'little insects that gnaw the hulls of ships . . . people who have no idea except making money.' They forced him to 'prostitute myself -- not to live, but in order not to die' (Welsh and Kramer 1978: 162-164). He never finished *Napoleon* or even began Christopher Columbus; his efforts to turn *Napoleon* and *J'Accuse* into sound films and shorten the former for mass appeal proved failures. His *Fin du Monde* (1929), a savage indictment of war and bourgeois materialism, was distorted by the people who owned the rights.

Ironically, Gance too, like the dead in *J'Accuse*, was able to arise, almost from the grave, and finally achieve recognition for *Napoleon*. Thanks to almost equally heroic efforts by Kevin Brownlow, who spent two decades reconstructing the film, it became an international sensation. A ninety-year-old Gance journeyed to Telluride, Colorado, where a crowd sat outdoors in below freezing weather until three o'clock in the morning to acclaim *Napoleon* and its creator. Participation in the Napoleonic enterprise continued. Gance listened to the applause over the telephone as the Francis Ford Coppola version -- for which his seventy-year-old father composed an Oscar-winning film score -- triumphed in Radio City. Through sheer longevity, Gance cheated fate and could die knowing that his great film would survive as a perpetual rebuke to an art which had failed to live up to its promise (Brownlow 1983: 229-234; 246-257).

Gance assumed two roles in his own films: in addition to Saint-Just, the purest of revolutionaries, he played Jean Novalic in *Fin du Monde*. Novalic appears as Jesus Christ in a passion 'play within a play' put on in a film where the spiritually-minded, ethical people he is leading are trying to save a corrupted world. It is safe to say Gance played these roles his entire life.

REFERENCES

Abel, Richard, 1982, 'Charge and Counter-Charge: Coherence and Incoherence in Gance's *Napoleon*,' *Film Quarterly* 35, 2-14.

Arroy, Jean, 1927, excerpt from *En tournant Napoleon avec Abel Gance,* translated in Kevin Brownlow, *Napoleon*, 34.

Brownlow, Kevin, 1983, *Napoleon: Abel Gance's Classic Film*, New York: Knopf.

Gance, Abel, 1927a, Interview with Jean Arroy, cited in Kevin Brownlow, *Napoleon*.

_____, 1927b, Letter to Marivaux spectators, cited in Kevin Brownlow, *Napoleon*.

_____, 1929, 'The Cinema of Tomorrow,' excerpted and translated in Norman King, *Abel Gance*, 62-79.

_____, 1954, 'Departure towards Polyvision,' excerpted and translated in Norman King, *Abel Gance*, 79-81.

_____, 1972, Letter of Abel Gance to Jacques Duhamel, translated in James M. Welsh and Steven P. Kramer, *Abel Gance*, 156-159.

_____, 1974, Interview with Abel Gance, translated in James M. Welsh and Steven P. Kramer, *Abel Gance*.

Grenier, Richard, 1981, '*Napoleon* Conquers America,' *Commentary*, April 1981, 65-70.

Hugo, Victor, 1874, English translation 1908: unknown edition of passage from *Ninety-Three*.

Kael, Pauline, 1981, 'Abel Gance,' *The New Yorker*, February 16, 1981, 114-123.

King, Norman, 1984, *Abel Gance: A Politics of Spectacle*, London: British Film Institute.

Moussinac, Leon, 1927, 'A French film: *Napoleon*,' translated in Norman King, *Abel Gance*, 34-41.

Peirce, Charles S., 1893, 'Evolutionary Love,' in CP 6.287-317. The abbreviation *CP* followed by volume number(s) separated from paragraph number(s) by a period, refers to the eight-volume *Collected Papers of Charles Sanders Peirce*, Vols. I-VI ed. Charles Hartshorne and Paul Weiss, Cambridge, MA: Harvard University Press, 1931-1935, Vols. VII-VIII ed. Arthur W. Burks, same publisher, 1958.

_____, c.1893, 'Materials for the Study of Napoleon,' Ms. 1319 in the microfilm edition of the Peirce Papers in the Houghton Library of Harvard University as catalogued by Richard S. Robin and described in his *Annotated Catalogue of the Papers of Charles S. Peirce*, Amherst: University of Massachusetts Press, 1967.

Vuillermoz, Emile, 1927, Writings on Gance and *Napoleon,* translated in Norman King, *Abel Gance*, 42-51.

Welsh, James M. and Kramer, Steven P., 1978, *Abel Gance*, Boston: Twayne.

Westerbeck, Colin, Jr., 1981, 'Film on Horseback: Abel Gance's Self-Made Dictator,' *Commonweal*, February 27, 1981, 115-116.

Chapter 21

Signs of William Walker:
Cinematic Views of Imperialism

Late in 1987, the film *Walker* directed by Albert Cox and purporting to tell 'The True Story of the First American Invasion of Nicaragua' opened with considerable publicity in New York and Los Angeles. Not many pictures are released in company with a 300-page paperback book. The first American feature film made in Sandinista Nicaragua, left-wing critics such as Gilbert Seldes and organs such as the *Village Voice* echoed the judgment of Nicaraguan Vice-President Sergio Ramirez that 'if this penetrates the commercial market in the United States, it is going to open some eyes and change some minds' (Wurlitzer 1987: front advertisements).

But *Walker* flopped, and did not even reach most communities. Its failure takes one back to 1970 and the almost unnoticed release of Gillo Pontecorvo's magnificent *Burn!* (*Queimada*), which depicted a British William Walker engineering a Latin American revolution and implicitly criticizing contemporary United States foreign policy. However, unlike *Walker*, *Burn!* (also a United Artists' film) received little publicity from its embarrassed company. If *Burn!* failed to make an impact because it made American audiences uncomfortable during the Vietnam War, *Walker* failed because it is a small, strange film, although an interesting one.

Comparison of the two films about different William Walkers can be a fascinating exercise in how film-makers perceive and interpret history. In both cases, presentist signs are dropped to indicate the film's relevance and to shape audience responses. *Burn!* does this more subtly. It also treats the Third World revolution and revolutionaries in question with more dignity, whereas *Walker*, by focusing exclusively on the American invasion of Nicaragua, paradoxically falls into a cinematic version of the very imperialism it sets out to condemn.

In some ways, *Walker* is the 'true story' it claims to be: 'in the big view, it's historically true' as Rudy Wurlitzer states (1987: 51). Ed Harris, dressed drably in black, in stark contrast to the dusty deserts of Mexico (which he invades first), his own motley supporters, and the colorful jungles and fires in Nicaragua, corresponds exactly with the historical Walker, the slight, quiet, puritanical man with 'grey eyes' and 'clergyman's ways' described in contemporary accounts and here in Ernesto Cardenal's poem 'With Walker in Nicaragua' (1950; excerpt quoted in Wurlitzer 1987: front pages). He is harsh with his own men, shooting plunderers and deserters and whipping other offenders, yet possessed of magnetism and courage which causes them to follow him into hopeless situations. Many of the details of Walker's career are told with reasonable accuracy, although telescoped and rearranged a bit to fit into an hour and a half. His romance with a liberal, intelligent deaf woman from New Orleans comes to life through, in part, Marlee Matlin's (*Children of a Lesser God*) fine performance, although the time between her death and Walker's deciding to become a filibuster is greatly compressed. Walker's expedition to Sonora, the Nicaraguan expedition, his troubled relation with Commodore Vanderbilt and his rivals to control the Central American route to California, the Battle of Rivas, Walker's conversion to pro-slavery to save his regime, and his capture and execution by the British are all ably depicted, although he never met Vanderbilt face to face and his two expeditions to Nicaragua are collapsed into one. Walker was shot in 1860 almost immediately on his return to Central America, three years after his short-lived republic (1855-1857) had collapsed.

Nevertheless, Cox moves so fast and oversimplifies so much that his characters emerge almost as caricatures, or as physical representations of certain political types. Walker was not hired by Vanderbilt as the film shows, although he did briefly work with him and double-crossed him. Vanderbilt is depicted as a crude, disgusting man swearing in twentieth century language, a parody of every nouveau riche who struck it big. The Central Americans are simply not there, except for Dona Yrena and the Legitimist (Conservative) Nicaraguan politician Corral, whom Walker executed after he reneged on a peace treaty. Dona Yrena is the power behind the weak Corral in the film, who goes from being his mistress to Walker's, neither of the Nicaraguans having a shred of patriotism. On the other side, Cox and Wurlitzer do not show that Walker had considerable Nicaraguan support as the outsider who could reconcile Legitimist and Democratic factions mired in bloody civil war, and that Corral's execution was prompted by his treachery. Nor do they do justice to Walker's initial, apparently sincere efforts to improve the lot of the lower classes by abolishing conscription and debt slavery. He only appears as tyrannical (we see Central Americans buried up to their necks with discarded Coca-Cola bottles nearby) and the reintroducer of slavery. Curiously, one can find the complexity of Walker in the fine biography by A. Z. Carr which comprises roughly three-quarters of the book accompanying the film's release!

By viewing Walker as a 'sign' of Ollie North and other 'white guys coming down to small countries thinking they can do anything,' Cox does more than distort the historical record. Walker becomes a tool of evil capitalists surrounded by a hideous crew of depraved villains who rape and pillage despite his orders (Contras), manipulating and manipulated by scheming native aristocrats. No character in the film emerges with any dignity except perhaps Walker's right-hand man Hornsby, who is erroneously turned into a black to drive home the irony of Walker's turning racist and pro-slavery to entice southern expansionists to emigrate and save his tottering government.   The resisters against Walker are not individuated; even though director Cox notes 'you got these incredible visuals for free' (Wurlitzer 1987: 32) the film for the most part might have been made anywhere. A handful of pro forma shots of the landscape are the only signs the film was in fact made in Nicaragua.

Not only does Cox ignore Nicaragua; other elements of the film suggest more than Nicaragua is being cheated. Three quarters of the book which boasts Rudy Wurlitzer's name in large letters on the cover is actually by historian A.Z. Carr, who is relegated to second billing like a bit part player at the bottom of the cover and on the reverse side of the title page. Unlike the magnificent score Ennio Morricone penned for *Burn*! (and for *The Mission*, another fine film about exploitation and rebellion in Latin America), Joe Strummer's soundtrack sounds like the sort of Latin music made popular by Xavier Cugat or Desi Arnaz -- bouncy, silly stuff which is either out of character with the film or a subtle ironic comment which backfires; the music, like the film, shows how Latin Americans are trivialized and ignored by North Americans. Finally, Cox and Wurlitzer almost brag about how cheaply they made the film, which frequently comes up in their interview (Wurlitzer 1987: 32, 39, 43, 46, 60-61). Interestingly, they even seem to suspect that they are in fact exploiting a revolution they are hoping to assist: 'The irony is that initially the Liberal party in Nicaragua invited Walker down to help them as, indeed, the Sandinistas encouraged our film. For their own ends, of course. And they might live to regret it.' 'We're probably kidding ourselves about the essential nobility of our efforts -- I mean, we were just a bunch of pigs, you know.' (Wurlitzer 1987: 23, 28). Are director and screenwriter engaging in a little staged false humility; are they consciously trying to cover for a film they probably knew was not the epic it should have been; or are they showing the ironic awareness perhaps present in Strummer's music -- that their film embodies as well as depicts the exploitation of Nicaragua?

One of the most interesting features of *Walker* is the frequent use of anachronisms to show how history repeats itself -- Vanderbilt uses all the expletives deleted from the Watergate publications, U.S. marines swoop down in a helicopter to save Walker's men (although Walker insists on staying, which did not really happen, but enables him to be executed on the first expedition) instead of their surrendering to the navy, the great publicity Walker received is symbolized by his appearance on the cover of *Time*, and atrocities then and now are related by the presence of modern debris around people buried up to their necks. Modern western civilization appears primarily through anachronistic signs of death. Cox himself expressed reservations about at least this last anachronism, but kept it in when his Nicaraguan taxi driver told him 'No way, that's really funny' (Wurlitzer 1987: 49). Indeed, these scenes are funny, but they rob power from a film that can afford to lose little.

Walker is in many ways a cinematic equivalent of the very foreign policy it seeks to denounce. It not only ignores the Nicaraguans as actors in their own destiny, it not only oversimplifies complex people and situations into ideological caricatures, but it also has the small-mindedness of a policy that pretends to recognize the Nicaraguan government while making war against it, that pretends to not make war by arming surrogates, who are alternatively given and denied money. Just as the United States has no consistent Latin American policy, *Walker* lacks a consistent point of view -- is it epic, ironic, humorous, or all three? It stands as a film beside the great Vietnam films (*Apocalypse Now, Platoon, The*

Deer Hunter, Full Metal Jacket) much as the war against Nicaragua stands to the Vietnam conflict.

Burn! is a much better film, perhaps a great one. Here we see the island and feel for the rebels. The film begins with a long scene in which a mother is bearing the executed body of her rebellious slave son back to a camp. It ends with William Walker (a fictional character although the name was probably deliberately chosen) being killed by a single rebel after he believes the rebellion has been put down. Revolution cannot be put down. Although Walker sets up the revolution by forcing its future leader, José Dolores, to take responsibility for a robbery and then instructing the revolutionary army, Dolores and his people emerge as both individuals and a community, fighting for a real cause, and rebelling a second time on their own.

Unlike the fanatical, one-dimensional Walker of *Walker*, the British Sir William Walker played by Marlon Brando is a complex, fascinating figure. He serves as an agent provocateur because it's a job he's paid to play a game he enjoys playing with no particular attachment to any cause. He foments a rebellion against a Portuguese sugar colony so the British government may trade with the independent nation; he cynically uses the slaves as the backbone of the revolt in alliance with the wealthy creole aristocracy, knowing full well they will not profit by their heroism. He comes to feel affection and admiration for the slaves, especially José Dolores, but this does not stop him from returning again to put down the second rebellion of blacks against creoles which is also interrupting British profits. Walker cannot understand why Dolores will not escape with his help after he is condemned to death when the rebellion is crushed -- 'If a man gives you freedom, it is not freedom. Freedom is something you take for yourself,' Dolores insists.

Walker, despite his title, refined accent, and intelligence, is paradoxically a desperate man who is only at ease plotting or fighting. He shows in his person the reality behind the refinements of western civilization. Between the insurrections he is brawling and drinking in London dives. He cares little for the economic or political rationale behind his activities: when the creoles protest that he burned their crops and the entire island when he put down the second revolt, Walker indifferently replies that was why he was hired and this was the only way he could do the job. He also spends some time in Indochina between the rebellions, which is Pontecorvo's anachronistic reference to similar imperialistic efforts in Vietnam -- first world nations tolerate third world independence in name only. He wears white, perhaps an ironic comment on the men in white hats of the westerns, the 'good guys.'

When I first saw *Burn!*, I was disturbed by the fact the revolution was begun and directed by a white man, who at first has to teach the slaves everything. Indeed, in the first revolt, they, as do the creoles, appear as puppets of the mastermind Walker who symbolizes the manipulations of a capitalist Britain forcing the world to dance to its tune in the nineteenth century. But the second half of the film redeems the first. The slaves fight on their own, Dolores turns from a clumsy tool of Walker into his moral superior and strategic equal, forcing the planters to call in the British army and lose both their wealth and independence to crush the revolt. *Burn!* thus shows us the creation of a people. And the death of this William Walker is a sign that revolution cannot be crushed permanently and ends on an inspiring note, whereas the execution of the real Walker by the British appears as a deus ex machina effect tacked onto the *Walker* film to end the story on a reasonably authentic note.

Semiotically, *Walker* fails because characters are presented as ideas and simplified, dogmatic ones at that. The context of place and the resisters' 'second' to the invaders 'first' are largely absent. Presentist signs are dropped into the film in a jarring, ironic manner at odds with the film's serious message. In *Burn!*, characters one can feel for and of some complexity evolve; groups and a well-presented setting give the story verisimilitude and continuity. Finally, *Walker* emerges as a sign of the very phenomenon (Americans exploiting Nicaraguans) it is criticizing. *Burn!*, on the other hand, was a commercial failure (but ultimately became a 'cult' film and something of a classic) precisely because it so effectively signified an immoral war.

REFERENCES

Pontecorvo, Gillo, 1970, *Burn!*, United Artists film, from an original story by Gillo Pontecorvo, Franco Solinas, and Giorgio Arlorio.

Wurlitzer, Rudy, and Cox, Alex, 1987, *Walker*, United Artists film, story by Rudy Wurlitzer, New York: Harper and Row.

Chapter 22

Ernesto Cardenal: Radical Priest as Semiotician

> If the history of humanity were 24 hours
>
> let's say
>
> private property, classes, division
>
> into rich and poor: these would be the last 10 minutes
>
> INJUSTICE/the last 10 minutes.
>
> -- 'Oracle Over Managua' 1973 --

Ernesto Cardenal, Nicaragua's former Minister of Culture, presents in his poetry a semiotics of history: the world of western capitalism is a deformation of the natural order of the universe and of human society. Its perversion can be seen, smelled, heard, and intellectually and morally discerned in the objects, behavior, and personalities it generates in opposition to the healthy cosmic order under God. In his poetry collections *Psalms* (1950) and *Homage to the American Indians* (1970) Cardenal draws attention to equivalent spiritual perversions in the Old Testament and Mayan civilizations, where greed and selfishness also challenged a communal world-view and a people living in harmony with their God. In this paper, I will focus on this conflict in recent times as Cardenal depicts it in 'With Walker In Nicaragua.'[1] Written in 1950 when he was twenty-five, the poem is purportedly written by a veteran of Walker's expedition of the 1850's some fifty years after the fact. Since Cardenal is in turn writing the poem a half century after its alleged composition, he calls our attention immediately to the continuity of experience in the 1850s, 1900s, and 1950s, the persistence of the struggle between two worlds.

Rollins is a filibuster who has gone native and forsaken the ways of his imperialist brethren. He has grown to like the Spanish-Americans, and describes their world as one of pleasant colors, odors, and sounds: 'that warm, sweet green odor of Central America'; 'The river turned leaf green'; 'the laughter of black women washing clothes and a Caribbean song' appear in the poem's first twenty-eight line section. But so does a storm, which Cardenal sets as an antithesis: 'a grey wave that comes blotting out the hills': 'a muffled sound of flood waters.' Monkeys howl and people go running to take in their clothes in response to the interruption of natural rhythms, and 'the heavy metallic beating of raindrops on the tin roofs' is heard before there is 'once again silence.' The storm's depiction as grey and metallic introduces the motifs of Walker's expedition, and articulates Cardenal's firm belief that the capitalist invasion, like the capitalist epoch, is but an interruption of a decent human order which will soon end.

No sooner has the natural storm passed than the men of Walker's expeditions appear. Not their leader, whose entrance is delayed both to heighten the effect and because such is the nature of imperialism: its dupes at home confront its victims abroad before the grand entrance, when it is safe, of the masters. Cardenal for the most part treats the invaders sympathetically when looking at them as individual human beings. They too are victims, a cross section of western civilization similar to the *Pequod's* contemporaneous crew of adventurers -- an aristocrat, a boxer, a prettyboy, a braggart, a bandit, a treasure hunter. Some of them die -- 'hanged from trees and left swinging beneath the stinking black vultures' or 'in the hot cobbled streets filled with shots -- or white, like shells on the seashore' or 'shot by Walker against a grey church.' Imperialist death is pitiless, black, white, and grey, reeking, steaming. It devours its own, whereas the survivors who escape the Nicaraguans' self-defense and Walker's own punishment of his 'traitors' dwell in peace, like our narrator surrounded by his grandchildren.

Before Walker appears, we are introduced to his advance man Hornsby, a satanic John the Baptist. He deludes the adventurers by confusing the color scheme. His description of Nicaragua begins with 'blue lakes amid blue mountains under a blue sky' and ends with 'blue stagecoaches.' This perversion of blue is the symbol of a predicted capitalist transformation -- Nicaragua is to 'teem with merchant ships and with foreigners speaking all tongues,' the 'pier of America,' the site of a future canal. In short, it is to be destroyed: the stanza ends with visions of saw mills, 'logs floating down the rivers,' the jungle transformed into piers and stagecoaches. For the capitalist, beauty is an object to be destroyed.

Enter Walker, whom Cardenal presents stripped of humanity. He has a face like a tiger, his eyes are grey 'without pupils,' like one who is blind -- as indeed Walker is to the world he sets out to conquer. His skin is pale, 'his voice colorless, cold, and sharp,' that 'calm voice of his announcing death sentences.' Nor does he drink, smoke, wear a uniform -- or smile. Walker is inhuman, unnatural, so much like the interchangeable drab-suited statesmen of the twentieth century who hide their atrocities behind straight faces, colorless rhetoric, and vapid abstractions. As a non-person seeking to reduce the cosmos to his own level, Walker is an extreme yet representative symbol of his world.

Walker's ship sets sail accompanied by portents of doom -- storms and volcanos. Cardenal hints that the world of the Mayans is still present in Nicaragua, as from 'behind blue islands' 'crumbling old volcanos like pyramids seem to be watching us.' As Cardenal in *Homage to the American Indians* treats the Mayan pyramid-builders as another civilization first healthy, then corrupted by greed and power, he is invoking a lesson Walker and his men could have profited from had they not been ignorant of history. For the invaders, neither the jungle sounds nor the volcanos are friendly -- the former are a 'constant moan.' Representatives of the perverted order find the friendly, natural order sinister.

Nevertheless, the land works its magic on its would-be despoilers. When they see Lake Nicaragua for the first time they exclaim 'Ometepe!' in awe of its beauty. By using the Indian word for the lake, they indicate their potential for integration into the truer universe they reject, especially when they react spontaneously, without thought, to what they perceive. Now the volcanos, hitherto hostile, grow friendly. In a proper setting they appear as 'breasts, joined at water level by their bases, which looked like they were sinking into the water.' The lake and its surrounding countryside have the appearance of a woman: one about to be raped, Cardenal implies, hinting at how the new conquistadors' minds are moving back to *their* reality. But initially, even the smoke from the villages and church steeples from the town of Rivas merge into the landscape, signs of the harmony man and nature have attained in Central America.

Although some of the filibusteros will eventually succumb to the temptations of an uncorrupted land, at this stage their appreciation of Nicaragua merely interrupts their dreams of wealth and conquest. They march on Rivas and see 'grey, walled streets,' notice 'silver plated revolvers' in use amid 'shouts and blood and fires.' What is better perceived as a 'blue port nestled in hills with their curved yellow coconut palms swaying' has turned into a cauldron of war. But there are signs of a mental transformation in some of the men -- Rollins is falling under the land's spell, and already one man is in a hospital bed -- 'angry at Walker.'

After Rivas, the expedition moves on to Leon where again we encounter society and nature in harmony. Cardenal has previously shown us this harmony in images and colors. Now we hear sounds and feel breezes: 'the nights were cool/with distant guitars below wrought-iron balconies and the wind swinging the golden lamps.' Even the sentries seem to sing, and they remind some of the invaders of the 'cheery, full, and clear' voices of watchmen in 'snow-covered' towns. Walker's men briefly recognize their common humanity with the Nicaraguans, and distantly sense the same spirit in North America's small, unpolluted towns at one with the natural world that they find in southern climates. This human solidarity is reemphasized when the Yankees fall immediately 'in love with the women of that land,' anticipating the unions some of them will later form. Through Leon, Nicaragua has given the Yankees a second chance to capitulate to its wonders; a vibrant yet serene civilization complements spectacular natural beauty.

But despite the changing perceptions of Yankees who are coming to love Nicaragua more as they know it better, capitalism and Walker march on to Granada. The volcanos turn into 'two blue guards,' resuming their sinister personae. The invaders advance in darkness wearing black uniforms, 'hearing every little noise as if a big racket.' Unlike in Leon, perceived by day and not as a military target, in Granada the exuberant song disappears and every noise is cursed, even the sounds of crickets. Granada's appearance is characterized by 'thick towers' and 'foreign streets, grave and empty.'

The stealthy approach works, for suddenly 'there was peace,' Cardenal notes ironically. After the town's surrender, Walker 'spoke of peace and National Reconciliation/and kneeling with Corral [the President] in church he swore to observe the Constitution.' Of course this is a false peace, but Cardenal is also suggesting the terms under which real peace (then as now) would be possible, with

North Americans as well as Nicaraguans respecting law and religion, the two groups treating each other as equals.

Even under the false peace, Granada completely changes its aspect. The streets literally merge with the natural world as vendors sell all sorts of fruits and water. Their very sounds 'cool the streets' as do stands with 'drinks of all colors.' Sensible commerce is not alien to man's nature. Its sounds mingle harmoniously with the songs of washerwomen, the *Salve Regina*, lovers' serenades, bells, people's conversations, and even the frogs' croaking. The sounds are distinctly individual yet do not jar as 'the air is pure': such are the pleasures of the rightly ordered world Rollins is discovering.

Again, harmony is but an interlude. Walker orders Corral executed, and remains deaf to his wife and daughters' pleas for mercy. He mocks their grief by allowing the man two additional hours of life, and once more the lake turns 'leaden,' like a wall. Walker's 'colorless eyes of ice' and his self-separation from the execution (he is not present) dominate this episode, along with the silent protest of some of his men, who wait expectantly for a positive decision on the pardon. One soldier voices a protest 'and he had to be taken off so he wouldn't be heard.' Not being heard, silence in the face of atrocity, is a key theme of this section, and contrasts poignantly with the laughter and life of the previous one. Cardenal subtly underlines the inability to speak meaningfully against immoral authority under capitalism, and the division of labor between those who order atrocities and those who carry them out. Only by distancing himself from his cruel deed can Walker accomplish it. Finally we hear mourning and weeping, and then 'a great calm, like the calm before a storm.'

The storm is not long in coming. Upon Corral's death, Walker 'proclaimed himself President/and he declared slavery and the seizure of estates.' Walker's order is presented starkly, suddenly, without justification or imagery, in contrast to the rest of the poem. Cardenal has reached the midpoint: until now, the invaders have been successful. Now their defeat will be recorded, as the next line indicates: 'Meantime enemy troops we didn't see were mustering around lagoons.' People in nature plan to recover the true world; the false world remains self-centered and oblivious.

Walker's regime is marked by both the plague (cholera) and war. The two intermingle, reflect each other, and establish themselves as principal signs of Walker's rule and world. There are 'piles of corpses,' 'bloodstained streets,' and 'stinking wells.' Symbols of beauty become terrifying, and vice-versa. The glorious sun 'rose up out of the lake like an island of gold' -- both a beautiful image and a mockery of the golden dreams of the besieged Yankees -- but for Walker's men it only heralds 'one more day of horror.' In turn, a bugle played by the newsboy -- named Dixie in honor of the slave society Walker is hoping to import to Central America -- that signals their rescue 'shined like a glorious light.' Religion, previously symbolized by hymns, is forsaken, to appear as 'a statue of the Virgin hanging on a black wall.' The blue lake turns 'white as ice' and then 'ash colored,' 'water the color of Walker's eyes.' From without, the invisible enemy '*boomed* (my emphasis) laughter and guitars.' Signs of perverted man and perverted nature merge in a hideous spectacle of destruction. As Granada is destroyed, Cardenal compares its appearance 'from afar' to the sight of holiday fireworks to complete the sequence of distorted images, the fruits of an insane regime, symbolizing the world he is forcing us to see as unnatural. Even as they destroy the town they must flee, Walker's men embody the 'civilized' nations which find the defeat pleasurable of those deemed less civilized.

Walker is not present at the scene of his greatest crime. He 'stayed on the boat,' 'taking dips in the ocean at San Juan del Sur!' as his men burned with thirst. Far from being a hero, the mastermind is a calculating opportunist, ready to flee virtually alone if necessary, anxious not to take personal responsibility for or experience the concrete effects of his machinations. Again, he exemplifies the capitalist elite. His commander on the spot is Henningsen, an Englishmen, who 'dug trenches day and night,' encouraged the men with a 'calm voice,' seems to have taken no joy in destroying the city, and was the last man out. His final message to Walker is 'Your order has been obeyed, sir: Granada is no more.' Henningsen is a soldier of fortune who fought both for the Czar and for the Hungarian patriots of 1848. Cardenal depicts him as a courageous if unprincipled man who sells himself to the highest bidder and then carries out his tasks as efficiently as possible without regard to their moral import. His courage, abilities, and 'stiff upper lip' sense of duty too are perverted by his world system. A final point -- he is English, and will fight for anyone, a martial equivalent of the free trade championed by his nation as beneficial to the world in the nineteenth century, but ultimately profitable to itself. If Henningsen profits from everyone's distresses, he does so by selling himself.

As Walker's first expedition is sent reeling back to the States, Cardenal tells us that 'they' -- the Nicaraguans? Walker's men who remained? -- 'loved Granada like a woman,' and that even 'today' -- fifty years later when the poem was supposedly written, they mourn the town 'where once there was love.' But the love remains in Nicaragua, for several of the men do not return and experience no hostility from the forgiving people.

Rollins/Cardenal relates Walker's final expedition at second hand. Although terser, it depicts Walker's moral growth under fire and hardship, glimmerings of humanity which emerge as he realizes too late the horror he has wrought. The American becomes much like the Englishman Henningsen -- staying up all night to tend a wounded man. Walker himself is finally wounded, and despite a fever that leaves him 'paler than ever' he is the last of his men to retreat from a battle.

He carries a crucifix as the British court-martial him and for the first time, as he stands beside his open grave, he speaks in Spanish: 'El Presidente de Nicaragua, es nicaraguense.' In short, he renounces the presidency. Walker recovers the symbols of life -- kindness, courage, Christianity, and identification with the land -- but too late. Cardenal then ends the poem quickly: 'All the bullets hit the mark. Out of ninety-one men only twelve made it back. And there, by the sea, with no wreaths or epitaph remained William Walker of Tennessee.' Walker's execution and ultimate oblivion is the inevitable fate of his kind: Nicaragua will be restored to its people, and recover the properties of the natural order under God. Yet in Walker's permanent internment in Nicaragua, his escape from his history, and his moral awakening, is Cardenal's hope and hint that Nicaragua can redeem the North which has so arrogantly tried to subdue it. Capitalist man has only the choices of Rollins and Walker, to love the real world and become part of it, or to rage against it and be defeated.

Cardenal's vision of a war of worlds is not new: Walker in many ways is Caliban to Nicaragua's Ariel, to use the dichotomy José Rodo coined in *Ariel*, the seminal essay contrasting Latin American spirituality with North American brutality and materialism. But Cardenal brings these worlds to sensual life, praising Latin Americans and comforting them not to be ashamed of their traditional way of life. He also confronts capitalism and its representatives with the perversion they have put in its place. These have been the lifelong themes of Cardenal's poetry and religious education work. Cardenal has juxtaposed the smells, sounds, and products of the modern world system with its antithesis, the just order of the universe under God, to emphasize the former's evil, but also its brevity and inevitable replacement. In 'Apocalypse' (a.1977), Cardenal rewrites the Book of Revelation to foretell the coming nuclear holocaust, but one in which annihilation yields to 'one sole organism/made up of men in place of cells.' 'And there was a new Canticle/and all other inhabited planets heard the Earth singing/and it was a love song.' 'The 'Prayer for Marilyn Monroe' (1971) brings this cosmic struggle to an individual level, as Cardenal prays that God may forgive someone who only 'followed the script we gave her,/that of our own lives, but it was meaningless.' In contrast, 'Joaquin Artola' (1950a) is a Nicaraguan peasant who returns as an old man to ask for work on a ranch at San Jacinto, where he had once inadvertently routed Walker's army by starting a stampede. This brief poem provokes reflection on how 'history' as made by statesmen and soldiers is a terrifying interruption of the natural rhythms of life. If it makes heroes of peasants, they only wish to be left alone.

In his testimony before the Permanent People's Tribunal (1984), an international organization dedicated to holding the world's nations to the standards they applied to the Nazis at Nuremburg, Cardenal mused as to why the United States would expend so much energy to destroy the Sandinista revolution, as trade with Central America is minimal (the region absorbs more in aid that it yields in profits) and Nicaragua is no military threat to anyone. 'U.S. hegemony at a world level is being questioned,' he answered his own question. 'They do not see us as a reality, but we are a ghost in the mind of a psychopath. And for the United States Nicaragua is only a symbol -- but a symbol that must be destroyed.' Thirty years before his testimony, Cardenal had described the reality, the symbol, the ghost, and the psychopath in 'With Walker in Nicaragua.' If his poem makes us aware that Nicaraguans know their history -- and ours -- and we do not, it will have fulfilled its purpose of locating the present struggle as one episode in the eternal war of good and evil.

ENDNOTE

1. William Walker invaded Nicaragua at the invitation of one of two rival aristocratic factions in 1855 and served as President of a perpetually threatened regime until 1857. Forced out of the country by local resistance, he returned in 1860 to Nicaragua's east coast and was promptly executed by the British. To save his tottering government, he tried to create a slave state in Central America and demonstrate to Southerners there was a real possibility of countering the preponderance of free states through southward expansion.

REFERENCES

Cardenal, Ernesto, 1950, 'With Walker in Nicaragua,' orig. Spanish poem, in *With Walker in Nicaragua and Other Early Poems*, trans. Jonathan Cohen, Middleton, CT: Wesleyan University Press, 1984, 42-71.

_____, 1950a, 'Joaquin Artola,' orig. Spanish poem, in *With Walker In Nicaragua and Other Early Poems*, trans. Jonathan Cohen, Middleton, CT: Wesleyan University Press, 1984, 74-75.

_____, 1969, *Salmos,* Buenos Aires: Ediciones C. Lohle, reprinted in a Nicaraguan edition, Ediciones El Pez y la Serpiente, 1979, trans. as *Psalms* by Thomas Blackburn et al., New York: Crossroad, 1981.

_____, 1970, *Homenaje a los Indios Americanos,* Chile: Editorial Universitaria, trans. by Monique and Thomas Alstchul as *Homage to the American Indians*, Baltimore: Johns Hopkins University Press, 1973.

_____, 1971, 'Oracion por Marilyn Monroe,' trans. by Robert Pring-Mill as 'Prayer for Marilyn Monroe' in *Apocalypse and Other Poems*, New York: New Directions, 1977, 30-32.

_____, 1973, 'Oraculo Sobre Managua,' trans. by Donald D. Walsh as 'Oracle Over Managua,' in *Zero Hour and Other Documentary Poems*, New York: New Directions, 1980.

_____, a.1977, 'Apocalypse,' orig. Spanish poem, in *Apocalypse and Other Poems,* trans. Robert Pring-Mill, New York: New Directions, 1977, 33-37.

_____, 1984, Testimony before the Permanent People's Tribunal, October, 1984, in Brussels, Belgium, printed as *On Trial: Reagan's War Against Nicaragua*, ed. Marlene Dixon, San Francisco: Synthesis, c.1985, 77-83.

Chapter 23

Stamping Out History:
National Identity on Postage Stamps

I decided to have some fun by entitling my final essay 'Stamping Out History.'
I could imagine people expecting some radical deconstructionist theory that history
is dead, unknowable, or meaningless, only to find I am merely talking about how
nations portray themselves on postage stamps. Stamps are small messages,
emblems of ruling groups' self-perceptions to be conveyed to the population at
home and correspondents abroad. The stamp is also a means of selectively
remembering those aspects of a nation's culture it deems valuable: what is not on
stamps can be an indication not only of what is unimportant, but of what the
powers that be are trying to hide.

For about half the history of the modern postage stamp -- which began with
the famous 'penny black' issued by Great Britain in 1840 bearing the likeness of
Queen Victoria -- that is, from the 1840s until the early twentieth century --
postage stamps were for the most part small, one-colored designs bearing the
images of symbols of national unity. The Queen of England, famous patriots in
the United States, and imperial eagles in Germany and Russia were images found
on letters in these nations decade after decade. The stamps were much like the
clothes of the bourgeois gentlemen who invented them -- functional, unelaborate,
and in their stability reflecting the nineteenth century's belief in an order which
admitted change reluctantly and believed it had found good government in the
contemporary nation-state.

But even with nations issuing only a handful of stamps over much of a century, patterns emerge.   Russia, with its ethnically diverse population and unpopular monarchy, never put a czar on a stamp before 1913, when a series of former monarchs appeared.   The incumbent Nicholas II was only depicted on a high, seldom-used denomination.   Did the avoidance of the contemporary ruler reflect timelessness, Russia the nation, or the need to downplay antagonism against the contemporary monarchy?   In nineteenth-century France, too, republicans and monarchists (who could not even agree on the same flag), avoided any depiction of persons or politically loaded symbols after the demise of Louis Napoleon removed his image from stamps.   The head of Ceres, symbol of the nation's agricultural productivity, and other icons representing commerce, peace, and freedom satisfied French postal needs.   And although Prussia had issued stamps bearing images of its king before German unification, after 1871 the national symbols (the eagle and Germania) replaced him.   They emphasized that this was a German, and united monarchy, not merely a Prussian one -- which, for the most part, it really was.

Austria and the United States did not hesitate to use people in controversial ways to appear on stamps.   Emperor Franz Josef served as a symbol for uniting a dual monarchy with two different flags, governments, and sets of icons.   His personal popularity as he aged was an unexpected bonus, but still one can imagine reactions to his image among Czech and Balkan nationalists.   Before the Civil War, the United States kept its stamps politically neutral.   Only Franklin, Washington, and Jefferson adorned the early issues -- none had belonged to a contemporary political party and all had mythic status as national unifiers.   In 1861, however, the Union proclaimed its idea of what the South ought to do by issuing a stamp of southerner Andrew Jackson, who had threatened to hang disunionists thirty years earlier.   The Confederacy responded with an Andrew

Jackson of its own, accompanied by states righters Thomas Jefferson, John C. Calhoun (the man Jackson threatened to hang), and its own President Jefferson Davis. In 1866, the nation proclaimed reunion with an Abraham Lincoln stamp, and the next thirty years witnessed the appearance of deceased Civil War heroes including Generals Winfield Scott, William Sherman, Ulysses S. Grant, and Lincoln's cabinet members Edwin Stanton and William Seward. This selection reflected Northern and Republican hegemony over the Democratic South. Only with the triumph of the Democratic Party during the administration of Franklin D. Roosevelt, in 1936, did rebel leaders Robert E. Lee and Stonewall Jackson finally appear on a stamp, and in the midst of a larger series honoring the United States Army at that. If European nations usually adopted a single symbol of their more united and bureaucratized lands, the more pluralist, decentralized United States similarly employed a wider variety of symbols of unity.

Two other remarks about the early stamps. First, with very few exceptions, only the head or bust of the ruler or other figure is visible. The ruler thus appears literally as the head, or figure-head, of the nation: it is the symbol, not the individual person, which matters. Similarly, many of the early figures are portrayed using idealized Roman-style busts, sometimes wearing laurel wreaths, further depersonalizing them and investing them with the timeless, classical, and imperial Roman values which resonated deeply with the nineteenth century bourgeoisie. The United States is particularly interesting in this respect. Washington, Jefferson, Franklin, and Jackson sometimes appear realistically, sometimes as heroic busts, whereas more modern figures (except for one series of 1870-1871) are given photographic representation. Two series (1894 and 1922 to 1925) have classical busts of Jackson, Washington, and Franklin amid more modern portraits. One can argue such depictions unconsciously reflected

Americans' belief that the founders were somehow members of a different, more stable, and perhaps better age.

The colonies of major powers usually issued imitations of the mother country's stamps. Congolese natives opened letters with King Leopold's image, those in India with Queen Victoria's, while Africans under French rule looked at the same symbols of agriculture, commerce, and navigation as Frenchmen at home. By the early twentieth century, however, especially after World War I as the movement to decolonize accelerated, the imperial powers granted on stamps the sort of token representation they hoped would suffice in government. It was not until 1931 that anything Indian appeared on Indian stamps -- and then it was British government buildings. Only in 1935 did a non-British symbol finally appear. On one occasion, this took a significantly comic form. The first series with Philippine sites issued by the United States in 1932 contained what ought to have been the image of Pagsanjan Falls in Laguna; instead, Vernal Falls from Yosemite Park in California was substituted, but allowed to stand for the duration of the series to complete the insensitivity. Some colonies did not even have the dignity of their own stamps, especially smaller territories, but had to make do with a special imprint added to the stamps of the mother country or a neighboring colony. Ever reminding Ireland of its inferior status, Britain issued no stamps for Ireland but used the regular series there. After independence, Eire took revenge by overprinting images of King George with Gaelic proclamations of independence. Such overprinting also signalled domestic revolution. Portugal and Austria, for example, temporarily blotted out the king's image as they became republics; Nasser's Egypt announced itself in 1952 with three heavy lines superimposed on the face of King Farouk.

Commemorative stamps first appeared at the end of the nineteenth century, but did so infrequently. The United States' first series was an elaborate 16-issue set in honor of the Columbian Exposition of 1893, its next in 1898 to honor the Trans-Mississippian Exposition. These early series, like those honoring the 1901 Pan American, 1903 Louisiana, and 1907 Jamestown Expositions, honored the contemporary commemoration rather than the event itself, and were sold in connection with the expositions. Perhaps because the United States was a new nation, its identity forged in a history most Americans regarded with pride rather than as a symbol of oppression or controversy, it could issue commemoratives as the monarchies did not. Aside from the World War Victory issue, a plain three-cent purple Victory Allegory, the first commemorative in the United States strictly honoring a past event was the three-issue series of 1920 for the Pilgrims' three hundredth anniversary. Other major nations only began to print special issues in the 1920s. Britain honored the Empire in 1924, but its next commemorative, other than royal jubilees, was to rejoice at the end of World War II. Britain, the last monarchy remaining of the nineteenth century great powers, has also adopted perhaps the world's most conservative approach to issuing stamps. Commemoratives are few, always bear the ruler's image, and in many cases honor the royal family to symbolize apolitical national unity. Not until 1964 did someone outside the royal family appear on a British stamp, and it took the four hundredth anniversary of Shakespeare's birth to accomplish this. In 1965, the Labor Party buried its partisanship to recognize the contribution of Winston Churchill to the cause of civilization. France's first commemoratives honored the 1924 Paris Olympics, Spain's the hundredth anniversary of painter Francisco Goya's death in 1928. Germany entered the world stage in this respect by honoring its lost colonies at the beginning of the Nazi era, in 1934.

But it was Soviet Russia which inaugurated a new era in stamp issuance, much as it marked a new type of society. As the bourgeois democracies continued to stamp out prominent historical figures, rulers, and honor fairly innocuous and conservative patriotic events, the Communist state poured out dozens of large, colorful stamps proclaiming the message of the new regime to the nations of the world.   Allegories 'Severing the Chain of Bondage,' of agriculture, industry, science and art, and 'Russia Triumphant' replaced a 1913 series honoring the czars soon after the Revolution of 1917.   Under Stalin, Russia honored contemporary workers, women, ethnic groups, soldiers, and revolutionary heroes with great frequency.   Russia pioneered in 'people's stamps' which hid the reality of Stalinism -- the dictator did not appear on a stamp until 1946, then in tandem with Lenin -- stamps as both propaganda and yet symbols of what Communism hoped to accomplish.

Sometimes stamps hide things. Stalin's pre-eminence could never have been guessed at from Russian postal history. Mussolini never adorned an Italian issue -- Julius Caesar, Augustus, and Victor Emmanuel hid the dictator's hand. He finally achieved postal immortality on a German stamp of 1940 where his image joined Hitler's.   Hitler, on the other hand, regularly issued stamps to commemorate his birthday among other events, a practice followed by Ghana's Kwame Nkrumah.   Spain's Franco, Indonesia's Sukarno and Suharto, and Nicaragua's Somozas have all portrayed themselves shamelessly as the essence of their country on the regular, long term, issues of their nations.

One of the most interesting phenomena in the world of stamps is what I call postal neo-colonialism.   Third World and small countries issue unnecessary commemoratives (for postal purposes) to sell to collectors in First World countries. The stamps frequently honor First World achievements and figures. For example, Mali, one of the world's poorest lands, has honored Konrad Adenauer, Leonardo da Vinci, Louis Braille and Marie Curie. Mali has publicized such diverse activities as the 1979 Judo Championship in Paris, horse breeding, contract bridge, and dominoes.   Mali also honors numerous medical and technological achievements most of its population have no idea of. Guatemala honored the fiftieth anniversary of Lindbergh's Trans-Atlantic Flight, Eleanor Roosevelt (in 1973, a year of no special importance for her), and the United States moon landing. Liechtenstein and Tonga are perhaps the most famous purveyors of stamps designed for philatelic rather than postal use. The former, a small European country with 24,000 inhabitants, issues twenty to thirty stamps a year depicting art works, scenery, and the royal family, especially geared to promote tourism. Tonga, a kingdom of Pacific Islands under British protection, issues enormous stamps edged in gold leaf in various odd shapes. Someone with a sense of irony must have designed the five-issue set of 1976 honoring Tonga's friendship with Germany in the form of the Star of David.

It is possible to trace political trends within a nation such as the United States using its stamps. The first American Indian -- other than Pocahontas, also the first woman on an American stamp in the 1907 Jamestown series -- appeared on a 14-cent stamp in 1923, one year before Indians became American citizens and at the height of anti-immigrant sentiment. A variety of stamps honoring the 150th anniversary of the American Revolution brought forth a protest from Polish-Americans concerning the omission of their contribution. In 1931, a belatedly issued commemorative honored the 150th anniversary (in 1929) of Casimir Pulaski's death. A 1933 stamp with a group of workers (one of whom may have been President Roosevelt with a moustache) was the government's first use of a stamp to promote a contemporary program, in this case the National Recovery Administration and the New Deal. Susan B. Anthony was the first woman to appear on a stamp thanks to her own achievements -- Martha Washington had previously appeared along with Pocahontas. But the timing -- 1936, honoring the sixteenth anniversary of the women's suffrage amendment -- suggests the political clout of Eleanor Roosevelt more than a real anniversary. George Washington

Carver was the first black American on a stamp; the date, 1948, fell between the integration of major league baseball in 1947 and the armed forces in 1950. American stamps now reflect the diverse wishes of the nation's interest groups, but timing can be significant.   Both conservatives like Robert Taft and Dwight Eisenhower and the liberals like Mrs. Roosevelt and Lyndon Johnson all had stamps within a year of their deaths, but it took until 1979 for Martin Luther King Jr. and Robert Kennedy, a decade after their assassinations, and the Democratic Presidency and Congress of Jimmy Carter's administration, to receive postal recognition.

As postage stamps have become big business throughout the world, colorful emblems to attract tourists and put a cheerful face on almost any government, it is salutary to note that stamps have made, as well as reflected, history.   A Nicaraguan stamp with the image of the nation's active volcano Mt. Momotombo was distributed to United States senators at the turn of the century to encourage a Panama Canal route by supporters of the latter.   In 1900, the Dominican Republic issued a stamp showing its boundary extending far into the territory of neighboring Haiti, which promoted intermittent conflict between the nations costing 15,000 lives for four decades. (Grossman: 114).   One can only wonder whether a militant image of Theodore Roosevelt in Rough Rider garb issued months before the 1959 Cuban Revolution may have unnecessarily reminded Cubans of their land's excessive dependence on the United States.   In the 1980s, Sandinista Nicaragua issued stamps depicting Lincoln and Washington along with Lenin and religious leaders to convince the world it was indeed a pluralist society.   Incidentally, Cuban stamps since 1962 are no longer listed in United States catalogues and cannot be legally bought, sold, or possessed in the United States.   Similar non-recognition was accorded to the People's Republic of China for years.   Recognition of a nation and its symbols go together semiotically.

REFERENCES

Grossman, Samuel, 1981, *Stamp Collecting Handbook*, New York: Grossman Stamp Company.

Scott, 1984, *Standard Postage Stamp Catalogue*, New York: Scott Publishing Company. This standard reference on stamps is the source for most of the information in this paper.

ACKNOWLEDGEMENTS

The author thanks the following for permission to reprint previously published material:

Semiotics, Proceedings of the annual meetings of the Semiotics Society of America, for: 'Charles S. Peirce and Arisbe' (1985); 'Carl Becker and the Semiotics of History' (1986); 'Legality, Legitimacy, and the American Middle Class' (1984); 'Peirce-suing Plato: The *Republic* as Semiotic Society' (1991); 'Of What Is Music a Sign: Toscanini, Fürtwangler, and Walter on Musical Interpretation and the Philosophy of History' (1987); 'Napoleonic Semiosis: *Napoleon vu par Abel Gance*' (1987); 'Ernesto Cardenal: Radical Priest as Semiotician' (1989); 'Stamping Out History: Images of National Identity on Postage Stamps' (1988).

Semiotica, Walter de Gruyter, Berlin, for 'Charles S. Peirce, Historian and Semiotician,' volume 83, #s 3-4, 1991, special issue on Semiotics and History edited by Brooke Williams and William Pencak.

Proceedings of the Thirteenth and Fourteenth World Congresses in Philosophy of Law and Social Philosophy (IVR), Franz Steiner Verlag, Stuttgart, for 'Dialogues and Dilemmas of Carl Becker: A Historian's Reflections on Liberty and Revolution' (Fourteenth Congress) and 'Thucydides as Semiotician' (Thirteenth Congress).

Law and Semiotics,* Plenum Publishers, New York, for 'Eric Voegelin and the Semiotics of History' (Volume II, 1989) and 'The United States Constitution: A Semiotic Interpretation (Volume I, 1988).

Law and Semiotics,* Peter Lang, New York, for incorporating shorter essays published: 'Thorstein Veblen's Semiotic Critique of American Capitalism' (Volume IV, 1991), and 'The Sign of Francis Lieber' (Volume VI, 1993).

Pennsylvania History, for 'The Declaration of Independence: Changing Interpretations and a New Hypothesis,' volume 57 (1990).

The American Journal of Semiotics for 'Christian Symbolism and Political Unity in the English Reformation: A Historical Interpretation of the Semiotics of Anglican Doctrine,' volume 9 (1992).

Opera Quarterly,+ Duke University Press, for 'The Operatic *Ulysses*,' volume 7 (1990); 'Cherubini Stages a Revolution,' volume 8 (1991).

* series editor, Roberta Kevelson.
+ series editor, Bruce Burroughs.

INDEX